WORDS/PUNCTUATION/ MECHANICS/RESEARCH

DOCUMENTATION IN ACTION

W9-AXQ-288

GUIDE TO COVERAGE OF COMMUNITIES OF WRITERS AND READERS

If you go to college, hold a job, and join a civic group, right now you're speaking, reading, and especially writing in the academic, work, and public communities discussed in this book. As you participate in these communities, you'll learn to recognize different community expectations—what readers want or need—and to tailor your choices as a writer to meet those expectations.

ACADEMIC COMMUNITY	WORK COMMUNITY	PUBLIC COMMUNITY
Students, teachers, researchers, and others create and exchange knowledge through analysis, interpretation, and research.	Co-workers, managers, clients, customers, and others exchange information, analyze and solve problems, and promote an organization.	Residents, local leaders, activists, volunteers, and others support a cause or issue, supply information, or participate in civic exchanges.

COMMUNITY ISSUES

COMMUNITY CHARTS

STRATEGIES FOR WRITERS AND READERS

STRATEGIES FOR COLLABORATION

MAKE THE CONNECTION

Good writing is all about making connections—and the connection between writer and reader is the most important of all. *The Longman Writer's Companion* will help you become a better writer by helping you make this connection in your writing. By focusing on your experience as a reader, and developing your abilities to recognize the expectations of your readers, it can help you learn strategies that will enable you to succeed in a variety of writing situations.

Using the text's unique "Read-Recognize-Revise" approach will help develop an intuitive understanding of grammar conventions. Consulting the "Strategies" that occur throughout will help devise concrete solutions to common problems. Understanding the text's emphasis on writing for different communities will help you become more attuned to the needs and requirements of various audiences and assignments—whether you're writing a college paper, composing a résumé, or designing a newsletter.

No matter what context you find yourself writing in, *The Longman Writer's Companion* prompts you to attend to your readers' expectations, providing you with the information and strategies you need to become a better writer.

THE "READ-RECOGNIZE-REVISE" APPROACH TO CORRECTING ERRORS

COMMA SPLICE   CBS was founded in 1928 by William S. Paley, his uncle and his father sold him a struggling radio network.
READER'S REACTION: At first I thought CBS had three founders: Paley, his uncle, and his father. Then I realized that Paley probably bought the network from his relatives.

EDITED   CBS was founded in 1928 by William S. Paley **;** his uncle and his father sold him a struggling radio network.

FUSED SENTENCE   The city had only one swimming pool without an admission fee the pool was poorly maintained.
READER'S REACTION: I can't decide whether the single pool in town is poorly maintained or the only free pool is in bad shape.

EDITED   The city had only one swimming pool **, but** without an admission fee, the pool was poorly maintained.

A **comma splice** links what could be two sentences (two main or independent clauses) by a comma alone. On the other hand, a **fused sentence** (or **run-on sentence**) joins what could be two sentences without any punctuation mark or connecting word to establish clear sentence boundaries. These errors are likely to occur when you draft quickly or when you write sentences with the same subject, related or contrasting ideas, or one illustrating the other. In academic, work, or public communities, these are serious errors because they may cause readers to misunderstand a passage.

22a Recognizing comma splices

To find comma splices, look for commas scattered between word groups that could stand on their own as sentences. Join these word groups by more than a comma alone.

STRATEGY   Check for commas that string word groups together.

COMMA SPLICE   The typical Navajo husband serves as a trustee, the wife and her children own the family's property.

EDITED   The typical Navajo husband serves as a trustee **, but** the wife and her children own the family's property.
READER'S REACTION: Until you added but, I missed your point about the woman playing a more important role than the man.

22b Recognizing fused sentences

Though fused sentences may be any length, look for long sentences with little or no internal punctuation. Such sentences may combine freestanding (main) clauses without signaling their relationships.

22b
cs/fs

Editing Comma Splices and Fused Se[ntences]

STRATEGY   Count the separate statements in a sentence.

If your sentence seems to contain more than one statem[ent] appropriate punctuation and connecting words.

FUSED SENTENCE   The scientists had trouble identifying the fossi[l] resembled that of both a bird and a lizard.

EDITED   The scientists had trouble identifying the fossil skelet[on] it resembled that of both a bird and a lizard.
READER'S REACTION: Adding because separates the two m[ain clauses] and makes the ideas easier to understand.

22c Editing comma splices and fused sentences

You can vary emphasis and create sentence diversity as you repair c[omma] splices and fused sentences. When the ideas in two main clauses are loose[ly re]lated, you can generally express them best in two sentences.

STRATEGY   Create separate sentences. (___ . ___)

COMMA SPLICE   The sport calls for a total of fourteen people (or twelve p[eo]ple and two dogs) divided into two teams, they throw a d[isk] called a Frisbee up and down a field.

EDITED   The sport calls for a total of fourteen people (or twelve peopl[e] and two dogs) divided into two teams **.** They throw a disk called a Frisbee up and down a field.

FUSED SENTENCE   Football does not cause the most injuries among student ath[letes] gymnastics is the most dangerous sport.

EDITED   Football does not cause the most injuries among student ath[letes] **.** **G**ymnastics is the most dangerous sport.

When main clauses convey equally important ideas, try linking them with a comma plus a coordinating conjunction telling how they relate.

STRATEGY   Use a comma plus and, but, or, for, nor, so, or yet.
(___ , and ___ .)

COMMA SPLICE   The finance department has reviewed the plan, the operations department is still analyzing it.

EDITED   The finance department has reviewed the plan **, but** the oper[ati]ations department is still analyzing it.

FUSED SENTENCE   The emergency room is understaffed it still performs well.

EDITED   The emergency room is understaffed **, yet** it still performs well.

READER'S REACTION notes help identify potential errors by showing how a reader may react to confusing passages.

STRATEGY SECTIONS offer practical advice on how to revise and edit.

gnize, and Revise
s Errors

WHY ARE THESE ERRORS SERIOUS?

re identified in our research as among those most likely to
readers in the academic community. Whether errors distort
ast carelessness, they distract readers from what you want to
ors can erode your relationship with your readers and
ess of your writing.

USING THE "READ, RECOGNIZE, AND REVISE" APPR

Use the read-recognize-revise pattern to identify and edit errors. Fi
example provided (column 1). Consider the Reader's Reaction, show
a reader might respond (column 2). Next use the handbook's advice
Strategies suggested, or your own strategy to help you recognize th
(column 3). Finally, select a Strategy to revise or repair the error (col

READ		RECOGNIZE	REVISE
potential problems d edit.	Consider the possible reactions of your community of readers.	Try strategies for recognizing problems—or invent your own.	Use strategies to edit, rep replace errors or problem
turned the parking area tranded thousands	READER'S REACTION: The second part seems disconnected. Now I've got to stop and figure out how it fits.	**Fragment:** Ask questions. Who (or what) does? Who (or what) is? (21a)	The heavy rain turned the par mud and stranded thousands
s called the insurance discovered their accidents was limited.	READER'S REACTION: I'm confused. Is this about some new insurance company that the promoters discovered?	**Fused Sentence:** Look for a long sentence without internal punctuation; count the separate statements it contains. (22b)	The promoters called the insu and they discovered their cove accidents was limited. (22c)
with the groundskeeper, hief said he would not be or the safety of the crowd.	READER'S REACTION: Who's he—the groundskeeper or the security chief?	**Unclear Pronoun Reference:** See whether your sentence contains two or more words to which a pronoun might refer. (23a)	After talking with the ground security chief said, "I will not for the safety of the crowd."
horities hadn't scarcely urces to cope with the	READER'S REACTION: Hadn't scarcely— this isn't the way a college graduate or a professional writes.	**Double Negative:** Check for combinations of negative words like no, not, scarcely, or don't. (20b-4)	The local authorities had scar resources to cope with the fl
ncing the cancellation ge, the crowd began g to the promoters.	READER'S REACTION: I know the crowd didn't announce the cancellation, but that's what this says!	**Dangling Modifier:** When a modifier begins a sentence, consider whether the person or thing modified is the subject of the main clause. (24a-2)	After the promoters announ cancellation from the stage, complaining about the deci
romoters promise to and honor tickets did p the crowds complaints.	READER'S REACTION: I can't read this without feeling irritated that apostrophes are missing.	**Missing Possessive Apostrophe:** Test for possession by trying to turn a noun ending in -s into an of phrase. (36a)	Even the promoters' promi and honor tickets did little complaints. (36b)
unds are slippery, the mayor d, "so please leave in an anner."	READER'S REACTION: Here are more missing marks! Didn't this writer bother to proofread?	**Missing Marks:** Look for marks often used in pairs such as quotation marks (37a) and commas. (34c, 34e, 34j)	"The grounds are slippery, announced, "so please lea manner." (37a)
n the microphone, the mayor ope the security chief or the s has a plan to help everyone ly."	READER'S REACTION: Promoters has? This careless writer didn't even make the effort to fit subjects and verbs together.	**Lack of Subject-Verb Agreement:** Find the subject (especially if separated, plural, or compound); match the verb. (19a–b)	Away from the microphon "I hope the security chief have a plan to help everyo (19b)
left the amphitheater quickly, d get to your car without long in the rain.	READER'S REACTION: Why is this sentence mixing people with you? Is you supposed to mean me?	**Shift:** Hunt for illogical or inconsistent shifts among I, we, you, he, she, it, or they. (25a)	If people left the amphith could get to their cars wi in the rain. (25b)
h, the muddy parking area problems, all the cars and left the grounds without	READER'S REACTION: It looks as if the writer just tossed in some commas here—and they make the sentence hard to read.	**Unnecessary Commas:** Check for un-needed commas after words like although or between subject and verb. (34l)	Although the muddy par problems, all the cars an grounds without inciden

"READ, RECOGNIZE, AND REVISE TEN SERIOUS ERRORS" CHART

Located in the back of the book for *quick reference on the most common
problems*, this chart also acts as a guide to using the Read, Recognize, Revise
approach.

THE THREE COMMUNITIES OF WRITERS AND READERS: ACADEMIC, WORK, AND PUBLIC

THREE MAJOR COMMUNITIES OF READERS AND WRITERS			
	ACADEMIC	**WORK**	**PUBLIC**
ROLES	Students Teachers Researchers Committees gathering expert opinions Readers interested in specialized knowledge	Co-workers Supervisors Organizational work groups (management, accounting, public relations) Clients and customers Government agencies Public target groups	Residents or group members Possible supporters Public officials or agencies Community activists Local groups Readers interested in an issue
GOALS	Creation or exchange of knowledge	Provision of information Analysis of problems Proposal of solutions Promotion of organization	Persuasion in support of a cause or issue Participation in democracy Provision of issue-oriented information
TYPICAL FORMS	Analysis of text or phenomenon Interpretation of text, artwork, or event Research proposal Lab report Scholarly article Annotated bibliography Grant proposal Classroom presentation	Description of object, event, situation, or problem Proposal Report of findings Memos, letters, minutes of meetings Guidelines or instructions Promotional materials Meeting presentation	Position paper Informative report Letter to group, supporters, officials, agency, organization, or publication Flyer, newsletter, pamphlet, or fact sheet Action or grant proposal Guidelines, charter, or principles Comments in public forum
WRITING CHARACTERISTICS	Detailed reasoning and critical analysis Fresh insights or conclusions Extensive evidence Accurate detail supporting conclusions Balanced treatment acknowledging other viewpoints Thoughtful, stimulating exploration of topic	Concentration on task, problem, or goal Accurate and efficient presentation of problem or issue Concise, clear, direct prose Promotion of product or service	Focus on shared values and goals Advocacy of cause Fair recognition of others' interests Relevant evidence supporting positions Concentration on own point of view or on need for information Orientation to actions or solutions

STRATEGY   Use TASALS to help you recognize electronic communities.

TOPIC. On what subject does the site focus? Do contributors belong to any organization or share any other affiliation?

ATTITUDE. Does the site have a clear point of view or set of values? Do contributors have similar perspectives or values?

STRATEGIES. Does the site use a particular written style or visual design?

Throughout the text there is an emphasis on writing for different communities, helping writers to be attentive to the expectations and demands of various audiences whether they are composing a research paper for class, a memo at work or a letter to the editor.

USING TECHNOLOGY AS A WRITER AND RESEARCHER

URLS IN THE TAKING IT ONLINE FEATURE

located on each tabbed divider, offer access to Web resources related to each section.

SECTION 3

Editing Grammar: Meeting Community Expectations

TAKING IT ONLINE

PURDUE ONLINE WRITING LAB (OWL)
http://owl.english.purdue.edu/
Visit this site for the most complete list of resources, handouts, and exercises about grammar and editing collected by any American university. The site also offers grammar advice for ESL writers.

THE GOOD GRAMMAR, GOOD STYLE© PAGES
http://www.protrainco.com/info/grammar.htm
Do you have a grammar question? Check this site's searchable database and "Articles & Answers" archive.

POP-UP GRAMMAR
http://www.brownlee.org/durk/grammar/
Pop-up Grammar is an online testing, instruction, and assessment site. To test your grammar skills, try the interactive grammar quizzes.

QUIZ ON SENTENCE TYPES
http://webster.commnet.edu/cgi-shl/quiz.pl/sentence_types_quiz.h
This site offers an interactive quiz on sentence types that tests your knowledge and checks your answers. You'll also find additional grammar instruction and writing advice.

WRITING TIPS
http://faculty.rmwc.edu/jabell/writing.htm
THE MARKETING DEPARTMENT'S TOP 10 LIST OF WRITING ERRORS AND THEN SOME
http://www.csun.edu/~hfbus023/errors.html
These guidelines from professors will help you recognize and edit co
writing errors.

DAVE'S ESL CAFE HINT OF THE DAY
http://eslcafe.com/webhints/hints.cgi
Read the hint of the day, and search the archive for past hints, too

NUMBERED WEB ICONS

appearing in the margins of the page show where exercises, Web research activities, and more can be found on the Companion Website.

32.2

---

182   Using Respectful Language

32a Recognizing and editing stereotypes based on gender
32.1

The most common form of sexist language uses *mankind* or *m* humankind; *he, his,* or *him* for all people; and words implying men in pations (*fireman*). When editing the generic *he*, try first to make the con tion plural (for example, use *their* for *his* or for the clumsy *his or her*).

SEXIST   Every trainee should bring **his** laptop with **him**.

AWKWARD   Every trainee should bring **his or her** laptop with **him** **her**.

BETTER   All trainees should bring **their** laptops with **them**.

Some guides suggest that a plural pronoun is better than the generic *he*, e if the pronoun does not agree in number with the subject (see 19b). So readers, however, object more strenuously to the agreement error than to t sexist language. Reword to avoid both problems.

ORIGINAL   **Everyone** has at some time squandered **his** money.

PROBLEMATIC **Everyone** has at some time squandered **their** money.

BETTER   **Most people have** at some time squandered **their** money.
               Everyone has at some time squandered money.

Your readers are likely to object to negative stereotypes based on gen der, such as assumptions that men are stronger or women are worse at math.

STRATEGY Watch for stereotyped roles and occupations.

STEREOTYPED The OnCall Pager is **smaller than most doctors' wallets and easier to answer than phone calls from their wives.**
READER'S REACTION: I'm a woman and a doctor. I'm insulted by the as-sumption that all doctors are male and by the negative reference to "wives." OnCall will never sell a pager in my office!

EDITED   The OnCall Pager **will appeal to doctors because it is small and easy to operate.**

32b Recognizing and editing racial, ethnic, and cultural stereotypes
32b
lang

Most readers won't tolerate racism and will stop reading material with **discriminatory language.** Don't rely on your intent; think about how your reader might construe your words.

STRATEGIES FOR FINDING INFORMATION IN THE HANDBOOK

Strategy 1: Use the index to search alphabetically for your topic and turn to the precise page where you can find it. The index also lists alternative terms (such as *run-on* and *fused sentence*) and cross-references to related terms and glossary entries.

Strategy 2: Use the menu inside the front cover to find the section or tabbed dividers you need. Each divider is labeled and color-coded for writing [red], grammar and usage [green], research [gold], and documentation [dark green]. URLs for Taking It Online appear on the front of the divider, with a TOC of that section on the back.

Strategy 3: Use the detailed table of contents inside the back cover to skim the book's coverage and find the section, chapter, or subtopic you need at a glance.

Strategy 4: Use the glossary to answer questions about usage—for example, whether to use *affect* or *effect* in your sentence.

Strategy 5: ESL Advice is integrated throughout the text. To find a particular topic, turn to the Guide to ESL Advice at the back of the book.

Strategy 6: Look for charts, checklists, and boxed summaries for quick and easy access to useful information.

HOW TO WORK WITH A HANDBOOK PAGE

Look for these elements and reference features to find information in the text.

Running head identifies the chapter topic on the left and the section topic on the right.

Web icons indicate interactive activities on the Website

Boldfaced terms are defined in the text.

Idioms are expressions, often with "forgotten histories," whose meanings differ from their literal definitions, as in *wipe the slate clean* for "start over." Overused idioms can lose their freshness, becoming **trite** or **clichéd**.

STRATEGY Replace trite idioms with precise words.

IDIOMATIC   The losers complained of **dog-eat-dog** politics.

EDITED   The losers consoled themselves after their defeat.

Strategy presents specific techniques to apply in your own writing.

ESL ADVICE: IDIOMS IN AMERICAN ENGLISH

Whether an expression is an **idiom** or a **phrasal verb** (see 15c), the meanings of its separate words will not reveal its meaning as a whole. Although memorizing idioms will enrich your spoken English, these expressions may be too informal in many writing situations. In class or at work, notice how many and which idioms appear in well-written papers by native speakers; adjust your usage accordingly.

ESL Advice provides additional information for nonnative speakers.

32 | Using Respectful Language

Chapter opener identifies the chapter topic.

To represent others fairly, writers and editors eliminate sexist and discriminatory language from their work.

DRAFT   Early in his career, Lasswell published his **seminal** work on propaganda.

READER 1: **Why do you have to use this word? It's offensive to associate originality and creativity with being male.**

READER 2: **You could replace** *seminal* **with** *important* **or** *influential.*

READER 3: **Aren't you overreacting? You wouldn't throw out** *matrimony* **just because it's related to the Latin word for** *mother* **or** *patriot* **because it comes from the word for** *father.*

No matter how you feel about diversity, as a writer you *must* consider how readers react to your representation of men, women, and members of minority groups. You don't want to alienate readers, prejudice people against your ideas, or perpetuate unhealthy attitudes.

THE LONGMAN WRITER'S COMPANION WEBSIT

Just as the text is meant to be a companion to writers, the Website is a companion to the text, offering a wealth of additional resources to help them become better writers and researchers.

The Companion Website includes:

- An easy-access menu to all the interactive exercises and Web research activities that correspond to the Web icons which appear in the text.
- Numerous additional exercises in all areas of grammar, style, punctuation, and mechanics.
- Interactive Tutorials on topics such as incorporating sources, following documentation styles, and other areas of writing.
- Links to a wealth of online resources relating to writing and research.

http://www.ablongman.com/anson

THE
Longman
Writer's Companion

SECOND EDITION

CHRIS M. ANSON

North Carolina
State University

ROBERT A. SCHWEGLER

University of
Rhode Island

MARCIA F. MUTH

University of
Colorado at Denver

Longman

New York San Francisco Boston
London Toronto Sydney Tokyo Singapore Madrid
Mexico City Munich Paris Cape Town Hong Kong Montreal

Senior Vice President and Publisher: Joseph Opiela
Acquisitions Editor: Susan Kunchandy
Development Director: Janet Lanphier
Development Editor: Michael Greer
Supplements Editor: Donna Campion
Media Supplements Editor: Nancy Garcia
Marketing Manager: Christopher Bennem
Senior Production Manager: Bob Ginsberg
Project Coordination, Text Design, and Electronic Page Makeup:
    Nesbitt Graphics, Inc.
Cover Design Manager and Cover Designer: John Callahan
Manufacturing Buyer: Lucy Hebard
Printer and Binder: Quebecor World Taunton
Cover Printer: Coral Graphic Services, Inc.

For permission to use copyrighted material, grateful acknowledgment is made to the copyright holders on pp. 422–423, which are hereby made part of this copyright page.

Library of Congress Cataloging-in-Publication Data

Anson, Christopher M.
   The Longman writer's companion / Chris M. Anson, Robert A. Schwegler, Marcia F. Muth.—2nd ed.
      p. cm.
   Includes index.
   ISBN 0-321-09726-2
   1. English language—Rhetoric—Handbooks, manuals, etc. 2. Report writing—Handbooks, manuals, etc. I. Schwegler, Robert A. II. Muth, Marcia F. III. Title.

PE1408 .A61848 2002
808'.042—dc21

                                                              2002073419

Please visit our website at http://www.ablongman.com/anson.

ISBN 0-321-09726-2

12345678910—WCT—05040302

PREFACE FOR STUDENTS AND INSTRUCTORS

We've prepared this book for people who will be called on to write for different audiences and purposes—in short, for all writers. We know from experience and research that the demands of writing situations vary in important ways. We know, too, that writers need a range of concrete strategies in order to work successfully with the expectations and possibilities posed by each writing situation.

In response, we have produced a handbook filled with advice about writing and revising, creating correct and effective sentences, researching and reasoning, documenting and evaluating sources, representing yourself as a writer and speaker, and navigating the electronic world—all within three important communities: academic, work, and public. And we've made this advice easy to locate and use. We hope that you'll find this handbook to be just what its title promises—a true writer's companion.

New in this edition

In preparing the second edition of *The Longman Writer's Companion*, we have relied on the advice of those who have used this handbook, strengthening the book's innovative features while responding to the changing needs of student writers.

Early coverage of critical reading. Chapter 2 focuses immediately on reading as a means of joining the dialogue of a community. This early chapter illustrates analytical and critical reading with an annotated sample, complementing Chapter 48, "Reading Critically and Evaluating Sources."

Expanded discussion of thesis statements. Besides showing writers how to complicate, qualify, or extend a thesis statement, Chapter 4 now illustrates four useful types of thesis statement: argumentative, general, academic, and informative.

New chapter on community style. Innovative Chapter 8, "Matching Style to Community," introduces elements of community, rather than personal, style. Its advice about academic, workplace, and public style focuses on both expectations and options.

New coverage of speaking. Chapter 11, "Presenting Yourself as a Speaker," outlines how to prepare and deliver an effective oral presentation. A useful chart reviews "speaking" in Three Major Communities (p. 55) while later sections add strategic advice about speaking in academic (55h), workplace (58g), and public (59f) communities.

Even more practical editing advice. Sections 3–7 provide even sharper editing and proofreading Strategies that writers can apply to their own texts. Useful new material includes 39g on combining punctuation marks.

Updated research advice. Chapters 46–50 continue to advise about how to plan a research project, pose research questions, use keywords, find sources, assess search results, read analytically and critically, and evaluate print and electronic sources. New and timely advice includes organizing collaborative research, distinguishing types of periodicals (magazines, journals, and newspapers), selecting search engines, using advanced search strategies, and getting fewer, but better, search results.

Full chapter on crediting sources and avoiding plagiarism. Chapter 49, "Integrating and Crediting Sources," introduces community expectations for citing sources and suggests ways to integrate quotations, paraphrases, summaries, and visuals. Two sections, "Recognizing plagiarism" (49c) and "Avoiding plagiarism" (49d), include new Strategies for avoiding inadvertent plagiarism.

Expanded MLA and APA documentation coverage. Updated Chapter 51, "Using MLA Documentation Style," substantially expands illustrations for Internet resources. Chapter 52, "Using APA Documentation Style," presents the most current APA style, adding many examples of electronic sources and illustrating major APA style changes. Along with Chapters 53 and 54 on CMS and CSE (formerly CBE) styles, these additions enhance documentation coverage we believe to be among the most comprehensive available in a compact handbook, helping writers document sources accurately by using easy-to-follow models.

New student samples. A new student application letter and résumé (58f) now supply practical models for students seeking internships or jobs.

Continuing emphasis on writing in three communities— academic, work, and public

This handbook continues to approach written communication as a social act, taking place among communities of writers and readers. Within different communities—academic, work, or public—the kinds of writing employed are likely to vary considerably. So, too, are expectations for style, reasoning, diction, correctness, and documentation.

The Longman Writer's Companion is unique among compact handbooks in its attention to writing within different communities and in its concrete strategies to help writers understand and respond to the needs of these communities. While the text highlights the importance of the academic setting, it recognizes writing as an essential tool for both occupational success and participation as an involved citizen.

This emphasis on writing for communities appears in discussions, examples, and boxes throughout the handbook and frames the text—with coverage at the very outset, in Chapter 1, and again at the very end in Section 12.

Using the "read, recognize, and revise" approach to correcting errors

It is hard to correct an error if you don't first recognize it as a problem. We have designed *The Longman Writer's Companion* to help writers develop the ability to recognize problems in their work by viewing it as readers do. We pay attention both to the importance of following conventions and to the way conventions may vary from community to community. Finally, we provide practical advice that is easy to find and easy for writers to apply to their own texts.

"Read, recognize, and revise" pattern. This unique approach to grammar and usage organizes the chapters in Sections 3–7, first helping writers identify problems and then suggesting how to revise or edit to repair them.

Reader's reactions. These comments, following examples of errors, convey possible responses to confusing or irritating sentences or passages, helping to explain errors or flaws in terms of their effects on readers.

Strategies. Concrete, practical Strategies apply general advice, showing how to recognize and remedy problems and how to select among alternatives.

ESL advice. Integrated ESL Advice for nonnative speakers strategically supplements discussions of both rhetoric and grammar.

Writing and researching with technology

This handbook offers practical advice for writing and conducting research in technologically enhanced environments.

Taking it online. The Taking It Online feature, located on the front of each tabbed section divider, identifies Web resources related to the section topic. Web icons in the margin note material on the book's Web site.

Writing in electronic communities. Because the vast majority of college students routinely use computers and access the Internet, the handbook supplies pertinent advice throughout, such as "Finding an Online Voice" (Chapter 12), which includes email messages, online class conferences, and Web pages.

Conducting online research. The research chapters (46–49) emphasize conducting keyword searches, selecting search engines, and critically evaluating electronic resources.

Reading, writing, and critical thinking

This handbook, a compact version of *The Longman Handbook for Writers and Readers,* incorporates the distinct philosophy toward reading, writing, and thinking that helped to make its parent text a success.

Writing for readers. This handbook emphasizes the importance of real or potential readers who are present (or ought to be) from the earliest stages of writing to the final proofreading. Specific strategies help writers develop the ability to keep communities of readers and their likely responses in mind during planning, drafting, revising, and editing (Sections 1, 2, 3–7, and 12).

Critical thinking and reading. Reading, thinking, and audience are intertwined in discussions of the roles and expectations of readers, analytical and critical reading, and critical thinking (Sections 1, 2, 8, and 12).

Collaboration and feedback. One way to understand how readers respond to a text is to collaborate with other writer-readers. We offer practical advice about giving and receiving constructive criticism and about collaborating with other writers, whether in the classroom or in work and public settings (Sections 1, 3, 8, and 12).

Reading and writing in research communities. The research chapters (46–50) focus on research processes, resources, and the critical reading, evaluation, and integration of sources. Chapter 48 includes analytical techniques such as summary and paraphrase as well as critical techniques such as synthesis and interpretation, giving special emphasis to critical evaluation of both print and electronic resources. Chapter 49, "Integrating and Crediting Sources," explains how to integrate both text material and visuals while recognizing and avoiding plagiarism. Chapter 50 turns to fieldwork, briefly presenting ethnographic studies, interviews, and other methods.

Representing yourself in a community

In the unique Section 2, "Representing Yourself," we include six chapters that address ways student writers represent themselves—always with an eye toward the three communities.

Chapter 8 identifies the features of community style, while Chapter 9 treats language variation, including home and community varieties. Chapter 10 shows writers how their reasoning and its presentation in a written document affect their readers, working in conjunction with Chapter 56, "Making Persuasive Arguments."

The rest of Section 2 turns to oral, virtual, and visual contexts that may complicate the tasks of contemporary writers. Chapter 11, "Presenting Yourself as a Speaker," advises about effective oral presentations. Chapter 12 helps writers attend to audience, purpose, and community conventions in online contexts such as email, electronic mailing lists, online class conferences, and Web pages. Chapter 13 on document design examines the role and impact of visual presentation, featuring full-color annotated model documents.

Easy access

Even if a handbook is authoritative, flexible, and up to date, it still must be easy to use. We have paid special attention to the handbook's design, tabbed dividers, index, glossary, and pages inside the front and back covers to help users locate the advice they need. For more on these devices for easy access, see "Strategies for finding information in your handbook" on page ix.

Ancillaries

The ancillary package for *The Longman Writer's Companion* is designed to bring helpful resources to both instructors and students.

Print resources FOR STUDENTS

- *Researching Online*. Sixth Edition, by David Munger and Shireen Campbell, gives students detailed, step-by-step instructions for performing electronic searches; for using email, electronic mailing lists, Usenet newsgroups, IRC, and MUDs and MOOs to do research; and for assessing the validity of an electronic source.
- *Literacy Library Series*. Three brief supplements offer additional models and guidelines for writing in different communities: *Public Literacy*, Second Edition, *Workplace Literacy*, Second Edition, and *Academic Literacy*.
- *Visual Communication*, Second Edition, by Susan Hilligoss and Tharon Howard (both of Clemson University) features practical discussions of space, type, organization, pattern, graphic elements, and visuals along with planning worksheets, design samples, and exercises.
- *Exercises to Accompany The Longman Writer's Companion* offers activities on everything from paragraph coherence to comma splices to paraphrasing. *Developmental Exercises to Accompany The Longman Writer's Companion* provides practical activities for developmental writers.

- The **Documentation Guide** provides coverage of MLA, APA, CMS, and CSE styles in a pocket-sized format, as well as a full sample MLA paper and an APA paper.
- **The Penguin Program:** Longman is proud to offer a variety of Penguin titles at a significant discount when packaged with any Longman title. Popular titles include Mike Rose's *Lives on the Boundary* and *Possible Lives* and Neil Postman's *Amusing Ourselves to Death.*
- *A Guide for Peer Response*, Second Edition, by Tori Haring-Smith (Brown University) and Helon H. Raines (Armstrong State University), supplies guidelines for peer critiques and specific forms for different stages in the writing process and for various types of papers.
- Either **Merriam-Webster's Collegiate Dictionary**, Tenth Edition, hardcover dictionary, or **The New American Webster Handy College Dictionary**, Third Edition, paperback dictionary, is available with *The Longman Writer's Companion.*

Print resources FOR INSTRUCTORS

- *The Instructor's Resource Manual* by Stephen Parks (Temple University) includes course design strategies, sample syllabi, writing assignments, classroom and online activities and resources, and much more. Separate Answer Keys are also available for both the Exercises and the Developmental Exercises described above.
- *Comp Tales*, edited by Richard Haswell (Texas A&M, Corpus Christi) and Min-Zhan Lu (Drake University), collects stories that college writing teachers tell and retell about their teaching experiences, organized by current topics of debate in composition studies and on key issues for new writing teachers.
- *Teaching in Progress: Theories, Practices, and Scenarios*, Second Edition, by Josephine Koster Tarvers (Winthrop University) and Cindy Moore (St. Cloud State University)
- *Teaching Writing to the Non-Native Speaker* by Jocelyn Steer
- *Teaching Online: Internet Research, Conversation, and Composition*, Second Edition, by Daniel Anderson (University of North Carolina, Chapel Hill) and Bret Benjamin, Chris Busiel, and Bill Paredes-Holt (University of Texas, Austin)

Media resources FOR STUDENTS AND INSTRUCTORS

- *The Longman Writer's Companion Online* at <http://www.ablongman.com/anson>, a Companion Website, includes practice exercises for every chapter; helpful links; brief writing samples illustrating key concepts of many chapters; and an interactive module on Internet searching methods. Teachers will also find sample syllabi, teaching notes, *PowerPoint* presentations, and more at this site.

- **A CD-ROM featuring *The Longman Writer's Companion*** includes a searchable online version of the handbook with additional practice exercises for students. Please contact your local sales representative for more information.

Acknowledgments

First we wish to thank the students who have generously allowed us to present their writing as an inspiration to others: David Aharonian, Summer Arrigo-Nelson, Jeanne Brown, Amy Burns, Zachary Carter, Kimlee Cunningham, Christine Reed Davis, Melanie Dedecker, Robin Edwards, Jennifer Figliozzi, Shane Hand, Tammy Jo Helton, Norrie Herrin, Andrea Herrmann, Kris Lundell, Brian Schwegler, Meghan Tubridy, Kimberly Tullos, and Ted Wolfe. Marcia Muth also thanks the students in her writing workshops, which she offers through the School of Education at the University of Colorado at Denver.

A community of special consultants assisted us in the initial development of this handbook. We remain grateful for the advice of Victor Villanueva of Washington State University at Pullman, Christina Haas of Kent State University, and Elizabeth Ervin of the University of North Carolina at Wilmington. We have also continued to build on earlier assistance from Mick Doherty and Sandye Thompson on online writing and the Taking It Online feature, Daniel Anderson of the University of North Carolina on electronic research, Jim Dubinsky on document design and Eric Pappas on workplace writing, both of Virginia Polytechnic Institute and State University, Charlotte Smith of Adirondack Community College on research, and Ellen Bitterman of the State University of New York, The College at New Paltz, on the ESL advice. For this edition, we appreciate updated advice on workplace writing from Stevens Amidon of the University of Rhode Island and on research strategies and resources from Mary Finley of the University Library at California State University Northridge.

Our special thanks go to the following reviewers: William Carroll, Texas A & M University; Leona Fisher, Georgetown University; Darrin L. Grinder, Northwest Nazarene University; Kathleen Kelly, Northeastern University; John Connors Kerrigan, Fort Hays State University; Leslie Lydell, University of Minnesota; Susan Smith Nash, University of Oklahoma; Laura Bearrie Pogue, Hardin-Simmons University; and Deborah Coxwell Teague, Florida State University.

Our Longman team has been skillfully guided by Susan Kunchandy, our resourceful sponsoring editor, and by Michael Greer, our tenacious developmental editor. Thanks to both of you for respecting and encouraging the vision of this book as it moves into its second edition. We also appreciate the assistance of Rebecca Gilpin, especially with the Taking It Online feature, and of Kim Dozier for her industrious aid with documentation entries. We remain grateful for the many long-standing contributions of Bob Ginsberg, a production manager of infinite patience, and for the conscientious and thoughtful orchestration of Susan McIntyre, Project Manager, Nesbitt Graphics. The attentive support of Jerilyn Kauffman, Nesbitt Graphics, designer, and Kathy Graehl, copyeditor, has once again helped to ensure an attractive, accessible, and consistent book.

Chris Anson thanks Geanie, Ian, and Graham for enduring yet another book project and for always being understanding (well, almost always) when long phone calls, hours at the computer, or thickets of manuscript got in the way of backyard soccer, a leaking faucet, or something more than thirty minutes for dinner. Your patience has been my inspiration.

Bob Schwegler would like to acknowledge above all Nancy Newman Schwegler for sharing her understanding of readers, reading, and writers. "And I'll be sworn up 't that he loves her; / For here's a paper written in his hand, / A halting sonnet. . . ." He would also like to thank Brian and Tara Schwegler for their advice, Christopher for his smiles, and Ashley Marie for inspiration.

Marcia Muth thanks her family: her son, Anderson, whose friends, crises, inspirations, and inventive papers continue to enlighten her about the rich and varied lives of student writers, and her husband, Rod, who remains the most patient, steadfast, and inspirational of friends, advisors, and companions.

CHRIS M. ANSON
ROBERT A. SCHWEGLER
MARCIA F. MUTH

TAKING IT ONLINE

THE VIRTUAL COMMUNITY
http://www.rheingold.com/vc/book
Howard Rheingold's best-selling book *The Virtual Community* is available for free on the Web. It will give you insight into how electronic resources like the Web have affected "the rules of community."

WEB EXHIBITS
http://www.webexhibits.org
Browse this site for links to interesting reading and visuals on widely varied topics, academic and otherwise.

THE ONLINE WRITERY
http://www.missouri.edu/~writery/
Visit *The Online Writery* at the University of Missouri at Columbia for help with your general questions about writing.

OVERCOMING WRITER'S BLOCK
http://leo.stcloudstate.edu/acadwrite/block.html
Can't get started? Try the ideas on this page, or turn to the other suggestions available at *The Write Place*.

WORKING WITH TOPICS
http://writing.colostate.edu/references/processes/topic/
Here's advice across the academic disciplines for finding, narrowing, and working with topics.

DEVELOPING A THESIS STATEMENT
http://www.english.uiuc.edu/cws/wworkshop
Click on "Tips & Techniques" and then on "Developing a Thesis." This guide uses pairs of original and revised sentences to illustrate how to refine a thesis statement.

SECTION 1
Joining Communities: Participating as Critical Readers and Writers

1 Readers, Writers, and Community Expectations

Someone created the Web page you browsed yesterday—writing its text, planning its design, and anticipating readers' reactions. Someone else wrote the newsletter in your mailbox, the forms for your car loan, and the waiver you signed before the technician X-rayed your ankle. Because writing and reading surround us, shaping our lives, choices, responsibilities, and values, this book looks at the roles of writers and readers in contemporary culture. It offers concrete strategies for writing, for critical reading and thinking, and for understanding your readers' expectations.

Whether you're drafting a psychology paper, an email message at work, or a neighborhood flyer, try to envision a **community of readers and writers**, people with shared—though not necessarily identical—goals, settings, preferences, and uses for verbal and visual texts. This book will help you develop your skill at recognizing different needs and expectations of writers, readers, and speakers in the academic, work, and public communities in which you may be active throughout your life.

1a Recognizing academic, work, and public communities of readers and writers

1.1

In a Denver suburb, pets have been disappearing. The culprits have been coyotes or other predators, crowded by new homes and industrial parks. Alarmed local residents wonder if a young child will be the next victim.

In such situations, problem solving often begins with written and oral presentations. City officials and citizens may turn to the **academic community** for studies of the habitat and feeding habits of coyotes and other predators, documents that may sound like this:

> This report summarizes and compares data from two studies of the habits of predators in areas with significant population growth and urbanization over the past ten years.

The scientific reports focus on one question: how do coyotes behave in a shrinking habitat? But parents, pet owners, and others in the **public community** are likely to ask a different question: how can we protect our children and pets without harming local wildlife? Tips created by the Colorado Division of Wildlife apply scientific knowledge to residents' concerns.

1

> *If you see a coyote:*
> - Leave it alone; do not approach it.
>
> *If a coyote approaches:*
> - Use an animal repellent such as pepper spray to ward off the coyote.
> - Throw rocks or sticks at the coyote to scare it away.
>
> - Use a loud, authoritative voice to frighten the animal away.
>
> *How to coexist with coyotes:*
> - Keep your pet on a leash.
> - Do not let pets out between dusk and dawn, when most predators are active. . . .
>
> *(The Denver Post, 30 July 1998, 15A)*

Neighborhood groups might distribute leaflets and organize meetings.

> ## COYOTE ALERT!
>
> Are your children safe in their own backyards? Coyotes attacked seven dogs and cats last summer. Find out what we can do. Join the Committee to Safeguard Our Children on Tuesday, October 2, at 7:00 p.m. in the high school gym.

Other reports might circulate in the **work community**, analyzing the frequency of complaints, summarizing business perspectives, or presenting policy options to help people, pets, and coyotes live in balance.

1 Consider academic, work, and public communities

Participating within and across academic, work, and public communities means talking, listening, reading, and, especially, writing. To communicate effectively within a community of readers and writers, consider its roles, goals, forms, and writing characteristics. (See the chart on the facing page.) Although community considerations sometimes overlap, they can help you recognize readers' expectations and your limitations and choices as a writer.

ESL ADVICE: CIVIC PARTICIPATION

Many schools encourage students to join clubs, participate in campus governance, and volunteer on or off campus. Local civic participation is a rewarding tradition that provides many opportunities to improve your reading, writing, and speaking in English.

2 Consider electronic communities

The broad academic, work, and public communities all cohabit the intriguing world of the Internet. A click of a mouse connects you with large and small electronic communities, each organized around a shared interest in a topic, point of view, or issue.

THREE MAJOR COMMUNITIES OF READERS AND WRITERS			
	ACADEMIC	**WORK**	**PUBLIC**
ROLES	Students Teachers Researchers Committees gathering expert opinions Readers interested in specialized knowledge	Co-workers Supervisors Organizational work groups (management, accounting, public relations) Clients and customers Government agencies Public target groups	Residents or group members Possible supporters Public officials or agencies Community activists Local groups Readers interested in an issue
GOALS	Creation or exchange of knowledge	Provision of information Analysis of problems Proposal of solutions Promotion of organization	Persuasion in support of a cause or issue Participation in democracy Provision of issue-oriented information
TYPICAL FORMS	Analysis of text or phenomenon Interpretation of text, artwork, or event Research proposal Lab report Scholarly article Annotated bibliography Grant proposal Classroom presentation	Description of object, event, situation, or problem Proposal Report of findings Memos, letters, minutes of meetings Guidelines or instructions Promotional materials Meeting presentation	Position paper Informative report Letter to group, supporters, officials, agency, organization, or publication Flyer, newsletter, pamphlet, or fact sheet Action or grant proposal Guidelines, charter, or principles Comments in public forum
WRITING CHARACTERISTICS	Detailed reasoning and critical analysis Fresh insights or conclusions Extensive evidence Accurate detail supporting conclusions Balanced treatment acknowledging other viewpoints Thoughtful, stimulating exploration of topic	Concentration on task, problem, or goal Accurate and efficient presentation of problem or issue Concise, clear, direct prose Promotion of product or service	Focus on shared values and goals Advocacy of cause Fair recognition of others' interests Relevant evidence supporting positions Concentration on own point of view or on need for information Orientation to actions or solutions

STRATEGY Use TASALS to help you recognize electronic communities.

TOPIC. On what subject does the site focus? Do contributors belong to any organization or share any other affiliation?

ATTITUDE. Does the site have a clear point of view or set of values? Do contributors have similar perspectives or values?

STRATEGIES. Does the site use a particular written style or visual design?

AUTHORITY. Does the site support claims or information? Do contributors reason carefully, offering evidence rather than opinion?
LINKS. Do postings or links refer to related online resources?
SUMMARIZE. How can you sum up the qualities of the community, it
expectations of participants, and its conventions?

1b Joining communities of readers and writers

Participating in communities of readers and writers brings personal
academic, and professional rewards whether your involvement just happens
or you actively seek it.

STRATEGY   Become involved in communities of readers and writers.

- **Become an active, critical reader.** Read widely—newspapers, special-
interest magazines, campus newsletters, neighborhood flyers, electronic
exchanges, or Web texts. Note especially effective passages. Reread them
as a writer, trying to figure out why they work so well.
- **Look for opportunities to write as a citizen, employee, and student.** Create an email study group for a class. Contribute to a company or group newsletter or the school paper. Keep a journal, record
ideas in a notebook, or send email messages. Write letters to the newspaper or public figures about issues that simplify or complicate your
life as a citizen. Attend public meetings, and voice your ideas.
- **Turn to your readers.** Do they expect your text to be short or long,
simple or elaborate? Do they want sources or opinions, analysis or argument, formal style or chatty prose? Ask readers to respond to your draft:
Is it clear or confusing? Which parts read well? Which are awkward?
- **Develop a portfolio.** As you look ahead to demonstrating your skills
for potential employers, begin building a portfolio. Include samples of
your best academic papers, work documents, materials from civic or
volunteer activities, and taped oral presentations.

1c Recognizing myths and realities about the writing process

Successful writing is almost never a matter of just recording your
thoughts in finished form. Instead, it begins with a response: to an idea or
experience, a reading, or a problem. It calls for planning, defining a purpose
and thesis, considering community and readers, drafting, revising, editing,
and proofreading. And it rarely moves in a straight line. Revising may mean
further drafting, or editing may mean collaborating with readers.

Replace your self-defeating habits with reliable strategies that increase
your impact and flexibility writing in different communities.

Myth: People easily succeed in the real world without having to write.
Reality: It's a popular myth that executives don't need to write because their assistants do this work. In Fortune 500 companies, however, over half the employees spend between eight and forty hours writing each week. As more employees carry laptops and send email, their writing time is likely to increase, making writing ability even more crucial for success.

Myth: Writing is easy for people born with the knack.
Reality: If we looked over other writers' shoulders, we'd know what researchers know: good writers draft and redraft, succeeding through hard work.

Myth: You can be a good writer without doing much reading.
Reality: It's not likely. The more you read, the better you understand the writing that works in specific communities and your options as a writer.

Myth: It's cheating to ask others to read your paper before you turn it in.
Reality: It certainly is cheating if you have someone else write a paper or parts of it and then claim the work as your own. But successful writers always depend on readers for feedback. Especially at work and in civic groups, key documents are likely to be written collaboratively.

Myth: Good writing is effective for all readers.
Reality: All good writing is clear, coherent, and correct, but what works in one community may not work as well in another. Your sociology research paper will differ in tone, style, and content from the proposal you write at work or the email you send to your running group.

ESL ADVICE: EFFECTIVE WRITING

Another myth is that you can't be an effective writer if English is not your first language. Of course, the more you read and write, the more your English will improve. But effective writing takes hard work whether you're a native or nonnative speaker. And powerful writing from the heart moves readers no matter what the writer's language background.

2 | Reading

When you read, you almost always respond. You may highlight in your textbook, revise a collaborative report at work, or jot a civic event on your calendar. Whatever you read—essays, articles, memos, reports, Web pages—responsive reading is bedrock, supporting speaking and writing.

2a Reading to join the community dialogue

A systematic approach to reading can help you identify expectations o readers and practices of writers in your community.

1 Preread before reading

Preview the form. Locate features that suggest the text's approach: long paragraphs or short, opening abstract, headings, sidebars, frames, glossary, references, links, visuals, one column or more.

Preview the organization. Skim a book's table of contents. Look for headings in articles, reports, or memos. Click on the site map.

Examine the context. Note the author's background, the original readers and situation, the place and date of first publication, or a Web site's sponsor.

Sample and predict. Scan the text to activate your own knowledge and prepare for interpreting unfamiliar words and examples in context. Look up baffling words before you read. Recall similar texts; try to predict where the reading will go.

Learn some background. Talk to peers, co-workers, or others who know a difficult subject. Find an encyclopedia entry on key concepts.

Plan ahead. When you read Web pages or library articles, consider printing or duplicating the text so you can write on your own copy.

2 Stay alert while reading

Pause and assess. Where are you? What have you learned so far? What confuses you? Jot down your answers; then skim what you've just read.

Share insights. Meet with classmates or co-workers to discuss a text. Compare reactions, considering how the others reached their interpretations.

Summarize in chunks. Glance back over a section, and state the main point so far. Guess where the reading will go next.

Find what's important. Read first—*without highlighting*—to capture the essentials. Go back again to note or highlight what's *really* important.

Read the visuals. Examine graphs, charts, diagrams, or other illustrations; analyze what they say and how they relate to the written text.

3 Follow up after reading

Record main ideas. Use a file card, journal, or computer file so you can review without leafing through copies, printouts, or books.

Add your own responses. Note what you already know as well as your own views about the topic. Don't simply accept what the author says.

Reread and review. Reread difficult material, first skimming more quickly and then studying the passages you've highlighted.

Write in your text. If a book or other text isn't yours, don't write in it. If it—or a photocopy or printout—is yours, annotate it.

- Interpretations: What does the author or speaker mean?
- Confusions: At what points are you puzzled?
- Questions: What more do you need to know?
- Objections or counterarguments: Where do you disagree?
- Restatements: How can you say it in your own words?
- Evaluations: What do you like or dislike about the reading?
- Applications: What can you use for class, work, or activities?
- Expectations: How does this reading resemble or differ from others typical in your academic, work, or public community?

2b Reading analytically and critically

Your purposes and context shape your responses as a reader. If you are gathering details for an oral presentation or essay, your **analytical reading** will focus on *understanding* the content—the ideas, purposes, information, organization, perspective, and approaches. (See 48a.)

STRATEGY Read analytically: Discover what a text says.

- **Summarize:** How can you sum up or restate its key ideas?
- **Paraphrase:** How can you state its main points in your own words?
- **Synthesize:** How can you connect its information with that in other texts?
- **Quote:** Which of the text's exact words make powerful statements?

Next, your **critical reading** will focus on *interacting* with the text, adding to it your knowledge and insight, analyzing what it does—and doesn't—address, relating it to other texts within the community, and assessing its strengths and limitations. (See 48b.)

STRATEGY Read critically: Interact with a text.

- **Question:** What answers do you still want or need?
- **Synthesize perspectives:** How can you relate it to other views?
- **Interpret:** What do you conclude about its outlook and bias?
- **Assess:** How do you evaluate its value and accuracy?

2.1

The passage below illustrates both analytical and critical comments.

ANALYTICAL COMMENTS		CRITICAL COMMENTS
Compares health care choices to grocery shopping	How is health care like going to the grocer? The more you put in the cart, the higher the bill. But unlike your grocery expedition, where all you pay for are the items in your own cart, with health care the other customer's cart is on your tab, too.	Sounds good, but is it fair overall? Need t[o] read more
Admits benefits but claims costs will increase Supplies supporting evidence	Nor will the tab get any better with the patient protection legislation being considered in Washington. Sure, Americans will get guaranteed access to emergency rooms, medical clinical trials and specialists. Senate legislation even provides the right to sue your insurer and and be awarded up to $5 million in punitive damages.[. . .]	Lots of coverage problems—like my emergency room bill
Projects costs and effects	The litigation costs, and the efforts by some employers to avoid liability, could lead to an additional 9 million uninsured Americans by 2010.	Does everyone agree on estimates?
	—"Restrict Right to Sue or We'll Pay in the End," *Atlanta Journal-Constitution*, July 19, 2001.	What's this paper's usual viewpoint?

3 | Planning

Imagine trying to build a house without drawing up any plans before-hand or going into the playoffs without a team strategy, just to "see what hapens." Success would depend on luck, not design. The same is true for peaking and writing. For almost any formal project—in college, for a civic roup, or on the job—you need to "rough out" ideas before you really get arted. **Planning** before you write a full draft—often called **prewriting**—ves you a map of where you want to go in your writing.

SL ADVICE: PLANNING

Try planning in your first language; move to English as ideas grow.

3a Generating ideas

Whatever your writing task, you will want to ask, "What do I know bout what I'm writing? What else do I need to know?" Gather ideas from our existing resources—your journal or notebook entries, readings anno-ated with your responses, class or meeting notes, your assignment sheet or ob description, and any similar projects. (See also 4a.)

STRATEGY **Try freewriting.**

Write by hand or at the computer for five or ten minutes *without stop-ing*, even if you only repeat "I'm stuck." As such empty prose bores you, ou'll almost magically slip into more engaging ideas. Or begin **focused freewriting** with an idea you already have—"I guess I support antigambling aws"—to start productively exploring the topic.

3.1

Listing can help you draw out your own knowledge, create ideas through association, and generalize from details. For her history paper on Soviet espionage during the Cold War, Annie Hanson listed her main points and, under her final point, key supporting details.

1. Cold War background from Yalta to Berlin Wall
2. Western vs. Soviet technology
3. Role of KGB training operatives and recruiting
4. Espionage examples (Fuchs, De Groot, Philby)

STRATEGY **Use listing.**

Write your topic at the top of a page, and then list ten thoughts, facts, impressions, ideas, or specifics about it. For example, begin with a general idea or a major part of your project, and list supporting details and new asso-ciations. Repeat the process with your other ideas or parts.

Especially for proposals and recommendations, **strategic questioning** can pull information from your memory and suggest more to gather. Brian

Corby asked questions as he began his letter to the zoning board opposing high-rise apartment next to a public park.

What?
  * Proposed high-rise apt.—18 stories, 102 units
  * East side of Piedmont Park by Sunrise Ave.
  * Planning by Feb., groundbreaking by June, done in a year

Why?
  * Developers profit
  * Provides medium-cost housing in growing area
  * Develops ugly vacant lot by park

Why Not?
  * "Citifies" one of the few green patches in town
  * Traffic, crime rate, park use
  * New zoning opens the door to other high-rises

STRATEGY Ask strategic questions.

Begin with *what*, *why*, and *why not*. Ask *who*, *where*, *when*, and *how*, i they apply.

ESL ADVICE: CLEAR AND FORCEFUL DETAILS

Most writing in English tends to be direct rather than abstract. Especially in the academic and work communities, a writer often makes a clear assertion about a topic, problem, or event and then supports that idea with facts, details or research. In a sense, the writer must "prove" the point, and readers won't accept it on faith or by virtue of the writer's authority. If readers find your writing too broad, indirect, or poorly supported, compare their expectations with those of readers in your first language. American teachers and workplace supervisors generally want writers to ask questions about writing projects and are used to explaining what they expect.

3b Structuring ideas and information

Ideas and information alone will get you started, but most writing and speaking projects require **structure**—a pattern, outline, or plan to shape and organize. Use the structure expected by readers in projects such as reports, or create a structure from the ideas you've generated. As she began her researched argument paper, Marianne Kidd used clustering to relate her ideas about censoring rock music lyrics. (See Figure 3.1 on p.11.)

STRATEGY Draw a cluster.

Circle a concept, idea, or topic in the center of a page. Then jot down associations with this kernel topic, circling and connecting them with lines to the center, like the spokes of a wheel, or to each other to show interconnec-

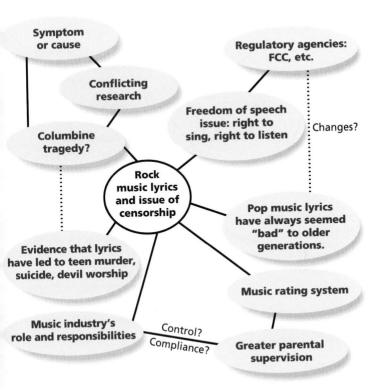

FIGURE 3.1   A simple conceptual cluster

tions. To create clusters in cycles, use each subsidiary idea as a new kernel topic.

Tree diagrams resemble clusters, but their branches tend to be more linear and hierarchical. Each main branch of Bill Chen's diagram became a "chunk" or section in his paper on possible uses of virtual reality. (See Figure 3.2 on p.12.)

STRATEGY Create a tree diagram.

Start with your topic as the trunk. Create main branches for central points and smaller branches for related ideas. Then "revise" your diagram into a working plan or outline for the paragraphs or sections of your project.

If your project involves chronology, use a **time sequence**. For example, in planning a self-guided tour of a museum exhibit, James Cole drew a time sequence detailing Andy Warhol's artistic life.

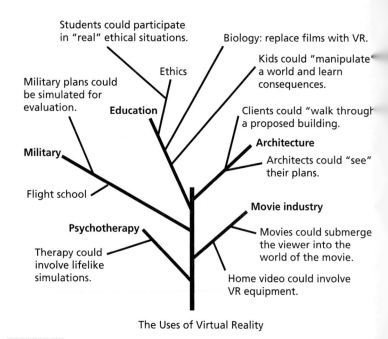

The Uses of Virtual Reality

FIGURE 3.2 A simple tree diagram

STRATEGY Build a time sequence.

Frame each event along a line, noting dates, ages, or other time markers. If you wish, add thick connecting lines to mark pivotal events that led to or caused other events and thin lines to show simple time links.

___

Position papers, business reports, and other persuasive pieces often follow **a problem-solution sequence**, outlining a problem, offering workable solutions, or advocating one solution rather than another. Paula Masek used a problem-solution grid to plan her editorial exploring temporary solutions to the problem of feeding the homeless. Later she discussed each boxed item in a separate section or paragraph of her draft. (See Figure 3.3.)

STRATEGY Create a problem-solution grid.

First state the problem. Underneath, in boxes or columns, identify possible solutions. Below these, identify problems each solution might create and then their solutions. Generate as many layers as you wish.

___

The best-known planning technique is the trusty **outline**, complete with Roman numerals. The traditional outline may help writers label or arrange

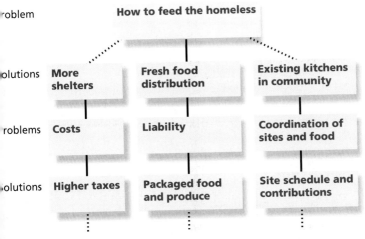

Problem — **How to feed the homeless**

Solutions — **More shelters** — **Fresh food distribution** — **Existing kitchens in community**

Problems — **Costs** — **Liability** — **Coordination of sites and food**

Solutions — **Higher taxes** — **Packaged food and produce** — **Site schedule and contributions**

FIGURE 3.3 A problem-solution grid

ideas but doesn't do much to help *generate* them. A **working outline**, however, can help you generate information or identify missing pieces.

STRATEGY Invent an outline.

With a simple topic as your main heading, commit yourself to three second-level headings by writing *A, B,* and *C* underneath. (Leave a lot of space in between.) Then fill in the subheadings. Now develop third-level headings by writing *1, 2,* and *3* beneath *each* letter. Fill them in, too.

3.2

Mitch Weber used a working outline to plan a brief history of the nonprofit organization where he had a summer internship.

> **CREATION OF THE FAMILY HEALTH CENTER**
> A. Founding Work of Susan and Roger Ramstadt
>   1. The "vision"
>   2. Finding the money
>   3. Support from the Crimp Foundation
> B. The Early Years (1982-95)
>   1. Building momentum
>   2. The great financial disaster
>   3. Rebirth
> C. Toward Maturity
>   1. Fund-raising in the late 1990s
>   2. State recognition and the big award
>   3. The new vision: health and sustenance

Whatever your planning strategies, use all available tools.

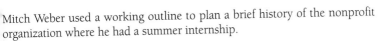

3b plan

4a
rpose

STRATEGY Use electronic planning to expand your options.

- Use your computer for planning so that you can easily reorganize an develop your ideas into a draft.
- Try interactive questions or prompts from your software, the Web, (the campus computer lab or tutoring center.
- Use a search engine to browse for Web sites on your topic.
- Skim links, gathering possible ideas from varied sites.

4 | Defining Your Purpose, Thesis, and Audience

Think about what writing or speaking on the job, in school, and in civic groups actually *does*. It helps communicate ideas, produce commodities, provide services, or make things work. It can sell, buy, or negotiate things. It can be coolly informative or passionately persuasive. It can do public good or make private profit. And it can produce knowledge that will delight and entertain, lead to personal wisdom, or save lives.

4a Analyzing your purpose

Given all that writing *can* do, one of your early steps is to decide just what a particular piece of writing *needs* to do.

1 Define the focus of your task or assignment

In many writing situations, someone else hands you a task or assignment, and it's your job to produce decent prose. Meg Satterfield began this process by underlining a key noun phrase in her assignment.

> Most of us have volunteered at some time—helping family or friends or joining a service-learning project. Tell your audience (our class) about <u>some unexpected outcome</u> of your experience as a volunteer.

Meg decided that her assignment left the topic open but valued something ("unexpected outcomes") that would surprise or engage readers.

STRATEGY Target your topic.

On your assignment sheet or job description, underline any nouns or noun phrases; use them to invent and narrow possibilities (see 3a).

Define the purpose of your task or assignment

Focusing on a topic—a noun—gives you a clear sense of what your writing is *about*. But nouns don't act, and your writing needs to *do* something, too. Its **purpose** usually takes the form of an action statement—a verb or verb phrase like these two in Cory Meta's assignment.

> Find a magazine ad that catches your attention. Analyze the ad for its hidden cultural assumptions, being sure to describe exactly what is happening in the ad. Note techniques such as camera angle, coloration, and focus.

STRATEGY Pinpoint what you need to *do*.

In your assignment sheet or job description, underline any verbs or verb phrases that tell you what to *do*. (See the chart on p. 16 for a list of verbs frequently used in academic writing situations.) Then use planning strategies to generate material related to these verbs (see 3a).

3 Rough out a purpose structure

In planning a student housing guide, Carol Stotsky specified her purposes by developing a tentative order for her section on options.

BEGINNING	Persuade students to consider housing options carefully.
MIDDLE	Explore advantages and disadvantages of each in detail.
ENDING	Recommend that traditional students move gradually from security (home or dorm) to independence (off campus).

STRATEGY Use simple categories to shape your purpose.

A sequence such as "1-2-3-4" or "beginning-middle-ending" can help you decide what each part should do. Use verbs that clarify your purpose: *show, explain, claim, counter, build up to.*

4b Creating a thesis

Just as readers may look for an executive summary with a report or an abstract before an article, they may expect you to clarify your point right away in a college paper, too. For this reason, a thesis statement often ends the first paragraph. The **thesis**, usually a single sentence, is the controlling idea that you then explore, support, or illustrate using specific examples or arguments. You may draft a paper with a clear thesis in mind, discover your thesis later on and revise accordingly, or modify your thesis as you look for evidence or ideas to back up your assertions.

KEY VERBS USED TO SPECIFY WRITING PURPOSES

Analyze: Divide or break something into constituent parts so you can observe, describe, and study their relationships.

Analyze the relationships between form and color, light and shadow, and foreground and background in one of Titian's paintings.

Argue: Prove a point, or persuade a reader to accept or entertain a position. (See Chapters 10 and 56.)

In a letter to the College Senate, argue your position on a campuswide smoking ban.

Compare and contrast: Show similarities and differences for two or more things.

Compare and contrast costs at local hospitals for ten surgical procedures.

Describe: Show how something is experienced through sight, sound, taste, touch, or smell.

Describe obstacles encountered in local historic homes by visitors in wheelchairs.

Discuss: Provide an intelligent, focused commentary about a topic.

Discuss current transit needs in the metropolitan region.

Evaluate: Reach conclusions about something's value or worth, using substantiating evidence based on observation and analysis.

Evaluate the effectiveness of camera technique in Hitchcock's *The Birds*.

Extend: Apply an idea or concept more fully.

Extend last year's production figures to take into account the April work slowdown.

Inform: Present facts, views, phenomena, or events to enlighten your reader.

Inform homeowners about the hazards of lead paint.

Show: Demonstrate or provide evidence to explain something.

Show how Pip, in his later years, is influenced by Joe's working-class values in Dickens's *Great Expectations*.

Synthesize: Combine separate elements into a single or unified entity.

Synthesize this list of facts about energy consumption.

Trace: Map out a history, chronology, or explanation of origins.

Trace the development of Stalinism.

Use: Focus on the designated material, selecting specifics from it to explain and illustrate your broader points.

Use the three assigned poems to illustrate contemporary responses to death.

To begin defining a thesis, first narrow the topic to some specific angle or perspective. Then begin turning the topic from a noun (a "thing") into a statement that contains a verb. Notice how Lynn Tarelli developed a thesis for her brochure for a parenting group.

VAGUE TOPIC	`Ritalin`
STILL A TOPIC	`Ritalin for kids with attention-deficit disorder (ADD)`
STILL A TOPIC	`The problem of Ritalin use for kids with ADD`
ROUGH THESIS	`Parents should be careful about using medicines such as Ritalin for kids with ADD.`

Lynn progressively sharpened the topic and brought the fourth version to life by expressing an assertion about it, seeing it from a specific perspective.

Complicate, qualify, or extend your rough thesis

Lynn's thesis still didn't make a clear suggestion to parents about Ritalin: Should it not be used for kids with ADD? Should it be used judiciously?

FINAL THESIS	`Although Ritalin is widely used to treat children with ADD, parents should not rely too heavily on such drugs until they have explored both their child's problem and all treatment options.`

Lynn *complicated* her rough thesis by accepting Ritalin as a legitimate treatment for ADD; her cautions about overreliance and other options *qualified* and *extended* it to create a clearer, more complex statement.

2 Shape an appropriate thesis

You may also refine your thesis to suit your purpose or readers.

4.2

Argumentative thesis. Readers will expect you to indicate your opinion on an issue and perhaps to acknowledge other views.

> `Although bioengineered crops may pose some dangers, their potential for combating worldwide hunger and disease justifies their careful use in farming.`

General thesis. Readers will expect to learn your conclusions or special perspectives and perhaps their importance as well.

> `Sooner or later, teenagers stop listening to parents and turn to each other for advice, sometimes with disastrous results.`

Academic thesis. Readers will expect your specific conclusion and you plan to support it, both using terms appropriate to the field.

> My survey of wedding announcements in local newspapers from 1960 to 2000 indicates that religious background and ethnicity have decreased in importance in mate selection but education and social background remain significant factors.

Informative thesis. Readers will expect to learn why information is inter esting or useful and how you'll organize or synthesize it.

> For parents who want to choose kids' videos based on the moral lessons they teach, the job of selection is simplified by watching for the three main categories of videos.

3 Develop and modify your thesis

As your ideas evolve, be ready to modify or change your thesis. Afte outlining his contribution to a library publication on computer literacy, Joe Kitze modified his thesis to give readers more to consider.

THESIS In spite of expanding technology, computers will never replace books as the chief medium of written literacy.

SUPPORTING IDEA 1 Books are more democratic, since not everyone can afford a personal computer.

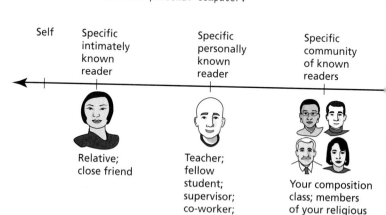

Self   Specific intimately known reader   Specific personally known reader   Specific community of known readers

Relative; close friend   Teacher; fellow student; supervisor; co-worker; acquaintance from school, work, or group   Your composition class; members of your religious group; your division at work; other grou bound by situation

FIGURE 4.1 The audience continuum

JPPORTING IDEA 2   Books can be enjoyed anywhere--on a bus or beach, in bed.

JPPORTING IDEA 3   Children enjoy the physical comfort of reading with adults, a comfort harder to achieve with computers.

MODIFIED THESIS   Although computer technology allows masses of information to be stored and conveyed electronically, it will never replace the bound book as the most affordable, convenient, and magical medium for print.

STRATEGY Develop your thesis.

Help your reader anticipate and organize information in your writing, itting separate chunks—paragraphs and sections—into your larger purpose. Use planning strategies (see Chapter 3) or research (see 46g) to create a series of points that support, expand, or illustrate your thesis. Then extend and modify your thesis by asking why, how, and for what reason.

4c Considering your readers

Like an oral presentation, a written text addresses a specific **audience** that includes your actual or implied readers. (See Figure 4.1.)

Specific publicly known reader	Specific unknown reader	Specific community of unknown readers	General community of unknown readers

Senator Kennedy; Whoopi Goldberg; president of your university; editor of your local newspaper	Personnel director at Inland Chemicals; editor of the *Journal of Economics*; chair of the university committee on animals in research; others known by name and affiliation	Board of directors at Inland Chemicals; members of the local PTA; the choir's electronic mailing list; readers of *Hunting Magazine*; other groups with shared interests	Democrats; educated Americans; readers of popular fiction; concerned citizens; working parents

4.3

1 Analyze your readers

Begin your audience analysis by asking, "Who are my readers?"

STRATEGY Characterize your readers.

- **Size and familiarity.** How large is your audience? How close to you Use the audience continuum to define levels of familiarity and formalit
- **Community.** Which expectations of readers are typical of the commu nity in which you are writing? Which are specialized or local? Wha roles in the community do your readers play or expect you to play?
- **Knowledge.** What do readers already know about your topic? Ar they novices or experts?
- **Social context.** What characterizes your readers socially, culturally and educationally? How do they spend their time?
- **Intellectual disposition.** How do your readers think? Are they con servative? radical? apathetic?
- **Conditions of reading.** Under what conditions will they read?
- **Power.** What is your status relative to readers? Are they peers or supe riors? Do you expect them, or do they expect you, to do something?

2 Adapt to your readers

Because academic, work, and public communities are broad groups, also ask, "Exactly what do my readers expect?"

- **Select the genre readers expect.** The type of text you choose to write— the **genre**—depends on your purpose and readers. If you request funds for a volunteer project, readers will expect a grant proposal, not a poem.
- **Shape your content to the context.** If you're explaining how to re- move mildew for a neighborhood newsletter, skip the history of mildew unless it's relevant to the remedies.
- **Adjust your structure to the situation.** In a letter to your invest- ment firm's client whose stock has tumbled, you might lead up to this news with the circumstances of the loss. A lab report, however, should move directly to the conventional sections.
- **Anticipate possible responses of readers.** Will readers expect you to be clinical and detached, informal and chatty, or in between? How might they react if you're emotional, hostile, or legalistic?

ESL ADVICE: APPROPRIATE FORMALITY

Spoken English, even in the classroom and the office, may be quite in- formal. Written English may vary in formality, but readers other than friends and relatives generally expect it to be more formal than spoken language. If you're uncertain about what is appropriate, look at comparable writing done by others, or ask your teacher or supervisor for advice.

5 | Drafting

If planning resembles storyboarding a movie, then drafting begins the filming, even though you may retake entire scenes and cut lots of footage. **Drafting** is the challenging process of stringing words together into sentences and paragraphs that make sense to a reader.

5a Moving from planning to drafting

Although all your planning (see Chapters 3–4) prepares you for drafting, you may not know how and where to begin writing. As Amy Burns reviewed a cluster she drew for her paper on superstition, she began jotting notes on "rabbit's foot," one of her "cases of superstition." Using these notes, she began drafting simply with a series of phrases.

> Rabbit's foot—common lucky charm. Omen of good fortune. Brasch says thumping noise from hind paws = communication. Thought to have magical powers. Newborns brushed to chase evil spirits.

Using a simple three-part scheme, Amy then developed a preliminary structure for grouping her ideas on superstition.

INTRODUCTION	Fear, people who believe, origins
BODY	Examples (black cat, #13, ladder, rabbit's foot, etc.)
CONCLUSION	Truth and falsity, mystery of superstitions

Amy used her plan as a way to start, writing an introduction about how superstitions originate in a fear of the unknown.

STRATEGY **Group your ideas.**

Use your planning material to place ideas, topics, or terms into one of three categories: introduction, body, and conclusion. If your project has a required or expected structure, use it to define your groups. You might set up separate computer files so that you can work on these parts one section at a time. Later you can cut and paste the files into a single text.

5.1

As you draft, consider whether you're achieving your general purposes (persuading someone or explaining something) or your more specific purposes for different parts (enlivening a paragraph or illustrating a point). Given her specific purpose, to "grab my readers' attention and interest them in superstition," Amy added to her informative but dull opening.

21

```
     Do you knock on wood after making a prediction? shiver
when a black cat crosses your path? consider 13 unlucky? If so,
you have already been swept into the world of superstitions.
Many people practice some of the bizarre rituals of
superstition, but few know why.
```

STRATEGY **Use your purpose and audience as your guide.**

What readers expect first, second, and third may help you determine how to organize to achieve your purpose. You'd probably arrange a local history of a ballpark chronologically but organize an argument for its preservation logically, using your paragraphs to support your assertions.

5.2

5b Using strategies for drafting

Strategies for getting words down on paper can simplify drafting.

STRATEGY **Write about your writing.**

Begin not by writing your paper but by writing *about* it. What concerns you most? What do you hope to do? How might you start? As you jot notes, you'll be less anxious about starting—after all, you *have* started.

As you begin drafting, don't worry about writing perfect sentences and paragraphs. Just get as much on paper as you can. Try to write quickly so that you develop momentum.

STRATEGY **Try semidrafting.**

Write full sentences until you're about to stall out. Then simply write *etc.* in place of the full text, and continue with your next point. Or add directions to yourself in brackets, noting what to do next.

For documented projects or research papers, use semidrafting to note what you need to integrate from sources as Kavita Kamal did when writing about "wild children" (supposedly raised by animals in the woods).

```
The first case was that of Victor, the "Wild Boy of Aveyron."
Victor first appeared in a village in southern France in
January 1800. His age was estimated at eleven or twelve years.
[Explain his adoption by Itard and Guerin and their subsequent
studies.] People assumed that he was a mute because he did not
```

```
speak. [Now go into the stuff from Shattuck about no
malformation of the tongue, mouth, etc.]
```

ESL ADVICE: SEMIDRAFTING AND PHRASING

If you find composing in English difficult, type *XXX*, draw a circle, or make a note in your first language where you need to rework your phrasing. Continue semidrafting so that you get your main ideas down on paper, and fill in the small points later.

5c Drafting collaboratively

If you get stuck, leave your draft, but rejuvenate your ideas.

STRATEGY Find a community sounding board.

- Try talking or emailing about your writing with someone in your writing community. Explaining what you're trying to do may alleviate tension, suggest solutions, or draw ideas from your listener that will help you get started again.
- You might also try *imagining* the most sympathetic listener you can. Then tell him or her all about your project. Focus on this interested friend, and banish that critical reader who peers over your shoulder.

When you write with a work team or a civic or academic group, look for collaborative strategies that suit the group and the context.

STRATEGY Draft with others from your community.

- Organize **parallel drafting**, dividing up the project, perhaps by group members' specialties, so that each is responsible for drafting a particular section. You can exchange drafts as you revise and edit, but one person may need to act as editor, integrating the drafts.
- Try **team drafting** when writers share similar ideas and approaches, assigning two writers for each section. The first drafts until he or she gets stuck, and then the second begins where the first stopped. Recirculate the drafts when revising and editing.
- Consider **intensive drafting** when working with a close friend or colleague. Assemble materials in a space where you can work undisturbed. Decide where each will begin drafting, and exchange sections at a certain time or as you finish segments. Continue exchanging drafts, or vary your pattern by having one person compose aloud as the other types.

6 | Revising

Because so much of what we read is in final, published form, we forget the hours the author has spent **revising**—reconsidering content and structure in terms of community expectations, redrafting whole sections, and struggling to find just the right words. Revision is more than fine-tuning style, grammar, and sentence problems (**editing**) or searching for missing apostrophes and typographical errors (**proofreading**), important though these activities may be (see Chapter 14). Instead, revision means *reading* your draft critically and *reworking* it to make effective changes. It means stepping outside the draft to assess its strengths and weaknesses and then deciding what to expand, clarify, reword, restructure—or just plain cut.

CHECKLIST FOR REVISING, EDITING, AND PROOFREADING

Major revision	Focus on sections and chunks as part of the whole. Redraft, reorganize, add, and delete.
Minor revision	Focus on passages and paragraphs. Revise for sense, style, and economy.
Editing	Focus on paragraphs, sentences, and words. Edit for correctness and conventions (grammar, sentences, wording, punctuation, mechanics). Edit for clarity, style, and economy.
Proofreading	Focus on details and final appearance. Proofread for spelling, punctuation, and typographical errors.

6a Making major revisions

Concentrate first on **major revision**, large-scale changes that make your draft as a whole more effective. For example, if your report seems too informal for your work community, you may decide to redraft its introduction, delete an anecdote, or add more on alternative solutions. Think critically about content, structure, tone, style, appeals to audience, and purpose.

1 Redraft workable material

Rework ineffective parts, as Jessica White did with her opening.

ORIGINAL DRAFT   I was a cheerleading captain and I loved basketball. I put a lot of work into my cheerleading season. We had great team spirit between the cheerleaders and the teammates. We led our crowd to great enthusiasm and spirit.

WRITER'S ASSESSMENT: **I want people to feel what it was like after the state quarter-finals. This doesn't even say where I was or what was happening.**

REVISED DRAFT   There we were, a bunch of cheerleaders packed into Rebecca's car. Everyone's spirits were soaring; we had won the quarter-final game of the state basketball championship. It was a bitterly cold night, but we laughed, joked, and endlessly replayed the highlights of the game.

STRATEGY   **Target your weak spots.**

Let your draft sit for a few hours or days, and then read it (preferably aloud). Place a question mark next to any ineffective section. After you finish reading, go back to each question mark, and bracket the passage where the writing loses vitality or meaning. Ask yourself what you want to accomplish there, take out a new page (or open a new file), and say it again.

6.1

2 Reorganize paragraphs or sections

An early draft may reflect your process of discovery instead of the best order for your readers or subject. Keyshawn Williams drafted a memo from a committee looking for ways to cut company expenses. He originally opened with the committee's conclusions, but the group revised to give readers more context—concise background on the committee's task, a clear statement of the problem, and then the recommendations.

STRATEGY   **Summarize your paragraphs.**

Number the paragraphs in your draft, and write a phrase or sentence to sum up the main point of each. Use this list to spot paragraphs that you could combine or reorganize to create a clearer flow of ideas. Consider whether points at the end belong at the beginning. (See 3b and 7f.)

3 Add new material

An addition can develop a paragraph (see 7f), enliven a dull passage, clarify or extend a point, or supply missing detail. When Gina Giacomo revised her Web page explaining the transfer to a new email system, she added material to clarify the transition for readers.

```
        Your new email address is listed below. It should be easy
to remember because it consists of the first six letters of
your name. You may send your new address to people or groups
that send you messages, but you don't need to. Our server will
automatically forward any mail directed to your old address.
```

STRATEGY   **Check the paragraph flow.**

Highlight the first and last sentence in each paragraph. Read through these highlighted sentences, identifying any gaps where a paragraph doesn't connect clearly to the one before or after it or where information or detail is missing within the paragraph. (See 7d.)

4 Delete unnecessary material

Don't be afraid to slash away large chunks if they're unnecessary, illogical, or redundant, as Brian Corby did in his letter to the zoning board.

```
        With eighteen stories, Regency Towers will cast a long,
wide shadow over Piedmont Park. The building will be quite tall
and very wide. For several hours a day, the toddler play area
will be darkened. On summer afternoons, the shadow will cut
across the baseball diamond. This could be dangerous.
```

STRATEGY   **Trim the fat.**

Imagine that your draft will be published if you trim at least 10 percent of the fat. Mark sentences where you can cut or paragraphs where you might merge the essentials. (See 30b.)

6b Making minor revisions

Minor revisions are fairly small changes, mostly refining and polishing passages for three reasons: *sense, style,* and *economy.*

1 Revise for sense

When you're immersed in your writing, you may forget what your reader *doesn't* know or think, leading to illogical or puzzling statements.

STRATEGY   **Read critically to check your logic.**

Does each passage *make sense* in the context of the whole project? Try to look at the text as your readers might, not in your own way. If possible, ask peer readers to place question marks next to anything confusing.

aul Tichey asked his peer group to read his draft on Nevada's environmen-
lly threatened wild mustangs. Paul revised after his readers pointed out that
ney couldn't tell whether the Air Force was helping or harming the animals.

The Air Force ~~,~~ *, which* was partly responsible for the ~~reduction in the~~ *demise*
~~number~~ *the* of ~~∧~~ wild mustangs on the Tonopah missile range ~~,~~ *, has now* ~~The Air~~
~~Force is part of a team that also includes~~ *joined forces with* the Bureau of Land
Management and a group of wild-horse preservationists. ~~All three~~
~~groups have banded together~~ to help ~~∧~~ *save* the wild mustangs ~~in this~~ *from dehydration and*
~~period of drought and dehydration.~~ *death during the duration of the drought.*

2 Revise for style

Consider how your prose "sounds"—its rhythm and complexity.

STRATEGY   **Smooth out your sentences and words.**

In any rough paragraph, place a +, √, −, or ? next to each sentence to
indicate whether you feel positive, neutral, negative, or uncertain about it.
Rewrite what you don't like; try to get readers' advice on questionable sentences. When in doubt, try an alternative. (See 29b and 31b.)

Paul placed a minus sign next to the sentence below. He decided that too
many words began with *d*, and *during the duration* seemed redundant.

The Air Force, which was partly responsible for the demise of
the wild mustangs on the Tonopah missile range, has now joined
forces with the Bureau of Land Management and a group of wild-
horse preservationists to help save the mustangs from ~~∧~~ *fatal*
dehydration ~~∧~~ *while the drought persists.* ~~and death during the duration of the drought.~~

3 Revise for economy

Cut what you can without losing sense or coherence. Paul reduced
seventy-eight words to thirty-six—a cut of over 50 percent!

**SECOND
DRAFT**   A serious problem confronting groups who want to manage
wild mustangs on military sites in Nevada is the relative
inaccessibility of the sites, since many require security
passes or are fenced off, and environmentalists can't
come and go as they please, as they can on public or even

6c
evise

some private land. It's simply harder to study or help horses on restricted military installations. Open rangeland has easier access, and inspectors can simply move in and out at will.

THIRD DRAFT
(REVISED FOR
ECONOMY)
Restricted access to Nevada military sites presents a serious obstacle to successful horse management. Unlike open rangeland, where inspectors can come and go as they please, military sites are often fenced off and require security clearance.

STRATEGY   **Count your words.**

Total the words in a passage that lacks economy. Then start cutting See what percentage you can trim without changing meaning. (See 30b.)

6c   Revising collaboratively

Ask at least one person you respect to give you honest feedback. In return, promise to read drafts for your reader.

1 Respond helpfully

6.2

When you act as a peer reader—or ask someone to read for you—begin by establishing the writer's purpose, audience, and concerns.

- What sort of project is it? What is the writer trying to do?
- For what community is it intended? What do readers expect?
- What does the writer want to learn from a reader?

Jot notes that balance praise with helpful criticism. Don't simply say, "It was really good," or give directions like "Move this to page 2." Instead, offer diplomatic advice: "What would happen if you moved this to page 2?"

2 Turn to your readers for their responses

Accept constructive comments from an honest reader gracefully. If you are defensive, your reader is unlikely to give you more feedback. But if a reader questions something you like, remember that you have the final say.

STRATEGY   **Make the most of collaborative revision.**

- Give your readers a list of your specific concerns about the draft.
- Minimize apologies. Everyone feels anxious about sharing a draft.
- If time is limited, consider taping reactions, meeting briefly to take notes on responses, emailing, or exchanging comments jotted on the drafts.

- Use responses to plan how to revise. If readers didn't like a section, do you want to change it, delete it, or write it another way?
- Recirculate a collaborative draft, or meet again to revise.

ESL ADVICE: PEER READERS

You may worry about editing grammar or spelling before you share a draft. Review these details quickly, and look for a peer reader who is willing to ignore the small points in a rough draft. Ask this reader to focus on specific issues (such as the order of ideas) or on common problems (such as weak first paragraphs). Consider sharing your draft with several readers, including native speakers of English, so you get a range of responses.

7 | Shaping Paragraphs

Every time you indent to begin a new paragraph, you give readers a signal: watch for a shift in topic, another perspective, or a special emphasis. Whether you are writing a history paper, a letter to the editor, or a memo at work, readers will expect your paragraphs to guide them. Revising paragraphs to increase *focus, coherence,* and *development* helps readers figure out what's important, how ideas and details logically connect, and what's coming up.

7a Recognizing unfocused paragraphs

When you concentrate on a main idea throughout, you create a paragraph that is **focused** because it doesn't stray into unrelated details. A paragraph is **unified** when all its sentences directly relate to its point.

STRATEGY Check your paragraph focus.

- What is the main point (or topic) in this paragraph?
- How many different topics does this paragraph cover?
- Is the focus announced to readers? Where? How?
- Does the paragraph elaborate on the point? Do details fit the topic?

Jeanne Brown used questions to analyze a paragraph on color analysis.

UNFOCUSED

> A color to look at is the color red. Red is often considered a very fast and sporty color for cars. Porsches that are red are likely to be chosen over blue ones. Red ties are often called "power ties." Red can also be a very daring color to wear. A woman who wears a long red dress and has painted fingernails to match is not a shy woman. She is going to be noticed and will revel in the attention.

WRITER'S REACTION: *My main point?* I want to talk about the strong effects red can have on people. I don't think that the focus on red's power is clear. *Focus announced to readers?* Not really. I need to say that I am discussing the effects red has, not simply that it is a color worth looking at. *Elaboration on the point?* No, not very much. I need to help readers understand how each example explains my view of red's effect on moods and attitudes.

REVISED

> Red is a color that can affect how people feel and react. Red makes heads turn, and the person associated with the color often ends up feeling important and influential. A red Porsche draws more attention than a blue one. A red tie, or "power tie," can be bold and assertive. Worn with a blue or gray suit, the touch of red makes the wearer stand out in a crowd and builds self-confidence. A woman wearing a long red dress with nails painted to match is probably not shy. She is going to be noticed and will revel in the attention because it reinforces her positive self-image.

7b Revising for paragraph focus

Help your readers recognize a paragraph's focus by stating your topic and your main idea or perspective in a **topic sentence**. Begin with this sentence when you want readers to grasp the point right away.

<u>When writing jokes, it's a good idea to avoid vague generalizations.</u> Don't just talk about "fruit" when you can talk about "an apple." Strong writing creates a single image for everyone in the crowd, each person imagining a very similar thing. But when you say "fruit," people are either imagining several different kinds of fruit or they aren't really thinking of anything in particular, and both things can significantly reduce their emotional investment in the joke. But when you say "an apple," everyone has *a clear picture,* and thus a feeling.
                                     —JAY SANKEY, *Zen and the Art of Stand-Up Comedy*

xperiment with other topic sentence options: placing it at the end of the
ragraph, repeating it at the end from a different perspective, implying it if
ur point is unmistakably clear, or adding a limiting or clarifying sentence
narrow your point. Supplement your topic sentences with section head-
gs if readers expect them in a report or proposal.

STRATEGY **Highlight topic sentences to sharpen your focus.**

Skim your draft, using a highlighter (or bold type) to mark each topic
entence. When you note that one is missing or inadequate, read critically to
ecide whether to revise the topic sentence or refocus the paragraph. Skim
our topic sentences again, tracing your explanation or argument through
he draft as a whole.

SL ADVICE: PARAGRAPH CONVENTIONS

In English, readers expect a paragraph to have a specific focus and of-
en look to a topic sentence for guidance. In Hindi, however, paragraphs may
lack a sharply defined topic and may contain loosely related ideas. In some
languages, a topic sentence does not begin a paragraph or is not stated directly. As you write in a second language, adjust your paragraphs so they do
what readers in that language expect.

7c Recognizing incoherent paragraphs

A paragraph is **coherent** if each sentence clearly leads a reader to the
next or if the sentences form a recognizable, easy-to-understand arrangement. Paragraphs may lack coherence if sentences are out of logical order or
so abruptly change topic that readers must struggle to follow the thought.

LACKS COHERENCE

Captain James Cook discovered the island of Hawaii in 1779.
Mauna Kea, on Hawaii, is the tallest mountain in the Pacific. Cook
might have noticed the many mountains on the island as he sailed into
Kealakekua Bay. The island also has five major volcanoes. Mauna Loa,
another mountain on the island, is a dormant volcano that last erupted
in 1984. Kilauea is the most active volcano on earth. It continues to
enlarge the land that makes up this largest island in the Hawaiian
chain. The volcano sends forth lava continuously.

READER'S REACTION: **This paragraph provides lots of information, but it's hard
to follow because it jumps from sentence to sentence.**

REVISED

In 1779, Captain James Cook sailed into Kealakekua Bay an discovered the island of Hawaii. As he entered the bay, did Cook **notic** the many **mountains** on the island? Perhaps he **noticed** Mauna Ke the tallest **mountain** in the Pacific. Perhaps he **spotted** one or more **o** the five major **volcanoes**. **One of these**, Mauna Loa, is a dorman **volcano** that last erupted in 1984. **Another**, Kilauea, is the most activ **volcano** on earth. It sends forth lava continuously. **In addition**, keeps adding to the landmass of what is already the largest island in th Hawaiian chain.

STRATEGY Check your paragraph coherence.

- What words name the topic and main points? Are they repeated?
- What transitions alert readers to relationships among sentences?
- What parallel words and structures highlight similar or related ideas?
- Does the arrangement of ideas and details clarify their relationships?

7d Revising for paragraph coherence

By repeating key words, phrases, synonyms, and related words that re- fer to your topic and main point, you keep readers aware of your focus.

According to recent research, **people married for a long time** often develop similar **facial features**. The **faces** of **younger couples** show only chance resemblances. As **they** share emotions for many years, however, most **older couples** develop similar **expressions**.

STRATEGY Position your key words for effective repetition.

Place key words prominently, beginning or ending sentences. Avoid burying them in the middle of sentences.

7.2

Transitional expressions like *in addition, therefore,* and *on the other hand* also alert readers to relationships among sentences.

Many people still consider your college choice your most impor- tant career decision. These days, **however**, graduate school is the most important choice **because** the competition for jobs has grown fiercer. **For example**, business positions at the entry level often go to people with MBAs and law degrees. **In addition**, many good jobs require ad- vanced training and skills. **Moreover**, employers pay attention **not only** to the presence of an advanced degree on your résumé **but also** to the program of study **and** the quality of the school.

Patterns of arrangement also build coherence by emphasizing how details are related. A **spatial** organization guides readers through the details of a scene, a work of art, or a mechanism in an easy-to-follow order such as left to right or top to bottom. Presenting events in time sequence, first to last, is the clearest **chronological** arrangement. Signal simple rearrangements, such as flashbacks or simultaneous events, with wording like *at the same time, next,* and *earlier.* A **question-answer** or **problem-solution** sequence alerts readers to a **logical order**. In a **general-to-specific** pattern, you offer broader generalizations first and then move to more specific details. In a **specific-to-general** pattern, you reverse the order, moving from specific examples and details toward

USEFUL TRANSITIONS FOR SHOWING RELATIONSHIPS

Time and Sequence	next, later, after, while, meanwhile, immediately, earlier, first, second, shortly, in the future, subsequently, as long as, soon, since, finally, last, at that time, as soon as
Comparison	likewise, similarly, also, too, again, in the same manner, in comparison, equally
Contrast	in contrast, on the one hand . . . on the other hand, however, although, even though, still, yet, but, nevertheless, conversely, at the same time, despite, regardless
Examples	for example, for instance, such as, specifically, thus, to illustrate, namely, in fact
Cause and Effect	as a result, consequently, accordingly, if . . . then, is due to this, for this reason, because, as a consequence of, thus
Place	next to, above, behind, beyond, near, here, across from, to the right, there, in front, in the background, in between, opposite
Addition	and, too, moreover, in addition, besides, furthermore, next, also, finally, again
Concession	of course, naturally, it may be the case that, granted, it is true that, certainly, though
Conclusion	in conclusion, in short, as a result, as the data show, finally, therefore
Repetition	to repeat, in other words, once again, as I said earlier
Summary	on the whole, to summarize, to sum up, in short, therefore, in brief

a generalization. You can also link elements by using **parallelism**—repeating th same grammatical structures to highlight similar or related ideas (see 27b).

7e Recognizing poorly developed paragraphs

Paragraph development provides the examples, facts, concrete details explanations, or supporting arguments that make a paragraph informativ enough to support your ideas, opinions, and conclusions. Short paragraphs are not always underdeveloped, nor are long paragraphs always adequate—yet length can be an important cue. More than two sentences are generally necessary for a paragraph to explore a topic and support a generalization.

> **UNDERDEVELOPED**
>
> Recycling is always a good idea—or *almost* always. Recycling some products, even newsprint and other paper goods, may require more energy from fossil fuels and more valuable natural resources than making them over again.
>
> **READER'S REACTION: I'd like to know more before I agree with this. What are these products? How much energy does it take to recycle them? What natural resources do they consume?**

Readers from different fields and communities favor different kinds of supporting information. The detail expected in a lab report obviously differs from that expected in a job application or a grant proposal, but the success of all three depends on clear and powerful supporting detail.

STRATEGY   Check your paragraph development.

- Does the paragraph present enough material to *inform* readers?
- Does the paragraph adequately *support* any generalizations?

7f Revising for paragraph development

Examples, whether brief or extended, help clarify a concept, explain a generalization, or provide reasons to support your position. They help a reader see an idea in action and its consequences.

> One day in 1957, the songwriter Johnny Mercer received a letter from Sadie Vimerstedt, a widowed grandmother who worked behind a cosmetics counter in Youngstown, Ohio. Mrs. Vimerstedt suggested Mercer write a song called "I Want to Be Around to Pick Up the Pieces When Somebody Breaks Your Heart." Five years later, Mercer got in touch to say he'd written the song and that Tony Bennett would record it. Today, if you look at the label on any recording of "I Wanna Be Around," you'll notice that the credits for words and music are shared by Johnny Mercer and Sadie Vimerstedt. The royal-

ties were split fifty-fifty, too, thanks to which Mrs. Vimerstedt and her heirs have earned more than $100,000. In my opinion, Mercer's generosity was a class act.   —JOHN BERENDT, "Class Acts"

7f
¶ dev

STRATEGY Add details and specifics to develop paragraph content.

- **Examples.** Use brief or extended illustrations.
- **Concrete detail.** Recreate sights, sounds, tastes, smells, movements, and sensations of touch.
- **Facts and statistics.** Offer precise data from your fieldwork or authoritative sources, perhaps in numerical form.
- **Supporting statements.** Explain your own interpretations or quote people or sources that readers will trust.
- **Summaries.** Present other people's opinions, conclusions, or explanations in compressed form (see 48a), showing how your conclusions agree, disagree, or supplement theirs.

   Patterns of development help you accomplish familiar tasks so that readers can readily recognize the purpose and arrangement of a paragraph or a cluster of paragraphs.

7.3

PATTERNS FOR PARAGRAPH DEVELOPMENT

TASK	DEVELOPMENT STRATEGY
Tell a story; recreate events; present an anecdote	Narrating
Provide detail about a scene or object; portray someone's character; evoke a feeling	Describing
Explore similarities or differences; evaluate alternatives	Comparing and contrasting
Provide directions; explain the operation of a mechanism, procedure, or natural process	Explaining a process
Separate a subject into parts; explore the relationships among parts	Dividing
Sort things or people into groups; explain the relationships among the groups	Classifying
Explain the meaning of a term or concept; explore and illustrate the meaning of a complicated concept or phenomenon	Defining
Consider why something did happen (or might); explore possible causes and results	Analyzing causes and effects

Narrating. Turn to **narration** to recount past or present events, recreate an experience, tell an anecdote, or envision the future.

> Suddenly the ground thundered, and, as if called, a train caught up with Uncle Clark. It slowed only a little, but not enough to be caught, even by my uncle, strong and sleek as he was. Undaunted, Uncle Clark let out a piercing whistle. Out of the black square shadow of one boxcar shot a long arm. In a flash my uncle grabbed and was hoisted inside the wide door. We never saw the other hobos; we only heard them laughing at the show they'd given us townies.
>
> —Brenda Peterson, "Vaster Than Empires and More Slow"

Describing. You can create images of a place, an object, or a feeling or sketch a person's character through **description**, emphasizing emotional impact (**subjective description**) or physical details (**objective description**).

> With its shed roof sloping north, the cabin sits low and compact in the snow, a pair of moose antlers nailed above a window in the high south wall. There are four dog houses to the rear of it, each of them roofed with a poke of snow-covered hay. A meat rack stands to one side, built high between two stout spruces, and a ladder made of dry poles leans against a tree next to it. A hindquarter of moose hangs from the rack; it is frozen rock hard and well wrapped with canvas to keep it from birds. Just the same, I see that camp-robbers have pecked at it and torn a hole in the canvas. Nothing else can reach it there seven feet above the ground.
>
> —John Haines, "Three Days"

Comparing and contrasting. Paragraphs that **compare** and **contrast** can evaluate alternative policies or products, examine pros and cons, or compare qualities and explanations. A **point-by-point organization** examines each comparable feature for first one subject and then the next.

Topic sentence	But biology has a funny way of confounding expectations. Rather than disappear, the evidence for innate sexual
Feature 1	differences only began to mount. In medicine, researchers documented that heart disease strikes men at a younger age
Feature 2	than it does women and that women have a more moderate
Feature 3	physiological response to stress. Researchers found subtle neurological differences between the sexes both in the brain's
Feature 4	structure and in its functioning. In addition, another generation of parents discovered that, despite their best efforts to give baseballs to their daughters and sewing kits to their sons, girls still flocked to dollhouses while boys clambered into tree forts. Perhaps nature is more important than nurture after all. —Christine Gorman, "Sizing Up the Sexes"

A **subject-by-subject organization** considers each subject in its en-
ety, within a paragraph or a series of paragraphs.

>   For everyone, home is a place to be offstage. But the
> comfort of home can have opposite and incompatible mean-
> ings for women and men. For many men, the comfort of
> home means freedom from having to prove themselves and
> impress through verbal display. At last, they are in a situation
> where talk is not required. They are free to remain silent. But
> for women, home is a place where they are free to talk, and
> where they feel the greatest need for talk, with those they are
> closest to. For them, the comfort of home means the freedom
> to talk without worrying about how their talk will be judged.
> —DEBORAH TANNEN, "Put Down That Paper and Talk to Me!"

topic sentence
subject 1

subject 2

Explaining a process.   To give directions, show how a mechanism or procedure works, or explain other processes, label the steps or stages clearly.
Arrange them logically, usually chronologically. Devote a paragraph to each
part of the process if you wish to emphasize its stages.

>   Stage One sleep is very light—just the other side of wakeful-
> ness. Stage Two (which makes up about half our total slumber time)
> is a transitional phase into either slow-wave or REM sleep, while
> stages Three and Four are slow-wave sleep. In slow-wave, or deep,
> sleep, brain activity slows to a crawl. In REM, or dreaming sleep, on
> the other hand, the brain bursts into high activity virtually identical
> to being awake—though the muscles are temporarily paralyzed from
> the neck down.   —ROYCE FLIPPIN, "Tossing and Turning"

Dividing and classifying.   When you divide a subject, you split it into parts,
explaining it and the relationships of its parts.

DIVISION

>   Sunglasses should be more than cheap plastic frames with dark
> lenses. A good pair has three important features: it protects, adds a
> touch of style, and costs a lot more than $1.99. Eye-damaging ultra-
> violet rays make protection essential. Your sunglasses should guard
> against both UV-A rays and the shorter, more damaging UV-B rays.
> The racks of sunglasses, many sporting designer names, offer styles
> from wraparound to wire frames, from amber tints in red rims to
> gray on gray. You can create almost any impression: debonair, retro,
> sexy, athletic, Hollywood, even owlish and scholarly. Yet trendy ap-
> pearance and effective protection come at a price. Be ready to pay at
> least $20 for a pair of sunglasses coated to protect from all the harm-
> ful rays and ten times as much (or more) for designer styles from this
> year's collection.   —MEGHAN TUBRIDY, College Student

To classify, you sort several subjects into groups, exploring similarities *within* groups and differences and relationships *between* groups.

CLASSIFICATION

   Men all have different styles of chopping wood, all of which are deemed by their practitioners as the only proper method. Often when I'm chopping wood in my own inept style, a neighbor will come over and "offer help." He'll bust up a few logs in his own manner, advising me as to the proper swing and means of analyzing the grain of the wood. There are "over the head" types and "swing from the shoulder" types, and guys who lay the logs down horizontally on the ground and still others who balance them on end, atop of stumps. I have one neighbor who uses what he calls "vector analysis." Using the right vectors, he says, the wood will practically *split itself*.

—JAMES FINNEY BOYLAN, "The Bean Curd Method"

Defining. When you introduce a term or concept to your readers, you may need to contrast its definition with others or to stipulate the one of multiple meanings it will carry in your writing.

   When they hear the word *crystal*, many people think of a mineral dug from the ground. But the lead crystal used to make beautiful plates, glasses, and vases does not come from this source. The crystal in these objects—artworks, actually—is glass with a high lead content. The glass is made from a mixture of sand and other ingredients like potash (potassium) or soda that help the mixture melt. The various minerals also affect the color and clarity of the glass. Lead crystal must contain at least 30 percent to 35 percent lead oxide (by weight) in its ingredients. The resulting material is easier for artists to work with as they grind intricate facets into the surface to create designs that sparkle and intrigue like a finely cut diamond.

—ANDREA HERRMANN, College Student

Analyzing causes and effects. You may explain why something has occurred (causes), explore consequences (effects), or combine both.

   Of all the habits I have, there is one my friends simply cannot understand. I always set my clock ahead fourteen minutes. "What for?" everyone asks when they notice that my clock is running so far ahead. The habit started in my first year of high school. I was so nervous about being late for the first day of "real" school that I moved the clock hands ahead—fourteen minutes ahead. When I got into bed, I had a secure feeling that everything would work out fine. Since then, I feel rushed and hurried every time I set my clock to regular time, but relaxed and secure when I set it to my time, fourteen minutes fast.

—KRIS LUNDELL, College Student

7g Using special-purpose paragraphs

Paragraphs help begin, end, and link the parts of a text.

Introductory paragraphs. Your opening builds your relationship with readers, motivating them to continue reading. It can establish the tone, approach, and degree of formality expected by readers in a given community.

STRATEGY **Tailor your opening to engage your reader.**
- What is the main idea or purpose of this project?
- What precise topic (problem, issue) will this text address?
- Why should readers be interested in this topic?

This anecdote introduces the environmental threat posed by Las Vegas.

> It was advertised as the biggest non-nuclear explosion in Nevada history. On October 27, 1993, Steve Wynn, the State's official "god of hospitality," flashed his trademark smile and pushed the detonator button. As 200,000 Las Vegans cheered, the 18-story Dunes sign, once the tallest neon structure in the world, crumbled to the desert floor.
>
> —MIKE DAVIS, "House of Cards"

CREATING INTRODUCTORY PARAGRAPHS

Provide background, context, or history.	Tell an anecdote or story, or recall an event.
Explain an issue.	Supply a definition.
Present the sides in a controversy.	Ask a question.
Use an extended example.	Offer an intriguing analogy.
Quote from an authority.	Quote someone's opinion.
Compare another situation, time period, or issue.	Provide statistics to define the issue or problem.
Describe a mysterious or interesting phenomenon.	Cite pertinent or little-known facts.

Avoid obvious generalizations, shopworn phrases, apologies, and references to your own title.

7g
dev

Concluding paragraphs. Your ending may remind readers of key ideas an encourage them to think about information presented or actions proposed

> So if it's any consolation to those of us who just don't manag to fit enough sleep into our packed days, being chronically tire probably won't do us any permanent harm. And if things get desper ate enough, we just might have to schedule a nap somewhere on ou busy calendars. —DANIEL GOLEMAN, "Too Little, Too Late

---

CREATING CONCLUDING PARAGRAPHS

Summarize main points briefly.

Restate the thesis, or repeat proposed recommendations.

Echo the introduction.

Use a quotation.

Offer a striking example, anecdote, or image.

Predict future events or speculate.

Avoid apologies, overstatements, new ideas, and simply rewording your thesis statement.

Linking paragraphs. Paragraphs work together to form a coherent whole. Add links to clarify their relationships within a cluster or section.

STRATEGY Connect your paragraphs to guide readers.

- Announce your purpose to help readers anticipate your reasoning.
- Provide a **boundary statement**—a sentence beginning one paragraph but acting as a bridge from the paragraph before. Remind the reader of material covered earlier as you present the topic sentence.
- Create transition paragraphs to help readers move forward.

> **Signal paragraphs** alert readers to a major change in direction or the beginning of a new section.
> Brief **summary paragraphs** mark the end of a discussion or review main points for readers.
> Short **planning paragraphs** help readers anticipate the arrange- ment of the upcoming discussion.
> **Highlight paragraphs** call attention to ideas and information.

TAKING IT ONLINE

PRESENTATIONS
http://www.rpi.edu/dept/llc/writecenter/web/presentation.html
Review the solid advice here on oral presentations.

TEN TIPS FOR SUCCESSFUL PUBLIC SPEAKING
http://www.toastmasters.org/tips.asp
These tips from Toastmasters International can help you feel less nervous before an oral presentation.

CRITICAL THINKING CONSORTIUM
http://www.criticalthinking.org/
This Web site provides a variety of resources, including materials on critical thinking in academic and business contexts.

SAMPLE CRITICAL REASONING PAPERS
http://www.siu.edu/departments/cola/psycho/intro/samples.html
These eight student papers, written by first-year college students at Southern Illinois University, show critical reasoning skills in action.

THE NET: USER GUIDELINES AND NETIQUETTE
http://www.fau.edu/netiquette/net/
This guide helps you with style demands in electronic communication.

DOCUMENT DESIGN MAGAZINE
http://www.wcdd.com/dd/ddindex.html
This online magazine focuses on document design, relating writers, readers, written text, and visuals.

SECTION 2
Representing Yourself:
Creating Your Place in a Community

8 | Matching Style to Community

Should you use *I* or *we* to describe yourself? Should you address readers as *you*? If you use technical terms, will readers find them pompous or appropriate? Choices like these are questions of community style.

DRAFT   I'm as thrilled as a grizzly in a trout pond to offer 20 percent off.

> READER'S REACTION: **What's with the bear and the trout? Isn't this a discount on an oil change?**

REVISED   Mill Motors appreciates loyal customers like you. Please enjoy 20 percent off your next oil change.

Style often refers to choices reflecting individual preferences—your "voice" or personal style. Here, however, it refers to preferences taken for granted by communities of readers and writers—frameworks growing from their values, goals, and typical relationships. These frameworks should help guide—but not dictate—your choices as a writer or speaker.

8a Recognizing community style

8.1

Identifying the elements of a community's typical framework can help you decide how and when to accept them or alter them so that you represent yourself effectively and achieve your purpose.

Values. Are writers expected to address values, preferences, and emotions directly or leave them in the background? Will writers and readers expect to share values or need to negotiate differences?

Language. What **diction**—word choices—will readers expect? Will they appreciate vivid, imaginative phrasing or prefer careful, neutral terms? Do they rely on careful, logical links among statements (*however*, *in addition*, *consequently*), or find such terms needlessly formal? Which technical terms—how many, how often—will they expect or accept?

Formality. Will readers expect writing that is formal, complicated, and somewhat technical or relaxed, direct, and everyday?

Writer's stance. What pronouns, if any, do writers use to identify themselves, readers, and subject matter: *I*, *we*, *you*, *he*, *she*, *it*, *they*?

Distance. Is a writer typically distant from or personally involved with the issue, problem, or topic? an insider or outsider? a participant observer? a member of the group addressed, familiar with it, removed in time, space, or interests?

8b Adjusting to community style

Although specific written or spoken texts may have their own variations, each major community has a typical approach to style.

8b style

1 Reflect academic fields and methods

Academic readers typically appreciate formal, complicated writing that supports careful analysis. They expect writers to reflect a field's knowledge, values (such as scientific objectivity), and methods (such as Freudian psychoanalysis). The use of *I* varies from field to field, but readers are seldom addressed directly. Academic writers usually stand at a distance from a subject (*he, she,* or *it*), acting as spectator, observer, or participant observer. Some fields such as social work, family counseling, or women's studies may accept political or social activity.

STYLE IN THREE MAJOR COMMUNITIES		
	ACADEMIC	**WORK**	**PUBLIC**
APPROACH	Complex, formal, or detailed analysis	Clear, everyday, or informal explanation	Emotional, value-laden, but reasoned argument
VALUES	From the discipline's knowledge base or methods	From organizational goals such as service and efficiency	From cause, issue, or group's area of interest
LANGUAGE	Technical terms and methods of the field	Plain or technical terms but little vivid, figurative wording	Lively and emotional with few technical terms and little slang
FORMALITY	Formality supports analytical approach and values of the field	Informality reflects or builds sense of team-work or closeness	Informality reveals personal involvement with serious issues
STANCE	Observer (*he, she, it*) or participant (*I, we*)	Team member (*we*) with personal concern (*I, you*)	Involved individual (*I, you*) or representative (*we, you*)
DISTANCE	Objective and dispassionate, not personal or emotional	Supportive, committed closeness with mutual respect	Personal and passionate about cause, issue, or group

STRATEGY Adopt the style of your academic community.

8.2

- Rely on sources and information that show your effort to understand the discipline's knowledge and methods.
- Use appropriate technical terms accepted by the field.
- Look for models—other readings that illustrate the formality, stance, and distance typical or acceptable in the field.

Reflect workplace goals

9
lang

Work communities begin with or work toward shared values like efficiency, service, and respect. These values may be reflected in terms such as *we* (to reinforce relationships and teamwork) and in the narrow distance between writers and readers, in reality or as a goal. Depending on the work and background of those involved, diction may be straightforward or technical, though vivid language is often restricted to passages urging action. To ensure directness, even formal reports may use everyday expressions. Internal documents may be quite informal in diction and tone, reflecting (or building) closeness, commitment, and support.

Reflect public commitment

Values, either shared or divergent, are often in the forefront of public writing, conveyed by emotion- and value-laden language. Writers may be engaged personally with the issues and audiences they address (*I, we, you*), using informal language to reflect this closeness. Real informality (such as slang) is usually avoided because it may undercut serious issues. Writers may use a few complicated or technical expressions but generally avoid exclusionary formal diction. Reasoning and argument, often part of public exchanges, are embodied in terms like *thus, however,* and *nonetheless.*

9 | Adapting to Community Language Variety

How do you talk at school, at work, at home, or in your neighborhood? Do you use language to represent yourself differently with friends, teachers, or bosses? Every speaker of English uses a particular variety of the language shaped by region, culture, exposure to other languages, and home

community. Where they're used, these varieties seem natural. In most academic, business, and broad public settings, however, variations aren't seen
acceptable but as "errors" or sloppiness.

HOME VARIETY   Unless **if** RayCorp ordered the resistors, the shipment wa
sent out **on** accident.

READER'S REACTION: **Who made all these mistakes in a compan
memo?**

EDITED   **Unless** RayCorp ordered the resistors, the shipment was ser
out **by** accident.

**9a
lang**

Except in casual, personal situations, writers substitute more general star
dards for their regional, cultural, and home language varieties. Readers, eve
in a local area, expect most writing to conform to general standards, partl
because it can readily move to other settings. Becoming a flexible write
means developing awareness of differences between the habits of your ow
community and the expectations of more general readers.

9a Recognizing home and community language varieties

Every major language is spoken in a variety of ways called **dialects**
English has dozens of dialects that vary between countries (like England and
the United States) and between regions (like Tuscaloosa, Alabama, and Bar
Harbor, Maine). Dialects can also vary by culture, ethnicity, and ancestry
Cuban and Puerto Rican Americans in New York City not only speak differ-
ent dialects, but their dialects may vary between the Bronx and Brooklyn.

1 Learn to see dialect variations as "rules"

9.1

What counts for a "rule" in one dialect may break a rule in another.
This is how all language works—the rules are simply structures and conventions that people within a group agree, unconsciously, to use in their speech.
Pronouncing *pen* to rhyme with *hen* is a rule of Northern speech, but much
of the South rhymes it with *tin*. Each group follows the *rules* of its own community. To break them is to be an outsider.

2 Understand "standard" English as a function of power and prestige

If every community has its own language rules, then who's to say why
the so-called standard language should be "better"? Why *should* it be any

ore correct to say "There isn't anyone who can tell me anything" than to say ain't no body gon' tell me nuffin'"?

Around the world, languages have a prestige dialect considered more orrect" or "proper" than other dialects. How this dialect came to be preferred is almost always a matter of historical, political, and social forces. If our home dialect differs from this standard, you may be unfairly stereotyped or discriminated against by those in positions of power. Even unbiased people may not listen to you because they can't: they aren't part of your dialect group. Whether or not society ever accepts more language varieties, people without power will stay powerless if they can't communicate in the language of the powerful. But if they can gain positions of power, maybe they can help change public views of language.

9b
lang

Distinguish accents from written variations

While Americans don't usually mind differences in leaders' *accents*, people might balk at a president who said, "Them senators ain't ready for this-here veto." In writing, the most glaring (and least forgiven) variations are *grammatical*, followed by *lexical* differences (word choice, slang, jargon). Readers may unfairly see these as signs of ignorance or laziness.

9b Meeting language expectations

To avoid stereotypes and get others to listen to your ideas, you'll need to edit home or community language variations not widely shared.

1 Learn how to code-shift

One way speakers and writers adjust to differing expectations is by **code-shifting**. Many people use a home or community language with friends but shift into formal language in a college essay, letter to the mayor, or company report. There they adopt a variety that works across many communities, often called standard edited American English.

> **STRATEGY** Seek advice from a community member.

Turn to someone from your home language community who also has good facility with standard edited American English. Ask for advice about how to edit one of your papers for readers who expect this form of English. As you work together, try to figure out this person's techniques for using several language varieties successfully.

2 Focus on grammatical variations

Grammatical variations in your home dialect can be tricky to notic
after all, they may not look the least bit problematic—to you. But someor
who isn't a member of your dialect community will see them right away.

HOME VARIETY	Miss Brill **know** that the lovers **making** fun of her, but sh **act like** she **don't** care.
EDITED	Miss Brill **knows** that the lovers **are making** fun of her, bu she **acts as if** she **doesn't** care.

9b lang

STRATEGY Look for the "rules" of your home language.

On the left side of a notebook page, record examples of patterns i
your home language; on the right side, note corresponding examples in star
dard English. Explain the differences in your own terms.

Rule in KY: The lawn needs mowed.

Rule elsewhere: The lawn needs to be mowed.

3 Resist hypercorrection

9.2

Worrying about language habits that aren't seen as the norm can leac
you to **hypercorrection**—unconsciously creating new errors by guessing
that a construction is wrong and ironically substituting an error.

HYPERCORRECTED	Stuart gave the petitions to Mary and **I**.
EDITED	Stuart gave the petitions to Mary and **me**.

Similarly, if you try too hard to be formal and sophisticated, you may end up
writing tangled prose that frustrates readers.

CONVOLUTED	That the girl walks away, and the showing of the parrot to the restaurant owner who, having closed shop, will not let her inside, is indicative of that which characterizes the novel, i.e., denial and deception.
EDITED	The central theme of denial and deception is illustrated when the girl tries to show the parrot to the restaurant owner and is turned away.

STRATEGY Check uncertainties to avoid new errors.

When you feel unsure about your writing, circle the words or put a
star in the margin. Then check the rule, or ask for advice. List any cases of
hypercorrection you (or a reader) note; explain them in your own words.

10 | Representing Yourself Through Critical Reasoning

What convinces people to accept your conclusions, to share your view, to follow your recommendations, or to trust your explanations? An important factor is your **critical reasoning** or **critical thinking**: the careful, logical, insightful thought your writing (or speaking) embodies.

WRITER 1   Foreign language classes are a waste of money. Anybody with a brain knows that all our kids need is English.

> READER'S REACTION: **Don't children need language skills for business or travel—or for talking with family or others who don't speak English? And why attack people without giving any reasons or evidence?**

WRITER 2   Although foreign language requirements motivate some students, others are discouraged by required courses. For example, a survey of recent graduates showed . . .

> READER'S REACTION: **I'm not sure about this, but the writer notes several views and sounds reasonable. Let's see the evidence.**

Writer 1 opens with an opinion—and then simply restates it while attacking others. In contrast, Writer 2 begins to reason—presenting a point of view, recognizing other views, providing reasons and evidence. When you write or speak, the quality of your thinking contributes to your **persona**, the representation of yourself you create for an audience. Do you present yourself as thoughtful, informed, fair—hence persuasive? Or do you seem illogical, careless, imprecise, or uninterested in other views?

10a Recognizing critical reasoning

Critical reasoning, a process of thinking through a problem, asking a question, or explaining, has four major characteristics.

- Reaches logical or reasonable conclusions supported by evidence
- Questions assumptions and tries to see differing outlooks
- Draws on precise information and clearly defined ideas
- Desires to go beyond the superficial to reach fresh insights

Good critical thinking means that you search for better evidence, consider alternatives, and check your logic to confirm, modify, or even reverse your conclusion. (See also Chapter 56.)

47

STRATEGY Use insights of others to improve your reasoning.

- Use face-to-face or electronic discussions (see 12b–c) to identify issue conclusions, evidence, and possible objections to your view.
- Put your tentative thoughts on paper, and then read what others say i order to identify gaps in your evidence or logic.
- Ask others to read your drafts critically and to identify reasonable ob jections so you can address them as you revise.
- Put your work aside for a while; then read it as your readers migh Note any gaps that undermine clarity, persuasiveness, or credibility.

10b
ason

10b Reasoning critically in your community

Even for the same subject, goals and methods of critical reasoning ma differ with audience and occasion. For example, researchers testing alternative fuel vehicles take different paths with their reasoning than do public official creating regulations or automakers developing products.

CRITICAL REASONING IN THREE MAJOR COMMUNITIES			
	ACADEMIC	**WORK**	**PUBLIC**
GOAL	Analysis of text, phenomenon, or creative work to interpret, explain, or offer insights	Analysis of problems to supply information and propose solutions	Participation in democratic processes to contribute, inform, or persuade
REASONING PROCESS	Detailed reasoning, often explained at length with tight logic leading to conclusions	Accurate analysis of problem or need with clear explanation of solution	Plausible reasoning, not ranting, focused on supporting own point of view
SPECIAL INTERESTS	Crucial citations of others as well as insights beyond common knowledge	Sharp focus on task, problem, or goal that promotes organization	Shared values and goals, often local, that support a cause or policy
EVIDENCE	Specific references to detailed evidence, gathered and presented to support conclusions	Sufficient evidence to show the importance of the problem and to justify an appropriate solution	Relevant evidence, often local or interest-oriented, to support claims and substantiate probabilities
VIEWPOINT	Balanced treatment recognizing and explaining other views	Awareness of alternatives and likely results of actions	Fair recognition of other views, interests, and goals

10c Building a chain of reasoning

Critical thinking works toward a **chain of reasoning**, the path you take in linking observations, interpretations, conclusions, and evidence as you explore an academic topic, recommend a change at work, or urge people to take a stand. Some links in your chain may supply *information*: examples, facts, details, data. Others may offer *ideas*: reasons, comments by authorities, other views, analysis, logical argument. (See 56c.)

Reach conclusions

The important end point of a chain of reasoning—your **main conclusion**—is likely to be stated in an argumentative or academic thesis (see 4b-2). You may even offer multiple conclusions, such as adding workstations *and* upgrading software to track inventory.

10c
reaso

TYPES OF CONCLUSIONS YOU MIGHT DRAW

- **Interpretations** of meaning (experience, film, literature), importance (current or past event), or cause and effect (problem, event)
- **Analyses** of elements of a problem, situation, phenomenon, scientific topic, academic subject, issue, or disagreement
- **Propositions** about an issue, problem, policy, or disagreement
- **Judgments** about "right" or "wrong" (action, policy), quality (performance, creative work), or effectiveness (solution, proposed action)
- **Warnings** of consequences of action or failure to act
- **Recommendations** for guidelines, policies, or solutions
- **Plans** for further study, direct action, or involvement of others

TYPES OF INFORMATION THAT CAN SUPPORT CONCLUSIONS

- **Background** to supply the scope and substance of an issue, subject, or problem through history, context, or consequences
- **Evidence** to provide reasons for accepting conclusions as accurate, valuable, or important
- **Subject knowledge** to provide in-depth understanding

STRATEGY Focus on conclusions to strengthen reasoning.

- List all your conclusions (interpretations, opinions, and so on). Use an outline, colored highlighters, a cluster or tree diagram, or two columns to identify and relate main and supporting conclusions.
- Review your conclusions. Do others come to mind? Are any important ones missing? Do you need to develop them?

- Think as readers might. Will they see any assertions as interpretation or judgments? Will they expect—and accept—your conclusions?

2 Provide supporting information

A chain of reasoning needs both information and inferences. **Information** includes facts of all kinds—examples, data, details, quotations—that you present as reliable, confirmable, or generally undisputed. Information turns into **evidence** when it's used to persuade a reader that an idea is reasonable. **Inferences** or **generalizations**, often stated in a thesis (see 4b), are your conclusions based on and supported by information.

> ### TYPES OF EVIDENCE
>
> **Examples** of an event, idea, person, or place, brief or extended, from personal experience or research
>
> **Details** about an idea, place, situation, or phenomenon
>
> **Information** about times, places, participants, numbers, surroundings, consequences, and relationships
>
> **Statistics,** perhaps presented in tables or charts
>
> **Background** on context, history, causes, or effects
>
> **Quotations** from experts, participants, or other writers

STRATEGY Distinguish between information and inference.

- List the key facts about your subject. Which will readers see as undisputed? Which can you confirm with observation or reliable sources? If facts are disputed, what reasons support your presentation?
- Next list your inferences. Which reflect your understanding? Which do the facts imply? Which *might* happen as a result of the facts?

3 Assess evidence and reasoning

Readers expect you to select evidence carefully and to link it reasonably with assertions—that is, to proceed logically.

STRATEGY Evaluate the evidence as you read and write.

- How *abundant* is the evidence? Is it *sufficient* to support your claim?
- Does it *directly* support the claim?
- How *relevant*, *accurate*, and *well documented* is the evidence?

Proceeding logically is complicated when evidence persuades one audience but not another. Consider, for example, how two citizen groups might respond to a proposed greenway between parks in two neighborhoods, one in economically depressed Coolidge and the other in wealthy Lake Stearns. Starting from the assumption that the generally law-abiding residents of Coolidge are deprived of shopping and services that have left the area because of a high crime rate, the Coolidge Consortium logically supports the greenway because it will give residents access to recreation and shopping in Lake Stearns. In contrast, starting from the assumption that the balance of a peaceful, low-crime neighborhood can easily be upset, a Lake Stearns group argues logically that, though most Coolidge residents are law-abiding, the greenway will draw habitual criminals who will undermine the quality of life in both neighborhoods. Each side reasons logically, but each starts with different assumptions and arrives at different conclusions. (See also 56e.)

10c
reaso

STRATEGY **Ask questions to evaluate your assumptions.**

- How do I view the groups of people on each side of this issue?
- What will my readers want in a plan that addresses this problem?
- What do specialists in the field see as questions worth investigating?
- What might my peers suggest about my answers to these questions?

---

4 Consider assumptions

Some of your assumptions and values are easy to identify, but others are unspoken. After hearing the talk at work about efficiency, you might think your readers there want only to cut costs. But saving jobs and offering a quality product are also goals. The success of your reasoning may depend on how closely your assumptions match those of your audience.

STRATEGY **Anticipate readers' responses.**

- List your assertions that identify cause-effect links, classify, compare, connect generalizations and examples, or define (see 7f). Delete or rethink any that are weak or possibly illogical (see 56e).
- To spot weak reasoning, imagine a skeptical reader's reactions.

  WEAK Violence in schools is rising because of increased violence in movies and on TV.

  READER'S REACTION: Is this true? My kids watch TV, but they aren't more violent than I was as a kid when TV was far less violent.

10d Representing your reasoning

Compare these excerpts from letters to the editor about the controversial greenway proposal (see 10c-3).

WRITER 1

City planners must be out of their minds to cook up this crazy idea. Drug pushers and thieves will run wild, preying on people who use Lake Stearns Park. Soon the whole neighborhood will be destroyed by crime. We must stop these insane public officials before they totally destroy our way of life.

WRITER 2

The proposal to create a greenway between Coolidge and Lake Stearns Parks appears to bridge the gap between these two communities. But the greenway will not solve existing problems in Coolidge Park. Residents near Lake Stearns are unlikely to ride bikes or jog into Coolidge, and the presence of Coolidge residents in Stearns will only create a feeling, unjustified though it may be, of defensiveness. City funds could be better used to update the Coolidge Park lighting, basketball courts, and community center.

Both letters argue the same point: the greenway proposal is shortsighted. But think about the way these two writers present themselves.

WRITER 1	**WRITER 2**
Attacks proposers and Coolidge residents	Focuses on the proposal and likely outcomes
Uses emotionally charged words (*insane, crazy*)	Uses balanced language (as in sentence 3)
Comes up with vague ideas (stopping officials)	Offers specific alternatives (park improvements)
Stereotypes Coolidge residents	Suggests Coolidge benefits
Seems impulsive, shallow	Seems balanced, thoughtful

1 Be well informed

Issues, ideas, and insights are embedded in the social, occupational, historical, or disciplinary contexts around a topic. (See also 56b–c.)

STRATEGY Develop your knowledge.

List what you know about your topic and its context. Note key areas, given your purpose. Then define what's unclear and how to fill the gaps.

Anticipate readers' perspectives and reactions

If you fail to acknowledge other views, contrary arguments, conflicting evidence, or different solutions, your readers may find your presentation one-sided and question your credibility. By anticipating such reactions, even in a thesis (see 4b), you complete your chain of reasoning and build readers' confidence in your conclusions. (See 56d.)

Be balanced and reasonable

Emotional language may be just right for urging public action. The same language might irritate, even offend, co-workers or academic readers expecting critical analysis. As you pick the words and tone to represent your thinking, you create an image of yourself—a **persona**—whose qualities may make readers trust you, dislike you, or find your views rash.

UNCONSIDERED   The greenway will transport the Coolidge low-lifes into Lake Stearns Park and destroy its peace and quiet.

> READER 1: What's a "low-life"? Is this term based on race? or class? Is everyone in Coolidge a "low-life"?
>
> READER 2: Why—and how—would people from Coolidge destroy the "peace and quiet" of Lake Stearns?

4 Assess the appropriateness of strong bias

Writing effectively means knowing when to be cool and logical and when to show emotion. At work, bias is expected when you represent an organization but not when you write objective reports. In public, your devotion to a cause generally will be accepted as such, but your academic writing should favor unimpassioned reasoning. (See 8b.)

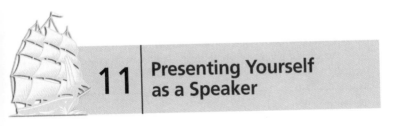

11 | Presenting Yourself as a Speaker

Surveys show that people fear public speaking more than almost anything else, including losing a relative or being fired. Fear often comes from too little preparation, trying to "wing it" and hoping for the best.

SPEAKER   I can't get the computer to project the latest sales figures, bu
                 most of them are going up.
                 LISTENER'S REACTION: **What a disorganized waste of time—especiall**
                 with our supervisor here.

Good speakers use practice and experience to turn apprehension into energ
presenting themselves and their ideas enthusiastically and clearly. (See 55
on group, 58g on committee, and 59f on public presentations.)

11a Recognizing types of oral presentations

Oral presentations aren't limited to formal occasions when someone
stands at a lectern on a stage to deliver a polished address. You might presen
your portfolio to your class or sum up a project's status at work. At a town
meeting, you might express your views from the audience. In such settings
listeners expect speakers to follow accepted patterns.

STRATEGY   Notice speaking conventions.

- How long do others speak? How formal is the usual style?
- What evidence and what persuasive strategies do others use?

11b Connecting speaking and writing

Many strategies apply to both verbal and written texts.

STRATEGY   Transfer your skills from writing to speaking.

- Apply your planning and organizing skills (see 3a and b).
- Analyze your listeners and your purpose (see 4c).
- Draft your speaking notes (see 3b and 5a).
- Write out powerful opening and key sentences (see 29b).
- Practice and revise your oral presentation (see 5a and c).
- Add well-designed visuals (see 13b and f).

11c Preparing an effective oral presentation

You can greatly improve your performance—and your confidence—if
you prepare in four stages: *planning, practice, delivery, reflection.*

SPEAKING IN THREE MAJOR COMMUNITIES			
	ACADEMIC	**WORK**	**PUBLIC**
AUDIENCE EXPECTATIONS	Explore or advance knowledge	Advance product, service, or company goals	Support position, policy, or proposal
	Develop clear topic with evidence	Present clear information on problem or task	Present position with reasons and evidence
GOALS OF ORAL EXCHANGES	Develop and exchange information or interpretations	Make decisions or solve problems to improve product or service	Publicize issue and promote views or position
	Reflect on and respond to shared interests	Inform about products and services	Explore issues and options
TYPES OF INFORMAL ORAL EXCHANGES	Class, peer, or collaborative discussion	Work group, client, or committee discussion	Civic exchange or committee discussion
GOALS OF ORAL PRESENTATIONS	Present creative, applied, or theoretical work	Analyze problems and recommend solutions	Advocate position, policy, or proposal
	Analyze, synthesize, or interpret sources or findings	Promote product development, assembly, marketing, or delivery	Inform group, officials, or community about issue or proposal
	Engage interest of group	Inspire employees or customers	Motivate to care or act
TYPES OF FORMAL ORAL PRESENTATIONS	Description, explanation, or demonstration	Progress report, proposal, or recommendation	Public statement on issue, action, or proposal
	Conference panel or poster session	Telephone, video, and personal job interviews	Interviews or press statements on issue

1 Plan ahead when you speak formally

Keep a list of information about your presentation; let it shape your plans. For example, your time limit will help you decide what detail, points, and materials (such as handouts) to include. (See 4a and c.)

STRATEGY Analyze your speaking situation.

- What's the occasion? How many people will be there?
- How long is the event? How long will you speak?
- What place or space will you speak in? Where will you be?

- How will you know when to speak?
- What do you hope your presentation will do?
- What will your audience expect to find out or experience?
- What do you know—or need to find out—about your topic?

Begin to organize by grouping or outlining your remarks.

1. *Introductory remarks*: introduce yourself and give your audience a preview of what you'll say, show, or cover.
2. *Content or substance of the presentation*: present your main ideas, illustrations, and supporting material (see 7f).
3. *Conclusion*: sum up, restate your purpose, and remind your audience of what you have shown or offered.

Next, write out your **talking points**—key phrases, words, visual cues, or other reminders to guide you as you speak.

11c
peak

STRATEGY **Develop your talking points.**

- Jot down both your main points and signals to help you coordinate your talk: "Check time," "Show overhead."
- Use transitions (*next* or *to sum up*; see 7d) to link the parts and guide your audience: "As we've seen, the Valdez oil spill initially devastated the Alaskan shoreline. I want to turn now to its long-term impact."
- Match your style to your situation, audience, and topic.
- Estimate the time for each group of talking points. If necessary, consolidate, trim, or use a handout.
- Transfer your final talking points—content and cues—to 3" × 5" cards. Write out your first and last sentences to begin and end confidently.
- Number your cards so you always know where you are. At the top of every fifth card, estimate the time used by that point.

To engage your audience, have them read a handout, view a slide, talk in pairs, or tackle an activity—but allow the *time* for participation.

2 Rehearse your presentation

Stand up to match the physical conditions of your talk—body position, foot placement, breathing, eye movements. Rehearse alone first; then invite a few trusted listeners. Ask advice on pacing, volume, body movements, transitions, and the like. Videotape or record a rehearsal to spot problems, distracting habits, or unclear points. Keep rehearsing until you know every transition, dramatic pause, and reminder to look around.

Deliver your presentation

Although reading a printed paper aloud is common in some fields, most audiences prefer speakers to *present* their ideas instead of *read* them. This **extemporaneous** or **conversational speaking** emphasizes greater interaction among the speaker, audience, and ideas.

STRATEGY Focus on your delivery.

- Use your talking points to recall what to say, not to read out loud.
- Speak loudly and clearly, projecting your voice over the audience.
- Vary pitch and cadence for emphasis; don't exaggerate emotions.
- Avoid distracting verbal habits—"um," "like," or "you know."
- Move around if you wish, but don't pace, drum on the podium, or jingle your change.

11d
spea

Vary your eye contact so you don't favor the same person, group, or part of the room. Look directly at listeners (for only a few seconds unless you're answering a question). Glance at your visuals, but focus on your audience. Don't make them wait while you write out a transparency.

STRATEGY Use visuals to enhance your speech.

11.2

- Prepare your visuals ahead, whether you use a chalkboard, flip chart, overhead transparency, or audiovisual projection.
- Try to rehearse with any equipment to figure out how to run it, where to stand, and how to coordinate your visuals with your remarks.
- Use a large readable font, or pass out copies to simplify taking notes.
- If you use software such as *PowerPoint*, practice with the technology, avoid too much glitz, and always bring backup overheads.
- Let listeners read visuals for themselves. Paraphrase, note, or sum up in bulleted points what you present in detail.

4 Assess your results

Look for feedback on what you did well and what you can improve. If possible, ask someone to attend and honestly appraise your presentation. Your instructor may provide a scoring guide, evaluation sheet, or advice. Write out a self-assessment to strategize about future problems.

11d Managing speech anxiety

Like pilots with thousands of flight hours, experienced speakers have learned to control their apprehension. Giving oral presentations in college provides you with experience and confidence.

STRATEGY Reduce your anxieties about speaking.

- Write down your fears; look for strategies to overcome them.
- Before presentations, rest and eat well despite your anxiety.
- Sweaty palms and butterflies don't predict the quality of your talk.
- Take long, deep breaths to slow your heart rate, calm your nerves, an provide oxygen to your brain. Deliberately relax any tense spots.
- Focus on your ideas, not your looks or your worries.
- Move confidently to your speaking position. Face your audience be fore you begin; take a few seconds to organize or adjust a microphone
- Don't panic if you get lost or distracted: pause, breathe, cope.

11e Fielding questions

Presentations often end with questions—a dialogue with listeners. Anticipate what your audience might ask, plan brief answers, and remain flexible. Ask for clarification if you don't understand a question. Respond directly, not evasively. If you don't know an answer, say so, and don't make one up. Answer any hostile questions diplomatically, with "Yes," "No," or "I'm not sure," and move on.

12 | Finding an Online Voice

Technology has many sounds—hums, pings, whirs, and clicks. However, the most important sound is still that of your own personal or professional "voice" as you represent yourself in electronic communities.

TOO CASUAL   Hiya, Prof.! Sorry I slept late and missed your test. I really, really hope I can do the makeup this week. —Drake
READER'S REACTION: **Sounds like a goof-off to me.**

REVISED   Prof. Jones: Unfortunately, I missed the test today in Physics 130. Is it possible for me to do a makeup this week at your convenience? —Drake Long

Each online community has accepted standards for group members, language and customs to help you represent yourself appropriately.

12a Recognizing online expectations

Expectations of participants may be as specific as the shared interest uniting an online community. A brief period of "lurking" (reading without participating) is a good way to discover who participates, what rules govern participation, and whether your expectations match the community's.

Identify the type of online community

The **domain name** in an electronic address identifies an organization or other entity on the Internet, indicating the origin of material you access. For instance, the National Association for the Advancement of Colored People maintains the domain name *naacp.org*, which follows *www* in its Web site address and @ in its email addresses. Some suffixes also identify material from other countries (such as *.ca* for Canada, *.no* for Norway).

12a
onlin

> ### COMMON DOMAIN SUFFIXES IN INTERNET ADDRESSES
>
> | | | | |
> |---|---|---|---|
> | .com | commercial sites | .edu | educational groups |
> | .gov | governmental sites | .net | network sites |
> | .org | nonprofit organizations | | |

2 Use netiquette as a guide to community standards

Netiquette defines the behavior and politeness expected online.

STRATEGY Respect a site's netiquette guidelines.

- **Think before you act.** Once sent or posted, a message is open to friends, relatives, instructors, or employers.
- **Learn the norms.** Read a site's FAQ (frequently asked questions) page, and lurk before you participate.
- **Respect a group's interests.** Avoid personal attacks ("flames"), off-topic messages, hoaxes, inappropriate jokes, and spamming (sending unsolicited email to groups).
- **Use conventional grammar and usage.** Avoid creating a sloppy persona with careless wording or a rude one with ALL CAPS.
- **Remember the Golden Rule of netiquette.** Real people receive your email or access your Web site. Be considerate of them.

12.1

3 Define your persona for writing online

Consider how to tailor your **persona**, the image of yourself that you present to readers. In a public online community, you may remain anonymous, use a pseudonym (false name), choose a style or voice, and contribu rarely or often. Represent yourself as you wish, but do so honestly eve though others may not do the same. Neither school nor work offers th anonymity of a chat room. Adjust your persona accordingly.

12b Recognizing email conventions

Flexible and fast, email can create so much information that other may be irritated if you ignore conventions or lack purpose (see 4a).

1 Use the elements and functions of email

Online readers expect conventional elements in messages.

STRATEGY Save time with standard email components.

- **From.** State your identity in this line. Your email program may auto-matically show your address or your screen name.
- **Sent.** The date and time you send can help you track correspondence.
- **To.** Record the names of primary recipients. For copies sent to others, use the lines for **Cc:** (carbon copy) and **Bcc:** (blind carbon copy, sent without the knowledge of the main recipients).
- **Subject.** Use a short, clear subject line, like a news headline. If you're replying or forwarding from another message, keep this line current.
- **Message body.** Be concise. In a reply, clarify your topic, but follow the community's convention about including previous messages.
- **Signature or sig file.** Sign email for a reader's benefit. If you use a sig file to add your full name and contact details, consider your credibility and your readers before adding clever sayings, lyrics, or jokes.
- **Reply and reply-all.** Select "Reply" to answer the sender and "Reply-All" to include everyone who got the original. To avoid posting a per-sonal note, check the "To:" and "Cc:" lines before hitting "Send."
- **Forward.** Use discretion if you send messages on to others.
- **Attach.** If you attach files, spreadsheets, or video clips, recall that not all recipients will be able to open these documents.

2 Tailor your messages to the community

Individual email is like a letter; you specify who receives your message. List-based email, like contributions to printed newsletters, goes to all the list's subscribers. Individual mail isn't necessarily more "personal" or list mail more "professional." Recipients may expect different levels of formality, but most appreciate specificity, relevance, and brevity.

STRATEGY **Write brief messages that focus on essentials.**

- Identify your *most essential* point. Present it early and briefly.
- Clarify what you want readers to do or think as they respond.
- Break long blocks of text into short, readable paragraphs. Separate paragraphs with a blank line; consider adding headings.
- Replace detailed explanations with sources or an attached file.
- Reply economically, repeating only key material from prior messages. Consider how you're adding to what's come before.

Casual exchanges may use shortcuts inappropriate in professional or academic writing. Tilt your head to the left to see how **emoticons** (*emotion* + *icon*) add a jolt of feeling through faces drawn with keyboard characters.

:-) grin   :-(frown   ;-) wink   8-0 bug-eyed surprise

Abbreviations and **acronyms** (pronounceable abbreviations for common phrases) may also speed up casual communication. (See 44a-2.)

BTW by the way   F2F face-to-face   FYI for your information

12c onlir

12c Participating in online communities

Common formats encourage online exchanges.

1 Join electronic mailing lists and newsgroups

To join an electronic mailing list, email the host service. You'll then automatically receive all posted messages—individually or grouped in the day's "digest"—at your email address. Popular in the academic community, these lists allow private, focused discussion by a group. In contrast, you access a **newsgroup** directly, and messages are immediately posted for anyone to read. These popular resources for public and civic groups generally welcome participants.

2 Access Web-based forums

Web-based forums allow access to sites where users converse about shared interests. Some are moderated, many ask you to set up a user name and password, and a few charge fees. Forum readers may expect informal language, emoticons, acronyms, and citation of prior material for context.

3 Try real-time communication

Real-time discussion takes place instantly; words appear on each participant's screen as they are typed. The most popular real-time communities are **chat rooms**, informal conversations hosted by private Internet service or available via the Internet Relay Chat (IRC) network. The academic community often uses a **MUD**, or multi-user domain, which requires a series of commands for communication in a carefully described text environment. Users may adopt characters ("avatars") as they interact.

4 Participate in class conferences

Many classes are now offered online or include online requirements. If you don't routinely use the communication functions expected, allow time to learn how they work. Find out the purposes of online exchanges, conventions expected, ways to submit questions or post responses, resources required (online or print), deadlines for postings, and methods of assessment (numbers or types of postings, quiz scores). If you attach a file for others to read, use the required format so that everyone can access it.

12d Web

12.2

12d Writing for the World Wide Web

Different Web pages offer different types of writing.

TYPES OF WEB SITES

- **Personal home pages** sponsored by individuals to present personal, family, hobby, or special-interest news
- **Commercial sites** sponsored by corporations, businesses, or other enterprises to promote shopping or to explain products and services
- **Educational sites** sponsored by schools, colleges, libraries, scholarly journals, and other groups to supply access to resources or information
- **News or entertainment sites** sponsored by newspapers, magazines, and other media to supply breaking news or information archives
- **Search engines** dedicated to indexing Web pages for users

---

1 Design your Web page for readers

When building a Web page, first consider its format and purpose. Is it a class project on coral reef preservation, designed as a resource for those with similar interests? Is it an "online business card" limited to background and contact listings? Is it an autobiography for your friends and family?

Then consider how you want to present yourself. How will you establish your credibility? How will you react if an outsider comments on a site designed for your fellow students? Will you be comfortable if an employer or instructor visits your personal site? What might readers want to find? How are they likely to navigate? How will you expect its pages to relate? Finally, name your site carefully because search engines index words in the title and text. When your site is ready, visit the home pages of major search engines to register it so people can find your work.

STRATEGY Turn to your community to help you develop your site.

Before building a Web site, search for sites with similar purposes. Analyze how they work, listing what you like or dislike. Politely contact authors of notable pages for advice. Ask peers or colleagues for ideas, too.

Organize and manage your site

Maintain your site so you engage readers and encourage visits.

- **Keep content key.** Web users want information, not "cool" graphics. Don't overcrowd pages; allow ample "white space." When appropriate, list information. Use visuals to reinforce your topic, not fill space.
- **Stay updated, not outdated.** Publish when ready; update as needed.
- **Check your links.** Regularly test any links to supporting documents, data, or related sites to make sure they still work.
- **Consider visitors.** Use multiple platforms and browsers to test user interfaces. Include contact details, preferably an automatic email link.

13
desi

12e Behaving ethically online

Work ethically and professionally online. When you use a school email account—even if you access it away from campus—you are responsible for abiding by the institution's policies and regulations. You are also obligated by the terms of a public Internet service provider's contract. If you use your employer's Internet account, your employer may monitor what sites you access, and you probably have no legal expectation of privacy for anything you write or post. You may also be responsible under local, state, federal, or international law. (See also 49b-3 and 49c.)

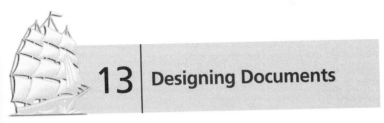

13 | Designing Documents

How can you prepare a report, a portfolio, or a visual aid that's clear and easy to read? How can you create a memorable document that engages readers and represents you as an effective writer or speaker?

DRAFT

PREVENTING VIOLENCE
Through **EARLY CHILDHOOD EDUCATION**

READER'S REACTION: Why does this title change type so often?

EDITED   Preventing Violence Through Early Childhood Education

The power of attractive, readable documents often lies in design: how yo present your text on the page and how you integrate visual aids.

13a Recognizing goals of document design

Your document often creates a reader's first impression of you. Its de sign can help convey your ideas and information effectively.

- Emphasize key points or ideas.
- Help readers readily locate and visualize information.
- Assure readers that you've considered their needs.
- Signal readers about your knowledge and perspective.
- Create a positive, persuasive image of you (a persona).

13b Recognizing principles of document design

Consider how the page looks and how readers process information.

Presentation matters. If a document is crowded or hard to understand, a reader may not bother to read it. If it's easy to follow, with clear headings, graphics, and other design elements, readers will respond positively.

Documents are visual. Visual elements include layout, space, headings, type, and cues provided by letters or numbers on a page as well as any visual aid (such as a photo, chart, or graph).

13c Planning your document

Readers need different things from different documents. The same reader approaches an air pollution report quite differently from chainsaw directions. And an engineer for a chemical plant and a homeowner living downwind from it will read the air pollution report very differently. Readers vary by community, too. While your academic readers expect to read a text from beginning to end, some readers at work may just skim the opening and conclusion.

STRATEGY Sketch a mock-up version of your document.

- What type of format or document do readers expect?
- How will you lay out the pages? Will you use headings or color?
- How will you show the organization? Will you add a table of contents?
- What font, typeface, and type size will you use?
- Will you use visuals? Which ones? How will you integrate them? What copyright issues or legal concerns must you address to use them?

13d Laying out your document

Layout is the arrangement of words, sentences, headings, lists, tables, graphs, and pictures on a page or computer screen.

Use visual cues

For readability, supply visual cues but avoid too many elements.

STRATEGY Use highlighting to direct the reader's eye.

Typographic devices such as **boldface**, *italics*, shading, rules, and boxes signal distinctions; they emphasize items and parts. Use *italics*, **boldface,** CAPITALS, and exclamation marks (!!) sparingly to create emphasis. Limit underlines (especially online where links are underlined).

Connotations of colors may vary with the context and reader.

COLOR	ENGINEERING	MEDICINE	FINANCE
blue	cold/water	death/not oxygenated	reliable/corporate
red	danger	healthy/oxygenated	loss
green	safe/environmental	infection	profit

STRATEGY Use color to communicate rather than decorate.

- Accomplish specific goals such as warning or caution.
- Prioritize and order; readers go to bright colors first.
- Symbolize, based on your knowledge of your readers.
- Identify a recurring theme, or connect a sequence.
- Show a pattern or relationship in a chart or graph.
- Code symbols or sections to simplify finding information.

2 Arrange information effectively

Use **white space**, open space not filled by other design elements, to organize text into chunks and guide the reader's eye. Consider the spaces around graphics and between letters, words, lines, or paragraphs. Note the margins (usually one inch to an inch and a half at the top, bottom, and sides). Try **lists** to break up dense text, emphasize points, itemize information, and group items, making it easy for readers to absorb ideas quickly. Consider highlighting items with bullets or numbers.

Headings, brief phrases that forecast or announce upcoming content, often are larger and darker than the rest of the text. Use them to move readers along so they see the organization and quickly find information.

13.2

STRATEGY **Design effective headings.**

- Use a consistent font and style for headings.
- Allow white space between headings and text.
- Position your headings consistently (for example, centering first-level headings and beginning second-level headings at the left margin).
- Focus headings for your specific content, task, or reader: *Deducting Student Loan Interest* rather than *Student Loans*.
- Make comparable headings parallel in structure (see 27a).
- Avoid clutter by using only the headings you need.

   Depending on the community you're addressing and the document you're writing, readers may expect specific features. Academic papers often use MLA or APA conventions (see Chapters 51–52); letters, reports, brochures, and other documents all follow their own visual conventions (see pp. 70–72, 364–65, and 369 for examples).

13e Using type

   Take judicious advantage of the fonts, typefaces, and type sizes available to highlight, organize, or connect text elements. A few—two or three fonts in a document—are generally better than too many.

Type size and weight. Select a readable typeface or font that enhances content. Type smaller than 8 points is hard to read; both 10- and 12-point type are easy to read. The latter is most common in academic texts. The larger the type, the more important the ideas will seem, but save sizes above 12 for special purposes and documents, such as overheads.

   8 point   10 point   12 point   16 point

Because some fonts have thicker or wider letters, you can use type weight to highlight without changing type style (**boldface**, *italics*, shadow).

Typefaces. Serif typefaces have little "feet" or small strokes at the end of each letterform. Sans serif fonts lack them.

   N serif   **N sans serif**

Readers tend to find serif typefaces easier to read in long documents but sans serif fonts effective in titles, headings, labels, and onscreen material. Serif typefaces include Times New Roman, Courier, Garamond, and Century Schoolbook. Sans serif faces include Arial, **Impact**, and Futura.

onts. Use decorative fonts and symbols with discretion. *Mistral*, **Sixpack**, **Cooper Black**, or *SigLight* can add engaging or emotional touches to brochures, invitations, or posters. Symbol fonts (such as those in Zapf Dingbats, Monotype Sorts, or Wingdings) can direct a reader's attention, emphasize a point, or add simple graphic flourishes. In your software's list of fonts, you may find symbols and icons like these.

13f Using visuals

Sometimes words aren't as efficient in making a point as tables, graphs, charts, photographs, maps, and drawings. Memorable visuals entice readers, are absorbed quickly, and communicate what words cannot.

Use tables, graphs, and charts to organize information

Tables concisely present information—usually text or numbers in columns and rows (see Table 1). **Graphs** rely on two labeled axes (vertical and horizontal) using **lines** (see Fig. 13.1) or **bars** (see Fig. 13.2) to compare items or relate variables. **Pie charts** show percentages of a whole (see Fig. 13.3). Title, number, and label tables as such in your text; number and label all other graphics as figures, and supply a brief caption. In MLA style, abbreviate a label (fig. 1); in APA style, spell it out (Figure 1).

Table 1 Services on the Campus WWW Site (percentages, by sector)					
	PUBLIC UNIVERSITY	**PRIVATE UNIVERSITY**	**PUBLIC 4-YR. COLLEGE**	**PRIVATE 4-YR. COLLEGE**	**COMMUNITY COLLEGE**
Undergraduate application	76.3	78.8	69.4	54.1	39.1
Course catalog	86.4	91.3	75.7	62.2	54.7
Program/degree requirements	83.1	69.5	73.9	68.4	46.0
Course registration	52.5	39.1	27.0	10.7	16.1
Library catalog	84.4	95.7	83.8	68.4	37.3
Student transcripts	44.1	43.5	22.5	12.2	8.7
Instructional software	57.5	60.9	26.1	26.5	5.0
e-Commerce (new)	18.5	13.0	1.8	4.1	3.1
Bookstore (new)	49.2	52.2	28.8	28.5	9.9

Source: Casey Green, The Campus Computing Project.

13f desig

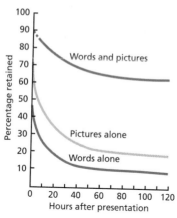

Fig. 13.1 Audience retention of information

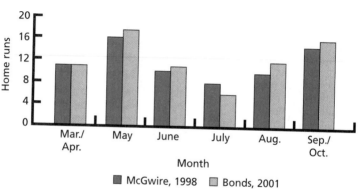

Fig. 13.2 Bonds versus McGwire: Chasing history

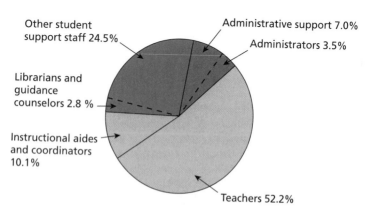

Fig. 13.3 Distribution of elementary and secondary education staff, by category

Use other visual devices

Drawings and diagrams can show physical features, connect parts, and ustrate spatial relationships so readers *see* what to do or how something orks. Photographs or illustrations record reality, as in newspapers and magzines. Simple drawings called "clip art," from software or the Web, are easy paste into a document to enhance a point.

STRATEGY **Integrate visual aids with your text.**

- Choose simple, appropriate visuals, not decorative filler.
- Use each visual to illustrate one main point that it clearly supports.
- Set off visuals with white space. Don't crowd them.
- Position graphics close to pertinent text. Supply verbal cues (labels, numbers, and captions) to link visuals and text.
- Credit sources for graphics. (Get permission to borrow, if needed.)
- For an oral presentation, use short phrases, bulleted points, and large type to keep your visuals simple, direct, and easy to read.

13g desig

13g Sample documents

The following three sample documents—an academic paper in MLA ormat, a workplace Web site, and a public poster—show how the principles f document design work. Each document has been annotated to point out ts features and layout.

13.3

Sample Document: Academic Paper, MLA Format

1 inch

⟨1⟩ 1/2 inch
Herrin 1 ⟨2⟩

Norrie Herrin ⟨3⟩
Dr. I. Job Thomas
Art 102
5 May 1999

13g
esign

⟨5⟩
1 inch

The Highlight of Pallavas Sculpture: <u>The Descent of the Ganges</u> ⟨4⟩

The Pallavas of South India are famous for the sculptures
that they created in the large granite outcroppings in
Mahabalipuram. During the reign of Narasimha Varman I
(c. 630 CE), the best examples of these immense sculptures,
such as <u>The Descent of the Ganges</u> (fig. 1), were carved into
the living granite off the shores of the Bay of Bengal
(Craven 145). The massive sculptures of the Pallavas often
depicted mythological stories from their Hindu traditions.
⟨6⟩ <u>The Descent of the Ganges</u> exemplifies the Pallava's new
sculptural and narrative genius.

The Descent of the Ganges is carved in relief on the surface
of an enormous granite rock. The sculpture tells the mythical
story of the Ganges falling to earth from her heavenly source
in the Himalaya to bless humanity (Lee 223). Over one hundred
figures are carved into the rock. They all face toward the cleft
in the center of the sculpture, where the water flows.

⟨7⟩

⟨8⟩ Fig. 1. <u>The Descent of the Ganges</u>, Mahabalipuram, Tamil Nadu,
India, seventh century

⟨1⟩ 1/2-inch margin at top

⟨2⟩ Author's last name and page number on every page including the first

⟨3⟩ Name, instructor's name, course, and date

⟨4⟩ Title centered with no extra space before or after

⟨5⟩ 1-inch margin at left, right, and bottom

⟨6⟩ Text double-spaced throughout, including long quotations and works cited list

⟨7⟩ Photo of sculpture taken by student writer duplicated using the "photo" setting on the copier

⟨8⟩ Numbered figure with label that properly credits the artist, giving work's title and location when the artist is unknown

Sample Document: Workplace Web Site

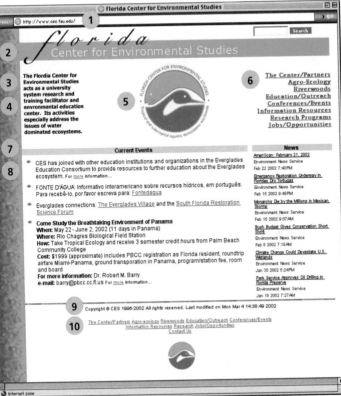

1 Descriptive title in window frame (used by search engines for indexing) that lets readers know where they are

2 Title repeated on the Web page creates a visual tone for the site

3 Textured background that adds appeal without diminishing legibility

4 Opening block of text identifies organization and its mission

5 Icon represents organization and reveals illustrations of menu options

6 HTML tables used to create a menu on the side of the page

7 Up-to-date news presented first in box so users don't have to scroll to it

8 Textual summaries that describe links

9 Date that tells visitors how current the information is

10 Contact information for organization and staff

13g
desig

Sample Document: Public Poster

THE POWER OF ONE
Alcohol Awareness Week
March 1 - 4, 1999 • UNC Charlotte

SPECIAL EVENTS:

MONDAY, MARCH 1ST
Alcohol Insanity Tour '99
with Wendi Foxx
Nationally renowned comedienne
Wendi Foxx will entertain with Alcohol
Aware Educational Comedy.
McNight Hall 8pm

TUESDAY, MARCH 2ND
Copacabana Mocktail Bar
Representatives from RSA and SGA
will provide refreshing alcohol-free
"mocktails" in a tropical setting right
here on campus!
After Hours 11:30am-1:30pm

WEDNESDAY, MARCH 3RD
DUI: Decisions
Under the Influence
Campus Police will demonstrate the
hazards of drinking with sobriety
exercises performed on real life
students.
Poplar Hall 2nd floor 8pm

THURSDAY, MARCH 4TH
Pledge Card Drive
Join the campus community in
pledging not to drink and drive.
Belk Tower 11am-3pm

Sponsored by the Department of Housing &
Residence Life, Resident Students

Mine is the Power of One
The power to make my own
  decisions
The power to achieve all of my
  goals

Mine is the Power of One
The power to create the life I want
The power to impact the lives of
  others

Mine is the Power of One
The power to set responsible limits
The power to drink without
  driving

The Power that is Mine
Comes from within

The Power that is Mine

① Unusual font drawing attention to headline

② Date and description of the event prominently placed

③ Open space keeping focus on key elements

④ Clear format for scheduling information

⑤ Interesting original artwork

⑥ Poem in more legible font that complements the headline

TAKING IT ONLINE

PURDUE ONLINE WRITING LAB (OWL)
http://owl.english.purdue.edu/

Visit this site for the most complete list of resources, handouts, and exercises about grammar and editing collected by any American university. The site also offers grammar advice for ESL writers.

THE GOOD GRAMMAR, GOOD STYLE™ PAGES
http://www.protrainco.com/info/grammar.htm

Do you have a grammar question? Check this site's searchable database and "Articles & Answers" archive.

POP-UP GRAMMAR
http://www.brownlee.org/durk/grammar/

Pop-up Grammar is an online testing, instruction, and assessment site. To test your grammar skills, try the interactive grammar quizzes.

QUIZ ON SENTENCE TYPES
http://webster.commnet.edu/cgi-shl/quiz.pl/sentence_types_quiz.htm

This site offers an interactive quiz on sentence types that tests your knowledge and checks your answers. You'll also find additional grammar instruction and writing advice.

WRITING TIPS
http://faculty.rmwc.edu/jabell/writing.htm

THE MARKETING DEPARTMENT'S TOP 10 LIST OF WRITING ERRORS AND THEN SOME
http://www.csun.edu/~hfbus023/errors.html

These guidelines from professors will help you recognize and edit common writing errors.

DAVE'S ESL CAFÉ HINT OF THE DAY
http://eslcafe.com/webhints/hints.cgi

Read the hint of the day, and search the archive for past hints, too.

14 | Editing and Proofreading

After revising your writing (see Chapter 6), you're ready to edit and proofread. **Editing** means adjusting sentences and words for clarity, style, economy, and correctness. A final polish, **proofreading**, eliminates distractions such as misspelled words and typographical errors.

14a Correcting errors: Expectations of readers and options for writers

Writing correctly means recognizing and using the **conventions**—the options for grammar, sentence structure and style, word choice, punctuation, and mechanics—that readers expect you to use. Some conventions don't vary much across communities, such as using complete sentences or standard spelling in formal prose. In these cases, most writers try to avoid challenging readers' strongly held expectations. After all, a reader irritated by errors isn't likely to give you a high grade, promote you, join your civic crusade, or view you as an attentive writer.

Other conventions, however, vary with the context. For example, newspaper readers wouldn't be surprised to find only one comma in this sentence: *The suspect jumped from the car, evaded the officers and ran into the motel*. But many academic readers would expect a second comma to follow *officers*, perhaps citing the well-known guides of the Modern Language Association (MLA) and the American Psychological Association (APA) as authorities on this comma issue (see Chapters 51–52). Likewise, a chemist would use numerals (such as *12* or *84*) in a lab report, while an art historian might spell out *twelve* and *eighty-four* in an interpretive paper. Effective writers learn how to recognize and edit flexible conventions to meet readers' expectations.

14b Editing your own writing

You can improve your editing skills each time you prepare a college paper, a work project, or a public communication. Allow plenty of time to read carefully, and shift your attention from content (what's said) to form (how it's said). Noticing readers' reactions during class or meetings can alert you to their individual and community sensitivities. Check your writing for both the problems readers identify and the features they admire.

As you edit, focus on one issue at a time—commas, perhaps, or wordiness—while you scour your text for specific cases. Then repeat the process for the next issue. Read your text several times to avoid being overloaded b too many problems at once.

1 Edit for clarity, style, and economy

14.1

Most writing profits from final cosmetic surgery. If your grant pro posal, oral presentation, letter to the editor, or other writing project has length limit, edit ruthlessly to meet this expectation.

DRAFT   The aligned pulleys are lined up so that they are located up abov the center core of the machine.
          READER'S REACTION: **This seems repetitive and boring.**

EDITED   The aligned pulleys are ~~lined up so that they are located~~ **positione** ~~up~~ above ~~the center core of~~ **the machine's core.**

STRATEGY Ask questions as you edit.

- **Are my sentences clear and easy to read?** Try reading out loud. When ever you stumble over the wording, rephrase or restructure.
- **Do I repeat some sentence structures too often?** If too many sen tences begin with nouns or *I*, start some with prepositional phrase (see 16b-1) or subordinate clauses (see 16c and 28b–c).
- **Do any words seem odd or inappropriate?** If so, reword. Turn to a dictionary or thesaurus for help. (See 31b, 33b.)
- **If I had to cut ten words per page, which could I drop?** Cut, but avoid new problems (such as short, choppy sentences). (See 29b.)

2 Edit for grammatical problems

Editing for grammatical problems challenges you first to *recognize* the problem and then to *edit* to repair or eliminate it. The chart on pages 426– 427 lists ten errors identified by academic readers as likely to irritate readers and call into question a writer's skills. This chart and this handbook's editing advice use the read-recognize-revise pattern to help you identify errors and select a useful editing strategy.

STRATEGY Read to recognize errors and suspected errors.

- Read your paper from start to finish, circling or marking any errors in grammar, punctuation, and sentence logic. If you can quickly correct an error, do so. Otherwise, finish identifying problems, and then look up the relevant advice in this handbook or other references.
- Read your paper again, this time marking all suspected problems in your text. Follow your instincts if you feel that a sentence is weak or flawed. Then look up the pertinent advice, and edit the errors or flaws. Stick to the possible errors unless you want to improve an awkward or

wordy sentence. Ask a teacher, tutor, peer editor, colleague, or friend for advice as needed.

aragraphs from Jim Tollefson's newsletter for his local nature conservancy ow his circled errors and his edited version.

RAFT WITH
RRORS
ARKED

Critics of the endangered species act think it is too broad. Because some specie's may be less vital to environmental balance than others. They want to protect species selectively, however, scientists do not know which species are more important.

caps
fragment
apostrophe
who?
comma splice

DITED

Critics of the Endangered Species Act think it is too broad because some species may be less vital to environmental balance than others. Our critics want to protect species selectively. However, scientists do not know which species are more important.

Look for patterns—repeated errors—that you recognize or that readers point out. Then you can make many corrections simply by identifying and repairing a specific type of error.

STRATEGY **Build your own editing checklist.**

- Analyze your papers, keeping track of your repeated errors.
- Ask a teacher or expert writer to identify your *patterns* of error.
- Use the strategies in this book or create your own for *recognizing* and *editing* your errors. Collect these in a personal editing checklist.
- Use your checklist; replace items you master with new ones.

After editing her report on the effects of loud music, Carrie Brehe added this item to her editing checklist.

A lot sounds like one word but is actually two. Think of its opposite, a little. From the noise paper: "Alot of teenagers do not know how their hearing works." Strategy: Search for alot.

14c   Editing collaboratively

When you edit collaboratively, you identify and talk about specific problems with "consulting readers," usually friends, peers, or colleagues who

14c
edit

help you improve a particular writing project while you learn to identify and repair errors on your own.

STRATEGY Observe guidelines for collaborative editing.

GUIDELINES FOR WRITERS

- Revise content and organization first to prepare your draft for editing. (If necessary, ask your reader for feedback on larger revisions instead. See 6c.)
- Supply a clean draft; don't waste your reader's time on sloppiness.
- Share your requirements or writing concerns with your reader.

GUIDELINES FOR READERS

- Use familiar labels and symbols for comments. (The terms in this handbook are generally accepted in academic, work, and public communities. See the list of symbols inside the back cover flap.)
- Just note possible errors. Let the writer use a dictionary, a style guide, or this handbook to identify and repair each problem.
- Be specific; *awkward* or *unclear* may not tell the writer exactly what's wrong. Briefly tell why something does or doesn't work.
- Identify outright errors, but don't "take over" the draft. Rewriting sentences and paragraphs is the writer's job.
- Look for patterns of error, noting repetition of the same mistakes.

14e
edit

14d Editing on the computer

14.2

Many computer programs claim to offer shortcuts for editors. Some can identify features like verbs in the passive voice or calculate the average length of sentences. Despite their claims, most are no match for human readers and editors. Besides taking time to run, they may question correct sentences while they skip errors (such as typing *the* for *they* because both words are spelled correctly). They also can't help you adjust to different community expectations or readers.

14e Proofreading

After you've edited as thoughtfully as possible, it's time for **proofreading**, your last chance to make sure that errors in presentation don't annoy your reader or undermine your ideas and credibility as a writer. If mistakes accumulate in a college paper or project at work, these errors can lead to a poor assessment or hinder your advancement.

STRATEGY Proofread for the details.

- Read out loud or even backwards from the last sentence to the first.

- Look for missing words, incorrect prepositions, missing punctuation marks (especially half of a pair of commas or parentheses), and accidental duplicates.
- Consciously fix your eyes on each word to be sure it doesn't contain transposed letters, typographical errors, and the like.

15 | Recognizing How Words Work to Create Sentences

To edit effectively, you need to recognize sentence components and their working relationships. At the simplest level, sentences consist of different types of words, often called *parts of speech*: nouns, pronouns, verbs, adjectives, adverbs, prepositions, conjunctions, and interjections.

STRATEGY   **Look for connections to your editing.**

This chapter is a resource for recognizing the roles of words in sentences. Look for ways to apply its information as you edit.

15a
gr

- Use this chapter to review the terms that describe the functions of words in sentences (the parts of speech). (See also Chapter 16.)
- Follow the cross-references in the chapter to relate its explanations to editing errors and options.
- Return here if you find later explanations confusing, even though this book tries to limit technical language.
- Turn also to the index to find unfamiliar terms used by an instructor, classmates, or others.

15a Recognizing nouns and articles

You can recognize a **noun** by looking for a word that names a person, a place, an idea, or a thing. For most nouns, form the **plural** (two or more) by adding -s or -es to the **singular** (one): *cow* + -s = *cows; gas* + -es = *gases.* Some nouns are irregular: *child, children; deer, deer.* Use a noun's **possessive** form to express ownership (see 36a–b on apostrophes).

SINGULAR	SINGULAR POSSESSIVE ('S)	PLURAL	PLURAL POSSESSIVE (')
student	student's	students	students'

ESL

15a
gr

TYPES OF NOUNS

Count noun	Names individual items that can be counted: *four cups*, *a hundred beans*
Noncount noun (mass noun)	Names material or abstractions that cannot be counted: *flour, water, steel*
Collective noun	Names a unit composed of more than one individual or thing (see 19b-2 on agreement): *group, board of directors, flock*
Proper noun	Names specific people, places, titles, or things (see 40b on capitals): *Miss America; Tuscaloosa, Alabama; Microsoft Corporation*
Common noun	Names nonspecific people, places, or things (see 40b on capitals): *children, winner, town, mountain, company, bike*

A noun often requires an **article**: *the, a* (before a consonant sound), or *an* (before a vowel sound).

> An **intern** prepared a **report** for the **doctor** at **Hope Hospital**.

ESL ADVICE: THE ARTICLES *A*, *AN*, AND *THE*

Remember that you'll still communicate your meaning even if you choose the wrong article or forget one. Notice as you read how the **indefinite articles** (*a* or *an*) and the **definite article** (*the*) are used.

NOUNS AND THE USE OF ARTICLES

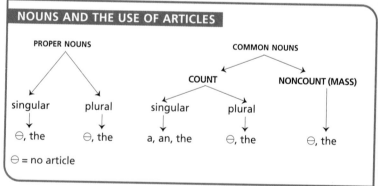

⊖ = no article

Singular proper nouns generally use no article, and **plural proper nouns** usually use *the*.

SINGULAR	Rosa Parks helped initiate the civil rights movement.
PLURAL	**The** Everglades have abundant wildlife and plants.

ingular count nouns use *a, an,* or *the* and cannot stand alone.

INGULAR   **The** <u>pig</u> is **an** intelligent <u>animal</u>.

lural count nouns use either no article (to show a generalization) or *the* to refer to something specific).

GENERALIZATION   <u>Books</u> are the best teachers. [books in general]

PECIFIC   **The** <u>books</u> on his desk are due Monday. [specific books]

Noncount (mass) nouns use either no article or *the*, never *a* or *an*. **General noncount nouns** sometimes stand alone. **Specific noncount nouns**, which have been limited in some way, use *the*.

FAULTY   A <u>laughter</u> is good medicine.

GENERAL   <u>Laughter</u> is good medicine. [laughter in general]

PECIFIC   **The** <u>laughter</u> of children is good medicine. [specific type of laughter]

ESL

15a
gr

STRATEGY   Select *a, an,* or *the.*

- Use *a* or *an* when you are not referring to any specific person or thing (using a nonspecific, singular count noun). Use *a* before a consonant sound and *an* before a vowel sound.

  I need **a** <u>car</u> to go to work. [unknown, nonspecific car or any car]

- Use *the* when you are referring to an exact, known person or thing (using a specific, singular noun).

  I need **the** <u>car</u> to go to work. [specific, known car]

  The <u>car</u> that she bought is metallic gray. [specific, known car]

- Generally use no articles with plural count and noncount nouns.

  COUNT   <u>Airline tickets</u> to Chicago are at half price.

  NONCOUNT   <u>Information</u> about flights to Chicago is now available.

- Use *the* when a plural count noun or a noncount noun is followed by a modifier, such as an adjective clause (see 16c-1) or prepositional phrase (see 16b-1), that makes the noun specific.

  COUNT   **The** <u>airline tickets</u> <u>that you bought</u> are at half price.

  NONCOUNT   **The** <u>information</u> <u>on the flight board</u> has changed.

15b Recognizing pronouns

To recognize a **pronoun**, look for a word like *them*, *she*, *his*, or *it* that takes the place of a noun and can play the same roles in a sentence. You can use a pronoun to avoid repeating a noun, but the pronoun's meaning depends on a clear relationship to the noun to which it refers—its **antecedent** or **headword**. (See 19c on agreement and 23a on pronoun reference.)

      antecedent   pronoun
    Jean presented **her** proposal to the committee.

You can also use a pronoun to modify a noun or another pronoun.

    This part has been on order for a month, and **that** one for a week.

A pronoun changes form to show **number** (singular or plural), **gender** (masculine, feminine, or neuter), and role in a sentence—**subject**, **object**, or **possessive** (see 16a on sentence structure and 18a on pronoun form).

15c Recognizing verbs

To identify **verbs**, look for words that express actions (*jump*, *build*), occurrences (*become*, *happen*), and states of being (*be*, *seem*). Change a verb's form to reflect person and number (see 19a on agreement) and to signal relationships in time (see 17a–g on **tense**).

PERSON	She **restores** furniture.	They **restore** furniture.
NUMBER	The copier **makes** noise.	The copiers **make** noise.
TENSE	They **prepare** the invoices.	They **prepared** the invoices.

Other forms show voice (see 17i and 29b-3 on sentences) and mood (see 17h).

ACTIVE VOICE	The pump **cleans** the water.
PASSIVE VOICE	The water **is cleaned** by the pump.
INDICATIVE MOOD	The report **was** on the desk.
SUBJUNCTIVE MOOD	If the report **were** on the desk, I would have found it.

You can use a **main verb** alone or with one or more **helping (auxiliary) verbs**, which include the forms of *be*, *do*, and *have*. A helping verb and a main verb form a **verb phrase**. You can also use **modal auxiliary verbs** as helping verbs but never as main verbs. They include *will/would*, *can/could*, *shall/should*, *may/might*, *must*, and *ought*. (See 17d.)

PRONOUNS AND THEIR FUNCTIONS

Personal pronouns
Designate persons or things using a form reflecting the pronoun's role in the sentence (see 18a)

SINGULAR
I, me, you, he, him, she, her, it

PLURAL
we, us, you, they, them

Possessive pronouns
Show ownership (see 18a on pronouns and 36a–b on apostrophes)

SINGULAR
my, mine, your, yours, her, hers, his, its

PLURAL
our, ours, your, yours, their, theirs

Relative pronouns
Introduce subordinate clauses that modify or add information to a main clause; these **relative clauses** act as **adjectives** and answer the questions "What kind of?" and "Which one?" (see 16c and 28b on subordination, 19b-6 on agreement, 34e–f on commas)

who, whom, whose, which, that

Interrogative pronouns
Introduce questions
who, which

Reflexive pronouns and intensive pronouns
End in *-self* or *-selves* and enable the subject or doer also to be the receiver of an action
End in *-self* or *-selves* and add emphasis

SINGULAR
myself, yourself, herself, himself, itself

PLURAL
ourselves, yourselves, themselves

Indefinite pronouns
Refer to people, things, and ideas in general rather than a specific antecedent (see 19b-6)

SINGULAR
anybody, each, every, neither, none, something

PLURAL
both, few, fewer, many, others, several

VARIABLE
all, any, enough, more, most, some

Demonstrative pronouns
Point out or highlight an antecedent; can refer to a noun or a pronoun or sum up an entire phrase or clause

this, that, these, those

Reciprocal pronouns
Refer to individual parts of a plural antecedent
one another, each other

15c
gr

MAIN VERB	The city **welcomes** tourists all year round.
HELPING + MAIN	The tourist agency **is planning** a video.
MODAL + MAIN	They **might decide** to include the Old Courthouse.

Use **action verbs** to show an action or activity: *swim, analyze, dig, tur* Use **linking verbs** (or **state-of-being verbs**) to express a state of being or a occurrence: *is, seems, becomes, grows*. These verbs link a subject with a **com plement** that renames or describes it (see 16a-2).

ACTION	The company and the union **negotiated** a contract.
LINKING	The flowers **smelled** musky.

Phrasal verbs include a verb plus a closely associated word that seem like a preposition but is known as a **particle**, as in *run down* ("exhaust") Unlike verb-plus-preposition combinations, whose meanings are the sums their parts (*run* = action + *by* = direction), phrasal verbs have meanings tha differ from those of the separate words. For example, *clear out* means "depart and *run by* means "consult."

ESL

15d
gr

phrasal verb	verb + preposition
I **ran** the idea **by** the committee.	I **ran by** the house.

15d Recognizing adjectives

To identify **adjectives**, look for words that modify nouns, pronouns, or word groups acting as nouns. They answer questions like "How many?" "Which one?" or "What kind?" (see 20a on adjective features).

HOW MANY?	The **three** meetings will last all day.
WHICH ONE?	Our report is the **last** one.
WHAT KIND?	Their proposal was **unacceptable**.

Adjectives come in three degrees of comparison: *high, higher, highest; crooked, more crooked, most crooked* (see 20a on adjective forms).

ESL ADVICE: ADJECTIVE FORMS

Adjectives in English never use a plural form.

DRAFT	Santo Domingo is renowned for beautiful beaches.
EDITED	Santo Domingo is renowned for beautiful beaches.

15e Recognizing adverbs

To identify **adverbs**, look for words that modify verbs, adjectives, other adverbs, or entire sentences. They answer such questions as "When?" "Where?" "Why?" "How often?" "Which direction?" "What conditions?" and "What degree?" (see 20a on adverb features).

WHEN?	Our committee met **yesterday**. [modifies verb *met*]
WHAT DEGREE?	We had a **very** long meeting. [modifies adjective *long*]
HOW OFTEN?	I attend board meetings **quite** frequently. [modifies adverb *frequently*, which modifies verb *attend*]

Many adverbs consist of an adjective plus *-ly* (*quickly, blindly, frequently*) though some adjectives also end in *-ly* (*neighborly, lovely*). Other common adverbs include *very, too, tomorrow, not, never, sometimes,* and *well*. Adverbs come in three degrees of comparison: *quickly, more* (or *less*) *quickly, most* (or *least*) *quickly* (see 20a on adverb forms).

You can use **conjunctive adverbs** such as *however, moreover, thus,* and *therefore* to indicate logical relationships. (See 28a for a list.)

They opposed the policy; **nevertheless**, they implemented it.

15f
gr

15f Recognizing prepositions

To recognize a **preposition**, look for a word like *in* or *at* followed by a noun or pronoun, forming a **prepositional phrase** (see 16b-1) and adding precise, detailed information to a sentence.

The office in **this region** sells homes priced above **$90,000**.

www
15.2

COMMON PREPOSITIONS

about	at	despite	near	to
above	before	down	of	toward
across	behind	during	off	under
after	below	except	on	until
against	beneath	for	out	up
along	between	from	outside	upon
among	beyond	in	over	with
around	by	into	past	within
as	concerning	like	through	without

ESL (margin)

15f
gr (margin)

ESL ADVICE: PREPOSITIONS

PREPOSITIONS OF TIME: *AT*, *ON*, AND *IN*

- Use *at* for a specific time.
- Use *on* for days and dates.
- Use *in* for nonspecific times during a day, month, season, or year.

Brandon was born **at** 11:11 a.m. **on** a Monday **in** 1991.

PREPOSITIONS OF PLACE: *AT*, *ON*, AND *IN*

- Use *at* for specific addresses.
- Use *on* for names of streets, avenues, and boulevards.
- Use *in* for names of areas of land—states, countries, continents.

She works **at** 99 Tinker Street **in** Dayton.

The White House is **on** Pennsylvania Avenue **in** Washington, D.C.

In general, use prepositional phrases in this order: place, then time.

place + time
The runners will start **in the park** on Saturday.

PREPOSITIONS OF PLACE: *IN*, *AT*, *ON*, AND NO PREPOSITION

IN	AT	ON	NO PREPOSITION
(the) bed*	the mall*	the bed*	downstairs
the bedroom	home	the ceiling	downtown
the car	the library*	the floor	inside
(the) class*	the office	the horse	outside
the library*	school*	the plane	upstairs
school*	work	the train	uptown

*You may sometimes use different prepositions for these locations.

TO OR NO PREPOSITION TO EXPRESS GOING TO A PLACE

- When you express the idea of going to a place, use the preposition *to.*

I am going **to** work.   I am going **to** the office.

- In the following cases, use no preposition.

I am going home.   I am going downstairs (downtown, inside).

FOR AND SINCE IN TIME EXPRESSIONS

- Use *for* with an amount of time (minutes, hours, days, months, years) and *since* with a specific date or time.

The housing program has operated **for** many years.

The housing program has operated **since** 1971.

REPOSITIONS WITH NOUNS, VERBS, AND ADJECTIVES

- Nouns, verbs, and adjectives may appear with certain prepositions.

NOUN + PREPOSITION He has an <u>understanding</u> **of** global politics.

VERB + PREPOSITION Managers <u>worry</u> **about** many things.

ADJECTIVE + PREPOSITION Life in your country is <u>similar</u> **to** life in mine.

NOUN + PREPOSITION COMBINATIONS

approval of	confusion about	hope for	participation in
awareness of	desire for	interest in	reason for
belief in	grasp of	love of	respect for
concern for	hatred of	need for	understanding of

VERB + PREPOSITION COMBINATIONS

ask about	differ from	pay for	study for
ask for	grow into	prepare for	think about
belong to	look at	refer to	trust in
care for	participate in	step into	work for

ADJECTIVE + PREPOSITION COMBINATIONS

afraid of	careless about	interested in	similar to
angry at	familiar with	made of	sorry for
aware of	fond of	married to	sure of
capable of	happy about	proud of	tired of

ESL

15g
gr

15g Recognizing conjunctions

To recognize **conjunctions**, look for words that join other words and word groups, signaling their relationships.

Coordinating conjunctions. You can use *and, but, or, nor, for, yet,* and *so* to link grammatically equal elements (see 28a).

WORDS analyze **and** discuss, compare **or** contrast

PHRASES over past sales **yet** under current hopes

CLAUSES They petitioned the board, **but** they lost their appeal.

Subordinating conjunctions. Use words such as *because* or *if* to create a **subordinate** (or **dependent**) **clause.** Such a clause cannot stand on its own as a sentence; you need to attach it to a **main** (or **independent**) **clause** that it qualifies or limits. (See 28b for a list of conjunctions.)

main clause   subordinate clause
Li spoke persuasively, **though** the crowd favored her opponent.

Correlative conjunctions. These pairs include *not only ... but also, either
... or, both ... and,* and similar combinations. They join sentence elements
that are grammatically equal. (See 27b on parallelism.)

15h Recognizing interjections

To recognize **interjections**, look for expressions that convey a strong
reaction or emotion, such as surprise (*Hey!*) or disappointment (*Oh, no!*)
They may stand alone or be loosely related to the rest of a sentence.

16 | Recognizing How Sentence Parts and Patterns Work

Careful editing depends on your ability to recognize the different parts
of sentences so that you can change their relationships or choose among alternative patterns. See also Chapter 15, which reviews the functions of the
words combined to form phrases, clauses, and sentences.

STRATEGY   Look for sentence alternatives.

This chapter is a resource for recognizing sentence parts and patterns
as you create varied and correct sentences.

* Use this chapter to review terms that describe sentence parts and structures (such as *predicate* or *main clause*).
* Look at the examples here as options. Try to recognize or experiment
  with similar sentences in your drafts.
* Follow the cross-references in the chapter to locate more examples as
  well as related editing advice.
* Return here if you need to clarify later explanations or look up unfamiliar terms used by others.

16a Recognizing subjects and predicates

Look for a subject and a predicate in each of your sentences.

Look for sentence subjects

To recognize a **simple subject**, look for one or more nouns (or pronouns) naming the doer or the topic. To identify a **complete subject**, find the simple subject *plus* all its modifying words.

SIMPLE SUBJECT   **Email** has changed business communication.

COMPLETE SUBJECT   **All the sales staff on this floor** left early.

A subject may be singular, plural, or compound (linked by *and* or *or*).

SINGULAR SUBJECT   **She** put the monitor on the desk.

PLURAL SUBJECT   **These pills** are difficult to swallow.

COMPOUND SUBJECT   **John and Chifume** are medical students.

In most sentences, the subject comes before the verb. Beginning with an expletive construction (*there is/are* or *here is/are*) delays the subject until after the verb (see 29b-2).

USUAL ORDER   **Homeless people** <u>camped</u> here.

EXPLETIVE   There <u>were</u> **homeless people** camping here.

To invert sentence structure for emphasis, you reverse subject and verb.

INVERTED   In this tiny house <u>was born</u> **a leader**.

Questions often place the subject between helping and main verbs.

QUESTION   <u>Did</u> **the board** <u>approve</u> the light-rail proposal?

In an imperative sentence expressing a request or command, the subject *you* generally is implied but not stated (see 16d).

IMPERATIVE   **[You]** <u>Put</u> the insulation around the door frame.

2 Look for sentence predicates

The **predicate** indicates an action or relationship expressed in a sentence and may specify consequences or conditions. A **simple predicate** includes only a verb (see 15c) or verb phrase (see 17d).

VERB   The bus **stopped**.   **VERB PHRASE**   The bus **might stop**.

The verb may be single or compound (linked by *and* or *or*).

SINGLE   The client **slipped**.   **COMPOUND**   The client **slipped and fell**.

To recognize a **complete predicate**, look for a verb or verb phrase *plus* modifiers and other words that receive the action or complete the verb.

16a
gr

Object patterns. With a **transitive verb**, you will often include a **direct object** in the predicate, telling *who* or *what* receives the action.

> **predicate**
> **subject**   **verb (direct object)**
> The bank officer **approved** the loan.

A sentence with a transitive verb can also include an **indirect object**, a noun or pronoun telling readers *to whom* or *for whom* the action is undertaken.

> **direct**
> **subject**   **verb**   **indirect object**   **object**
> The Marine Corps Reserve **gives** needy children toys.

You can add information to a predicate with an **object complement**, a noun or adjective that renames or describes the direct object.

NOUN   His co-workers elected **Jim** project leader.

ADJECTIVE   Critics judged **the movie** inferior.

Subject complement patterns. With a **linking verb**, such as *is*, *seems*, or *feels* (see 15c), you can include a **subject complement**, "completing" the subject by describing or renaming it.

> **subject**
> **subject**   **verb**   **complement**
> The grant proposal **is** too complicated.

Intransitive verb patterns. An **intransitive verb** doesn't take an object or a complement; neither is needed to complete the meaning.

> Our team **lost**.   Last week, the ferryboat **sank**.

16.1

FIVE BASIC PREDICATE STRUCTURES

1. **Subject + intransitive verb**
   The bus crashed.

2. **Subject + transitive verb + direct object**
   A passenger called the police.

3. **Subject + transitive verb + indirect object + direct object**
   The paramedic gave everyone a blanket.

4. **Subject + transitive verb + direct object + object complement**
   Officials found the driver negligent.

5. **Subject + linking verb + subject complement**
   The quick-thinking passenger was a hero.

16a
gr

16b Recognizing phrases

A **sentence** is a word group with a subject and a predicate that can stand alone (see 16d). In contrast, a **phrase** is a word group that lacks a subject, a predicate, or both. A phrase cannot stand alone and must be integrated within a freestanding sentence. If you capitalize and punctuate a phrase like a sentence, you create a fragment (see 21a).

16.2

1 Look for prepositional phrases

To recognize a **prepositional phrase**, look first for a **preposition**—a word like *at, for, under,* or *except* (see the list in 15f). Then identify the **object of the preposition**—the noun, pronoun, or word group that follows the preposition.

to <u>the beach</u>   **near** <u>her</u>   **after** <u>a falling out</u>   **inside** <u>the case</u>

A prepositional phrase can act as an adjective (almost always following the noun or pronoun it modifies) or as an adverb (placed next to the verb modified or elsewhere in the sentence). (See also 30b on conciseness.)

AS ADJECTIVE   The coupons **in the newspaper** offer savings **on groceries**.

AS ADVERB   Her watch started beeping **during the meeting**.

During the meeting, her watch started beeping.

16b
gr

2 Look for absolute phrases

An **absolute phrase** includes (1) a noun, pronoun, or word group acting as a noun and (2) a present or past participle and any modifiers (*the deadline approaching quickly*). You can use the phrase to modify a sentence as a whole rather than a word or element within the sentence.

They fought the fire, **the dense smoke slowing their efforts**.

3 Look for appositive phrases

To recognize an **appositive**, look for information added by renaming a noun or pronoun. An **appositive phrase** consists of an appositive (generally a noun) along with its modifiers. (See also 34e.)

Ken Choi, **my classmate**, won an award for his design.

He used natural materials, **berry dyes**, for example.

4 Look for verbal phrases

You can build phrases around participles, gerunds, and infinitives. These three verb parts, known as **verbals**, can function as nouns, adjectives, or adverbs—but they can never stand alone as verbs. A **verbal phrase** consists of verbal plus its modifiers, object, or complements.

Participial phrases. Look for **participial phrases** with *-ing* (present participle) or *-ed/-en* (past participle) forms of a verbal, using them as adjectives to modify a noun or pronoun.

Few neighbors **attending the meeting** owned dogs.

They signed a petition **addressed to the health department**.

Gerund phrases. To recognize a **gerund phrase**, look for the *-ing* form of a verbal (present participle) used as a noun in a subject, object, or subject complement.

sentence subject   object of preposition
Closing the landfill may keep it from **polluting the bay**.

ESL

6b
gr

ESL ADVICE: GERUNDS

You can use only a gerund, not an infinitive, after some verbs.

GERUND   Children enjoy **reading** fairy tales.

COMMON VERBS TAKING GERUNDS			
admit	consider	finish	postpone
anticipate	delay	imagine	practice
appreciate	deny	keep	quit
avoid	discuss	mind	recommend
can't help	enjoy	miss	suggest

You must use gerunds with some idiomatic expressions.

- After *go* (any tense): I **go** <u>swimming</u>.   I **went** <u>kayaking</u>.
- After *spend time*: Volunteers **spend** a lot of **time** <u>helping</u> others.
- After *have + noun*: Pilots **have difficulty** <u>flying</u> in bad weather.
- After a preposition: Midwives are trained **in** <u>assisting</u> at childbirth.

In each of the following examples, *to* is not part of an infinitive. *To* acts like a preposition and must be followed by a gerund ending in *-ing*.

I look **forward** to <u>working</u> at the museum.

He is **accustomed** to <u>designing</u> exhibits.

Patrons are **used** to <u>viewing</u> complex displays.

Infinitive phrases. To recognize an **infinitive phrase**, look for the *to* form of a verbal used as an adjective, adverb, or noun.

ADVERB   He used organic methods **to raise his garden**.

NOUN (SUBJECT)   **To live in the mountains** was his goal.

ESL ADVICE: INFINITIVES

Some verbs take only an infinitive, not a gerund.

INFINITIVE   Some students **need** to work part time.

COMMON VERBS TAKING INFINITIVES

agree	expect	need	refuse
ask	fail	offer	seem
choose	hope	plan	venture
claim	intend	pretend	want
decide	manage	promise	wish

Use an object-infinitive pattern after some verbs.

subject + **verb** + **object** + **infinitive**
Doctors often **advise** <u>their patients</u> <u>to eat</u> well.

COMMON VERBS TAKING AN OBJECT + INFINITIVE

advise	encourage	need	teach
allow	expect	permit	tell
ask	force	persuade	urge
convince	help	require	want

When *make*, *let*, and *have* suggest "caused" or "forced," they follow a different model using the infinitive without *to* (the base form).

She   **made/let/had** me   clean my room.

Use infinitives after certain adjectives.

I	**am**	<u>delighted</u>	to meet you.
The report	**is**	<u>easy</u>	to understand.
The volunteers	**are**	<u>pleased</u>	to help.

Gerund or infinitive phrases. You can follow some verbs with either gerund (the *-ing* form used as a noun) or an infinitive.

ESL ADVICE: GERUNDS OR INFINITIVES

The meaning stays the same when you use most verbs that can be followed by either a gerund or an infinitive.

GERUND   Developers prefer **working** with local contractors.

INFINITIVE   Developers prefer **to work** with local contractors.

COMMON VERBS TAKING EITHER GERUNDS OR INFINITIVES

begin	hate	like	start
can't stand	intend	love	try
continue	learn	prefer	

Remember, *forget*, *regret*, and *stop* change meaning with a gerund or an infinitive.

GERUND   I **remembered** meeting Mark. [I recall an event in the past.]

INFINITIVE   I **remembered** to meet Mark. [I did not forget to do this in the past.]

GERUND   I will never **forget** visiting Texas. [I recall a past event.]

INFINITIVE   I never **forget** to study for exams. [I remember to do something.]

GERUND   I **regret** telling you about her. [I'm sorry I told you in the past.]

INFINITIVE   I **regret** to tell you that you were not hired. [I'm sorry to tell you now.]

GERUND   I **stopped** smoking. [I do not smoke anymore.]

INFINITIVE   I **stopped** to smoke. [I paused to smoke.]

16c Recognizing subordinate clauses

A **main clause** (or **independent clause**) is a word group that includes a subject and a verb and can act as a complete sentence.

MAIN CLAUSE   I had many appointments last Friday.

n contrast, a **subordinate clause** contains both a subject and a predicate et cannot stand on its own as a sentence because it begins with a subordi- ating word such as *if*, *although*, or *that*. (See the list in 28b.)

JBORDINATE CLAUSE   **because** I was busy

ONNECTED TO SENTENCE   **Because I was busy**, I didn't call.

ubordinate clauses are also called **dependent clauses** because they "de- pend" on the main clause to which they are attached. If you punctuate a sub- ordinate clause as a sentence, you create a fragment (see 21a).

1 Look for subordinate clauses as adjectives

You can use a subordinate clause as an adjective, generally following right after the noun or pronoun it modifies. Choose either a **relative pro- noun** (*who*, *which*, *that*, *whom*, *whose*) or a **relative adverb** (*when*, *where*) as a subordinating word.

Many people **who live in Erie** came to the meeting.

They opposed the road **that the county plans to approve**.

Who, *whom*, *whose*, and *that* modify people. *Which*, *whose*, and *that* modify an- imals, places, and things. In spoken English *whom* generally is optional, but it is used in formal writing, especially in the academic community.

Adjective clauses can enrich description in your writing.

ESL

16c
gr

STRATEGY   **Use adjective clauses to combine short sentences.**

CHOPPY   I have an aunt. Her book is on the best-seller list.

COMBINED   I have an aunt **whose** book is on the best-seller list.

ESL ADVICE: ADJECTIVE CLAUSES

Place an adjective clause as close as possible to the noun (**antecedent**) it modifies. (See 24b.)

DRAFT   The actor is dynamic **who plays Romeo**.

EDITED   The actor **who plays Romeo** is dynamic.

You may include or drop a relative pronoun if it is not the subject of the clause. Either way is correct.

INCLUDED   The Web site **that** we designed was very popular.

OMITTED   The Web site we designed was very popular.

When a relative pronoun is the subject of an adjective clause, the clause can be changed to an **adjective phrase**. To make this change in a clause with *be* verb, omit the relative pronoun and the *be* verb.

                                      X   X

CLAUSE (WITH *BE*) He is the man **who is studying German**.

PHRASE He is the man **studying German**.

With another verb, omit the relative pronoun, and change the verb to a present participle. (See 16b-4 on participial phrases.)

                                      X

CLAUSE (NOT *BE*) He is the man **who wants to study German**.

PHRASE He is the man **wanting to study German**.

2 Look for subordinate clauses as adverbs

You can use subordinate clauses as adverbs (modifying verbs, adjectives, or adverbs). Begin with a subordinating conjunction such as *because*, *although*, *since*, or *while* (see the list in 28b).

WHY? She volunteered **because she supports the zoo**.

WHEN? **As the rally continued**, Jean joined the picket line.

ESL

**16c
gr**

ESL ADVICE: ADVERB CLAUSES

Adverb clauses explain time, reason, contrast, and condition.

TIME **When** the weather changes, the malls stock winter clothes.

REASON It is difficult to buy shorts **because** winter has started.

CONTRAST **Although** some shoppers turn to catalogs, others do not.

CONDITION Our online customers may do the same **unless** we expand our inventory.

SOME WORDS TO INTRODUCE ADVERB CLAUSES

TIME	REASON	CONTRAST	CONDITION
after	as	although	as long as
as, while	because	even though	even if
before	now that	though	if
once	since	while	only if
since	whereas		provided that
until			unless
when			

Look for subordinate clauses as nouns

Noun clauses begin with *who, whom, whose, whoever, whomever, what, whatever, when, where, why, whether,* or *how.* Look for them in the roles of nouns: subject, object, object of a preposition, or complement.

SENTENCE SUBJECT   **What she said** is interesting.

DIRECT OBJECT   You should pack **what you need for the trip**.

ESL ADVICE: NOUN CLAUSES

When you form a complex sentence by combining a noun clause with other sentence parts, the clause acts like a noun in the sentence.

THAT CLAUSE   I believe **that** <u>life exists in other solar systems</u>.

YES/NO QUESTION CLAUSE   I wonder **if** <u>life exists in other solar systems</u>.

I wonder **whether** <u>life exists in other solar systems</u>.

WH- QUESTION CLAUSE   I wonder **where** <u>signs of other life may be found</u>.

The third type above is formed by a question embedded into the sentence as a statement. It is introduced by a wh- question word such as *who, whom, what, where, when, which, why, how, how much,* or *how many.* When the noun clause follows an introductory clause, the noun clause uses question word order.

QUESTION   Who discovered the fire?

NOUN CLAUSE   Do you know **who discovered the fire**? [question word order]

Change to statement order when the question includes a form of *be* and a subject complement, a modal, or the auxiliary *do, does, did, have, has,* or *had.* Also use statement word order with *if* and *whether* clauses.

QUESTION   Who **are** your friends?

NOUN CLAUSE   I wonder <u>who</u> your friends **are**. [statement word order]

QUESTION   How **can** I meet them?

NOUN CLAUSE   Please tell me <u>how</u> I **can** meet them. [statement word order]

ESL

16c
gr

16d Recognizing different sentence types

Consider using various sentence structures and purposes.

16.

1 Look for sentence structures

Try to vary the kind and number of clauses you include.

Simple sentence. A sentence with one main (independent) clause and n subordinate (dependent) clauses is a **simple sentence**.

The mayor proposed an expansion of city hall.

Compound sentence. A sentence with two or more main (independent clauses and no subordinate (dependent) clauses is a **compound sentence** (See 28a on coordination.)

>   **main clause**   **main clause**
> **Most people praised the plans**, yet **some found them dull**.

Complex sentence. A sentence with one main (independent) clause and one or more subordinate (dependent) clauses is a **complex sentence**. (See 28b on subordination.)

>   **subordinate clause**   **main clause**
> <u>Because people objected</u>, **the architect revised the plans**.

Compound-complex sentence. A sentence with two or more main (independent) clauses and one or more subordinate (dependent) clauses is a **compound-complex sentence**.

>   **subordinate clause**   **subordinate clause**
> <u>Because he wanted to make sure</u> <u>that the expansion did not damage</u>
>
>   **main clause**
> <u>the existing building</u>, **the architect examined the frame of the older**
>
>   **main clause**
> **structure**, and **he asked the contractor to test the soil stability**.

2 Look for sentence purposes

You can also vary sentences according to the relationship you want to establish with readers. A **declarative sentence** makes a statement. An **interrogative sentence** poses a question. An **imperative sentence** requests or commands. An **exclamatory sentence** exclaims.

DECLARATIVE	The motor is making a rattling noise.
INTERROGATIVE	Have you checked it for overheating?
IMPERATIVE	Check it again.
EXCLAMATORY	It's on fire!

17 | Using Verbs

In casual speech, many different verb forms may be acceptable to listeners, especially those within your own dialect community.

CASUAL SPEECH
My daddy **be pushin'** me to do good in school.

Jimmy **should'a went** with them.

We **were fixin'** to eat dinner.

You **might could carpool** to work with Don.

LISTENER'S REACTION: What sounds fine when we talk might not be correct in a paper.

In your writing, however, nonstandard verb forms may distract readers who expect you to write fluently in standard English. Some readers may even assume that you are uneducated or careless if you don't edit the verb forms in your final drafts. Adjust to the expectations of your readers. After all, the formal language of the academic community is as inappropriate on the street corner as casual language is in a history paper or marketing report.

17a Recognizing simple present and past tense verbs

When you use a simple verb in a sentence, you put that verb into the **present tense** for action occurring now or the **past tense** for action that has already occurred. Most verbs form the past tense by adding -ed to the present tense form, also called the **base form**. Depending on the verb, this addition may be pronounced as -t (*baked*), -d (*called*), or -ed (*defended*).

ESL ADVICE: SIMPLE PRESENT AND SIMPLE PAST

Only these two tenses stand alone with no helping verbs. (See 17d.)

SIMPLE PRESENT   They **live** in the new dormitory.

SIMPLE PAST   They **lived** in an apartment last semester.

FAULTY   The chef **cooking** in the kitchen yesterday. [present participle without any helping verb]

EDITED   The chef **was cooking** in the kitchen yesterday.

17b Editing present tense verbs

You need no special ending to mark the present tense *except* in the third person singular form (with *he*, *she*, or *it* or a singular noun).

The customers **wait** in line until the cafeteria **opens**.

In the academic community, readers may expect special uses of the present tense.

STRATEGY Follow academic conventions for the present tense.

When writing for your humanities courses, use the present tense to discuss a piece of literature, a film, an essay, a painting, or a similar creative production. Treat events, ideas, characters, or statements from such works as if they exist in an ongoing present tense. (See 25h.)

In Erdrich's *Love Medicine*, Albertine **returns** to the reservation.

In the social sciences and sciences, use the present tense to discuss the results and implications of a current study or experiment, but use the past tense to review the findings of earlier researchers.

Although Maxwell (1991) **identified** three crucial classroom interactions, the current survey **suggests** two others as well.

ESL ADVICE: THE THIRD PERSON *-S* OR *-ES* ENDING

Be sure to add an *-s* or *-es* to verbs that are third person singular.

SUBJECT	VERB	SUBJECT	VERB + -S
I/you/we/they	**write**	he/she/it (animal, thing, concept)	**writes**

17c Editing past tense verbs

When you write the past tense of a regular verb, you usually add *-ed* to its base form. Sometimes you may leave off the *-ed* if you don't "hear" it, especially when a word beginning in *d* or *t* follows the verb.

DRAFT	The company **use** to provide dental benefits.
EDITED	The company **used** to provide dental benefits.

About sixty **irregular verbs** are exceptions to the "add *-ed*" rule; most change an internal vowel in the simple past tense (*run, ran*).

IRREGULAR VERB	The characters in the movie **sweared** constantly.
EDITED	The characters in the movie **swore** constantly.

STRATEGY List troublesome irregular verbs.

Use your personal list of difficult past tense forms as a guide for scanning your drafts or searching on the computer.

COMMON IRREGULAR VERBS

PRESENT	PAST	PAST PARTICIPLE
arise	arose	arisen
am/is/are	was/were	been
bear	bore	borne
begin	began	begun
bite	bit	bitten/bit
blow	blew	blown
break	broke	broken
bring	brought	brought
buy	bought	bought
catch	caught	caught
choose	chose	chosen
come	came	come
creep	crept	crept
dive	dived/dove	dived
do	did	done
draw	drew	drawn
dream	dreamed/dreamt	dreamt
drink	drank	drunk
drive	drove	driven
eat	ate	eaten
fall	fell	fallen
fight	fought	fought
fly	flew	flown
forget	forgot	forgotten
forgive	forgave	forgiven
get	got	got/gotten
give	gave	given
go	went	gone
grow	grew	grown
hang	hanged	hanged
hang	hung	hung
hide	hid	hidden
know	knew	known
lay	laid	laid
lead	led	led
lie	lay	lain
light	lit/lighted	lit

17c
verb

lose	lost	lost
prove	proved	proved/proven
ride	rode	ridden
ring	rang	rung
rise	rose	risen
run	ran	run
see	saw	seen
seek	sought	sought
set	set	set
shake	shook	shaken
sing	sang/sung	sung
sink	sank/sunk	sunk
sit	sat	sat
speak	spoke	spoken
spring	sprang	sprung
steal	stole	stolen
strike	struck	struck
swear	swore	sworn
swim	swam	swum
take	took	taken
tear	tore	torn
throw	threw	thrown
wake	woke/waked	woken/waked/woke
wear	wore	worn
write	wrote	written

ESL

17d
verb

17d Recognizing complex tenses and helping verbs

To recognize complex tenses, look for a **helping** or **auxiliary verb** (such as *is* or *has*) with a main verb in the form of the **past participle** (the *-ed/-en* form) or the **present participle** (the *-ing* form).

ESL ADVICE: VERB FORMS

In English, verbs can have the following forms.

PRINCIPAL PARTS OF VERBS IN ENGLISH

BASE FORM	PAST	PRESENT PARTICIPLE	PAST PARTICIPLE
REGULAR VERBS			
live	lived	living	lived
want	wanted	wanting	wanted
IRREGULAR VERBS			
eat	ate	eating	eaten
run	ran	running	run

he **present participle** is formed by adding -*ing* to the base form of the verb
he form with no endings or markers).

	helping verb	main verb (present participle)
He	was/will be/had been	**loading** the truck.

he **past participle** of most verbs is just like the simple past tense (base
orm + -*ed*). Because this form can be irregular, check the chart on irregular
erbs (see 17c) or the dictionary if you are uncertain of the form.

	helping verb	main verb (past participle)
EGULAR VERB	Mike has/had	**rented** the truck.
RREGULAR VERB	The copier has/had	**broken** down.

ESL ADVICE: HELPING VERBS

Most verbs combine one or more helping verbs (also called auxiliary
erbs) with a main verb to form a **verb phrase**.

HELPING VERB   I **was walking** to school during the snowstorm.

HELPING VERBS   I **have been walking** to school for many years.

Helping verbs include *am, is, are, will, would, can, could, have, has, had, was,*
were, should, might, may, must, do, does, and *did.* These words may be combined, as in *have been, has been, had been, will be, will have,* and *will have been.*

ESL

17d
verb

VERB FORMS AND HELPING VERBS
FOR COMMONLY USED VERB TENSES

The past, present, and future progressive use forms of *be.*

PROGRESSIVE FORM

	subject + *was/were* + present participle
PAST	I **was** working in my studio yesterday.
	subject + *am/is/are* + present participle
PRESENT	I **am** working in my studio right now.
	subject + *will* (modal) + be + present participle
FUTURE	I **will be** working in my studio tomorrow.

The past, present, and future perfect use forms of *have.*

PERFECT FORM

	subject + *had* + past participle
PAST	I **had** tried to call you all day.
	subject + *have/has* + past participle
PRESENT	I **have** tried to call you all day.
	subject + *will* (modal) + have + past participle
FUTURE	I **will have** called you by midnight.

17e Editing progressive and perfect tenses

When you use the **present**, **past**, and **future progressive** tenses, you can show an action in progress at some point in time.

PRESENT PROGRESSIVE	The carousel **is turning** too quickly.
PAST PROGRESSIVE	The horses **were bobbing** up and down.
FUTURE PROGRESSIVE	The children **will be laughing** from the thrill.

In progressive tenses, the main verb must take the *-ing* ending. In the future progressive tense, the verb must also include *be*.

STRATEGY Add or complete the helping verb.

Use correct, complete forms, even if your dialect omits them.

WORD OMITTED	The interview **starting** five minutes late.
EDITED	The interview **is starting** five minutes late.
WRONG FORM	The employees **was running** for the elevator.
EDITED	The employees **were running** for the elevator.

Turn to the three **perfect tenses** to show the order in which events take place. Use the **past perfect tense** for the first event to indicate that something had already happened before something else happened.

The fire **had burned** for an hour before the brigade arrived.

STRATEGY Check the form of the past participle.

Avoid substituting simple past tense for the past participle.

MISTAKEN PAST	Pierre **had rode** for six years before he got injured.
EDITED	Pierre **had ridden** for six years before he got injured.

Use the **present perfect tense** much like the past perfect, showing action that has happened before without a specific time marker or that you insist has already occurred.

I **have reported** the burglary already.

The present perfect also shows action begun in the past and continuing into the present. It differs from the simple past, which indicates an action already completed or specified in time.

ESENT PERFECT   I **have lived** in St. Louis for three weeks.

MPLE PAST   I **lived** in St. Louis in 1998.

elect the **future perfect tense** to show that something will have happened
y the time something else will be happening.

The chef **will have baked** all the cakes before noon.

SL ADVICE: SIMPLE PRESENT AND PRESENT PROGRESSIVE TENSES

Use the **simple present** tense to describe factual or habitual activities.
hese occur in the present but are not necessarily in progress.

HOWS FACT   The planets **revolve** around the sun.

HOWS HABIT   The bus usually **arrives** late.

COMMON TIME EXPRESSIONS FOR PRESENT TENSE HABITUAL ACTIVITIES

all the time	every holiday	every year	rarely
always	every month	frequently	sometimes
every class	every semester	most of the time	usually
every day	every week	often	never

Use the **present progressive** tense to describe activities in progress. If you
wish, you can add expressions to pinpoint the time of the activity.

am/is/are + present participle
DeVaugh **is testing** the process.

DeVaugh **is testing** the process **this month**.

COMMON PRESENT PROGRESSIVE TIME EXPRESSIONS FOR ACTIVITIES IN PROGRESS

at the moment	this afternoon	this month	this year
right now	this evening	this morning	today

When you choose between the simple present and present progressive
tenses, think about the time of the activity. Is it happening only at the

moment (present progressive) or all the time as a fact or habit (simple present)?

PRESENT (FACT)	All people communicate in some language.
PRESENT (HABIT)	The students speak their own languages at home.
PRESENT PROGRESSIVE (AT THE MOMENT)	Kim is studying Spanish this term.

VERBS THAT ARE TROUBLESOME IN PROGRESSIVE TENSES

	EXAMPLE	OTHER USAGES AND MEANINGS
SENSES		
see	I **see** the beauty.	I **am seeing** that doctor. (meeting with, visiting, dating)
hear	I **hear** the birds.	I **have been hearing** about the problem for a while. (receiving information)
smell	The flowers **smell** strong.	I **am smelling** the flowers. (action in progress)
taste	The food **tastes** good.	The cook **is tasting** the soup. (action in progress)
POSSESSION		
have	We **have** many friends.	We **are having** a lot of fun. (experiencing)
own	They **own** many cars.	
possess	She **possesses** wealth.	
belong	The book **belongs** to me.	
STATES OF MIND		
be	I **am** tired.	
know	I **know** the city well.	
believe	She **believes** in God.	
think	I **think** it is true. (know, believe)	I **am thinking** about relocating. (having thoughts about)
recognize	She **recognizes** him. (knows)	
understand	The professor **understands** the equation.	
mean	I **don't mean** to pry. (don't want)	I **have been meaning** to visit. (planning, intending)
WISH OR ATTITUDE		
want	We **want** peace.	
desire	He **desires** freedom.	

WISH OR ATTITUDE

need	We **need** rain.	
love	Children **love** snow.	I **have been loving** this book. (enjoying)
hate	Dan **hates** mowing.	
like	Lee **likes** skiing.	
dislike	She **dislikes** tests.	
seem	They **seem** kind.	
appear	He **appears** tired. (seems to be)	He **is appearing** at the theater. (acting, performing)
look	He **looks** tired. (seems to be)	We **are looking** at the map. (action of using eyes)

17f Editing troublesome verbs (*lie, lay, sit, set*)

Here are a few verbs confused even by experienced writers.

VERB	PRESENT	PAST	PARTICIPLE
lie (oneself)	lie	lay	lain
lay (an object)	lay	laid	laid
sit (oneself)	sit	sat	sat
set (an object)	set	set	set

ESL

17g
verb

DRAFT   I **laid** down yesterday for a nap. I **have laid** down every afternoon this week.

EDITED   I **lay** down yesterday for a nap. I **have lain** down every afternoon this week.

DRAFT   First Eric and Lisa **sat** the projector down on the table. Then they **set** down as the meeting began.

EDITED   First Eric and Lisa **set** the projector down on the table. Then they **sat** down as the meeting began.

17g Recognizing clear tense sequence

Conversation can jump from tense to tense with little warning. In writing, however, readers expect you to stick to one tense or to follow a clear **sequence of tenses** that relates events and ideas in time (see 25c–d).

                    present   past
LOGICAL   People **forget** that four candidates **ran** in 1948.

                    future   present
LOGICAL   I **will accept** your report even if it **is** a bit late.

LOGICAL   **past**
The accountant **destroyed** crucial evidence because no o[...]
past perfect
had asked him to save the records.

LOGICAL   **past perfect**
None of the crew **had recognized** that food stored in cans seale[...]
present (for generally true statement)
with lead solder **is** poisonous.

TENSES OF REGULAR AND IRREGULAR VERBS IN THE ACTIVE VOICE

Once you decide when actions or events occur, use this chart to help you select the appropriate verb tense.

PRESENT, PAST, AND FUTURE (showing simple actions)

PRESENT (action taking place now, including habits and facts)

I/you/we/they	examine/begin
he/she/it	examines/begins

PAST (action that has already taken place at an earlier time)

I/you/he/she/it/we/they	examined/began

FUTURE (action that will take place at an upcoming time)

I/you/he/she/it/we/they	will examine/begin

PRESENT, PAST, AND FUTURE PERFECT (showing order of events)

PRESENT PERFECT (action that has recurred or continued from past to present)

I/you/we/they	have examined/begun
he/she/it	has examined/begun

PAST PERFECT (action completed before something else happened)

I/you/he/she/it/we/they	had examined/begun

FUTURE PERFECT (action that will have happened before something else happens)

I/you/he/she/it/we/they	will have examined/begun

PRESENT, PAST, AND FUTURE PROGRESSIVE (showing action in progress)

PRESENT PROGRESSIVE (action in progress now, at this moment)

I	am examining/beginning
you/we/they	are examining/beginning
he/she/it	is examining/beginning

PAST PROGRESSIVE (action that was in progress earlier)

I/he/she/it	was examining/beginning
you/we/they	were examining/beginning

FUTURE PROGRESSIVE (action that will be in progress later on)

I/you/he/she/it/we/they   will be examining/beginning

PRESENT, PAST, AND FUTURE PERFECT PROGRESSIVE
(showing duration of action in progress)

PRESENT PERFECT PROGRESSIVE (action that has been in progress up to now)

I/you/we/they   have been examining/beginning
he/she/it   has been examining/beginning

PAST PERFECT PROGRESSIVE (action that had already been in progress before something else happened)

I/you/he/she/it/we/they   had been examining/beginning

FUTURE PERFECT PROGRESSIVE (action that will have been in progress by the time something else happens)

I/you/he/she/it/we/they   will have been examining/beginning

17h   Recognizing the subjunctive mood

Sentences can be classified by **mood**, the form of a verb that reflects the speaker's or writer's attitude. Most sentences are in the **indicative** (statements intended as truthful or factual like "The store closed at 10") or the **imperative** (commands like "Stop!"). Occasionally the **subjunctive** expresses uncertainty—supposition, prediction, possibility, desire, or wish.

SUBJUNCTIVE   **Were** the deadline today, our proposal would be late.

The subjunctive has faded from most casual speech and some writing. It is still expected by many readers in formal writing using **conditional statements**, often beginning with *if* and expressing the improbable or hypothetical.

DRAFT (PAST)   If Sandy **was** a biker who always wore a helmet, his family would be much less worried.

EDITED
(SUBJUNCTIVE)   If Sandy **were** a biker who always wore a helmet, his family would be much less worried.

Don't add *would* to the *had + verb* structure in the conditional clause, even if *would* appropriately appears in the **result clause** that follows the conditional.

EXTRA *WOULD*   If Sandy **would have worn** his helmet Sunday night, he **would have hurt** himself less seriously.

EDITED   If Sandy **had worn** his helmet Sunday night, he **would have hurt** himself less seriously.

Finally, some clauses with *that* require a subjunctive verb when they follo certain verbs that make demands or requests.

DRAFT (PAST) The judge asked that the witnesses **be swore** in.

EDITED The judge asked that the witnesses **be sworn** in.

STRATEGY Select the correct form for the subjunctive.

Use the present tense form with *that*, even in the third person singul

The court ordered that   I/you/he/she/it/we/they   appear.

For the verb *is*, the forms are *be* (present) and *were* (past).

17.1

ESL

17h
verb

ESL ADVICE: CONDITIONALS

Three types of **conditional statements** depend on a condition or a imagined. These may be (1) *true* in the present, (2) *untrue* or contrary to fac in the present, or (3) *untrue* or contrary to fact in the past. Each has an clause and a result clause that combine different verb tenses.

TYPES OF CONDITIONAL STATEMENTS

TYPE I: TRUE IN THE PRESENT

IF CLAUSE	RESULT CLAUSE

• **Generally true in the present as a habit or as a fact**

if + subject + present tense	subject + present tense
If I drive to school every day,	I get to class on time.

• **True in the future as a one-time event**

if + subject + present tense	subject + future tense
If I drive to school today,	I will get to class on time.

• **Possibly true in the future as a one-time event**

if + subject + present tense	subject + modal + base form verb
If I drive to school today,	I may/should get to class on time.

TYPE II: UNTRUE IN THE PRESENT

IF CLAUSE	RESULT CLAUSE
if + subject + past tense	subject + *would/could/might* + base form verb
If I drove to school,	I would arrive on time.
If I were a car owner,	I could arrive on time.

With Type II, the form of the verb *be* in the *if* clause is always *were*.

TYPE III: UNTRUE IN THE PAST

IF CLAUSE	RESULT CLAUSE
if + subject + past perfect tense	subject + *would/could/might* + *have* + past participle
If I had driven to school,	I would not have been late.

17i   Recognizing active and passive voice

17.2

To recognize a verb in the **active voice**, look for a sentence in which the doer of an action is the subject of the sentence (see 29b-3).

	AGENT (SUBJECT)	ACTION (VERB)	GOAL (OBJECT)
ACTIVE	The car	hit	the lamppost.
ACTIVE	Dana	distributed	the flyers.

In contrast, when a verb is in the **passive voice**, the goal of the sentence appears in the subject position, and the doer may appear in the object position, after the word *by* (in an optional prepositional phrase). The verb itself adds a form of *be* as a helping verb to the participle form.

	GOAL (SUBJECT)	ACTION (VERB)	[AGENT: PREPOSITIONAL PHRASE]
PASSIVE	The lamppost	**was hit**	[by the car].
PASSIVE	The flyers	**were distributed**	[by Dana].

The active and passive versions of a sentence create different kinds of emphasis because they use different words as sentence subjects.

ACTIVE	The city council banned smoking in restaurants.
PASSIVE	Smoking in restaurants was banned by the city council.
AGENT OMITTED	Smoking in restaurants was banned.

ESL

17i verb

ESL ADVICE: THE PASSIVE VOICE

All tenses can appear in the passive voice *except* these progressive forms: present perfect, past perfect, future, future perfect. In the following sentences, the agent of the action is not the subject *food*, but rather *chef*.

VERB FORMS IN THE PASSIVE VOICE

TENSES	SUBJECT + *BE* FORM + PAST PARTICIPLE
PRESENT	The food **is prepared** by the chef.
PRESENT PROGRESSIVE	The food **is being prepared** by the chef.
PAST	The food **was prepared** by the chef.
PAST PROGRESSIVE	The food **was being prepared** by the chef.
PRESENT PERFECT	The food **has been prepared** by the chef.
PAST PERFECT	The food **had been prepared** by the chef.
FUTURE	The food **will be prepared** by the chef.
FUTURE PERFECT	The food **will have been prepared** by the chef.

Each passive verb must have a form of *be* and a past participle (ending in -e for regular verbs). Sometimes the *-ed* ending is hard to hear when spoken, s edit carefully for it.

MISSING *-ED*   The young man was **call** by the draft board.

EDITED   The young man was **called** by the draft board.

18 | Using Pronouns

Readers count on you to use different forms of pronouns to guide them through your sentences. The wrong choices can mislead or irritate them.

DRAFT   **Him** and **me** will make a strong management team.

  READER'S REACTION: *Him and me* makes the writer sound careless and uneducated.

EDITED   **He** and **I** will make a strong management team.

Although most pronouns won't give you trouble, at times you may struggle with choices between *we* or *us*, *her* or *she*, and *who* or *whom*.

18a Recognizing pronoun forms

A pronoun changes form according to its role in a sentence: subject, object, or possessive, showing possession or ownership. (See also 15b.)

subjective possessive   objective
He and **his** design team created the furniture for **us**.

1 Look for subjective forms

Choose a subjective form if a pronoun acts as the subject of all or part of a sentence or if it renames or restates a subject.

She wants to know why the orders have not been filled.

Because **they** were unable to get a loan, the business failed.

Atco will be hiring people **who** are willing to work the night shift.

I attend class more regularly than **he** [does].

FORMS OF PRONOUNS

PERSONAL PRONOUNS

	SUBJECTIVE		OBJECTIVE		POSSESSIVE	
	SINGULAR	PLURAL	SINGULAR	PLURAL	SINGULAR	PLURAL
First person	I	we	me	us	my mine	our ours
Second person	you	you	you	you	your yours	your yours
Third person	he she it	they	him her it	them	his her hers its	their theirs

RELATIVE AND INTERROGATIVE PRONOUNS

SUBJECTIVE	OBJECTIVE	POSSESSIVE
who	whom	whose
whoever	whomever	
which	which	
that	that	
what	what	

INDEFINITE PRONOUNS

SUBJECTIVE	OBJECTIVE	POSSESSIVE
anybody	anybody	anybody's
everyone	everyone	everyone's

18a
pron

STRATEGY   **Check for pronouns that rename the subject.**

You create a **subject complement** when you follow a form of the verb *be* (*is, am, are, was, were*) with a pronoun renaming the subject (see 16a-2). Choose the subjective form of the pronoun.

SUBJECTIVE FORM   **The last art majors** to get jobs were Becky and **I**.

In conversation, people may use the objective form in complements. In writing, however, choose the correct form. If it sounds stilted or unnatural, rewrite the sentence.

CONVERSATION   The new traffic reporter is **him**.

STILTED   The new traffic reporter is **he**.

REWRITTEN   **He** is the new traffic reporter.

2 Look for objective forms

Use an objective form if a pronoun acts as, renames, or restates an objec

Maria needed software upgrades, so the company bought **them** for he

An accountant **whom** the firm hired helped **her** out.

Having called **us**, his survey was complete.

The report summarized interviews with two workers, **her and him**

You may find pronouns used with infinitives (*to* + a verb) tricky. In the exam
ple below, *us* is the direct object in the sentence (*Mr. Pederson asked* **us**), and
the objective form is correct.

OBJECTIVE FORM   Mr. Pederson asked **us** to review the minutes.

3 Look for possessive forms

When a pronoun shows possession or ownership, choose a possessive
form. The particular form you use depends on whether the pronoun appear
before a noun or *in place of a noun*.

BEFORE NOUN   The Topeka office requested a copy of **her** report.

REPLACING NOUN   **Hers** was the most up-to-date study available.

Check for possessive forms before gerunds (*-ing* verb forms that act as
nouns). Because this use of the possessive is often ignored in speech, you
may need to practice writing it until it begins to "sound right" to you.

CONVERSATION   Them requesting the report pleased our supervisor.

EDITED   **Their** requesting the report pleased our supervisor.

English nouns also vary in form to show possession, signaled by an apostrophe (*'s* or *'*): *the study/the study's conclusions.* (See 36a–b.) Don't confuse nouns
and pronouns by adding an apostrophe to a possessive pronoun.

STRATEGY   **Test your pronouns to choose *its* or *it's*.**

Its, not *it's*, is the form of the possessive pronoun. Test which you need
by replacing the pronoun with *it is* (the expansion of *it's*). If *it is* fits, keep the
apostrophe. If *it is* doesn't fit, omit the apostrophe.

DRAFT   The food pantry gave away (*its/it's*) last can of tuna.

REPLACEMENT TEST   The food pantry gave away **it is** last can of tuna.
It is doesn't make sense.

USE POSSESSIVE   The food pantry gave away **its** last can of tuna.

8b Editing pronoun forms

Sometimes you may find it difficult to choose the right form.

Check pronouns in compound subjects and objects

When you use a compound subject or object containing a pronoun, such as *the committee and I* or *Jim and me*, use the same case for the pronoun in the compound that you would use for a single pronoun in the same role.

COMPOUND SUBJECT	Denise or (*he? him?*) should check the inventory.
SUBJECTIVE FORM	Denise or **he** should check the inventory.
COMPOUND OBJECT	The coach selected (*she? her? and he? him?*) as captains.
OBJECTIVE FORM	The coach selected **her and him** as captains.

STRATEGY Try focus-imagine-choose.

- **Focus** on the pronoun whose form you need to choose.

    DRAFT   Anne-Marie and **me** will develop the videotape.
    FOCUS: *I or me?*

- **Imagine** each choice for the pronoun as the subject (or object).

    #1 (INCORRECT)   **Me** will develop the videotape.

    #2 (CORRECT)   **I** will develop the videotape.

- **Choose** the correct form for the compound subject (or object).

    EDITED   Anne-Marie and **I** will develop the videotape.

If the appropriate form is not immediately clear to you, see the chart in 18a. Choosing what "sounds right" may not work with compounds.

---

2 Focus on pronouns that rename or are paired with nouns

If you place a pronoun in an **appositive** (renaming a preceding noun or pronoun), the pronoun must match the form of the word it renames. If you pair a pronoun with a noun, match the form of the pronoun—*we, they* (subjective) or *us, them* (objective)—with the role played by the noun (subject or object).

STRATEGY Test alternatives.

- Edit pronouns that act as appositives by imagining alternative versions without the noun (or pronoun) that was renamed.

18.1

18b
pror

SENTENCE	The two book illustrators on the panel, (*she? her?*) an‍ (*I? me?*), discussed questions from the audience.
#1 (INCORRECT)	**Her and me** discussed questions from the audience.
#2 (CORRECT)	**She and I** discussed questions from the audience.
EDITED	The two book illustrators on the panel, **she and I**, dis‍ cussed questions from the audience.

- Edit a pronoun-noun pair by imagining alternatives without the noun‍

SENTENCE	The teaching evaluation should be conducted by (*us‍ we?*) students, not by the faculty or administration.
#1 (INCORRECT)	The teaching evaluation should be conducted by **we**. . .
#2 (CORRECT)	The teaching evaluation should be conducted by **us**. . .
EDITED	The teaching evaluation should be conducted by **us‍** students, not by the faculty or administration.

---

3 Align comparisons with *than* or *as*

When you end a comparison with a pronoun, choose the form that ac‍ curately signals the information left out. Use the subjective form for the sub‍ ject of the implied statement and the objective form for its object.

SUBJECTIVE	I gave her sister more help than **she** [did].
OBJECTIVE	I gave her sister more help than [I gave] **her**.

If readers may miss the grammatical signals, rewrite the sentence.

MAY BE AMBIGUOUS	I like working with Aisha better than she.
	READER'S REACTION: Does this mean that you prefer to work with Aisha? Or that you like to work with Aisha better than someone else does?
REWRITTEN	She doesn't like working with Aisha as much as I do.

4 Concentrate on *who* and *whom*

To begin subordinate clauses known as **relative clauses** or **adjective clauses** (see 16c), choose *who* and *whoever* when you use the pronouns as subjects; choose *whom* and *whomever* when you use them as objects.

SUBJECT	The boy **who wins the race** should get the prize.
OBJECT	Give this delicate assignment to **whomever you trust**.

Choose between *who* and *whom* according to the role the pronoun plays *within the relative clause*. Ignore the role the clause plays *within the sentence*.

(AFT   The fine must be paid by **whomever** <u>holds the deed</u>.
Although the whole clause is the object of the preposition *by*, within the clause the pronoun acts as a subject, not an object.

ITED   The fine must be paid by **whoever** holds the deed.

t the beginning of a question, you should use *who* when the pronoun is the abject of the sentence and *whom* when the pronoun is an object.

BJECT   **Who** is most likely to get the reader's sympathy at this point in the novel, Huck or Jim?

BJECT   **Whom** can Cordelia trust at the end of the scene?

19 | Making Sentence Parts Agree

Readers get mixed signals when sentence parts are not coordinated.

NCONSISTENT   The city council and the mayor is known for her skillful responses to civic debate.
READER'S REACTION: I thought the sentence was about two things—the city council and the mayor—but when I read *is* and *her*, it seemed to be about only one, the mayor.

EDITED   The city council and the mayor **are** known for **their** skillful responses to civic debate.

Readers expect you to help them understand how the ideas in a sentence relate by making the parts of a sentence work together grammatically—by showing **agreement** in number, person, and gender.

19a Recognizing agreement

Within a sentence, a subject and verb should agree in **number** (singular or plural) and **person** (first, second, or third).

<u>You</u> **know** our client. <u>She</u> **wants** to see the design next week.

In addition, each pronoun should agree with its **antecedent**, the noun or other pronoun to which it refers, in **number** (singular, plural), **person** (first, second, third), and **gender** (masculine, feminine, neuter).

The **crews** riding their snowplows left early; the **airport** needed i
runways cleared.

AGREEMENT: NUMBER, PERSON, AND GENDER

- *Number* shows whether words are singular (one person, animal, idea, or thing) or plural (two or more) in meaning.

  SINGULAR   This **community** needs its own recreation center.

  PLURAL   Local **communities** need to share their facilities.

- *Person* indicates the speaker or subject being spoken to or about.

  First person (speaker): *I, we*

  I operate the compressor.   **We** operate the compressor.

  Second person (spoken to): *you*

  You operate the forklift.

  Third person (spoken about): *he, she, it, they*; nouns naming things, people, animals, ideas

  He/she/it operates the drill.   **They** operate the drill.

- *Gender* refers to masculine (*he, him*), feminine (*she, her*), or neuter (*it*) qualities attributed to a noun or pronoun.

  MASCULINE/FEMININE

  The future father rushed for **his** car keys, while his wife packed **her** bag.

  NEUTER

  Despite **its** recent tune-up, the car stalled near the hospital.

19b Editing subject-verb agreement

Begin with either the subject or the verb; then edit to make the other agree. Watch for words that complicate simple agreement.

1 Start simply with number and person

First look for the subject. Identify its number (singular or plural) and person (first, second, or third). Then edit the verb so it agrees.

DRAFT   The clients is waiting.

BOTH PLURAL   The **clients** are waiting.

BOTH SINGULAR   The **client** is waiting.

STRATEGY   Check the *-s* and *-es* endings.

An *-s* or *-es* ending changes most nouns to plural but most present tense verbs to singular.

SINGULAR   The dam prevent**s** flooding.

PLURAL   The dam**s** prevent flooding.

EXCEPTIONS
- Nouns with irregular plurals (*person/people* or *child/children*)
- Nouns with the same form for singular and plural (*moose/moose*)
- Verbs with irregular forms, including *be* and *have* (see 17c)

In a **verb phrase** (a helping verb plus a main verb), the helping verb sometimes changes form for singular and plural, but the main verb remains the same (see 17d).

HELPING VERB CHANGES FORM	HELPING VERB DOES NOT CHANGE
SINGULAR The **park** <u>does seem</u> safer.	The **park** <u>might seem</u> safer.
PLURAL The **parks** <u>do seem</u> safer.	The **parks** <u>might seem</u> safer.

ESL

19b
s-v a

ESL ADVICE: SUBJECT-VERB AGREEMENT

Some troublesome verbs change form according to person or tense.

- ***Be* verbs** (present and past)
  I **am/was**.   He/She/It   **is/was**.   You/We/They   **are/were**.
- **Helping verb *be*** (present progressive and past progressive tenses)

I	**am** talking.	I/He/She/It	**was talking**.
You/We/They	**are** talking.	We/You/They	**were talking**.
He/She/It	**is** talking.		

- ***Have* verbs** (present)
  I/You/We/They   **have** a new home.   He/She/It   **has** a new home.
- **Helping verb *have*** (present perfect and present perfect progressive tenses)

  | I/You/We/They | **have** lived here for years. | **have** been living here since May. |
  | He/She/It | **has** lived here for years. | **has** been living here since May. |

- ***Do* or *does* to show emphasis**
  I/You/We/They   **do** want the job.   He/She/It   **does** want the job.

- ***Doesn't*** or ***don't*** **to show the negative**

  I/You/We/They   **don't** exercise   He/She/It   **doesn't** exercise
             enough.   enough.

19.1

2 Focus on a complex subject

Check for complicated or confusing subjects.

Collective nouns as subjects. A **collective noun** is singular in form yet identifies a group of individuals (*audience*, *mob*, *crew*, *troop*, *tribe*, or *herd*). When the
group acts as a single unit, choose a singular verb. When group members act individually, choose a plural verb.

ONE SINGLE UNIT   The **staff** is hardworking and well trained.

INDIVIDUAL   The **staff** have earned the respect of our clients.
MEMBERS

Titles and names as subjects. When your sentence subject is a book title
or company name, choose a singular verb even if the name or title is plural.
Think to yourself, "The *company* pays . . ." or "The *book* is. . . ."

ESL

Home Helpers **pays** high wages and **has** excellent benefits.

The White Roses **is** second on the best-seller list this month.

19b
/ agr

Nouns with plural forms and singular meanings. Nouns like *politics*, *physics*,
statistics, *mumps*, and *athletics* have *-s* endings but are singular.

Mathematics is an increasingly popular field of study.

STRATEGY **Use a pronoun to test your verb.**

Decide which pronoun accurately represents a complicated subject: *he*,
she, or *it* (singular), or *they* (plural). Read your sentence aloud using this replacement pronoun; edit the verb to agree.

DRAFT   The **news** about the job market _____ surprisingly good.
                   PRONOUN TEST: I could replace "The news" with "It" and say "It is."

EDITED   The **news** about the job market **is** surprisingly good.

3 Check subjects linked by *and*, *or*, and *nor*

Paired compounds or alternatives can be troublesome subjects.

Compound subjects. By joining two or more subjects with *and* or *both . . .
and*, you create a **compound subject**. Because *and* makes the subject plural
(even if its parts are singular), you generally need to choose a plural verb.

URAL   **Ham and eggs** <u>are</u> ingredients in this casserole.

WO PEOPLE   **My friend and my co-worker** <u>have</u> paintings in the show.

f the parts should be taken as a unit or if the parts designate a single person,
hing, or idea, you need to choose a singular verb.

NIT (SINGULAR)   **Ham and eggs** <u>is</u> still my favorite breakfast.

ONE PERSON   **My friend and co-worker** <u>has</u> paintings in the show.

Alternative subjects. When you use *or* or *nor* (*either . . . or, neither . . . nor*)
o connect alternative parts of the subject, the verb agrees with the closer
part. Putting the plural element closer to the verb often is less awkward.

PLURAL CLOSE   The auditor or **the accountants** <u>review</u> each report.
TO VERB

SINGULAR CLOSE   False records or **late reporting** <u>weakens</u> the review process.
TO VERB

ESL ADVICE: PAIRED CONJUNCTIONS

Both . . . and always needs a plural verb, whether the elements joined
are singular or plural.

Both the president **and** her advisor <u>are</u> in Tokyo this week.

Both the president **and** her advisors <u>are</u> in Tokyo this week.

Either . . . or, neither . . . nor, and *not only . . . but also* may take either a singular or a plural verb, depending on the subject closer to the verb.

Either the president **or** her <u>advisor</u> <u>is</u> in Tokyo.

Neither the president **nor** her <u>advisors</u> <u>are</u> in Tokyo.

4 Pay attention to separated subjects and verbs

When you separate subject and verb, make sure the two agree.

Subject and verb separated by other words. The verb should agree with
the subject, not intervening nouns.

FAULTY   The new trolley system, featuring expanded routes and lower
AGREEMENT   fares, are especially popular with senior citizens.

EDITED   The new **trolley system**, featuring expanded routes and
lower fares, <u>is</u> especially popular with senior citizens.

ESL

19
S-V

ESL ADVICE: SEPARATED SUBJECTS AND VERBS

Check for agreement if phrases or clauses separate subject and verb

PHRASE   A person **with sensitive eyes** has to wear sunglasses.

CLAUSE   A person **whose eyes are sensitive** has to wear sunglasses

When the subject is the same in both the main and subordinate clauses, the verbs must agree.

SAME SUBJECT   A **person** who **wants** to protect her eyes **wears** sunglasses.

Subjects within phrases. If you mistake a phrase like *as well as*, *in addition to*, *together with*, or *along with* for *and*, you may be tempted to treat a noun following it as the subject.

The **provost**, as well as the deans, has issued new guidelines.

If you mean *and*, use the word itself.

REWRITTEN   The provost **and** the deans have issued new guidelines.

STRATEGY Find the real subject.

Imagine the sentence without the intervening phrase.

DRAFT   A regular tune-up, along with frequent oil **changes**, prolong the life of your car.
         IMAGINE: A regular tune-up . . . **prolongs** the life of your car.

EDITED   A regular **tune-up**, along with frequent oil changes, prolongs the life of your car.

5 Match subjects and verbs as you vary sentence patterns

Check agreement when you use different sentence structures.

Inverted word order. The verb should agree with the subject even when you alter typical word order to create emphasis or ask a question.

QUESTION   Are **popular comedy and action films** mere escapism?

EMPHASIS   After victory comes **overconfidence** for many teams.

ESL

9b
agr

xpletive constructions such as *there are* and *it is* invert (reverse) the usual ubject-verb sentence order, allowing you to put the subject *after* the verb see 29b-2). Then the verb agrees with the subject that follows it.

NGULAR   There is **opportunity** for people starting service industries.

LURAL   There are many **opportunities** for service industries.

Linking verbs. When you choose a **linking verb** such as *is*, *appears*, or *feels* see 15c), the verb agrees with the subject, not with the **complement**, the noun or pronoun renaming the subject (see 16a-2).

                 subject   verb   complement

DRAFT   The chief **obstacle** to change are the **mayor and her allies**.

EDITED   The chief **obstacle** to change is the mayor and her allies.

ESL ADVICE: PRESENT TENSE VERB AGREEMENT

ESL

19k
S-V

In English, each present tense verb should agree with its subject.

- Check the subject and the verb in a simple sentence.

  The clerk **files** reports every afternoon.

- Check whether the subject and the verb are separated by phrases.

  The clerk from the office downstairs **files** reports.

- Check for compound verbs (more than one verb) in a simple sentence.

  The clerk **collects**, **sorts**, and **files** reports.

- Check for subject-verb agreement in a complex sentence (see 16d).

ADVERB CLAUSE   When the snow **falls**, we enjoy the scenery.

ADJECTIVE CLAUSE   The young man that I work with **lives** in town.

                   The young man that **works** with me **lives** in town.

- Check for correct selection of helping verbs.

THIRD PERSON DOES   That restaurant **does** give special dinner discounts.

MODAL   The president **might** give a speech this evening.

6 Concentrate on subject-verb agreement with troublesome words

Watch for words such as *all*, *everybody*, *who*, *that*, and *each*.

Indefinite pronouns (*all, everybody, none*) as subjects. These pronoun do not refer to specific ideas, people, or things. Most have clearly singula meanings and require singular verbs.

> **Someone** <u>is</u> mailing campaign flyers.

> **Everybody** <u>has</u> the duty to vote.

STRATEGY   **Find the word to which *all, any, most, none,* or *some* refers.**

Consider whether the pronoun refers to something that *cannot b counted* (singular) or two or more elements of something that *can be counted* (plural). Choose a verb accordingly.

SINGULAR   **All** of the <u>food</u> **is** for the camping trip next week.
food = food in general (not countable); *all* = singular

PLURAL   **All** of the <u>supplies</u> **are** for the camping trip next week.
supplies = many kinds of supplies (countable), such as baking mixes, bottled water, and dried fruit; *all* = plural

---

***Who, which,* and *that* as subjects.** The **relative pronouns** *who, which,* and *that* (see 15b) do not have singular and plural forms, yet the words to which they refer (their antecedents) generally do. Choose a singular or plural verb according to the number of the antecedent.

SINGULAR   He likes **a film** <u>that</u> **focuses** on the characters.

PLURAL   I prefer **films** <u>that</u> **combine** action and romance.

SOME INDEFINITE AND RELATIVE PRONOUNS

GENERALLY SINGULAR		PLURAL	EITHER SINGULAR OR PLURAL
another	neither	both	all
anybody	nobody	few	any
anyone	none	many	enough
anything	no one	others	more
each	nothing	several	most
either	one		some
every	other		that
everybody	somebody		which
everyone	someone		who
everything	something		whose
much			

ach and every. Your placement of *each* or *every* can create a singular or
lural meaning.

> *Each* before compound subject + singular verb
> **Each** supervisor and manager checks the logs daily.

> *Each* after compound subject + plural verb
> The supervisors and managers **each** check the logs daily.

ESL ADVICE: QUANTIFIERS

A **quantifier**—a word like *each*, *one*, or *many*—indicates the amount
or quantity of a subject.

> EXPRESSIONS FOLLOWED BY A PLURAL NOUN + A SINGULAR VERB
> Each of/Every one of/One of/None of   the **students** lives on campus.

> EXPRESSIONS FOLLOWED BY A PLURAL NOUN + A PLURAL VERB
> Several of/Many of/Both of   the **students** live off campus.

In some cases, the noun after the expression determines the verb form.

> EXPRESSIONS FOLLOWED BY EITHER A SINGULAR OR A PLURAL VERB
> noncount noun + singular verb
> Some of/Most of/All of/A lot of   the **produce** is fresh.

> plural noun + plural verb
> Some of/Most of/All of/A lot of   the **vegetables** are fresh.

MUCH AND MOST (NOT *MUCH OF* OR *MOST OF*) WITH NONCOUNT AND PLURAL NOUNS
NONCOUNT NOUN **Much traffic** occurs during rush hour.

PLURAL NOUN   **Most Americans** live in the cities or suburbs.

Other, others, and another. As pronouns, these words can act as subjects;
as adjectives, they can modify subjects.

ESL ADVICE: *OTHER*, *OTHERS*, AND *ANOTHER* AS PRONOUNS OR ADJECTIVES

PRONOUNS
Others + plural verb: adds points about a topic; there may be more points.

> I enjoy Paris for many reasons. Some reasons are the architecture and
> gardens; **others are** the wonderful people, culture, and language.

The others (plural) + plural verb; *the other* (singular) + singular verb adds the last point or points about the topic; there are no more.

> Some hikers favor Craig's plan; **the others want** to follow Tina's.

ADJECTIVES

Another + singular noun: adds an idea; there may be more ideas.
Other + plural noun: adds more ideas; there may be more ideas.

> One strength of our engineering team is our knowledge of the problem. **Another strength** is our experience. **Other strengths** include our communication skills, teamwork, and energy.

The other + singular or plural noun: adds the final point or points to be discussed.

> Of the two very important sights to see in Paris, one is the Louvre Museum, and **the other one** is the Cathedral of Notre Dame.

> One of the major sights in Paris is the Louvre Museum. **The other sights** are the Eiffel Tower, the Champs-Élysées, the Cathedral of Notre Dame, and the Arc de Triomphe.

ESL

19c **agr**

19c Editing pronoun-antecedent agreement

Begin with either the pronoun or its **antecedent** (the noun or pronoun to which it refers). Bring the other into agreement.

1 Focus on the pronoun and its antecedent

Match the pronoun with the antecedent to which it refers.

STRATEGY Find the specific word to which a pronoun refers.

If you are uncertain about which pronoun to use, circle or mark the specific word (or words) to which it refers. Then edit either the pronoun or the antecedent so that the two elements match.

INCONSISTENT Proposals should address its audience.

CLEAR **Proposals** should address **their audiences**.

CLEAR **A proposal** should address **its audience**.

A **collective noun** such as *team, group, clan, audience, army,* or *tribe* can act as a singular or plural antecedent, depending on whether it refers to the group as a whole or to the members acting separately.

SINGULAR   The **subcommittee** submitted **its** revised report.

PLURAL   The **subcommittee** discussed **their** concerns.

Check pronouns that refer to words linked by *and, or,* and *nor*

Antecedents linked as pairs or alternatives can be tricky.

Antecedents joined by *and*. When you form a **compound antecedent** by joining two or more antecedents with *and*, refer to them with a plural pronoun (such as *they*), even if one or more are singular.

> **Luis and Jenni** said that the lab tests they ran were conclusive.

> **The other students and I** admit that the tests we ran were not.

This guideline has two exceptions.

- If a compound antecedent refers to a single person, thing, or idea, use a singular pronoun.

  > **My colleague and co-author** is someone skilled at lab analysis.

- If you place *each* or *every* before a compound antecedent to single out the individual members of the compound, use a singular pronoun.

  > **Each** of the soil and water samples arrives in its own container.

Antecedents joined by *or* or *nor*. When you join the parts of an antecedent with *or* or *nor* (or *either . . . or, neither . . . nor*), make sure the pronoun agrees with the part closer to it.

> **Neither** the manager **nor** the **engineers** wrote their reports on time.

If one part is singular and the other plural, try putting the plural element second or rewriting to avoid an awkward or confusing sentence.

CONFUSING	Either Jim and Al or Dalhat will include the projections in his report.
	READER'S REACTION: **Will Jim and Al add to Dalhat's report? Or will the projections go into one of two reports, Dalhat's or Jim and Al's?**
EDITED	Either Dalhat or **Jim** and **Al** will include the projections in their report.
REWRITTEN	Either Dalhat will include the projections in his report, or Jim and Al will include them in theirs.

19c
p-a

3 Concentrate on pronouns that refer to other pronouns

When **indefinite pronouns** (such as *everyone* or *any*) are singular (se 19b-6), so are other pronouns that refer to them.

Somebody on the team left <u>her</u> racket on the court.

Each of the men has <u>his</u> own equipment.

To avoid either sexist language (see 32a) or inconsistency, use *both* a plura pronoun and a plural antecedent, especially when writing for the academ community.

SEXIST	**Everybody** included charts in **his** sales **talk**.
INFORMAL (SPOKEN)	**Everybody** included charts in **their** sales **talks**.
WRITTEN	**All presenters** included charts in **their** sales **talks**.

ESL ADVICE: DEMONSTRATIVE ADJECTIVES OR PRONOUNS

ESL

20 adv

Demonstrative adjectives or **pronouns** are either singular (*this*, *that*) or plural (*these*, *those*), depending on the noun being modified. (See 15b.)

INCONSISTENT	This crystals of water make snowflakes.
BOTH PLURAL	**These crystals** of water make snowflakes.
INCONSISTENT	Those snowflake crystal is made of frozen water.
BOTH SINGULAR	**That snowflake crystal** is made of frozen water.

20 | Using Adjectives and Adverbs

If you confuse adjectives and adverbs or use them improperly, many readers will notice these errors.

DRAFT	The new medication acts **quick**. READER'S REACTION: *Quick* doesn't fit here. Maybe the writer is careless or doesn't know what to use.
EDITED	The new medication acts **quickly**.

lthough academic readers may be especially alert to these differences, use
modifiers carefully in formal contexts, whatever the community.

20a Recognizing what adjectives and adverbs do

Adjectives and adverbs modify—add to, qualify, focus, limit, or extend
the meaning of—other words and thus are called **modifiers**.

FEATURES OF ADJECTIVES AND ADVERBS

ADJECTIVES
- Modify nouns and pronouns
- Answer "How many?" "What kind?" "Which one (or ones)?" "What size, color, or shape?"
- Include words like *blue*, *complicated*, *good*, and *frightening*
- Include words created by adding endings like *-able*, *-ical*, *-less*, *-ful*, and *-ous* to nouns or verbs (such as *controllable*, *sociological*, *seamless*, *careful*, *nervous*)

ADVERBS
- Modify verbs, adjectives, and other adverbs
- Modify phrases (*almost* beyond the building), clauses (*soon after* I added the last ingredients), and sentences (*Remarkably*, the mechanism was not damaged.)
- Answer "When?" "Where?" "How?" "How often?" "Which direction?" "What degree?"
- Consist mostly of words ending in *-ly*, like *quickly* and *carefully*
- Include some common adverbs that do not end in *-ly*, such as *fast*, *very*, *well*, *quite*, and *late*

**20a
adj/**

You can use most modifiers in three forms, depending on how many things
you compare—no other things, two things, or three or more.

POSITIVE	The cab drove **quickly** on the **smooth** road.
COMPARATIVE (2)	The cab drove **more quickly** on the **smoother** road.
SUPERLATIVE (3+)	The cab drove **most quickly** on the **smoothest** road.

COMPARATIVE AND SUPERLATIVE FORMS

ADJECTIVES

ONE SYLLABLE
Most add -er and -est (pink, pinker, pinkest).

TWO SYLLABLES
Many add -er and -est (happy, happier, happiest).
Some add either -er and -est or more and most (foggy, foggier, foggiest; foggy, more foggy, most foggy).

THREE (OR MORE) SYLLABLES
Add more and most (plentiful, more plentiful, most plentiful).

ADVERBS

ONE SYLLABLE
Most add -er and -est (quick, quicker, quickest).

TWO (OR MORE) SYLLABLES
Most add more and most (carefully, more carefully, most carefully).

NEGATIVE COMPARISONS

ADJECTIVES AND ADVERBS
Use less and least (less agile, least agile; less clearly, least clearly).

IRREGULAR COMPARATIVES AND SUPERLATIVES

ADJECTIVE	COMPARATIVE	SUPERLATIVE
bad	worse	worst
good	better	best
ill (harsh, unlucky)	worse	worst
a little	less	least
many	more	most
much	more	most
some	more	most
well (healthy)	better	best

ADVERB		
badly	worse	worst
ill (badly)	worse	worst
well (satisfactorily)	better	best

When you use two or more adjectives in a series, you need to place them in the appropriate order before the main noun.

;L ADVICE: ADJECTIVES IN A SERIES

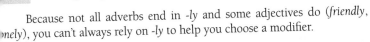

TERMINER	QUALITY	PHYSICAL DESCRIPTION	NATIONALITY	MATERIAL	QUALIFYING NOUN	MAIN NOUN
at	expensive	smooth black	German	fiberglass	racing	car
ur	little	round white		plastic	Ping-Pong	balls
veral	beautiful	young red	Japanese		maple	trees

20b Editing adjectives and adverbs

20.1

Because not all adverbs end in *-ly* and some adjectives do (*friendly*, *nely*), you can't always rely on *-ly* to help you choose a modifier.

Figure out what a modifier does in a sentence

First try to analyze what the modifier will do in your sentence.

STRATEGY Ask questions.

Do you need an adjective that answers "How many?" "What kind?" "Which one (or ones)?" or "What size, color, or shape?" Or do you need an adverb that answers "When?" "Where?" "How?" "How often?" "Which direction?" or "What degree?"

ESL

20b
adj/

> **DRAFT** Write **careful** so that the directions are clear.
> QUESTION: Write *how?* This word answers an adverb question.
>
> **EDITED** Write **carefully** so that the directions are clear.

The word modified also can tell you whether to use an adverb or adjective.

STRATEGY Draw an arrow.

Point to the word that is modified. If this word acts as a noun or pronoun, modify it with an adjective; if it acts as a verb, adjective, or adverb, modify it with an adverb.

> **DRAFT** The insulation underwent **remarkable** quick deterioration.
> CONNECTION: *Remarkable* modifies *quick* (and answers the adverb question "How quick?"). *Quick* in turn modifies *deterioration* (and answers the adjective question "What kind of deterioration?") Replace *remarkable* with an adverb.
>
> **EDITED** The insulation underwent **remarkably** quick deterioration.

2 Check your sentence pattern

A **linking verb** (*is*, *seems*, *becomes*) can tie together a subject and a **complement**, which can be a noun, pronoun, or adjective—but never an adverb. (See 15c, 16a-2.)

subject	linking verb	complement (adjective)
The room	smelled	musty.
The procedure	proved	unreliable.

STRATEGY   Select the right modifier for being or action.

Verbs such as *look*, *feel*, and *prove* can function both as **linking verbs** (showing states of being) and as **action verbs** (showing activities). For a state of being, use an adjective; for an action or activity, use an adverb.

ADJECTIVE (BEING)   The metal cover over the motor <u>turned</u> **hot**.

ADVERB (ACTION)   The large wheel <u>turned</u> **quickly**.

ADJECTIVE   The movement <u>grew</u> **rapid**. [The motion became quick.]

ADVERB   The movement <u>grew</u> **rapidly**. [The group spread its ideas.]

3 Choose the correct form for a troublesome word

Common uses of *real/really*, *bad/badly*, *good/well*, and *sure/surely* may be acceptable in speech but not in academic or other formal writing.

INFORMAL SPEECH   I feel **badly** that our group argues so much.
> READER'S REACTION: Someone who *feels badly* has a poor sense of touch.

BAD/BADLY; GOOD/WELL
- Use *bad* (adjective) with linking verbs such as *is*, *seems*, or *appears* (see 15c, 16a-2).

  I feel **bad** that our group argues so much. [not *badly*]
- Use *badly* (adverb) with action verbs.

  The new breathing apparatus <u>works</u> **badly**. [not *bad*]
- Use *good* (adjective) with linking verbs.

  The chef's new garlic dressing <u>tastes</u> **good**. [not *well*]
- Use *well* (adverb) with action verbs unless it refers to health.

  The new pump <u>works</u> **well**. [not *good*]

REAL/REALLY; SURE/SURELY

- Use *really* (adverb) to modify an adjective like *fast*, *efficient*, or *hot*.

    Lu Ming is **really** efficient. [not *real*]

- Use *surely* (adverb) to modify adjectives like *misleading*, *outdated*, or *courageous*.

    This diagram is **surely** misleading. [not *sure*]

4 Pay attention to comparative and negative forms

Someone with only two children may say, "She's my oldest," yet most communities expect more precise comparisons in writing.

20.2

STRATEGY Use precise comparative forms for facts and figures.

To compare two things, use the **comparative form** (*-er* or *more*); to compare three or more, use the **superlative form** (*-est* or *most*).

INACCURATE   The survey covered four age groups: 20–29, 30–44, 45–59, and 60+. Those in the older group smoked least.

READER'S REACTION: **Does this mean that the people in the older *groups* smoked least or that the people in the *oldest* group smoked least?**

PRECISE   The survey covered four age groups: 20–29, 30–44, 45–59, and 60+. Those in the **oldest group** smoked least.

Double comparatives. Most readers will not accept a double comparative (combining the *-er* form and *more*) or a double superlative (combining the *-est* form and *most*).

DRAFT   Jorge is the **most agilest** athlete in the squadron.

EDITED   Jorge is the **most agile** athlete in the squadron.

Illogical comparatives. Some adjectives and adverbs such as *unique*, *impossible*, *pregnant*, *dead*, *gone*, *perfectly*, and *entirely* cannot logically take comparative or superlative form.

STRATEGY Eliminate illogical comparative forms.

ILLOGICAL   Gottlieb's "Nightscape" is a **most unique** painting.

READER'S REACTION: **How can a thing be *more* or *most* if it is unique— the only one?**

LOGICAL   Gottlieb's "Nightscape" is a **unique** painting.

20b
adj/

Double negatives. Informal speech and dialects may combine negatives such as *no, none, not, never, hardly, scarcely,* and *haven't* and *don't* (formed with *n't,* abbreviating *not*). In writing, however, readers are likely to feel that two negatives used together—a **double negative**—cancel each other out.

STRATEGY   Reduce a double negative to a single negative.

DRAFT   The nurses **can't hardly** manage routine care, much less emergencies.

READER'S REACTION: This sounds more like a conversation than a staffing report.

EDITED   The nurses **can hardly** manage routine care, much less emergencies.

TAKING IT ONLINE

WHAT IS A SENTENCE FRAGMENT?

http://www.harpercollege.edu/writ_ctr/fragmnt.htm

This Web site includes examples, suggestions, and links to two simple tests for detecting fragments. Its conversational tone makes this site easy to understand and use.

ALMOST . . . EVERYTHING YOU WANTED TO KNOW ABOUT COMMA SPLICES

http://www.uark.edu/campus-resources/qwrtcntr/resources/handouts/commasp2.html

This site includes definitions, examples, and an exercise on comma splices, fused sentences, and fragments.

THE MISPLACED MODIFIER, AKA THE SENTENCE DANGLER

http://ace.acadiau.ca/english/grammar/mmodifier.htm

This page identifies one of the "ten most wanted" grammar outlaws and includes quizzes to help you rehabilitate this outlaw.

SEQUENCE OF VERB TENSES

http://ccc.commnet.edu/grammar/sequence.htm

Take a look at the handy charts on the sequence of tenses for active verbs, infinitives, and participles.

PARALLELISM

http://www.english.uiuc.edu/cws/wworkshop

Visit "Parallelism" in both the "Grammar Handbook" and "Tips & Techniques" for advice on what parallel structure is and how to use it effectively.

COORDINATION/SUBORDINATION

http://students.itec.sfsu.edu/ised783/Writing/coord.html

This site can help you use coordination and subordination well.

21 | Editing Sentence Fragments

If you present a group of words as a sentence when those words do not form a complete sentence, you are likely to irritate readers and undermine your authority as a writer.

PARTS MISSING   The insurance company processing the claim.

> READER'S REACTION: **Something is missing. What did the company do?**

EDITED   **The insurance company** processing the claim <u>sent</u> a check.

Despite having a capital letter at the beginning and a period at the end, a **sentence fragment** is only part of a sentence, not a complete sentence.

A fragment is considered the most serious sentence-level error by many college instructors as well as work and public readers. On occasion, an **intentional fragment** may create emphasis or a change of pace, especially in imaginative writing (see 21c). An unintentional fragment, however, forces readers to do the writer's job, mentally reattaching a word group to a nearby sentence or supplying missing information. If you make readers do your work, they may be too distracted to attend to your ideas and may harshly judge your writing (and you as a writer).

21a Recognizing sentence fragments

Before you can edit fragments effectively, you need to be able to distinguish complete sentences from word groups missing a subject or a verb (see 16a) and from clauses detached from sentences to which they belong.

1 Look for a subject and a verb

A **complete sentence** contains both a subject and a complete verb, expressed or implied. If a word group lacks either, it's a fragment.

STRATEGY Ask questions to test sentences.

Sentence Test 1: Ask *Who* (or *what*) *does*? Or *Who* (or *what*) *is*?

- Does a word group answer "Who?" or "What?" If not, it lacks a subject and is a fragment.

RECOGNIZING A SENTENCE

A **sentence**—also called a **main (or independent) clause**—is a word group with a subject and verb that can stand alone.

SENTENCE	**The hungry bears** <u>were hunting</u> food.
SENTENCE	Because spring snows had damaged many plants, **the hungry bears** <u>were hunting</u> food in urban areas.

A **subordinate (or dependent) clause** has a subject and a predicate, yet it cannot stand on its own as a sentence because it begins with a subordinating word like *because*, *although*, *which*, or *that* (see 28c).

FRAGMENT	Because **spring snows** <u>had damaged</u> many plants.

A **phrase** is a word group that lacks a subject, a predicate, or both. It cannot stand alone.

FRAGMENTS	were hunting	in urban areas	the hungry bears

FRAGMENT	Also needs a family counselor.
	READER'S REACTION: I can't tell *who* (or *what*) needs a counselor.
EDITED	**Hope Clinic** also needs a family counselor.

Exception: In an imperative sentence (see 16d-2), the subject *you* is understood and needn't be stated.

IMPERATIVE	[**You**] Use the spectrometer to test for the unknown chemical.

- Does a word group answer "Does?" or "Is?" If not, it lacks a verb and is a fragment.

FRAGMENT	The new policy to provide health care coverage on the basis of hours worked each week.
	READER'S REACTION: I can't tell what the new policy *does* or *is*.
EDITED	The new policy **provides** health care coverage on the basis of hours worked each week.

Sentence Test 2: Can you turn a word group into a question that can be answered *yes* or *no*? If you can, the word group is a sentence.

WORD GROUP	They bought a van to carry the equipment.
QUESTION	Did they buy a van to carry the equipment?
CONCLUSION	The word group is a sentence.

You may need to add or alter an element to create a question.

WORD GROUP	Bought the building for a warehouse.
QUESTION	Did _____ buy the building for a warehouse?
CONCLUSION	The question doesn't have a subject, so the word group is a fragment.
EDITED	**Johnson Plumbing** bought the building for a warehouse.
WORD GROUP	The company providing repairs for our computers.
QUESTION	Does the company **providing** repairs for our computers? CAUTION: **Do not begin the question with** *is, are, has,* **or** *have,* **or you may unintentionally provide a verb for the word group being tested.**
CONCLUSION	*Providing* can't act as the verb in its current form, so this is a fragment.
EDITED	The company **is** providing repairs for our computers.

Verbs and verbals. In checking for fragments, be careful not to confuse a verb and a **verbal**, part of a verb acting as a noun or modifier (see 16b-4). Verbals include participles (*testing, tested*), infinitives (*to test*), and gerunds (*testing*). A verbal alone can never act as the verb in a sentence. When combined with a **helping verb** such as *is, has, can,* or *should* (see 17d), a verbal can be part of a complete verb (*was testing, should test*).

Missing and implied elements. Sometimes a verb appears near the beginning of a word group (often following *and* or *but*) and its subject is nearby—but in another sentence. Readers consider this subject missing, not implied. A fragment like this occurs if you split off the last element of a **compound predicate** with two or more verbs (I *closed* the door. And *locked* it. [fragment]). Other patterns clearly imply a verb rather than repeat it.

VERB IMPLIED	Pedro moved to Detroit, Regina [**moved**] to Tucson.

21a
frag

2 Look for subordinating words

A word group containing both a subject and a complete verb may still be a fragment if it is controlled by a subordinating word. A subordinator introduces a word group, telling readers it is part of a larger statement.

STRATEGY **Hunt for a subordinating word.**

Look for a word group beginning with a subordinating conjunction such as *although, if, because, unless,* or *since* (see the list in 28c) or with a relative pronoun (*that, what, which,* or *who;* see 18a). If this word group is not attached to a main clause, it is a fragment.

FRAGMENT	Residents love the mild climate. <u>Which</u> **has encouraged ou** **door events**.
EDITED	Residents love the mild climate, **which** has encouraged ou door events.

21.1

21b Editing sentence fragments

Often a fragment is simply disconnected from a nearby sentence. When verbal—a participle (*asking, asked*), an infinitive (*to ask*), or a gerund (*asking*)—creates a fragment, the fragment can be connected to a sentence or rewritten.

STRATEGY Attach the fragment to a sentence, or rewrite.

FRAGMENT	Trauma centers give prompt care to heart attack victims <u>Because</u> **rapid treatment can minimize heart damage**.
ATTACHED	Trauma centers give prompt care to heart attack victim **because** rapid treatment can minimize heart damage.
FRAGMENT	**Introducing competing varieties of crabs into the same tank**. He did this in order to study aggression.
REWRITTEN	He **introduced** competing varieties of crabs into the same tank in order to study aggression.

When a fragment begins with *for example* or *such as*, decide whether to attach the examples or emphasize them in their own sentence.

FRAGMENT	Some sports attract many participants in their fifties, sixties, and even seventies. **For example**, **tennis and bowling**.
EDITED (ATTACHED)	Some sports, **such as tennis and bowling**, attract many participants in their fifties, sixties, and even seventies.
REWRITTEN (EMPHASIZED)	Some sports attract many participants in their fifties, sixties, and even seventies. For example, **tennis and bowling appeal to older adults year-round**.

You can also edit words to turn fragments into sentences.

STRATEGY Drop a subordinating word.

FRAGMENT	**Although** several people argued against the motion. It still passed by a majority.
EDITED	Several people argued against the motion. It still passed by a majority.

Add a missing sentence element to complete a sentence.

STRATEGY Supply a missing subject or verb.

FRAGMENT **The judge allowing adopted children to meet their natural parents**.

EDITED (VERB ADDED) The judge **favors** allowing adopted children to meet their natural parents.

21c Using partial sentences

In magazines, campaign literature, advertisements, and even well-written essays, you may encounter **partial sentences**—sentence fragments used intentionally, effectively, but sparingly. Partial sentences can call attention to details ("Deep rose, not red."), emphasize ideas ("Wilson. For the future."), heighten contrasts ("And in the last lane, my brother."), or add transition ("Next, the results."). Other uses include informal questions and answers ("Where?" "On my desk.") and exclamations ("Too bad!").

STRATEGY Use a partial sentence only when appropriate.

- Use partial sentences only when readers are likely to accept them.
- When in doubt, seek a reader's advice, or look at comparable writing.
- Have a clear purpose—describing, emphasizing, or contrasting.
- Be sure readers can supply missing elements or connect word groups.
- Make sure readers won't mistake your partial sentence for a fragment.

22
cs/fs

22 | Editing Comma Splices and Fused Sentences

You can easily confuse and annoy readers if you inappropriately join two or more sentences using either a comma only (**comma splice**) or no punctuation at all (**fused sentence**). If you don't clearly mark the parts and boundaries of a sentence, readers may have to puzzle over its meaning.

COMMA SPLICE   CBS was founded in 1928 by William S. Paley, his uncle ar
his father sold him a struggling radio network.

READER'S REACTION: **At first I thought CBS had three founders: Pale
his uncle, and his father. Then I realized that Paley probab
bought the network from his relatives.**

EDITED   CBS was founded in 1928 by William S. Paley **;** his uncle an
his father sold him a struggling radio network.

FUSED SENTENCE   The city had only one swimming pool without an admissic
fee the pool was poorly maintained.

READER'S REACTION: **I can't decide whether the single pool in town i
poorly maintained or the only free pool is in bad shape.**

EDITED   The city had only one swimming pool **, but** without an admis
sion fee, the pool was poorly maintained.

A **comma splice** links what could be two sentences (two main or indepen
dent clauses) by a comma alone. On the other hand, a **fused sentence** (o
run-on sentence) joins what could be two sentences without any punctua
tion mark or connecting word to establish clear sentence boundaries. Thes
errors are likely to occur when you draft quickly or when you write sen
tences with the same subject, related or contrasting ideas, or one illustratin
the other. In academic, work, or public communities, these are serious error
because they may cause readers to misunderstand a passage.

22a Recognizing comma splices

To find comma splices, look for commas scattered between word group
that could stand on their own as sentences. Join these word groups by more
than a comma alone.

STRATEGY **Check for commas that string word groups together.**

COMMA SPLICE   The typical Navajo husband serves as a trustee, the wife and
her children own the family's property.

EDITED   The typical Navajo husband serves as a trustee **, but** the wife
and her children own the family's property.

READER'S REACTION: **Until you added** *but,* **I missed your point about
the woman playing a more important role than the man.**

22b Recognizing fused sentences

Though fused sentences may be any length, look for long sentences
with little or no internal punctuation. Such sentences may combine freestanding (main) clauses without signaling their relationships.

TRATEGY   Count the separate statements in a sentence.

If your sentence seems to contain more than one statement, check for appropriate punctuation and connecting words.

SED SENTENCE   The scientists had trouble identifying the fossil skeleton it resembled that of both a bird and a lizard.

ITED   The scientists had trouble identifying the fossil skeleton **because** it resembled that of both a bird and a lizard.

READER'S REACTION: Adding *because* separates the two main points and makes the ideas easier to understand.

22c Editing comma splices and fused sentences

You can vary emphasis and create sentence diversity as you repair comma splices and fused sentences. When the ideas in two main clauses are loosely related, you can generally express them best in two sentences.

STRATEGY   Create separate sentences. (___. ___.)

OMMA SPLICE   The sport calls for a total of fourteen people (or twelve people and two dogs) divided into two teams, they throw a disk called a Frisbee up and down a field.

DITED   The sport calls for a total of fourteen people (or twelve people and two dogs) divided into two teams● **T**hey throw a disk called a Frisbee up and down a field.

USED SENTENCE   Football does not cause the most injuries among student athletes gymnastics is the most dangerous sport.

DITED   Football does not cause the most injuries among student athletes● **G**ymnastics is the most dangerous sport.

When main clauses convey equally important ideas, try linking them with a comma plus a coordinating conjunction telling how they relate.

STRATEGY   Use a comma plus *and, but, or, for, nor, so,* or *yet.*
(___ , and ___.)

COMMA SPLICE   The finance department has reviewed the plan, the operations department is still analyzing it.

EDITED   The finance department has reviewed the plan● **but** the operations department is still analyzing it.

FUSED SENTENCE   The emergency room is understaffed it still performs well.

EDITED   The emergency room is understaffed● **yet** it still performs well.

22c
cs/fs

Three or more closely related clauses can be punctuated as a series to emphasize their connection. Especially for the academic community, include both comma and a coordinating conjunction before the last item (see 34g).

SERIES OF CLAUSES	We collected the specimens, we cleaned them **,** **and** we measured them.

Subordinators such as *although*, *when*, *because*, *until*, *where*, and *unless* (see 28c) can specify a range of relationships between clauses, as can relative pronouns such as *who*, *which*, or *that* (see 18a). A subordinate clause includes the subordinator plus a subject and a verb; it cannot stand alone as a sentence.

STRATEGY Make one clause subordinate. (*Because* ____, ____.)

COMMA SPLICE	Automobiles are increasingly complex, skilled mechanics may spend several weeks a year in training.
EDITED	**Because** automobiles are increasingly complex **,** skilled mechanics may spend several weeks a year in training.
FUSED SENTENCE	Margaret Atwood is best known for her novels her essays and poems are also worth reading.
EDITED	**Although** Margaret Atwood is best known for her novels **,** her essays and poems are also worth reading.

ESL ADVICE: *BECAUSE* AND *BECAUSE OF*

ESL

The subordinator *because* introduces a clause with a subject and verb the preposition *because of* introduces a phrase with its object.

DRAFT	Because of the pay is low, José must look for another job.
EDITED	**Because** the pay is low, José must look for another job.
EDITED	**Because of** the low pay, José must look for another job.

Use a semicolon to join two main clauses and emphasize their similar importance. (See 35a.)

STRATEGY Use a semicolon. (____; ____.)

COMMA SPLICE	An autopilot is a device that corrects drift, the system senses and reacts to changes in the aircraft's motion.
EDITED	An autopilot is a device that corrects drift **;** the system senses and reacts to changes in the aircraft's motion.

ED SENTENCE	Most colleges offer alternatives to four years on campus study abroad, exchange programs with other schools, and coopera- tive programs are common.
TED	Most colleges offer alternatives to four years on campus **;** study abroad, exchange programs with other schools, and cooperative programs are common.

However, consequently, moreover, and other **conjunctive adverbs** (see 3a) specify relationships between clauses. You can use transitional expres- ons such as *in contrast* and *in addition* for similar purposes.

TRATEGY Use wording like *however, moreover, for example,* and *in contrast* plus a semicolon. (____; however, ____.)

22.1

OMMA SPLICE	To draw the human body, you must understand it, therefore, art students sometimes dissect cadavers.
DITED	To draw the human body, you must understand it **; therefore,** art students sometimes dissect cadavers.
USED SENTENCE	Chickens reach market size within months the lobster takes six to eight years.
DITED	Chickens reach market size within months **; in contrast,** the lobster takes six to eight years.

Conjunctive adverbs and transitional expressions can begin the second main clause or appear within it. Set them off with a comma or commas; join the clauses with a semicolon (see 35a-1).

BEGINNING OF CLAUSE	The Great Lakes were once heavily polluted **; however,** recently fish and other wildlife have returned.	**ESL**
MIDDLE OF CLAUSE	The Great Lakes were once heavily polluted **;** recently **, how- ever,** fish and other wildlife have returned.	**22c** cs/fs
END OF CLAUSE	The Great Lakes were once heavily polluted **;** recently fish and other wildlife have returned **, however**.	

ESL ADVICE: CONNECTING WORDS WITH THE SAME MEANING

Connecting words may have the same meaning but need different punc- tuation.

COORDINATOR	José likes his job **,** but it doesn't pay enough.
CONJUNCTIVE ADVERB	José likes his job **;** however **,** it doesn't pay enough.

When a clause summarizes, illustrates, or restates a preceding claus
you can join them with a colon. (See 35b-3.)

STRATEGY Use a colon. (____: ____.)

COMMA SPLICE   Foreign study calls for extensive language preparation, vacc
nations and a passport are not enough.

EDITED   Foreign study calls for extensive language preparation **:** va
cinations and a passport are not enough.

ESL ADVICE: SENTENCE VARIETY

American academic and workplace readers tend to prefer short sen
tences with varied sentence patterns. Native speakers usually avoid comm
splices and fused sentences by creating separate sentences, adding a coordinat
ing conjunction with a comma, or creating a subordinate clause. Sophisticate
writers sometimes use a semicolon or colon for special effect.

23 | Creating Pronoun Reference

Readers expect pronouns to make a sentence less repetitive and easier
to understand by taking the place of nouns (or other pronouns). For this
substitution to work effectively, your readers must recognize the word to
which a pronoun refers so they can tell exactly what the sentence means.

AMBIGUOUS
REFERENCE   Much of my life with the circus consisted of leading the ele-
phants from the cages and hosing **them** down.
    READER'S REACTION: **What got hosed down? elephants? cages? both?**

EDITED   Much of my life with the circus consisted of hosing the ele-
phants down after leading **them** from **their** cages.

The word to which the pronoun refers is known as its **antecedent** (or **headword**). When **pronoun reference**—the connection between pronoun and
antecedent—isn't clear and specific, readers may be confused. By creating
clear pronoun reference, you tie ideas and sentences together, clarify their relationships, and focus readers' attention.

23a Recognizing unclear pronoun reference

If readers say they "get lost" reading your work or "can't figure out what you are saying," make sure each pronoun refers *clearly* to one specific antecedent, either one word or several words acting as a unit.

Look for unclear pronoun reference

A pronoun may seem to refer to more than one possible antecedent (**ambiguous reference**) or may be too distant from its antecedent (**remote reference**) for a reader to recognize the connection.

AMBIGUOUS REFERENCE	Robespierre and Danton disagreed over the path the French Revolution should take. **He** believed that the Revolution was endangered by internal enemies.
	READER'S REACTION: I'm lost. Who's *he*? Robespierre or Danton?
EDITED	Robespierre and Danton disagreed over the path the French Revolution should take. **Robespierre** believed that the Revolution was endangered by internal enemies.

2 Look for unspecific pronoun reference

If readers have to guess what a pronoun refers to, you may have referred to the entire idea of an earlier passage (**vague** or **broad pronoun reference**) or to an **implied antecedent**, suggested but not stated.

IMPLIED ANTECEDENT	A hard frost damaged most of the local citrus groves, but **it** has not yet been determined.
	READER'S REACTION: I'm not sure what *it* means, though I guess it's related to the frost damage.
STATED	A hard frost damaged most of the local citrus groves, but **the extent of the loss** has not yet been determined.

STRATEGY Point out the specific antecedent.

Certain words—*it, they, you, which, this,* or *that*—are especially likely to refer to vague, implied, or indefinite antecedents. To spot imprecise references, search for these pronouns. In each case, see if you can find an antecedent stated in the passage.

23b Editing pronoun reference

To edit pronoun reference, focus first on the pronoun itself.

1 Clarify the pronoun

Replace the pronoun, reword around it, or move it as you edit.

STRATEGY Replace the pronoun with a noun, or reword.

If a pronoun might refer to two or more words or is distant from its antecedent, try replacing it with a synonym or with the word to which it refers. Or rewrite to eliminate any confusion.

| AMBIGUOUS REFERENCE | Detaching the measuring probe from the glass cylinder is a delicate job because **it** breaks easily. |
| | READER'S REACTION: Which is so fragile, the probe or the cylinder? |

| REPLACED WITH NOUN | Detaching the measuring probe from the glass cylinder is a delicate job because **the probe** breaks easily. |

| REWORDED | Because the measuring probe breaks easily, detaching it from the glass cylinder is a delicate job. |

In letters, email messages, appeals, directions, and other writing that addresses the reader directly, *you* is commonly accepted. It means "you, the reader." (See 25a.) When *you* refers to situations and people in general, however, it may lead to imprecise sentences.

| INDEFINITE ANTECEDENT | In Brazil, **you** pay less for an alcohol-powered car than for a gasoline-powered one. |
| | READER'S REACTION: Who is *you*? I'm not likely to buy a car in Brazil. |

| REPLACED WITH NOUN | In Brazil, **consumers** pay less for an alcohol-powered car than for a gasoline-powered one. |

| REWRITTEN | In Brazil, alcohol-powered cars cost less than gasoline-powered ones. |

STRATEGY Add clear wording right after the pronoun.

After *which*, *this*, or *that*, specify or explain the pronoun's referent.

| VAGUE REFERENCE | Redfish have suffered from oil pollution and the destruction of their mangrove swamp habitat. **This** has led to a rapid decline in the redfish population. |
| | READER'S REACTION: Does *this* refer to the destruction of habitat, to oil pollution, or to both? |

| SPECIFIED | Redfish have suffered from oil pollution and the destruction of their mangrove swamp habitat. **This combination** has led to a rapid decline in the redfish population. |

| EXPLAINED | Redfish have suffered from oil pollution and the destruction of their mangrove swamp habitat. **That increasingly serious pair of challenges** has led to a rapid decline in the redfish population. |

ometimes a pronoun does not have to be replaced, just moved—especially
position *who*, *which*, and *that* right after their antecedents.

STRATEGY Move the pronoun closer to its antecedent.

CONFUSING   In my old bedroom, I saw a stale piece of the bubble gum under
             the dresser that I loved to chew as a boy.

EDITED   In my old bedroom, I saw under the dresser a stale piece of
             the bubble gum that I loved to chew as a boy.

Clarify the antecedent to which the pronoun refers

Many academic readers will consider a possessive noun used as an antecedent an error, though the pattern appears often in informal writing. Pair a
possessive noun with a possessive pronoun (*Kristen's . . . hers*), or rewrite to
eliminate the possessive noun.

UNCLEAR   The **company's** success with a well-known jazz fusion artist
                     led **it** to contracts with other musicians.

EDITED   The **company's** success with a well-known jazz fusion artist
(POSSESSIVE PAIR)   led to **its** contracts with other musicians.

EDITED   Success with a well-known jazz fusion artist led the company
(NO POSSESSIVE)   to other contracts.

STRATEGY Rewrite to avoid using a possessive as an antecedent.

INAPPROPRIATE   In William Faulkner's *The Sound and the Fury*, he begins the
                 story from the point of view of a mentally retarded person.

EDITED   In *The Sound and the Fury*, **William Faulkner** begins the story
                 from the point of view of a mentally retarded person.

23b
pr re

3 Rework a passage to create a reference chain

Build a chain of pronouns whose antecedent is stated in the opening
sentence. Such a **reference chain** guides your readers through the passage,
clearly linking references to your topic.

UNCLEAR

Sand paintings were a remarkable form of Pueblo art. An artist would
sprinkle dried sand of different colors, ground flower petals, corn
pollen, and similar materials onto the floor to create **them**. The sun,
moon, and stars as well as animals and objects linked to the spirits

were represented in the figures **they** contained. **Their** purpose w
to encourage the spirits to send good fortune to humans.

Because *them* and *they* are buried at the ends of sentences in the middle
the paragraph, readers may lose sight of the topic, sand paintings.

EDITED TO CREATE A REFERENCE CHAIN

Sand paintings were a remarkable form of Pueblo art. To create **them**
an artist would sprinkle dried sand of different colors, ground flow
petals, corn pollen, and similar materials onto the floor. **They** con
tained figures representing the sun, moon, and stars as well as anima
and objects linked to the spirits. **Their** purpose was to encourage th
spirits to send good fortune to humans.

STRATEGY   Develop a reference chain.

- State the antecedent clearly in the opening sentence.
- Be sure no other possible antecedents interrupt the links in the chain
- Don't interrupt the chain and then try to return to it later.
- Call attention to the links by giving the pronouns prominent position
  (usually beginning sentences); vary their positions only slightly.

24 | Editing Misplaced, Dangling, and Disruptive Modifiers

Readers sometimes see a sentence like a string of beads. If the silver bead
is designed to reflect the red one, they expect to find those beads placed next to
each other just as they expect to find related parts of a sentence together.

MISPLACED MODIFIER

The wife believes she sees a living figure behind the wallpaper in the story by Charlotte Perkins Gilman, which adds
to her sense of entrapment.

READER'S REACTION: **How could a story add to a feeling of entrapment?**

MODIFIER MOVED

The wife **in the story by Charlotte Perkins Gilman** believes
she sees a living figure behind the wallpaper, which adds to
her sense of entrapment.

MODIFIER MOVED

In the story by Charlotte Perkins Gilman, the wife believes
she sees a living figure behind the wallpaper, which adds to
her sense of entrapment.

In the draft, the modifier is not positioned to relate clearly to the word modifies. Once the sentence is rearranged, the wife is "in the story," and the allpaper "adds to her sense of entrapment." Because a **modifier** qualifies, lds to, or limits the meaning of a word or word group, its location in a sentence tells a reader which word it modifies (its **headword**).

24a Recognizing misplaced, dangling, and disruptive modifiers

When a modifier is poorly positioned or illogically related to its headword, academic readers are especially likely to find a sentence vague, illogical, or unintentionally humorous.

Look for misplaced modifiers

To recognize a **misplaced modifier**, look for a word or word group hat is not close enough to its headword and instead appears to modify some ther word or *both* the word before it and the word after.

CONFUSING	The caterer served food to the directors standing around the room on flimsy paper plates. READER'S REACTION: Surely the directors weren't standing on the plates!
MODIFIER MOVED	The caterer served food **on flimsy paper plates** to the directors standing around the room.

2 Look for dangling modifiers

To find a **dangling modifier**, look for a sentence that begins with a modifier but doesn't name the person, idea, or thing modified. Readers will assume that this modifier refers to the subject of the main clause immediately following. If it doesn't, the modifier dangles.

DANGLING	Looking for a way to reduce complaints from nonsmokers, a new ventilation fan was installed. READER'S REACTION: How could a fan look for anything? The sentence never tells me *who* wants to reduce complaints.
SUBJECT ADDED	Looking for a way to reduce complaints from nonsmokers, **the company installed** a new ventilation fan.

3 Look for disruptive modifiers

Readers generally expect subjects and verbs to stand close to each other. The same is true for other sentence elements—verbs and their objects or complements, parts of infinitives, and verb phrases. To recognize a **disruptive modifier**, look for a long interruption between such elements.

DISRUPTIVE	The researcher, **because he had not worked with chimpanzees before and was unaware of their intelligence**, was surprised when they undermined his experiment.

However, a brief, relevant interruption can add variety and suspense.

CLEAR   The researcher, **unfamiliar with chimpanzees**, was surprise when they undermined his experiment.

STRATEGY Figure out which modifiers are disruptive.

How can you tell whether modifiers placed between subject and ver are disruptive? Modifiers that provide information related to both subjec and verb are likely to be disruptive because a reader can't tell which they re late to. Modifiers related to the subject alone generally aren't disruptive.

                subject   modifier
DISRUPTIVE   Work on the building, **due to problems with the construc**
                           verb
     tion permits, was completed three months late.

              subject   modifier   verb
NOT DISRUPTIVE   The youth center **that opened last month** has drawn crowds

---

ESL ADVICE: POSITION OF MODIFIERS

Some languages clarify the relationship between a modifier and its head-word through the form or ending of the words. Because modifiers in English tend to change location, not form, to show which words they describe, the posi-tion of a modifier can drastically change its meaning.

24.1

ESL

4b dm

24b Editing misplaced, dangling, and disruptive modifiers

A problem modifier may require only a simple repair.

1 Move the modifier

Try simply moving an ambiguous modifier. Place it near its headword, and avoid splitting other elements.

STRATEGY Place *who*, *which*, or *that* close to its headword.

For a clear connection, try to put *who*, *which*, or *that* immediately after its headword to avoid modifying the wrong word.

MISPLACED   The environmental engineers discovered another tank behind

                   the building that was leaking toxic wastes.
                   READER'S REACTION: I know a building can leak, but I'll bet the writer meant that the tank was the culprit.

MOVED AFTER
HEADWORD

Behind the building, the environmental engineers discovered another tank **that** was leaking toxic wastes.

In most cases, move a **limiting modifier** like *only*, *almost*, *hardly*, *just*, *merely*, *simply*, and *even* directly before the word to which it applies.

Only charities for children are maintaining their support.
They are the sole charities able to maintain support.

Charities for **only** children are maintaining their support.
The charities are for children from families with one child.

Charities for children are **only** maintaining their support.
They are not increasing the levels of support.

If a modifier appears to modify the wording both before and after it, move this **squinting modifier** to eliminate the ambiguity, or rewrite.

SQUINTING

People who abuse alcohol **often** have other problems.
READER'S REACTION: **Do they abuse alcohol *often* or *often* have other problems?**

EDITED

People who **often abuse alcohol** tend to have other problems.

REWRITTEN

People who abuse alcohol tend to have other problems **as well**.

STRATEGY Move a modifier that splits sentence elements.

Readers expect a subject and verb to stand together and an object or complement to come right after the verb.

CLUMSY

Joanne began collecting, **using her survey form**, data for her study of dating preferences.

EDITED

Using her survey form, Joanne began collecting data for her study of dating preferences.

If a modifier splits the parts of an infinitive (*to* plus a verb, as in *to enjoy*), readers may have trouble relating the parts. Some readers will find any **split infinitive** irritating, clear or not.

IRRITATING

The dancers moved **to** very rapidly **align** themselves.

EDITED

The dancers moved very rapidly **to align** themselves.

At times, however, a split infinitive may be the most concise alternative.

Our goal is **to** more than **halve** our manufacturing errors.

24
mn

2 Change the headword to which a modifier relates

If you can't move a modifier because the headword to which it shou
connect is not stated, find a way to state the headword.

STRATEGY Add or change the subject to connect a modifier.

DANGLING   While shopping, the stuffed alligator caught my eye.

SUBJECT ADDED   While **I was** shopping, the stuffed alligator caught my eye.

DANGLING   Jumping into the water to save the drowning swimmer, the crowe
applauded the lifeguard.

SUBJECT CHANGED   Jumping into the water to save the drowning swimmer, **the
lifeguard** was applauded by the crowd.

3 Rewrite the sentence

If your sentence still isn't clear, ask yourself, "What do I really mean:
Who's doing what?" Then state that point as directly as possible.

STRATEGY Focus and rework the entire sentence.

DANGLING   Having debated changes in the regulations for months, the
present standards were allowed to continue.
READER'S REACTION: *Who* is debating? Not the standards!

REWRITTEN   The commission debated changes in the regulations for
months but decided to continue the present standards.

25 | Making Shifts Consistent

Although readers are willing to shift attention many times, they expect
these shifts to be logically consistent and clearly signaled.

SHIFTED   If **parents** would call the school board, **you** could explain
why **we** oppose the proposal.
READER'S REACTION: I'm confused. Who's who? Who should do what?

EDITED   If **parents** would call the school board, **they** could explain
why **they** oppose the proposal.

EDITED   If **you** would call the school board, **you** could explain why
you oppose the proposal.

ITED If **all of us meeting tonight** would call the school board, **we** could explain why **we** oppose the proposal.

eaders can easily move from your point of view ("*I* recommend this") to the erspective of others ("*They* proposed changes") or from past to present vents. Although readers can follow logical shifts, they may doubt your authority as a writer if you make unexpected changes.

25a Recognizing shifts in person and number

Watch for unexpected shifts in person and number (see 19c). **Person** efers to the ways you use nouns and pronouns (*I, you, she, they*) to shape the elationship involving you, your readers, and your subject. Switching from one erson to another as you refer to the same subject can be illogical. **Number** hows whether words are singular (one) or plural (two or more). Look for con-using shifts between words like *person* and *people* that identify groups or their nembers.

INCONSISTENT When **a business executive is** looking for a new job, **they** often consult a placement service.

> READER'S REACTION: Does *they* mean business executives as a group? The sentence mentions only one executive.

EDITED When **business executives are** looking for **new jobs**, **they** often consult a placement service.

FIRST, SECOND, AND THIRD PERSON IN THREE COMMUNITIES

- **First person (*I, we*).** Use *I* to refer to yourself as the writer or the person whose experiences and perceptions are an essay's subject. Use *we* in a collaborative project with more than one author. In some academic papers, such as literary analyses, you may use *we* as you refer to ideas you and your readers share. You might use *we* at work to speak for your organization or in public to represent your group in a newsletter or press release.
- **Second person (*you*).** Use *you* to refer directly to the reader ("you, the reader"). In most academic and work writing, readers find *you* inappropriate. Some situations do call for *you*, as in instructions or a plain-language contract. In public writing that urges readers to act, *you* can engage the reader in a political, civic, or activist appeal.
- **Third person (*he, she, it, they; one, someone, each,* and other indefinite pronouns).** Use these pronouns for the ideas, things, and people you write about, including nouns (such as *people* or *person*) and names of groups of things, ideas, and people (such as *students* and *teachers*). In academic, work, and public communities alike, avoid sexist use of *he* and *she*. Be alert to exclusionary uses of pronouns, such as inappropriately pitting *we* against *they*.

25a
shif

25b Editing shifts in person and number

Check for illogical shifts between singular and plural forms, betwee first and second person, or between second and third person.

STRATEGY Refer to a subject in a consistent way.

INCONSISTENT NUMBER	If **a person has** some money to invest, **they** should seek advic from a financial consultant.
EDITED	If **a person has** some money to invest, **he or she** shoul seek advice from a financial consultant.
EDITED	If **people have** some money to invest, **they** should seek advic from a financial consultant.
INCONSISTENT PERSON	If a **person** is looking for a higher return on investments, **you** might consider mutual funds.
EDITED	If **you** are looking for a higher return on investments, **you** might consider mutual funds.

25c Recognizing shifts in tense and mood

The **tense** of a verb indicates time as past, present, or future (see 17g). When you change verb tense within a passage, you signal a change in time and the relationship of events in time. Illogical shifts can mislead your readers and contradict your meaning.

ILLOGICAL SHIFT	Scientists digging in Montana **discovered** nests that **indicated** how some dinosaurs **take care** of their young.
LOGICAL	Scientists digging in Montana **discovered** nests that **indicate** how some dinosaurs **took care** of their young.
	Although the actions of both the dinosaurs and the scientists clearly occurred in the past, *indicate* (present tense) is appropriate because researchers interpret the evidence in the present.

ESL ADVICE: VERB TENSE AND EXPRESSIONS OF TIME

Use both verb tense and expressions of time (*yesterday*, *today*, *soon*) to indicate changes in time. Make sure the two are consistent.

INCONSISTENT	I **study** English last year, and now **I worked** for an American company.
EDITED	I **studied** English last year, and now I **work** for an American company.

ESL

25c
hift

The **mood** of a verb shows the writer's aim or attitude (see 16d-2): to ɔmmand or request (**imperative**), to state or question (**indicative**), or to ffer a conditional or hypothetical statement (**subjunctive**; see 17h). If you hift mood inappropriately, your sentences may be hard to follow.

INCONSISTENT (IMPERATIVE AND INDICATIVE)
To reduce costs, **distribute** fewer copies of drafts, and **you should encourage** employees to replace paper memos with email messages.

CONSISTENT (IMPERATIVE)
To reduce costs, **distribute** fewer copies of drafts, and **encourage** employees to replace paper memos with email messages.

25d Editing shifts in tense and mood

25.1

Keep verbs consistent and logical within a passage.

STRATEGY Replace inconsistent verbs with logical tenses and moods.

If you begin narrating events in the past tense, avoid shifting suddenly to the present to try to make events more vivid.

INCONSISTENT TENSE
We **had been searching** for a new site for the festival when Tonia **starts yelling**, "I've found the place!"

EDITED
We **had been searching** for a new site for the festival when Tonia **started yelling**, "I've found the place!"

25e Recognizing shifts in active or passive voice

When a verb is in the **active voice**, the agent or doer of the action functions as the subject of the sentence. When a verb is in the **passive voice**, the goal of the action functions as the sentence's subject. (See 17i and 29b-3.)

25
shi

	subject	verb	object
ACTIVE	The lava flow	**destroyed**	twelve houses.
	agent	action	goal

	subject	verb	
PASSIVE	Twelve houses	**were destroyed**	[by the lava flow].
	goal	action	[agent]

25f Editing shifts in active or passive voice

Try to focus on either active or passive voice within a sentence.

STRATEGY	**Rewrite to use either active or passive consistently.**

INCONSISTENT   Among the active volcanoes, Kilauea **erupts** most frequentl
and over 170 houses **have been destroyed** since 1983.

READER'S REACTION: The first part mentions Kilauea, but the secon
part doesn't. Did Kilauea alone destroy the houses, or were som
other volcanoes also responsible?

EDITED   Among the active volcanoes, Kilauea **has erupted** most fre
quently in recent years, and it has destroyed over 170 house
since 1983.

Sometimes you may shift voice to emphasize or highlight a subject.

                                              active
                                                                              active
UNEMPHATIC   Volcanic activity **built** Hawaii, and the island still **has** active
volcanoes.

                              passive
                                                                              active
EDITED   Hawaii **was built** by volcanic activity, and the island still **has**
active volcanoes.

The first sentence shifts subjects from *volcanic activity* to *the island;* the second shifts between passive and active to keep Hawaii
as the focus.

25g Recognizing shifts in quotations

Through **direct quotation** you present someone's ideas and feelings in
that person's exact words, set off with quotation marks. Through **indirect
quotation** you report the substance of those words but in your own words
without quotation marks. Credit your sources either way (see 49b).

DIRECT QUOTATION   According to Aguilar, beachfront property "has wreaked havoc
on sea turtle nesting patterns" (16).

INDIRECT QUOTATION   Aguilar explained how beachfront property interferes with the
breeding habits of sea turtles (16).

25h Editing shifts in quotations

Within a sentence, shifts in quotation may be difficult to follow.

STRATEGY	**Rewrite awkward shifts between quotations.**

AWKWARD (INDIRECT + DIRECT)   Writing about the Teenage Mutant Ninja Turtles, Phil Patton
names cartoonists Peter Laird and Kevin Eastman as their
creators and **said,** "They were born quietly in 1983, in the
kitchen of a New England farmhouse" (101).

ITED　　Phil Patton **credits** cartoonists Peter Laird and Kevin Eastman with creating the Teenage Mutant Ninja Turtles, who "were born quietly in 1983, in the kitchen of a New England farmhouse" (101).

or indirect quotation, use past tense to report what someone has said.

RECT
UOTATION　　As Lan **notes**, "The region **is expected** to forfeit one of every three jobs" (4).

DIRECT
QUOTATION　　Lan **projected that** the area **would lose** one-third of its jobs during the next ten years (4).

ollow convention, however, and use present tense when you analyze events n a creative work, such as a novel, film, or television show. (See 17b.)

NCONSISTENT　　As the novel begins, Ishmael **comes** to New Bedford to ship out on a whaler, which he soon **did**.

CONVENTIONAL　　As the novel begins, Ishmael **comes** to New Bedford to ship out on a whaler, which he soon **does**.

26 | Editing Mixed and Incomplete Sentences

When someone switches topics or jumbles a sentence during a conversation, you can ask for clarification. When you are reading, however, you can't stop in the middle of a sentence to ask the writer to explain.

TOPIC SHIFT　　One **skill** I envy is **a person** who can meet deadlines.
　　　　　　　　REEADER'S REACTION: How can a *skill* be a *person*?

EDITED　　One **skill** I envy is **the ability** to meet deadlines.

Mixed sentences switch topics or sentence structures without warning, for no clear reason. They throw readers off track by undermining patterns that readers rely on. Similarly, **incomplete sentences** lack either grammatical (see 21a) or logical completeness. For example, if you begin a comparison with "*X* is larger," you should complete it: "*X* is larger *than Y.*"

26a Recognizing mixed and incomplete sentences

Spotting mixed and incomplete sentences may require extra effort.

26a
mix

1 Look for topic shifts

In most sentences, the subject announces a topic, and the predicate comments on or renames the topic. In a sentence with a **topic shift** (**faulty predication**), the second part of the sentence comments on or names a topic different from the one first announced. As a result, readers may have trouble figuring out the true focus of the sentence.

STRATEGY Ask "Who does what?" or "What is it?"

If the answer is illogical, clarify what you say.

TOPIC SHIFT	In this factory, **flaws** in the product noticed by any worker **can stop** the assembly line with the flip of a switch. QUESTION: Who does what? Flaws can't stop the line or flip a switch.
EDITED	In this factory, **any worker** who notices flaws in the product **can stop** the assembly line with the flip of a switch.

2 Look for mixed grammatical patterns

If you begin one grammatical pattern but shift to another, your sentence may confuse readers because it doesn't follow the pattern they expect.

STRATEGY Check who does what to whom.

- Read your sentences aloud. Pay attention to the *meaning*, especially how the subject and predicate relate.
- Ask, "What is the topic? How does the rest of the sentence comment on it or rename it?"

MIXED PATTERN	By wearing bell-bottom pants and tie-dyed T-shirts was how many young people challenged mainstream values in the 1960s. CHECK: *Who did what to whom* is not clear.
EDITED	By wearing bell-bottom pants and tie-dyed T-shirts, many young people challenged mainstream values in the 1960s.

3 Look for inappropriate omissions, especially in comparisons

Incomplete sentences leave out words necessary to meaning or logic, or they don't complete an expected pattern, such as a comparison.

STRATEGY Read aloud to identify missing words.

Listen for omissions such as needed articles, prepositions, pronouns, parts of verbs, or parts of a comparison.

COMPLETE   The new parking plan is much better.

READER'S REACTION: **Better than what? another plan? no plan?**

DITED   The new parking plan is much better **than the last plan**.

26b Editing mixed and incomplete sentences

Make sure the topic is the same in the subject and predicate.

Stick to a clear topic

When you use the verb *be* (*is*, *are*, *was*, *were*), you may use the sentence predicate to rename or define the subject. Balance the topics on each side of the verb; for example, pair a noun with a noun.

STRATEGY   Rename the subject.

If the topics on each side of *be* are not roughly equivalent, edit the second part of the sentence to rename the topic in the first part.

TOPIC SHIFT   **Irradiation** is **food** that is preserved by radiation.

EDITED   **Irradiation** is a **process** that can be used to preserve food.

Is when and *is where* make a balance on both sides of *be* impossible.

STRATEGY   Rewrite to eliminate *is when* or *is where*.

NOT BALANCED   **Blocking** is **when** a television network schedules a less popular program between two popular ones.

EDITED   **Blocking** is the **practice** of scheduling a less popular television program between two popular ones.

Readers find *the reason . . . is because* illogical because they expect the subject (topic) to be renamed after *is*. When *because* appears there instead, it cannot logically rename the subject.

STRATEGY   Rewrite to eliminate *the reason . . . is because*.

DRAFT   The **reason** he took up skating **is because** he wanted winter exercise.

• Drop *the reason . . . is*.

EDITED   He took up skating **because** he wanted winter exercise.

- Change *because* to *that*.

    EDITED   The **reason** he took up skating **is that** he wanted winte[r]
    exercise.

2 Stick to a consistent sentence pattern

26.1   If you mistake words between the subject and verb for the sentenc[e]
topic, you may mix up different sentence patterns.

> **STRATEGY** Make sure the subject and predicate are consistent despite
> any words between them.

TOPIC SHIFT   Programming **decisions** by television executives generally
think about gaining audience share.
READER'S REACTION: How can decisions think about viewers?

EDITED   **Television executives** making programming decisions generally think about gaining audience share.

EDITED   When **they are making** programming decisions, **television
executives** generally think about gaining audience share.

Watch for sentences in which you repeat a topic more often than the sentence structure allows or mistakenly start the sentence over again.

> **STRATEGY** Stick to one subject in sentences that begin twice.

MIXED   **The new procedures for testing cosmetics**, **we** designed
them to avoid cruelty to laboratory animals.

EDITED   **We** designed **the new procedures for testing cosmetics** to
avoid cruelty to laboratory animals.

EDITED   **The new procedures for testing cosmetics** were designed
to avoid cruelty to laboratory animals.

3 Make comparisons complete and logical

You create an **incomplete comparison** when you omit an item being
compared or the wording needed for a clear, complete comparison.

> **STRATEGY** Supply the words that complete a comparison.

INCOMPLETE   The senior members of the staff respect the new supervisor
more than their co-workers.
READER'S REACTION: Do the senior staff members respect the supervisor more than they respect their co-workers? Or do they respect
the supervisor more than their co-workers do?

EAR   The senior members of the staff respect the new supervisor
more **than do** their co-workers.

EAR   The senior members of the staff respect the new supervisor
more **than they respect** their co-workers.

---

n **illogical comparison** seems to compare things that cannot be reason-
bly compared.

STRATEGY   Add missing words or a possessive to compare logically.

LOGICAL   The amount of fat in even a small hamburger is greater than
a skinless chicken breast.

READER'S REACTION: I'm confused. Why is the writer comparing the
amount of fat in one food to another *kind* of food (chicken breast)?

DITED   The amount of fat in even a small hamburger is greater than
(WORDS ADDED)   **that in** a skinless chicken breast.

DITED   Even a small **hamburger's** fat content is greater than a skinless
(POSSESSIVE USED)   chicken **breast's**.

27 | Creating Parallelism

When you use consistent patterns, readers can easily follow and understand your ideas. They can concentrate on what you mean because they
know just what to expect and how your ideas relate.

WEAK   I furnished my apartment with what I purchased at discount
stores, buying items from the want ads, and gifts from my relatives.

READER'S REACTION: This list seems wordy and jumbled.

PARALLEL   I furnished my apartment with **purchases from discount stores**,
items from the want ads,
and **gifts from my relatives**.

Parallelism is the expression of similar or related ideas in similar grammatical form. Besides emphasizing the relationships of ideas, parallelism can create intriguing sentence rhythms and highlights. Academic readers value the
clarity or style that it brings even to everyday sentences, while workplace
readers appreciate its conciseness, and public readers its persuasive power.

27.1

27a Recognizing faulty parallelism

Once you begin a parallel pattern, you need to complete it. If you m
structures, creating incomplete or **faulty parallelism**, your sentences m
disappoint readers' expectations and be hard to read.

MIXED   Consider swimming if you want an exercise that **aids** cardiovascul
fitness, **develops** overall muscle strength, and **probably withou
causing** injuries.

PARALLEL   Consider swimming if you want an exercise that **aids** cardiova
cular fitness, **develops** overall muscle strength, and **causes** fe
injuries.

27b Editing for parallelism

Whether you create parallelism with words, phrases, or clauses, all th
elements need to follow the same grammatical patterns.

1 Rework a series, pair, or list using parallel forms

When you place items in a series, pair, or list, make sure they have th
same structure even if they differ in length and wording. Mixed grammatica
forms can make a series clumsy and distracting.

STRATEGY Rework a series so that its elements are parallel.

WORDS
MIXED   To get along with their neighbors, residents need to be patient, tact-
ful, and to display tolerance.

WORDS
PARALLEL   To get along with their neighbors, residents need to be patient, tact-
ful, and **tolerant**.

PHRASES
MIXED   The singer Jim Morrison is remembered for his innovative style,
his flamboyant performances, and for behavior that was self-
destructive.

PHRASES
PARALLEL   The singer Jim Morrison is remembered for his innovative style,
his flamboyant performances, and **his self-destructive behavior**.

CLAUSES
MIXED   In assembling the research team, Cryo-Com looked for engineers
whose work was creative, with broad interests, and who had boundless energy.

CLAUSES
PARALLEL   In assembling the research team, Cryo-Com looked for engineers
whose work was creative, **whose interests were broad**, **and whose
energy was boundless**.

Use parallelism with the seven **coordinating conjunctions** to heighten similarities or contrasts between the elements they link.

STRATEGY Join a parallel pair with *and, but, or, for, nor, so,* or *yet.*

WORDS
MIXED
A well-trained scientist keeps a detailed lab notebook and the entries made accurately.

WORDS
PARALLEL
A well-trained scientist keeps a **detailed and accurate** lab notebook.

PHRASES
MIXED
First-year chemistry teaches students how to take notes on an experiment and the ways of writing a lab report.

PHRASES
PARALLEL
First-year chemistry teaches students **how to take notes on an experiment** and **how to write a lab report**.

The **correlative conjunctions** call special attention to a relationship or a contrast between two elements.

STRATEGY Join a parallel pair with *both . . . and, not only . . . but also, either . . . or, neither . . . nor,* or *whether . . . or.*

DRAFT
Americans claim to marry "for love," yet their pairings follow clear social patterns. They choose partners from the same social class and economic level. Most marriages bring together people with similar educational and cultural backgrounds. Similarities in race and ethnic background are important as well.

EDITED
Americans claim to marry "for love," yet their pairings follow clear social patterns. They choose partners not only **with the same class and economic background** but also **with the same educational, cultural, racial, and ethnic background**.

27
//

A **list** can summarize key points, instructions, or stages.

STRATEGY Use parallel form for items in a list.

The early 1960s were characterized by several social changes.

UNEDITED (CONFUSING)
1. A growing civil rights movement
2. Emphasis increased on youth in culture and politics.
3. Taste in music and the visual arts was changing.

EDITED FOR PARALLELISM (CLEAR)

1. **A growing** civil rights movement
2. **An increasing** emphasis on youth in culture and politics
3. **A changing** taste in music and the visual arts

2 Build clear parallel patterns

Repeat or state words that complete grammatical or idiomatic patterns. You needn't repeat the same lead-in word for all items in a series.

Mosquitoes can breed **in** puddles, ~~in~~ ponds, and ~~in~~ swimming pools

STRATEGY State lead-in words needed for complete patterns.

INCOMPLETE   The main character from the novel *Tarzan of the Apes* has appeared on television, films, and comic books.
READER'S REACTION: **I doubt he was on films or on comic books.**

EDITED   The main character from the novel *Tarzan of the Apes* has appeared **on** television, **in** films, and **in** comic books.

3 Use parallelism to organize clusters

27.2

You can use parallelism to strengthen **sentence clusters**, groups of sentences that develop related ideas or information. The parallel elements can clarify difficult information, highlight the overall pattern of argument or explanation, link examples, or guide readers through steps or stages.

STRATEGY Build parallel elements in a sentence cluster.

Each of us probably belongs to groups whose values conflict. **You may belong to** a religious organization that **endorses restraint in** alcohol use or **in** relations between the sexes while **you also belong to** a social group with activities that **support contrasting values. You may belong to** a sports team **that supports** competing and winning and a club **that promotes** understanding among people.

You can also use parallelism, as simple as brief opening phrases, to reinforce the overall pattern of a cluster of paragraphs.

STRATEGY Try parallel paragraph openers.

One reason for approving this proposal now is . . .
A second reason for action is . . .
The most important reason for taking immediate steps is . . .

28 Using Coordination and Subordination

Suppose you were editing the following passage in a report.

California's farmers ship fresh lettuce, avocados, and other produce to supermarkets. They never send fresh olives. Fresh olives contain a substance that makes them bitter. They are very unpleasant tasting. Farmers soak fresh olives in a solution that removes oleuropein, the bitter-tasting substance. They leave just enough behind to produce the tangy "olive" taste.

READER'S REACTION: **This passage sounds choppy and disconnected.**

Using **coordination**, you could give equal emphasis to each statement.

California's farmers ship fresh lettuce, avocados, and other produce to supermarkets , **but** they never send fresh olives. Fresh olives contain a substance that makes them bitter , **so** they are very unpleasant tasting. Farmers soak fresh olives in a solution that removes oleuropein, the bitter-tasting substance ; **however** , they leave just enough behind to produce the tangy "olive" taste.

Using **subordination**, you could show the relative weight of ideas by beginning some sentences with words such as *because* and *though* and attaching these sentences to others.

California's farmers ship fresh lettuce, avocados, and other produce to supermarkets, **though** they never send fresh olives. **Because** fresh olives contain a substance that makes them bitter, they are very unpleasant tasting. **When** farmers soak fresh olives in a solution that removes oleuropein, the bitter-tasting substance, they leave just enough behind to produce the tangy "olive" taste.

28a Recognizing coordination

When you want to link words, clauses, or phrases and emphasize their equal weight, use coordination. When you coordinate main (independent) clauses, you create a single **compound sentence** (see 16d-1).

RELATIONSHIPS NOT SPECIFIED

Cats have no fear of water. They do not like wet and matted fur. Cats like to feel well groomed.

CLEAR RELATIONSHIPS

Cats have no fear of water , **but** they do not like wet and matted fur , **for** they like to feel well groomed.

163

CREATING AND PUNCTUATING COORDINATION

WORDS AND PHRASES

- Use *and*, *but*, *or*, *nor*, or *yet* (coordinating conjunctions).

  cut **and** hemmed   smooth **or** textured   intrigued **yet** suspicious

- Use pairs like *either . . . or*, *neither . . . nor*, and *not only . . . but also*.

  either music therapy **or** pet therapy

  neither spaghetti **nor** lasagne

  not only a nursing care plan **but also** a home care program

MAIN (INDEPENDENT) CLAUSES

- Use *and*, *but*, *or*, *for*, *nor*, *so*, or *yet* (coordinating conjunctions) preceded by a comma.

  The students observed the responses of shoppers to long lines **, and** they interviewed people waiting in line. Most people in the study were irritated by the checkout lines **, yet** a considerable minority enjoyed the wait.

- Use a semicolon (see 35a-1).

  The wait provoked physical reactions in some people **;** they fidgeted, grimaced, and stared at the ceiling.

- Use conjunctive adverbs like *however*, *moreover*, *nonetheless*, *thus*, and *consequently* preceded by a semicolon (see 35a-2).

  Store managers can take simple steps to speed up checkout lines **;** **however ,** they seldom pay much attention to the problem.

- Use a colon (see 35b-3).

  Tabloids and magazines in racks by the checkout counters serve a useful purpose **:** they give customers something to read while waiting.

EXPRESSING RELATIONSHIPS THROUGH COORDINATION

RELATIONSHIP	COORDINATING CONJUNCTION	CONJUNCTIVE ADVERB		
addition	, and	; in addition,	; furthermore,	
opposition or contrast	, but	; in contrast,		
	, yet	; however,	; nonetheless,	
result	, so	; therefore,	; consequently,	; thus,
cause	, for			
choice	, or	; otherwise,		
negation	, nor			

28b Recognizing subordination

Use subordination to create a sentence with unequal elements: one **main or independent clause** that presents the central idea and at least one

bordinate or dependent clause that modifies, qualifies, or comments on e main clause. You signal readers about this unequal relationship by beginng the subordinate clause with a word like *although* or *that* and by attaching to the main clause in a **complex sentence** (see 16d-1).

AIN CLAUSES Malcolm uses a computer to track clinic expenses. He knows how much we pay each year for lab tests.

JBORDINATED **Because** Malcolm uses a computer to track clinic expenses, he knows how much we pay each year for lab tests.

READER'S REACTION: **Now I know how the ideas relate—one is a cause and the other an effect.**

28c Editing for coordination and subordination

How can you tell if you're using too much or too little coordination or ubordination? Read your writing aloud. Watch for short, choppy sentences r long, dense passages. Check community expectations by noticing how eaders respond and what other writers do. Academic readers may favor subordination more than a work community that prefers directness.

28.1

STRATEGY Replace *and, so,* and *but* to add variety.

DRAFT Ripe fruit spoils quickly, **and** fresh grapefruit in markets is picked before it matures to avoid spoilage, **and** it can taste bitter, **but** grapefruit in cans is picked later, **and** it tastes sweeter.

EDITED Ripe fruit spoils quickly. Fresh grapefruit in markets is picked before it matures, **so** it may taste bitter. Grapefruit in cans is picked later; **consequently,** it tastes sweeter.

Simplify excessive subordination that overloads readers.

28c coor

STRATEGY Divide a sentence that has too much subordination.

CONFUSING The election for mayor will be interesting **because** the incumbent has decided to run as an independent **while** his former challenger for the Democratic nomination has decided to accept the party's endorsement **even though** the Republican nominee is her former campaign manager.

EDITED The election for mayor will be interesting. The incumbent has decided to run as an independent. His former challenger for the Democratic nomination has decided to accept the party's endorsement **even though** she will have to run against her former campaign manager.

CREATING AND PUNCTUATING SUBORDINATION

SUBORDINATING CONJUNCTIONS

- Use a subordinating conjunction such as *although* or *because* to create a subordinate clause at the beginning or end of a sentence (see 16c).
- Add a comma *after* an introductory clause that begins with a subordinating conjunction.

BEGINNING
Once she understood the problem, she easily solved it.

- At the end of a sentence, do not use a comma if the clause is *essential* to the meaning of the main clause (restrictive); use a comma if the clause is *not essential* (nonrestrictive). (See 34e.)

END (ESSENTIAL)
Radar tracking of flights began **after several commercial airliners collided in midair.**

END (NONESSENTIAL)
The present air traffic control system works reasonably well**, although accidents still occur.**

RELATIVE PRONOUNS

- You can use a relative pronoun (*who, which, that*) to create a relative clause (also called an adjective clause) at the end or in the middle of a sentence (see 16c-1).
- A relative clause that contains information *essential* to the meaning of the main clause is restrictive; do not set it off with commas.

RESTRICTIVE (ESSENTIAL)
The anthropologists discovered the site of a building **that early settlers used as a meetinghouse.**

RESTRICTIVE (ESSENTIAL)
The people **who organized the project** work for the Public Archaeology Lab.

- When the information is *not essential,* the subordinate clause is nonrestrictive; set it off with commas. (See 34e.)

NONRESTRICTIVE (NOT ESSENTIAL)
At one end of the site they found remains of a smaller building**, which may have been a storage shed.**

NONRESTRICTIVE (NOT ESSENTIAL)
A graduate student**, who was leading a dig nearby,** first discovered signs of the meetinghouse.

EXPRESSING RELATIONSHIPS THROUGH SUBORDINATION

Time	before, while, until, since, once, whenever, whereupon, after, when
Cause	because, since
Result	in order that, so that, that, so
Concession or contrast	although, though, even though, as if, while, even if
Place	where, wherever
Condition	if, whether, provided, unless, rather than
Comparison	as
Identification	that, which, who

Use the list of subordinating words (above) to expand your options.

STRATEGY   Replace inappropriate or ambiguous subordinating
words.

28.2

UNCLEAR
EMPHASIS   Since she taught middle school, Jean developed keen insight into
the behavior of twelve- and thirteen-year-olds.
**READER'S REACTION: Does *since* mean that she developed insight *because*
she was a teacher or *after* she quit teaching?**

EDITED   **Because** she taught middle school, Jean developed keen insight into
the behavior of twelve- and thirteen-year-olds.

Help readers see what matters most; put key ideas in a main clause and secondary ideas in a subordinate clause.

STRATEGY   Move your most important point to the main
clause.

DRAFT   His training and equipment were inferior, although Jim still set a
school record throwing the discus.
READER'S REACTION: Isn't Jim's achievement the key point?

EDITED   **Although** his training and equipment were inferior, Jim still set a
school record throwing the discus.

28c
coor
sub

ESL ADVICE: GRAMMATICAL STRUCTURES FOR COORDINATION AND SUBORDINATION

The following sentence has both a subordinator, *although*, and a coordinator, *but*. Use one pattern, not both at once.

MIXED
Although frogs can live both on land and in water, **but** the need to breathe oxygen.

CONSISTENT COORDINATION
main clause
Frogs can live both on land and in water, **but** they need to breathe oxygen.

main clause

CONSISTENT SUBORDINATION
subordinate clause
Although frogs can live both on land and in water, they need to breathe oxygen.

main clause

29 | Creating Clear and Emphatic Sentences

Most people would find the following sentence hard to read.

INDIRECT OR EVASIVE
It is suggested that employee work cooperation encouragement be used for product quality improvement.

READER'S REACTION: **Who is suggesting this? What is "employee work cooperation encouragement"?**

CLEAR
We will try to improve our products by encouraging employees to work cooperatively.

You can make sentences easier to read by creating clear subjects and verbs as well as direct sentence structures. In college papers, clarity helps readers follow even complex reasoning. At work, clear sentences present problems and solutions directly; in public, they support productive civic dialogue.

29a Recognizing unclear sentences

A clear sentence answers the question "Who does what (to whom)?" When a sentence doesn't readily answer this question, try to make its subject and verb easy to identify. (See 16a.)

ESL

29a
lear

AR

	subject	verb	object

The research team investigated seizure disorders in infants.

who?   **does what?**

AR

subject   verb

The seizures often become harmful.

who?   **does what?**

...u can create complex yet clear sentences by making the main elements—
...pecially subjects and verbs—easy for readers to identify.

...CLEAR   One suggestion offered by physicians is that there is a
need to be especially observant of a child's behavior during the first six months in order to notice any evidence of
seizures.

...EAR   Physicians suggest that parents watch children carefully
during the first six months for evidence of seizures.

29b Editing for clear sentences

As you edit for clarity, work on any recurring sentence features identi-
...ed by your readers, or test the strategies below.

Concentrate on nouns and subjects

Sentences whose subjects name important ideas, people, topics, things,
...r events are generally easy for readers to understand.

STRATEGY Ask questions to clarify significant subjects.

- Who (or what) am I talking about here?
- Is this what I want to emphasize?

UNFOCUSED   You run the greatest risk if you expose yourself to tanning
machines as well as the sun because both of them can
damage the skin.

READER'S REACTION: I thought the focus was the danger, whether
sunbathing or tanning. Why are they both buried in the middle?

**POSSIBLE
REVISION**   Either **the sun or a tanning machine** can damage the
skin, and you run the greatest risk from exposure to **both**
of them.

29b
clear

When you create a noun (*completion*, *happiness*) from another kind of wo[rd] such as a verb (*complete*) or adjective (*happy*), the result is a **nominalizatio[n]** often ending in *-tion*, *-ence*, *-ance*, *-ing*, or *-ness*. Nominalizations useful[ly] name ideas but may obscure information or distract readers from your foc[us.] Be sure each sentence tells who did what (to whom).

USEFUL   **Sleepiness** causes accidents at work and on the road.

STRATEGY Replace weak nominalizations with clear subjects.

WEAK   Stimulation of the production of serotonin by a glass of milk [or] a carbohydrate snack causes sleepiness.

> READER'S REACTION: **Why does this advice on getting a good night['s] sleep start off with *stimulation*?**

EDITED   **A glass of milk or a carbohydrate snack** stimulates the pro-duction of serotonin and causes sleepiness.

Sometimes one noun modifies another or nouns plus adjectives mod[-]ify other nouns: *sleep deprivation, jet lag, computer network server, triple bypas[s] heart surgery*. Although unfamiliar **noun strings** can be hard to understand[,] familiar ones can be concise and clear.

STRATEGY Specify the focus to rework a noun string.

Try turning the key word in a string (usually the last noun) into a verb[.] Then turn other nouns from the string into prepositional phrases.

CONFUSING   The team did a ceramic valve lining design flaw analysis.

> READER'S REACTION: **Did the team analyze flaws or use a special feature called flaw analysis? Did they study ceramic valves or valve linings made of ceramic material?**

EDITED   The team **analyzed** flaws **in** the lining design **for** ceramic valves.

Another option is to turn one noun into the sentence's subject.

EDITED   **Flaws** in the lining design for ceramic valves were analyzed by the team.

I, we, and *you*, though inappropriate in some academic settings, are com-monly used in work and public communities. (See 25a.)

| VAGUE AND
WEAK | The project succeeded because of careful cost control and attention to the customer's needs. |

| CLEAR AND
FORCEFUL | The project succeeded because **we** controlled costs carefully and paid attention to **our** customers' needs. |

STRATEGY Use *I*, *we*, and *you* when appropriate.

Analyze community expectations to see what other writers do and how readers respond—what they take seriously, what they find effective (see 8b).

Concentrate on verbs and predicates

Strong verbs can make sentences forceful and clear.

STRATEGY Replace weak verbs.

- Consider replacing the verb *be* (*is, are, was, were, will be*) with a more forceful verb, especially in sentences that list or identify qualities.

    | WEAK | Our agency **is** responsible for all aspects of disaster relief. |
    | STRONGER | Our agency **plans**, **funds**, and **delivers** disaster relief. |

- Replace **expletive** constructions, sentences beginning with *there is*, *there are*, or *it is* (see 16a-1), if they are wordy or obscure. (Leave them if they add variety, build suspense, or usefully withhold information about the doer.)

    | WEAK | **There is** a need for more classrooms at Kenny School. |
    | STRONGER | **Kenny School needs** more classrooms. |

- Turn predicate nouns into clear, specific verbs.

    | WEAK | The new recycling system is a **money saver**. |
    | STRONGER | The new recycling system **saves money**. |

- Eliminate general verbs (*do, give, have, get, provide, shape, make*) linked to nouns; turn the nouns into verbs.

    | WEAK | Our company **has done a study** of the new design project. |
    | STRONGER | Our company **has studied** the new design project. |

29b
clea

ESL ADVICE: *THERE* AND *IT* AS SUBJECTS

When you use *there* and *it* as the subjects of sentences, these pronouns may not have the object or place meanings usually attached to them. They may introduce new, unknown material, while *it* may introduce environmental conditions (including distance, time, and weather).

DRAFT	Although there was snowing, it was dancing after dinner.
EDITED	Although **it** was snowing, **there** was dancing after dinner.

Readers may find a sentence difficult if they have to hunt for the subject and verb (or parts of the verb) because a long phrase separates them.

STRATEGY Reorganize to keep the verb close to the subject.

CONFUSING	The veterinary association, **in response to the costly guidelines for disposal of medical waste**, has created a low-cost loan program for its members.
EDITED	The veterinary association has created a low-cost loan program for its members **in response to the costly guidelines for disposal of medical waste**.

---

3 Select active or passive voice

When you use a verb in the **active voice** (see 17i), the agent (or doer) is also the subject of the sentence.

agent   action   goal
The outfielder caught the towering fly ball.
subject   verb   object

When you choose the **passive voice** (see 17i), you turn the sentence's goal into the subject. You de-emphasize the doer by placing it in a prepositional phrase or by dropping an unknown or unimportant agent altogether.

goal   action   [agent]
The towering fly ball was caught [by the outfielder].
subject   verb   [prepositional phrase]

Many writers favor the active voice because it is direct and concise, and many readers find too much passive voice weak. On the other hand, the passive voice may be favored in lab reports and other scientific or technical writing in both academic and work communities. It avoids spotlighting the researcher or repeating the researcher's actions; instead it focuses on results—what happens, not who does it. It also may be used ethically to protect someone's identity, such as a child or the victim of crime or abuse. On the other

nd, it may inadvertently, or even deliberately, conceal a doer (or agent),
us obscuring responsibility for actions.

ENT
-EMPHASIZED
Federal tax forms have been mailed. [By the IRS, of course.]

ENT
NCEALED
Hasty decisions were made in this zoning case. [By whom?]

STRATEGY Rewrite sentences with unnecessary passive voice.

Reconsider sentences in the passive voice that add extra words, create
appropriate emphasis, or omit the doer (see 25e–f).

ASSIVE VOICE
5 WORDS)
subject
Three thousand people affected by the toxin were interviewed
agent
by **the Centers for Disease Control**.

CTIVE VOICE
13 WORDS)
agent (subject)
The Centers for Disease Control interviewed three thousand
people affected by the toxin.

Create variety and emphasis

If you feel that editing for clarity produces too many similar sentences,
ry some of the following options to direct the attention of your readers.

STRATEGY Polish your sentences for variety and emphasis.

- Emphasize material by shifting it to the places where a reader's attention gravitates—the **sentence opening or closing**.
- **Repeat key words and ideas** within a sentence or cluster of sentences to draw attention to them. (Avoid too much repetition that calls
  attention to itself rather than your ideas.)
- Try **climactic sentence order**—sentences that build to a climax—to
  create powerful emphasis. Such sentences can stress new information
  at the end or focus on the last element in a series.
- By piling up phrases, clauses, and words at the start, creating suspense
  by delaying the main clause, try an occasional **periodic sentence**.
- Consider creating a **cumulative sentence**. Start with the main clause,
  and then add, bit by bit, details and ideas in the form of modifying
  phrases, clauses, and words to build a detailed picture, an intricate explanation, or a cluster of ideas and information.
- Vary your **sentence length**. Add short sentences for dramatic flair. Use
  longer ones to explore relationships among ideas and build rhythmic

29b
clea

effects. Use middle-length sentences as workhorses, carrying the burden of explanation, but don't use too many in a sequence.

- Vary your sentence types (see 16d-2). **Declarative sentences** present, explain, and support ideas or information. An occasional exclamation (**exclamatory sentence**), a mild order (**imperative sentence**), or a question (**interrogative sentence**) can change your pace.
- Surprise your readers on occasion. Add **key words** to summarize and redirect a sentence. **Extend a sentence** that appears to have ended, adding new information or twists of thought. Use parallelism (see 27b) to highlight a contrast in a witty, dramatic, or ironic **antithesis**.

TAKING IT ONLINE

MERRIAM-WEBSTER ONLINE
http://www.m-w.com

THE AMERICAN HERITAGE DICTIONARY OF THE ENGLISH LANGUAGE
http://www.bartleby.com/61/
Each dictionary site encourages you to type in a word and find its definition, history, and pronunciation.

THESAURUS.COM
http://www.thesaurus.com/
Simply enter a word on the site, hit "Return" to see a list of synonyms, and then click on each of those for dozens more.

GENDER FAIR LANGUAGE
http://www.rpi.edu/dept/llc/writecenter/web/genderfair.html
Use the suggestions on this page to avoid sexist slips.

IDIOMS, PHRASAL VERBS, AND SLANG QUIZZES
http://www.aitech.ac.jp/~iteslj/quizzes/idioms.html
This Web site can help ESL students and native speakers alike learn some of the most common English idioms. More than fifty links to short quizzes are sorted by category.

WORLD WIDE WORDS
http://www.quinion.com/words/
This engaging site encourages you to think about word choice and precise meaning. Check out the "Topical Words" and "Weird Words" sections to see how new and strange words come into use.

A.WORD.A.DAY
http://www.wordsmith.org/awad/
Do you want to build your vocabulary? This site archives one of the Internet's most popular mailing lists, sending out a word each day.

SECTION 5
Editing Word Choice:
Matching Words to Communities

30 | Being Concise

Leaving extra words in your writing wastes valuable space—and your readers' time.

WORDY
> **There is evidence that the use of** pay **as an** incentive **can be a contributing or causal factor in** improvement **of the** quality **of** work.
> READER'S REACTION: Why is this so long-winded? What's the point?

TRIMMED
> Incentive pay improves work quality.
> READER'S REACTION: That's short and direct—but maybe too abrupt.

RESHAPED
> Incentive pay **often encourages** work **of higher** quality.
> READER'S REACTION: Now I'm gaining a fuller, more subtle perspective.

Conciseness means using only the words you need—not the fewest words possible, but those appropriate for your purpose, meaning, and readers. (See 29b and 31b.) Readers favor concise writing for efficiency at work, lucidity in college, and clear advocacy in public. Your situation may define the conciseness necessary: letters to the editor have word limits, speeches have time limits, and most grant proposals have page limits. Adhere to these limits—check length, run a word count, or rehearse an oral presentation.

30a Recognizing common types of wordiness

Imagine an ideal reader—a respected teacher, a savvy co-worker, or a wise civic leader. If a passage seems wordy, ask, "What would I need to tell X here?" Or think of X asking, "What's your point?"

Look for **wordy phrases** you can shrink to a word or two.

WORDY
> Carbon 14 can be used to date a site only **in the event that** organic material has survived. **In a situation in which** rocks need dating, potassium-argon testing is used.

CUT
> Carbon 14 can be used to date a site only **if** organic material has survived. **When** rocks need dating, potassium-argon testing is used.

Watch for **intensifying phrases** (*for all intents and purposes, in my opinion*), intended to add force but often carrying little meaning.

COMMON WORDY PHRASES

PHRASE		REPLACEMENT
due to the fact that	=	because
at the present moment	=	now
a considerable proportion of	=	many, most
has the capability of	=	can
regardless of the fact that	=	although
concerning the matter of	=	about

WORDY   **As a matter of fact**, most archaeological discoveries can b[e] dated accurately.

CUT   Most archaeological discoveries can be dated accurately.

Target clutter such as **all-purpose words** (like *factor, aspect, situation, type* *field, range, thing, kind, nature*) and **all-purpose modifiers** (like *very, totally major, central, great, really, definitely, absolutely*).

WORDY   In the short story, Young Goodman Brown is so **totally** over whelmed by **his own** guilt that he becomes **extremely** sus picious of the people around him. [25 words]

CUT   In the short story, Young Goodman Brown is so overwhelmed by guilt that he becomes suspicious of the people around him. [21 words]

REWRITTEN   In the short story, Young Goodman Brown's **overwhelming** guilt makes him **suspect everyone**. [13 words]

Simplify pairs that say the same thing twice (*each and every*) and **redundant phrases** in which adjectives repeat nouns (*final outcomes*), adverbs repeat verbs (*completely finished*), or specific words imply general (*small in size*).

WORDY   Because it was **sophisticated in nature** and **tolerant in style**, Kublai Khan's administration aided China's development in the 1200s.

CUT   Because it was **sophisticated and tolerant**, Kublai Khan's administration aided China's development in the 1200s.

REWRITTEN   Kublai Khan's **adept and tolerant administration** aided China's development in the 1200s.

30b Editing for conciseness

Edit both wordy expressions and wordy sentence patterns (see 29b).

Look for diction appropriate for a specialized context

Adjust your diction to your workplace or academic discipline, using
e specialized and precise language required in that context.

O GENERAL | [*in an analysis of a painting for an art history course*] Tiepolo's
Apotheosis of the Pisani Family (1761) is a lively painting typical of the period when it was painted with lots of action going
on and nice colors.

READER'S REACTION: **This wording seems too general for an analysis
in my field of art history.**

DITED | Tiepolo's *Apotheosis of the Pisani Family* (1761) shows affinities
with typical rococo frescoes of the period, including bright
colors with characters in highlighted actions set against dark
border accents.

Look for diction that meets your readers' expectations

In college and workplace writing that assumes a fairly formal diction,
void **colloquialisms**, informal expressions typical of a region or group. In
nformal and public contexts, avoid pretension.

OO INFORMAL | The stock market crash didn't seem to **faze** many of the inves-
tors with **megabucks stashed** in property assets.

READER'S REACTION: **This seems so informal that I'm not sure I trust
the writer's authority.**

DITED | The stock market crash did not profoundly affect investors with
extensive property assets.

3 Look for diction that supports your purpose

In order to inform or persuade readers, academic, work, and public communities alike may favor balanced reasoning over highly emotional language.

BIASED | Most proponents of rock-music censorship grew up listening
to pablum, thinking wimpy bands like the Beach Boys were a
bunch of perverts.

READER'S REACTION: **This writer seems too biased and emotional to
weigh all sides of the debate.**

EDITED | Proponents of rock-music censorship may unfairly stereotype
all of rock-and-roll culture as degenerate or evil.

4 Look for diction that suits your persona

Your **persona** is the role or character you assume in your writing. For
example, an objective, detached persona in a clinical report assures a reader
of accuracy, but this same persona might seem cold and impersonal in the
adoption column of the animal shelter newsletter.

31a
wor

TOO CLINICAL FOR CONTEXT   Three domestic canines, *Canis familiaris*, type Shetland shee[p] dog; age: 8 weeks; coloring: burnt umber with variegated blo[r] diameters; behaviorally modified for urination and defecatio[n] inoculated.

READER'S REACTION: **Why would someone at the shelter talk so unca[r]ingly about the puppies, treating them like laboratory specimen[s]**

EDITED   Three healthy sheltie puppies 8 weeks old, brown with lig[ht] spots, housebroken, all shots.

31b Editing for precise diction

When you choose among **synonyms**, words identical or nearly so i[n] meaning, consider their **connotations**—"shades" of meaning or association[s] acquired over time. Use concrete, direct wording unless the context calls fo[r] specialized language or more abstraction.

STRATEGY   **Pick precise, concrete, and direct words.**

- Replace an inexact word with an appropriate synonym.

  IMPRECISE   The senator **retreated** from the gathering.

  READER'S REACTION: **Did the senator feel attacked, bewildered, o[r] overcome? Or did she just leave?**

  EDITED   The senator **left** the gathering.

- Replace vague words with specific ones.

  VAGUE   [*in a do-it-yourself brochure on bathroom remodeling*] Do no[t] place flooring over uneven floor or damaged area.
  READER'S REACTION: **What's this about a damaged area?**

  EDITED   Do not **install** flooring over **existing** floors that are **uneven or show signs of wood rot**. **Replace** any damaged **flooring material before installing new flooring**.

- Stick mostly to simple, familiar words.

  STUFFY   The reflections upon premarital cohabitation promulgated by the courts eventuated in the orientation of the population in the direction of moral relaxation on this issue.
  READER'S REACTION: **How dull! Say it more plainly, please.**

  EDITED   Court decisions about living together before marriage led to greater public acceptance of this practice.

31.1

Idioms are expressions, often with "forgotten histories," whose meanings differ from their literal definitions, as in *wipe the slate clean* for "start over." Overused idioms can lose their freshness, becoming **trite** or **clichéd**.

STRATEGY **Replace trite idioms with precise words.**

IDIOMATIC The losers complained of **dog-eat-dog** politics.

EDITED The losers consoled themselves after their defeat.

ESL ADVICE: IDIOMS IN AMERICAN ENGLISH

Whether an expression is an **idiom** or a **phrasal verb** (see 15c), the meanings of its separate words will not reveal its meaning as a whole. Although memorizing idioms will enrich your spoken English, these expressions may be too informal in many writing situations. In class or at work, notice how many and which idioms appear in well-written papers by native speakers; adjust your usage accordingly.

32 | Using Respectful Language

To represent others fairly, writers and editors eliminate sexist and discriminatory language from their work.

DRAFT Early in his career, Lasswell published his **seminal** work on propaganda.

READER 1: Why do you have to use this word? It's offensive to associate originality and creativity with being male.

READER 2: You could replace *seminal* with *important* or *influential*.

READER 3: Aren't you overreacting? You wouldn't throw out *matrimony* just because it's related to the Latin word for *mother* or *patriot* because it comes from the word for *father*.

No matter how you feel about diversity, as a writer you *must* consider how readers react to your representation of men, women, and members of minority groups. You don't want to alienate readers, prejudice people against your ideas, or perpetuate unhealthy attitudes.

ESL

32
lan

32.1

32a Recognizing and editing stereotypes based on gender

The most common form of sexist language uses *mankind* or *men* f[or] humankind; *he*, *his*, or *him* for all people; and words implying men in occu[]-pations (*fireman*). When editing the generic *he*, try first to make the constru[c]-tion plural (for example, use *their* for *his* or for the clumsy *his or her*).

SEXIST	Every trainee should bring **his** laptop with **him**.
AWKWARD	Every trainee should bring **his or her** laptop with **him o**[r] **her**.
BETTER	All trainees should bring **their** laptops with **them**.

Some guides suggest that a plural pronoun is better than the generic *he*, eve[n] if the pronoun does not agree in number with the subject (see 19b). Som[e] readers, however, object more strenuously to the agreement error than to th[e] sexist language. Reword to avoid both problems.

ORIGINAL	**Everyone** has at some time squandered **his** money.
PROBLEMATIC	**Everyone** has at some time squandered **their** money.
BETTER	**Most people have** at some time squandered **their** money. **Everyone** has at some time squandered money.

Your readers are likely to object to negative stereotypes based on gen-der, such as assumptions that men are stronger or women are worse at math.

STRATEGY Watch for stereotyped roles and occupations.

STEREOTYPED The OnCall Pager is **smaller than most doctors' wallets and easier to answer than phone calls from their wives.**

> READER'S REACTION: I'm a woman and a doctor. I'm insulted by the as-sumption that all doctors are male and by the negative reference to "wives." OnCall will never sell a pager in my office!

EDITED The OnCall Pager **will appeal to doctors because it is small and easy to operate**.

32.2

32b Recognizing and editing racial, ethnic, and cultural stereotypes

Most readers won't tolerate racism and will stop reading material with **discriminatory language**. Don't rely on your intent; think about how your reader *might* construe your words.

DEMEANING

My paper focuses on the **weird** courtship rituals of a **barbaric** Aboriginal tribe in southwestern Australia.

READER'S REACTION: **Your paper sounds biased. How can you treat this topic fairly if you don't respect the tribe?**

EDITED

My paper focuses on the unique courtship rituals of an Aboriginal tribe in southwestern Australia.

Some racial and cultural stereotypes are so ingrained that you may not notice them at first. You may be used to hearing derogatory terms in others' speech, or you may not even know that a term is derogatory.

STRATEGY **Ask readers to help you spot biased terms.**

Trusted readers can circle stereotypes and derogatory wording for you, and you can do the same for them.

RACIST

The economic problems in border states are compounded by an increased number of **wetbacks** from Mexico.

READER'S REACTION: **This derogatory name is offensive. I object to characterizing a group of people this way.**

EDITED

The economic problems in border states are compounded by an increased number of illegal immigrants from Mexico.

HOMOPHOBIC

The talk show included a panel of **fags** who spoke about what it's like to be a **homo**.

READER'S REACTION: **Emotionally loaded names for people don't encourage reasonable discussion. You'll have to be more objective if you want me to pay attention to your ideas.**

EDITED

The talk show included a panel of gay guests who shared their thoughts about homosexuality.

DEROGATORY

In typical **white-male** fashion, the principal argued against the teachers' referendum.

READER'S REACTION: **The fact that white men are in the majority doesn't give you permission to stereotype them negatively.**

EDITED

The principal argued against the teachers' referendum.

DISCRIMINATORY

The Johnsons **welshed** on their promise.

READER'S REACTION: **What made you think that you could say this without offending people of Welsh descent? Casual stereotyping is just as offensive as deliberate insults.**

EDITED

The Johnsons broke their promise.

Deciding how to identify groups may be difficult. The term *American Indian* is still widely accepted, but *Native American* is preferred. In the 1960s,

32
lar

Negro gradually gave way to *black*, but *African American* has gained popular ity in its place. *Colored* has been out of use for some time, but *people of color* now preferred for members of any "nonwhite" group (though some object t *nonwhite*). Terms for those of Hispanic descent include *Chicano* (and its femi nine form, *Chicana*) for Mexicans and *Latino* and *Latina* for people from South and Central America in general.

STRATEGY Use community acceptance to help you identify groups.

- Whenever possible, use the term preferred *by the group itself.*
- When there is disagreement within the group, choose the *most widely accepted term* or one favored by a majority of the members.

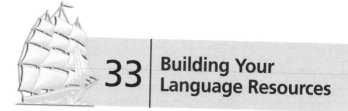

33 | Building Your Language Resources

The richer your vocabulary, the better you write and read.

CIVIC NEWSLETTER

Despite our efforts to lobby for a compromise, the senate en gaged in an **internecine** feud over the bill.

READER'S REACTION: I like *internecine* here to suggest the senate's de structive internal conflict.

WORK MEMO

Thanks to the marketing team for its **stellar** effort.

READER'S REACTION: What a nice way to say "job well done"!

A varied vocabulary is essential to effective writing and easier reading in aca demic, work, and public communities. The more extensive your language options, the more varied, accurate, and metaphoric your prose can be. And readers will appreciate your efforts to find just the right word.

33a Recognizing your language resources as a writer

The writer can rework this sentence for a grant proposal *because she has options*—words like *beneficence* or *sustenance.*

Without **help**, the food-shelf program may be **ineffective**.

Without the **aid** of the Talbot Foundation, the food-shelf program may become **obsolete**.

Without the **beneficence** of the Talbot Foundation, the food-shelf program may **die**.

Without the **financial** beneficence of the Talbot Foundation, the food-shelf program in Seattle may die **of starvation**.

Without the financial **sustenance** of the Talbot Foundation, Seattle's food-shelf program may **slowly** die of starvation.

STRATEGY Build a personal vocabulary list.

Use your **journal** (a record of your observations and insights) or any notebook to list unfamiliar words. Look them up, review them, incorporate them as you write, and cross them out when you can use them comfortably. Gather these words from whatever you read—public opinion pieces in the newspaper, textbooks for school, or technical materials at work.

33b Turning to the dictionary and the thesaurus

33.1

Hundreds of times you've flipped the dictionary open and checked a word's spelling or meaning. Look carefully to find much more. (See Figure 33.1, an example from *Merriam-Webster's Collegiate Dictionary*.) Like the printed versions, software dictionaries may also supply definitions, usage notes, word histories, and spelling correctors that can be personalized by adding words used often in a particular community (see 14d).

> Word Division   Pronunciation   Grammatical Function (Part of Speech)   Etymology (Origin or History)
>
> **col·lege** \'kälij\ *n often attrib* [ME, fr. MF, fr. L *collegium* society, fr. *collega* colleague—more at COLLEAGUE](14c) **1:** a body of clergy living together and supported by a foundation **2:** a building used for an educational or religious purpose **3a:** a self-governing constituent body of a university offering living quarters and instruction, but not granting degrees <Balliol and Magdalen *Colleges* at Oxford> **b :** a preparatory or high school **c:** an independent institution of higher learning offering a course of general studies leading to a bachelor's degree **d:** a part of a university offering a specialized group of courses **e:** an institution offering instruction usu. in a professional, vocational, or technical field <business~> **4:** COMPANY, GROUP; *specific:* an organized body of persons engaged in a common pursuit or having common interests or duties **5a:** a group of persons considered by law to be a unit **b:** a body of electors—compare ELECTORAL COLLEGE **6:** the faculty, students, or administration of a college

Meaning → (line 2)
Examples → (Colleges at Oxford)
Example in Context → (line <business~>)
Cross-Reference → (compare ELECTORAL COLLEGE)

FIGURE 33.1 Sample dictionary entry

33 dc

A **thesaurus**, printed or electronic, is a dictionary of **synonyms** an **antonyms**—words related or opposite in meaning. Under *funny*, for exan ple, *Webster's Collegiate Thesaurus* lists synonyms such as *laughable, comica ludicrous*, and *ridiculous*. Entries may also refer you to contrasted or con pared words and related alternatives.

STRATEGY   Develop your skills as a "wordsmith."

- **Use a dictionary**. Circle any words you've learned recently or rarel used; look them up to be sure you've used them correctly. Try an ES dictionary if you're not a native speaker.
- **Turn to a thesaurus**. Consider whether a new word choice is mor accurate, more flavorful, or less redundant than your original choice. I in doubt, stick with words you know.
- **Learn a new word every day**. Select a word you read or hear a school, at work, or in a public setting. Look up its definition and his tory. Work it into your speech or writing three times during the day, o make up sentences and repeat them to yourself.
- **Try the slash/option technique**. As you draft, note alternative words, separated with slashes. Decide later which word fits best.
- **Fight insecurity with simplicity**. Ask yourself which salesperson you would trust—one who talks in simple, honest language or one who uses fancy words for product features. Choose direct, concrete words yourself.
- **Ask a colleague or supervisor**. Someone more experienced may be able to tell you whether a term fits your community or context.

TAKING IT ONLINE

PUNCTUATION WORKSHOP

http://www.citadel.edu/citadel/otherserv/wctr/punct.html#practice

Beginning with an incorrectly punctuated paragraph, this site aims to help you revise that paragraph and learn more about punctuation.

PUNCTUATION QUIZZES FOR ESL WRITERS

http://www.pacificnet.net/~sperling/quiz/punctuation1.html
http://www.pacificnet.net/~sperling/quiz/punctuation2.html

These two quizzes are aimed at helping ESL students to distinguish the comma and the semicolon and to use other marks correctly.

PUNCTUATION MADE SIMPLE

http://chuma.cas.usf.edu/~olson/pms/

This Web site aims to help writers overcome their fear of punctuation, starting with a reassuring essay and covering the colon, semicolon, comma, dash, and apostrophe.

"DASH IT! THE ELUSIVE APOSTROPHE"

http://www.rightwords.co.nz/apos.html

The brief article on this New Zealand–based Web site outlines how and when to use apostrophes.

WHEN TO USE—AND NOT TO USE—QUOTATION MARKS

http://www.wilbers.com/quotes.htm

This handy list of rules and instructions from the *Writing for Business and Pleasure* Web site also includes a helpful article: "Quotation Marks Make Reading Easy, Writing Hard."

GRAMMAR, PUNCTUATION, AND SPELLING

http://www.owl.english.purdue.edu/handouts/grammar/index.html

Browse here for punctuation advice and exercises.

SECTION 6
Editing Punctuation: Following Community Guidelines

34 | Using Commas

Of all the punctuation marks in English, the comma is probably the easiest to misuse.

DRAFT   During the study interviews were used to gather responses from participants and, to supplement written artifacts.
READER'S REACTION: This sentence is hard to read. I can't tell where ideas end and begin.

EDITED   During the study **,** interviews were used to gather responses from participants and to supplement written artifacts.

The fewest commas are probably expected in the public community and some workplaces that favor very direct action-oriented prose. In the academic community and other formal contexts, some commas are optional, but others are mandatory. Readers who expect commas in certain situations find inappropriate commas confusing or disruptive.

34a Recognizing commas that join sentences

When you use *and, but, or, for, nor, so,* or *yet* (**coordinating conjunctions**) to link two word groups that could stand alone as sentences (**main clauses**), place a comma *before* the conjunction.

The election was close **, and** he couldn't tell who was winning.

He heard no cheering **, yet** he decided to return to headquarters.

Precincts were still reporting **, but** the mayor's lead had grown.

34b Editing commas that join sentences

Join main clauses with a comma *plus* a coordinating conjunction. If you omit the conjunction and join the clauses with only a comma, you create a **comma splice** (see 22a). Readers will react more strongly if you omit a conjunction than a comma, but they'll see both as errors in formal writing.

COMMA SPLICE   The rain soaked the soil **,** the mud slide buried the road.

EDITED   The rain soaked the soil **, and** the mud slide buried the road.

34c
^
,

STRATEGY Examine the pair joined by a coordinating conjunction.

When a coordinating conjunction links two word groups, how can you decide whether to add a comma? Analyze the word groups. If both can stand on their own as sentences (main clauses), add a comma *before* the conjunction.

main clause, **(and, but, or, for,** main clause
nor, so, yet)
We wanted to deliver the order **,** **but** the weather was too bad.

If one or both of the groups *cannot* stand alone as a sentence (main clause), do *not* separate the items in the pair with a comma.

PAIR SPLIT	We sanded **,** and stained the old oak table.
EDITED	We **sanded** and **stained** the old oak table.
PAIR SPLIT	I bought the wood stain because it was inexpensive **,** and easy to clean up.
EDITED	I bought the wood stain **because it was inexpensive** and **easy to clean up.**

When two main clauses are very short, a comma is always appropriate but sometimes can be omitted, especially in public and informal contexts. Some academic readers, however, will expect you to use this comma in nearly every case to show your mastery of this convention.

The temperature dropped **and** the homeless shelters reopened.

34c Recognizing commas that set off sentence elements

A comma can help your readers distinguish potentially confusing sentence parts. The simplest sentences, consisting of a noun phrase and a verb phrase, need no comma.

noun phrase   verb phrase
Dr. Bandolo is my physician.

When you add another layer to the beginning—an **introductory word or word group**—you may need to signal the addition with a comma.

Although I am healthy , I see my doctor for a regular checkup.

For the past decade , Dr. Bandolo worked in an HMO.

Nonetheless , she may open her own practice.

The basic structure of a sentence can be interrupted with all sorts of **parenthetical expressions** that add information: **conjunctive adverbs** (*however, moreover;* see 28a), **transitional expressions** (*on the other hand, for example*),

nd **parenthetical remarks** or **interrupters** (*in fact*, *more importantly*). Use
ommas to set off these expressions.

RANSITIONAL	**On the other hand,** the hail caused severe damage.
TERRUPTER	It broke, **I think,** a dozen stained glass windows.
ONJUNCTIVE DVERB	We hope, **therefore,** that someone starts a repair fund.

also set off tag questions, statements of contrast, and direct address.

AG QUESTION	We should contribute, **shouldn't we?**
ONTRAST	The church's beauty touches all of us, **not just the members**.
DIRECT ADDRESS	Recall, **friends of beauty,** that every gift helps.

34d Editing commas that set off sentence elements

Readers usually expect a comma to simplify reading by signalling
where introductory wording ends and the main sentence begins.

STRATEGY Test an introductory word group for readability.

| CONFUSING | Forgetting to alert the media before the rally Jessica rushed to the park. |
| EDITED | Forgetting to alert the media before the rally, Jessica rushed to the park. |

In contrast, these sentences are easy to understand without a comma.

| CLEAR | By noon Jessica will be finished with her speech. |
| CLEAR | Suddenly it started raining, and Jessica quit speaking. |

In general, put a comma at the end of a long introductory element introduced
by a subordinating conjunction (*although*, *because*, *when*; see 28b–c), a preposition (*during*, *without*; see 15f), or a verbal (see 16b-4). Also use a comma if a
short introductory element might briefly confuse readers.

| CONFUSING | By six boats began showing up. |
| EDITED | By six, boats began showing up. |

Use a pair of commas around a parenthetical expression in the middle
of a sentence; use a single comma with one at the beginning or end.

STRATEGY Set off word groups that interrupt a sentence.

| DRAFT | Teams should meet even spontaneously as often as needed. |
| EDITED | Teams should meet, even spontaneously, as often as needed. |

34e Recognizing commas that set off nonessential modifiers

Modifiers qualify or describe nouns, verbs, or other sentence elements. You change the meaning of a sentence when you decide whether to set off modifying word or phrase with commas. You use a **restrictive modifier** to present essential information. Add it *without* commas so that readers see it as a necessary, integral part of the sentence.

RESTRICTIVE   The charts **drawn by hand** were hard to read.

> READER'S REACTION: I assume that the other charts, maybe generated on a computer, were easier to read than these.

You use a **nonrestrictive modifier** to add information that is interesting or useful but not necessary for the meaning. Set it off *with* commas so that readers regard it as helpful but nonessential detail.

NONRESTRICTIVE   The charts **,** **drawn by hand** **,** were hard to read.

> READER'S REACTION: All the charts were hard to read. The detail that they were hand drawn doesn't necessarily relate to readability.

STRATEGY   Test for nonrestrictive and restrictive modifiers.

Drop the test modifier from the sentence. If you can do so without altering the essential meaning, even if the sentence is less informative, the modifier is *nonrestrictive*. Set it off with commas.

DRAFT   Their band **which performs primarily in small clubs** has gotten fine reviews.

DROP TEST   Their band has gotten fine reviews.

> The meaning is the same, though the sentence does not offer as much interesting information. The modifier is nonrestrictive.

COMMAS ADDED   Their band **,** **which performs primarily in small clubs** **,** has gotten fine reviews.

If dropping the modifier changes the meaning of the sentence, the modifier is *restrictive*. Delete any commas with it.

DRAFT   Executives **,** **who do not know how to cope with stress** **,** are prone to stress-related illness.

DROP TEST   Executives are prone to stress-related illness.

> The intended meaning is that *some* executives are prone to stress-related problems; in contrast, the shortened sentence says they *all* are. The modifier is restrictive.

COMMAS
OMITTED   Executives **who do not know how to cope with stress** are prone to stress-related illness.

though the terms for these modifiers may be hard to remember, the distinction they identify is important to readers in all communities.

STRATEGY Memorize the modifiers formula.

*non*restrictive = *non*essential = *not* integrated (separated by commas)
restrictive   = essential   = integrated (not separated by commas)

34f Editing commas that set off nonessential modifiers

Readers expect you to connect punctuation and meaning for a **restrictive modifier** (with information essential to meaning) or a **nonrestrictive modifier** (with interesting, useful, but nonessential information).

STRATEGY Place commas before, after, or around nonrestrictive modifiers.

| | nonrestrictive | |
| main clause begins, | modifier, | main clause ends |

The public hearing **,** set for 7 p.m. **,** will address cable TV rates.

| nonrestrictive modifier, | main clause |

Because of rising costs **,** the companies have requested a rate hike.

| main clause, | nonrestrictive modifier |

Many residents oppose the hike **,** which is larger than last year's.

Clauses with *who*, *which*, and *that*. Use commas to set off nonrestrictive clauses beginning with *who*, *which*, *whom*, *whose*, *when*, or *where* (see 16c). Because *that* can specify rather than simply add information, it is used in restrictive (essential) clauses. *Which* is often used to add nonessential information but can be used both ways.

NONRESTRICTIVE	Preventive dentistry **,** **which is receiving great emphasis ,** may actually reduce visits to the dentist's office.
NONRESTRICTIVE	At the heart of preventive dentistry are toothbrushing, flossing, and rinsing **,** **which are all easily done**.
RESTRICTIVE	Dentists **who make a special effort to encourage good oral hygiene** often supply helpful pamphlets.
RESTRICTIVE	They also provide samples of toothbrushes and floss **that encourage preventive habits**.

Appositives. An **appositive** is a noun or pronoun that renames or stands for a preceding noun. Most are nonrestrictive and need commas.

34h
∧
⌄

| NONRESTRICTIVE | Amy Nguyen**,** **a poet from Vietnam,** recently publishe her latest collection of verse. |
| RESTRICTIVE | The well-known executive **Louis Gerstner** went from head ing RJR Nabisco to the top job at IBM. |

34g Recognizing and editing commas that separate items in a series

34.2

When you list items of roughly equal status in a series, separate th items with commas. Readers expect such commas because reading a serie can be difficult, even confusing, without them.

> The human relations office has forms for medical benefits**,** insuranc options**, and** retirement contributions.

If an item has more than one part, put a comma after the entire unit.

> The human relations office has forms for medical and dental benefits**,** disability and insurance options**, and** retirement contributions.

Avoid confusion by placing a comma before the *and* that introduces the last item in a series. Outside the academic community, this comma is often omitted, especially in a short, clear list. Within the academic community, however, both the MLA and APA style guides recommend this comma because it reduces ambiguity (see Chapters 51 and 52).

CONFUSING	New members fill out applications, interest-group surveys, mailing labels and publication request forms.
	READER'S REACTION: **Does** *mailing labels and publication request forms* **refer to one item or two?**
EDITED	New members fill out applications, interest-group surveys, mailing labels**,** and publication request forms.

Punctuate a numbered or lettered list in a sentence as a series. If items in a list contain commas, separate them with semicolons (see 35a-3).

> You should (a) measure the water's salinity**,** (b) weigh any waste in the filter**,** and (c) determine the amount of dissolved oxygen.

34h Recognizing and editing commas that separate adjectives in a sequence

When you use a pair of **coordinate adjectives**, each modifies the noun (or pronoun) on its own. Separate these adjectives with commas to show their equal application to the noun.

| COORDINATE (EQUAL) | These drawings describe a **quick,** **simple** solution. |

hen you use **noncoordinate adjectives**, one modifies the other, and it, in rn, modifies the noun (or pronoun). Do not separate these adjectives with comma.

NONCOORDINATE
(UNEQUAL)   We can use **flexible plastic** pipe to divert the water.

If you answer one of the following questions with *yes*, the adjectives e coordinate. Separate them with a comma.

STRATEGY Ask questions to identify coordinate adjectives.

- Can you place *and* or *but* between the adjectives?

COORDINATE   Irrigation has turned dry infertile [*dry and infertile?—yes*] land into orchards.

EDITED   Irrigation has turned dry , infertile land into orchards.

NOT   The funds went to new computer [*new and computer?—no*] equipment.
COORDINATE

- Is the sense of the passage the same if you reverse the adjectives?

COORDINATE   We left our small cramped [*cramped small?—yes, the same*] office.

EDITED   We left our small , cramped office.

NOT   We bought a red brick [*brick red?—no, not the same*] condo.
COORDINATE   **Because *brick red* is a color, the condo could be wooden.**

34i Recognizing and editing commas with dates, numbers, addresses, place names, people's titles, and letters

Readers will expect you to follow conventional practice.

Dates. Put a comma between the date and the year, between the day of the week and the date, and after the year when you give a full date.

I ordered a laptop on May 3 , 2002 , that arrived Friday , May 21.

You don't need commas when a date is inverted (5 July 1973) or contains only month and year, month and day, or season and year.

We installed the software after its June 2002 test.

Numbers. To simplify long numbers for readers, use commas to create groups of three, beginning from the right. You may choose whether to use a comma with a four-digit number, but be consistent within a text.

We counted 1 , 746 sheep on a ranch worth $1 , 540 , 000.

34k
∧
,

Omit commas in addresses and page numbers of four digits or more.

18520 South Kedzie Drive   page 2054

Addresses and place names. Separate names of cities and states with commas. For an address within a sentence, place commas between all elements *except* the state and zip code. Do not place a comma after the zip code unless some other sentence element requires one.

If you live in South Bend**,** Indiana**,** order locally from Frelle and Family**,** Seed Brokers**,** Box 389**,** Holland**,** MI 30127.

People's names and titles. When you give a person's last name first, separate it from the first name with a comma: *Shamoon, Linda K.* Use a comma before and after a title that *follows* a person's name.

We hired **Cris Bronkowski**, **A.I.A.**, to design the building.

Openings and closings of letters. Use a comma after the opening of a personal letter, but use a colon in a business or formal letter. Use a comma after the closing, just before the signature.

Dear Nan**,**   Dear Tennis Team**,**   Dear Hardware Customers**:**

Sincerely**,**   Best wishes**,**   With affection**,**   Regards**,**

34j Recognizing and editing commas with quotations

When you introduce, interrupt, or conclude a quotation with a source or context, use commas to distinguish explanation from quotation.

At the dedication, she stated**,** "This event celebrates Oakdale."

"Our unity**,**" said the mayor**,** "is our strength."

"Tomorrow the school can reopen**,**" the principal reported.

If your explanation ends with *that* just before a quotation, do not include a comma. If you quote a person's words indirectly (rather than word for word in quotation marks), do not use a comma after *that*.

Lu introduced her by saying that "calamity followed Jane." Jane replied that she simply outran it.

34k Editing commas to make your meaning clear

Even if no rule specifies a comma, add one if necessary to clarify your meaning, to remind readers of deleted words, or to emphasize.

CONFUSING   When food is scarce, animals that can expand their grazing territory at the expense of other species.

DITED   When food is scarce, animals that can⸲ expand their grazing
territory at the expense of other species.

34I   Editing to eliminate commas that do not belong

Avoid scattering commas through a paper; add them as required.

STRATEGY Remove extra commas.

- Omit commas after words like *although* and *because*. These subordinating conjunctions (see 28b–c) introduce a clause and should not be set
off with commas. Conjunctive adverbs (like *however*; see 28a) and transitional expressions (like *for example*) should be set off with commas.

EXTRA COMMA   **Although**⸲ Jewel lost her luggage, she had her laptop.

EDITED   **Although** Jewel lost her luggage, she had her laptop.

- Remove commas between subjects and verbs unless a modifier separates
them.

**SPLIT SUBJECT
AND PREDICATE**   Cézanne's painting *Rocks at L'Estaque*⸲ hangs in the
Museu de Arte in São Paulo, Brazil.

EDITED   Cézanne's painting *Rocks at L'Estaque* hangs in the Museu
de Arte in São Paulo, Brazil.

Today most readers prefer a style in which commas are not used heavily. Too
many commas, even correctly used, can create choppy prose.

**TOO MANY
COMMAS (7)**   Rosa⸲ always one⸲ like her mother⸲ to speak her mind⸲
protested the use of force⸲ as she called it⸲ by two store detec-
tives⸲ who had been observing her.

EDITED (2)   Always one to speak her mind⸲ like her mother⸲ Rosa protested what she called the use of force by two store detectives.

35 | Using Semicolons
and Colons

Semicolons and colons help readers make connections.

TWO SENTENCES   On April 12, 1861, one of Beauregard's batteries fired on Fort
Sumter• **The** Civil War had begun.

READER'S REACTION: Maybe these two sentences present a dramatic moment, or maybe they simply state facts, but they don't *necessarily*
connect these events.

SEMICOLON   On April 12, 1861, one of Beauregard's batteries fired on Fo
Sumter ; the Civil War had begun.
READER'S REACTION: **The semicolon encourages me to link the batter
firing to the Civil War beginning.**

COLON   On April 12, 1861, one of Beauregard's batteries fired on Fo
Sumter : the Civil War had begun.
READER'S REACTION: **Now I see the guns' firing as a dramatic momen
the beginning of the Civil War.**

All three examples are correct, yet each encourages a different perspective
Readers expect you to use punctuation, especially semicolons and colons, t
shape their responses and show them how your ideas relate.

35a Recognizing and editing semicolons

35.1

A semicolon can dramatically highlight a close relationship or a contrast as it creates a brief reading pause. Because it can't specify the logical link
as a word might, be sure the relationship won't puzzle readers.

1 Join main clauses with a semicolon

A semicolon joins main clauses that can stand alone as complete sentences. Make sure you could convert both clauses into sentences.

TWO SENTENCES   The demand for paper is at an all-time high ● Businesses alone
consume millions of tons each year.

ONE SENTENCE   The demand for paper is at an all-time high ; businesses alone
consume millions of tons each year.

STRATEGY Test both sides of the semicolon.

DRAFT   The demand for recycled paper increased greatly ; with manufacturers rushing to contract for scrap paper.

TEST CLAUSE 1   The demand for recycled paper increased greatly.
The first clause is a complete sentence.

TEST CLAUSE 2   With manufacturers rushing to contract for scrap paper.
The second part is a sentence fragment.

EDITED   The demand for recycled paper increased greatly ; manufacturers rushed to contract for scrap paper.

Exception: In some cases, elements within a second clause can be omitted if
they "match" elements in the first clause. Then the two can be joined with a
semicolon even though the second could not stand alone.

ELEMENTS
INCLUDED   In winter, **the hotel guests enjoy** the log fire ; in summer, **the
hotel guests enjoy** the patio overlooking the river.

EMENTS
MITTED

In winter, **the hotel guests enjoy** the log fire **;** in summer, the patio overlooking the river.

Use a semicolon with transition words

When you use a semicolon alone to link main clauses, you ask readers) recognize the logical link between the clauses. When you add words like *owever* or *on the other hand*, you create a different effect on readers by speci- ʋing how the clauses relate.

assertion → semicolon → transition → assertion
(*pause*) (*consider relationship*)

I like apples **;** **however ,** I hate pears.
assertion **pause**   **contrast** **assertion**

To specify the transition between clauses, you can choose a **conjunctive ad- ʋerb** such as *however, moreover, nonetheless, thus,* or *therefore* (see 28a) or a **transitional expression** like *for example, in contrast,* or *on the other hand.* ʋary the punctuation depending on where you place such wording.

BETWEEN CLAUSES Joe survived the flood **;** **however ,** Al was never found.

WITHIN CLAUSE Joe survived the flood **;** Al **,** **however ,** was never found.

AT END OF CLAUSE Joe survived the flood **;** Al was never found **,** **however**.

3 Use a semicolon with a complex series

When items in a series contain commas, readers may have trouble de- ciding which commas separate parts of the series and which belong within items. To avoid confusion, put semicolons between elements in a series when one or more contain other punctuation.

CONFUSING I interviewed Debbie Rios, the attorney, Rhonda Marron, the accountant, and the financial director.
READER'S REACTION: How many? Three, four, or five?

EDITED I interviewed Debbie Rios, the attorney **;** Rhonda Marron, the accountant **;** and the financial director.

35b Recognizing and editing colons

Use a colon to introduce, separate, or join elements.

35.2

1 Use a colon to introduce examples, lists, and quotations

The words *before* the colon generally form a complete sentence while those after may or may not. When the words after the colon don't form a sen- tence, begin with a lowercase letter. When a sentence follows, begin with ei- ther a capital or lowercase letter. Stick to one style in a text.

Examples. Commonly, a colon follows a statement or generalization that th[e] rest of the sentence illustrates, explains, or particularizes.

> She has only one budget priority: teacher salaries.

Lists. A colon can introduce a list or series following a sentence. Following [a] word group other than a complete sentence, do not use a colon.

DRAFT   The symptoms are: sore throat, fever, and headache.

EDITED   She had three symptoms: sore throat, fever, and headache.

EDITED   The symptoms are sore throat, fever, and headache.

Quotations. Whether you integrate a short quotation with your own word[s] or set off a longer one in your text (see 49b-1), a complete sentence mus[t] precede a colon. If not, use a comma.

> Ms. Nguyen outlined the plan: "Boost sales, and cut costs."

2 Use a colon to separate in accord with convention

Colons separate main titles from subtitles.

Designing Your Web Site: *A Beginner's Guide*   "Diabetes: Are You at Risk?"

Colons also separate hours from minutes (10:32); chapters from verses, as in the Bible (John 8:21–23); the salutation from the text of a business letter (Dear Ms. Billis:); parts of a ratio (2:3); parts of an electronic address (http://www.nytimes.com); and parts of references in some documentation styles (see Chapters 51–54).

3 Use a colon to join sentences

You can most effectively use a colon to join main clauses (see 22c) when the second clause sharply focuses, sums up, or illustrates the first.

> The blizzard swept across the prairie: **the Oregon Trail was closed.**

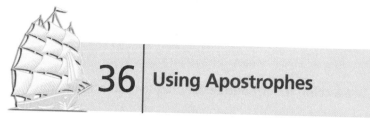

36 | Using Apostrophes

Like the dot above the *i*, the apostrophe may seem trivial. But without it, irritated readers would stumble over your sentences.

ˀAFT Though its an 1854 novel, Dickens *Hard Times* remain's an ageless critique of education by fact's.

READER'S REACTION: I can't tell possessives from plurals and contractions. This is too annoying to bother reading.

ˀTED Though **it˒s** an 1854 novel, **Dickens˒s** *Hard Times* **remains** an ageless critique of education by **facts**.

all three communities, readers view apostrophes as conventional, not flex-le. Hunt consciously for them if you tend to misuse or omit them.

36a Recognizing apostrophes that mark possession

A noun that expresses ownership is called a **possessive noun**. Mark ossessive nouns to distinguish them from plurals.

ˀSSING The **cats** meow is becoming fainter.

READER'S REACTION: I expected something like "The cats meow all night." Do you mean many cats or the meow of one cat?

ˀITED The **cat˒s** meow is becoming fainter.

STRATEGY Test for possession.

If you can turn a noun into a phrase using *of*, use a possessive form. If ot, use a plural.

ˀRAFT The officers reports surprised the reporters.

ˀEST The reports **of** the officers? [yes, a possessive]

ˀEST Reports surprised **of** the reporters? [no, a plural]

ˀITED The officers˒ reports surprised the reporters.

36b Editing apostrophes that mark possession

Decide whether to add an apostrophe plus *-s* or just an apostrophe.

36.1

STRATEGY Check the ending of the noun.

- **Does the noun end in a letter other than -s**? When you write a sin- gular possessive noun, usually follow it with an apostrophe plus *-s*.

  Bill˒s coat   Connecticut˒s taxes   the dog˒s collar

Possessive indefinite pronouns (see 15b) follow the same pattern.

  nobody˒s report   everybody˒s office   someone˒s lunch

A few nouns form their plurals (*mice*, *fish*) without ending in *-s* or *-es*.

  oxen˒s habitat   children˒s toys   women˒s locker room

- **Does the noun end in -s, and is it plural** (more than one person item)? Most plural nouns end in -s or -es. To make one possessive, simply add an apostrophe after the -s.

    the Solomon**s'** house   the rose**s'** petals   the bus**es'** rout

- **Does the noun end in -s, and is it singular** (one person or item Stick to one of two options in a paper. The preferred convention is add an apostrophe and another -s, as with another singular noun.

    Chri**s's** van   Elliott Nes**s's** next move

    Alternatively, simply add an apostrophe to the final -s.

    Chri**s'** van   Elliott Nes**s'** next move

- **Does the noun end in -s and sound awkward?** Occasionally, addir a possessive -s (Hodges**'s**) to a word already ending in that sound wi seem awkward to say ("Hodges-es"). If so, use only the apostroph (Hodges**'**) to indicate only one -s sound, or avoid the awkwardnes (*the Adams County Schools**'s** policy*) by rewriting (*the policy of the Adam County Schools*).

Even though third person singular verbs end in -s, these are not nouns and do not have possessive forms. They don't require an apostrophe.

DRAFT   The contractor **order's** all material early.

EDITED   The contractor **orders** all material early.

Don't add apostrophes to personal pronouns; they're already possessive. (See 36c-1.)

If this car is **yours**, why did you take **hers** and dent **its** fender?

In general, treat **hyphenated** and **multiple-word nouns** as a single unit. marking possession on the last word.

HYPHENATED   My **father-in-law's** library is extensive.

MULTIPLE-WORD The **union leaders'** negotiations collapsed.

When you use a **compound noun phrase** (two or more nouns connected by *and* or *or*) as a possessive, decide whether the nouns function as separate items or as a single unit.

Billy's and Harold's lawyers were ruthless. [separate lawyers]
Billy and Harold's lawyers were ruthless. [same legal team]

6c Recognizing and editing apostrophes that mark contractions and omissions

You can use an apostrophe to indicate the omission of one or more let-
rs when two words are brought together to form a **contraction**.

Use an apostrophe to contract a verb form

You can contract pronouns and verbs into a single unit (you'll = you +
ill) or splice nouns followed by *is*. If this informal style seems inappropriate
, your class or workplace, always err on the side of formality.

FORMAL	**Shoshana's** going, but her **seat's** in the last row.
ORE FORMAL	**Shoshana is** going, but her **seat is** in the last row.

STRATEGY **Expand contractions to test the form.**

they're	=	they + are	there	=	an adverb
you're	=	you + are	your	=	a possessive pronoun
who's	=	who + is	whose	=	a possessive pronoun
it's	=	it + is	its	=	a possessive pronoun

or example, test the contraction *it's* by expanding the expression (*it + is*); if
he expansion doesn't make sense, use *its*.

RAFT	**Its** the best animal shelter in **its** area.
XPANSION TEST	**It is** [yes, a fit] the best animal shelter in **it is** [no, not a fit] area.
DITED	**It's** the best animal shelter in **its** area.

2 Use an apostrophe to mark plural numbers and letters

Make letters and numbers plural by adding an apostrophe + *-s*.

LETTERS	Mind your **p's** and **q's**. The **x's** mark missing lines.
NUMBERS	I'll take two size **10's** and two size **12's**.

Sometimes the apostrophe is omitted if it risks making a term look like a
possessive (*TAs* or *TA's*). The MLA and APA styles (see Chapters 51–52) omit
it from numbers and abbreviations (*1980s* and *IQs*).

3 Use an apostrophe to abbreviate a year or show colloquial pronunciation

Informally abbreviate years by omitting the first two numbers (*the '90s*
or *the class of '05*) if the century is clear to readers. Also use apostrophes to
indicate omissions in colloquial speech and dialects.

DIALECT	I'm **a-goin'** out for some **o'** them shrimp **an'** oysters.

36.2

37 | Marking Quotations

Quotation marks play many conventional roles.

QUOTATION NOT FULLY MARKED

"Thanks to the navigator," the pilot said, we made the landing.
READER'S REACTION: **Without quotation marks, I didn't realize at first that t**
pilot said the last part, too.

EDITED

66Thanks to the navigator,**99** the pilot said, **66**we made the landing.**9**

Although conventions may vary slightly by field, readers in academic, wor**k**
and public communities expect you to use quotation marks precisely. How
you use these marks tells readers who said what. (See 49b.)

37a Recognizing and editing marks that indicate quotations

Quotation marks tell readers which words are someone else's (and
which words are your own).

1 Direct quotations and dialogue

Whenever you directly quote someone's exact words, spoken or written, use double quotation marks (" ") both before and after the quotation
Long quotations for research papers are an exception (see 49b-1).

37.1

SPOKEN QUOTATION

66The loon can stay under water for a few minutes,**99** the ranger said

WRITTEN QUOTATION

Gross argues that **66**every generation scorns its offspring's culture**99**
(9).

Use quotation marks within a sentence to separate quoted material from the
words you use to introduce or comment on it.

QUOTATION INTERRUPTED

66Every generation,**99** according to Gross, **66**scorns its offspring's culture**99** (9).

When you are writing dialogue and a new person speaks, indent as if you're
starting a new paragraph. Begin with new quotation marks.

L ADVICE: QUOTATION MARKS

If your native language uses other marks for quotations or if you are
ed to British conventions, try using your computer's search capacity to find
ch of the marks so you can check for American usage.

Quotations inside quotations

Whenever one quotation contains another, use single marks (' ') for the
side quotation and double marks (" ") for the one enclosing it.

De Morga's account of the sinking of the *San Diego* described the
battle that **"**caused his ship to **'**burst asunder**' "** (Goddio 37).

Indirect quotations

Whenever you paraphrase or summarize someone else's words, do not
se quotation marks. (See Chapter 49.)

INDIRECT QUOTATION (PARAPHRASE)
The pilot told us that the navigator made the safe landing possible.

INDIRECT QUOTATION (SUMMARY)
Samuel Gross believes that the social consequences of a major war
nearly vanish after just one generation (5).

37b Editing titles of short works

Use quotation marks to enclose titles of short works, parts of a larger
vork or series, and unpublished works. (See p. 204 and 41a.)

STRATEGY **Present your own title without quotation marks.**

Place only quoted material in quotation marks.

RAFT   **"**The Theme of the Life Voyage in Crane's **'**Open Boat**' "**

DITED   The Theme of the Life Voyage in Crane's **"**Open Boat**"**

37c Editing quotation marks for special uses

You can use quotation marks or italics (see 41b) to set off technical
erms, unusual terms, or words used in a special sense. Avoid too much high-
ighting; it distracts readers, and most terms don't require it.

In the real estate industry, **"**FSBO**"** (sometimes pronounced as
"fizbo**"**) refers to a home that is **"**for sale by owner.**"**

You can—*sparingly*—use quotation marks to indicate irony or sarcasm or to
show a reader that you don't "lay claim" to an expression.

37.2

38
•

QUOTATION MARKS WITH TITLES

ARTICLES AND STORIES

"TV Gets Blame for Poor Reading"	newspaper article
"Feminism's Identity Crisis"	magazine article
"The Idea of the Family in the Middle East"	chapter in book
"Baba Yaga and the Brave Youth"	story
"The Rise of Germism"	essay

POEMS AND SONGS

"A Woman Cutting Celery"	short poem
"Evening" (from *Pippa Passes*)	section of a long poem
"Riders on the Storm"	song

EPISODES AND PARTS OF LONGER WORKS

"Billy's Back"	episode of a TV series
"All We Like Sheep" (from Handel's *Messiah*)	section of a long musical work

UNPUBLISHED WORKS

"Renaissance Men—and Women"	unpublished lecture
"Sources of the Ballads in Bishop Percy's Folio Manuscript"	unpublished dissertation

38 | Using Periods, Question Marks, and Exclamation Points

When you speak, you mark sentence boundaries with changes in pitch or pauses. When you write, you use visual symbols—a period, a question mark, or an exclamation point.

LESS FORMAL   And why do we need your support❓ Without you, too many lovable pups will never find new homes❗

READER'S REACTION: **This bouncy style is great for our volunteer brochure but not for our annual report.**

MORE FORMAL   The League's volunteers remain our most valuable asset, matching abandoned animals with suitable homes•

Readers in all communities expect periods to mark the ends of sentences. Some readers may accept liberal use of question marks and exclamation points, but only in informal contexts.

38a Recognizing and editing periods

No matter how complicated, all sentences that are *statements* must end with periods—even if they contain clauses that appear to be something other an statements. The following sentence as a whole is a statement; it reports, ut does not ask, the question in the second half.

> Naomi thanked her supporters profusely but wondered whether they felt responsible for her defeat•

38.1

Periods also mark decimal points in numbers (22.6 or 5.75) and punctuate abbreviations by letting readers know that something has been eliminated from the word or term.

> Dr• Ms• Ph•D• C•P•A• pp• etc• a•m• B•C•

ome abbreviations may not require periods, especially **acronyms** whose letters form pronounceable words (*OSHA*, *NATO*), terms entirely capitalized GOP), and state names such as *OH*. When in doubt, turn to a dictionary.

When an abbreviation with a period occurs at the *end* of a sentence, hat period will also end the sentence. If the abbreviation occurs in the *middle* f a sentence, the period may be followed by another mark, such as a comma, lash, colon, or semicolon.

> Residents spoke until 10 **p•m•,** and we adjourned at 11 **p•m•**

38b Recognizing and editing question marks

Always end a direct question with a question mark. In a sentence with several clauses, the main clause usually determines the punctuation.

DIRECT	When is the train leaving**?**
DIRECT: QUOTED	Laitan asked, "Why is the air rising so quickly**?**"
DIRECT: TWO CLAUSES	Considering that the tax break has been widely publicized, why have so few people filed for a refund**?**

When you present an **indirect question**—a sentence whose main clause is a statement and whose embedded clause asks a question—end with a period.

INDIRECT	José asked if we needed help preparing the bid•

A question mark also may signal an uncertain date or other fact.

> David Robert Styles, 1632**?**–1676   Meadville, pop. 196**?**

Unless you're writing very informally, avoid adding question marks after other people's statements, using more than one question mark for emphasis, or combining question marks and exclamation points.

39a
( )

38c Recognizing and editing exclamation points

Exclamation points end emphatic statements such as commands or warnings but are rarely used in most academic or workplace writing.

STRATEGY **Use draft punctuation to guide your editing.**

Like question marks, exclamation points can be used informally. They can express dismay, outrage, shock, or strong interest. As you revise and edit, look for strong words to emphasize a point.

38.2

DRAFT   Rescuers spent hours (!) trying to reach the child.

EDITED   Rescuers spent **agonizing** hours trying to reach the child.

39 | Using Other Punctuation Marks

Most punctuation symbols make up a kind of toolbox for writing. You can use the tools to change the style, sense, and effect of your prose.

DASHES   When the boy—**clutching three weeks' allowance**—returned to the store, it had already closed.

READER'S REACTION: **Dashes emphasize how hard the boy worked to save his allowance.**

PARENTHESES   When the boy **(clutching three weeks' allowance)** returned to the store, it had already closed.

READER'S REACTION: **The parentheses de-emphasize the boy's savings, making the store hours seem more important.**

COMMAS   When the boy**,** **clutching three weeks' allowance,** returned to the store, it had already closed.

READER'S REACTION: **This straightforward account doesn't emphasize either the allowance or the store hours.**

Punctuation marks help guide readers through complex sentences.

39a Recognizing and editing parentheses

39.1

Parentheses *enclose* a word, sentence, or clause: you can't use just one. Readers interpret whatever falls between as an aside. Omit a comma *before* a parenthetical statement in the middle of a sentence. *After* the closing parenthesis, use whatever punctuation would otherwise occur.

WITHOUT PARENTHESES	When you sign up for Telepick**,** including Internet access**,** you will receive an hour of free calls.
WITH PARENTHESES	When you sign up for Telepick **(**including Internet access**),** you will receive an hour of free calls.

When parentheses *inside a sentence* come at the end, place the end punctuation *after* the closing mark. When enclosing a *freestanding sentence*, place end punctuation *inside* the closing parenthesis.

INSIDE SENTENCE	People on your Telepick list also get discounts **(**once they sign up**).**
SEPARATE SENTENCE	Try Telepick now. **(**This offer excludes international calls**.)**

You can also use parentheses to mark numbered or lettered lists or to enclose detail that is not part of the structure of a sentence.

DETAIL AND LIST	Harry's Bookstore has a fax number **(**555-0934**)** for **(**1**)** ordering books, **(**2**)** asking about new items, or **(**3**)** signing up for store events.

39b Recognizing and editing brackets

When you add your own words to a quotation for clarity or background, enclose this **interpolation** in brackets. (See also 39d on ellipses.) Also bracket the word *sic* (Latin for "so" or "thus") after an error in a source to confirm that you've quoted accurately.

INTERPOLATION	As Walters explains, "When Catholic Europe adopted the Gregorian calendar in 1582 and dropped ten days in October, Protestant England ignored the shift, still following October 4 by October 5 **[**Julian calendar**]**" (71).

Academic readers expect you to use brackets scrupulously to distinguish your words from those of a source (though nonacademic readers may find them pretentious).

If one parenthetical statement falls *within* another, use brackets for the inner statement.

Contact Rick Daggett **(**Municipal Lumber Council **[**Violations Division**]**, Stinson County Center**)** to report logging violations.

39c Recognizing and editing dashes

Dashes set off material with more emphasis or spark than parentheses supply. Too many dashes may strike academic readers as informal. In contrast, dashes add flair to work and public appeals, ads, or brochures. Type a dash as two unspaced hyphens, without space before or after: --. In print, the dash appears as a single line: —.

39d

Use one dash to introduce material at the *end* of a sentence; use dash in pairs to highlight words in the middle.

MATERIAL IN THE MIDDLE

After hours of service to two groups—**Kids First and Food Basket** Olivia was voted Volunteer of the Year.

Dashes can set off an idea or a series of items, especially to open or close dra matically or call attention to an assertion.

OPENING LIST

Extended visitation hours, **better meals**, **and more exercise**—the were the inmates' major demands.

STRATEGY Convert excessive dashes to other marks.

If your draft is full of dashes, circle those that seem truly valuable– maybe setting off a key point. Replace the others with commas, colons, parer theses, or more emphatic wording.

39d Recognizing and editing ellipses

The **ellipsis** (from Greek *elleipsis*, "an omission") is a series of three *spaced* periods showing that something has been left out. Academic reader expect you to use ellipses to mark omissions from a quotation. Readers in other communities may prefer complete quotations to ellipses.

PLACEMENT OF ELLIPSIS MARKS

- Use three spaced periods • • • for ellipses within a sentence or line of poetry. Bracket the ellipsis $\left[\,\bullet\ \bullet\ \bullet\,\right]$ if you are following MLA style (see 39b and Chapter 51).
- Use a period before an ellipsis that ends a sentence• • • •
- Leave a space before the first period • • • and after the last unless the ellipsis is bracketed.
- Omit ellipses when you begin quotations (unless needed for clarity) or use words or phrases that are clearly incomplete.
- Retain another punctuation mark before omitted words if needed for the sentence structure; • • • omit it otherwise.
- Bracket a series of spaced periods (in MLA style) to show an omitted line (or more) of poetry in a block quotation.

Ellipses mark material omitted from a quotation because it is irrelevant, too long, or located between two useful parts of the quotation. When you drop *part* of a sentence, keep a normal structure that readers can follow.

ORIGINAL INTERVIEW NOTES
Museum director: "We expect the Inca pottery in our special exhibit to attract art historians from as far away as Chicago, while the colorful jewelry draws the general public."

CONFUSING DRAFT
The museum director hopes "the Inca pottery • • • art historians • • • the colorful jewelry • • • the general public."

EDITED
The museum director "expect[s] the Inca pottery • • • to attract art historians • • • while the colorful jewelry draws the general public."

In fictional or personal narrative, you may want to indicate a pause or gap showing suspense, hesitation, uncertainty, or ongoing action.

FOR SUSPENSE   Large paw prints led to the tent• • • •

39e Recognizing and editing slashes

39.2

When indicating alternatives, the slash may translate as *or* or *and*.

Be certain that the **on/off** switch is in the vertical position.

This shorthand is common in technical documents, but some readers object to its informality or imprecision (and prefer *or* in its place).

To quote poetry *within* your text instead of using a block quotation (see 49b-1), separate lines of verse with a slash, with spaces before and after.

The speaker in Sidney's sonnet hails the moon: "O Moon, thou climb'st the skies! / How silently, and with how wan a face!" (1–2).

39f Recognizing and editing the symbols in electronic addresses

When you note an electronic address, record its characters exactly—including slashes, @ ("at") signs, underscores, colons, and periods.

j•bon@ceo•uc•edu

http://www•access•gpo•gov/su_docs

39g Combining marks

Follow the conventions your readers expect.

- **Pair marks that enclose:** **( ) [ ] " " ' '** Pair commas an dashes to enclose midsentence elements. Type a dash as a pair — hyphens.

- **Use multiple marks when each plays its own role.** If an abbrevi tion with a period falls in the *middle* of a sentence, the period may b followed by another mark.

  Lunch begins at **11 a.m.,** right after the lab.

- **Eliminate multiple marks when their roles overlap.** When an ab breviation with a period concludes a sentence, that one period als ends the sentence. Omit a comma *before* parentheses; *after* the paren theses, use whatever mark would otherwise occur.

- **Avoid confusing duplications.** If items listed within a sentence in clude commas, separate them with semicolons, not more commas.

  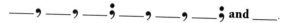

  If one set of parentheses falls within another, use brackets to enclose the internal element.

  —(—[—] —).

  Use one pair of dashes at a time, not dashes within dashes.

TAKING IT ONLINE

PROOFREADING
http://www.bgsu.edu/departments/writing-lab/goproofreading.html
http://reach.ucf.edu/~uwc/Writing%20Resources/handout_home.htm
Both sites supply practical tips to help you proofread more accurately
and efficiently.

OVERCOMING HYPHENPHOBIA
http://www.superconnect.com/wordsmit/hyphens.htm
The author of this site assures writers that "hyphens are our friends."
Here you'll find practical advice on how to use hyphens, as well as tips
on writing and common error patterns.

THE ACRONYM DATABASE
http://www.ucc.ie/info/net/acronyms/
The meanings of acronyms and abbreviations can differ from community
to community. To a sportswriter, *ERA* means something different than it
does in a discussion about gender. Use this searchable database to find
out what acronyms or abbreviations mean.

A SPELLING TEST
http://www.sentex.net/~mmcadams/spelling.html
This interactive spelling test of fifty of the most commonly misspelled
words in American English will tabulate your score automatically.
The site also offers advice on ways to become a better speller.

CANDIDATE FOR A PULLET SURPRISE
http://tenderbytes.net/rhymeworld/feeder/teacher/pullet.htm
There are many versions of this humorous but enlightening poem
published on the Internet. It reveals just how unreliable computer
spelling checkers can be. Can ewe right another verse or too?

40 | Capitalizing

Capitalization makes reading easier. Readers expect capital letters to signal where sentences start or to identify specific people, places, and things.

CAPITALS MISSING
thanks, ahmed, for attaching a copy of the 2001 plant safety guidelines. i'll review this file by tuesday.

READER'S REACTION: Even though email may be informal, the missing capitals here distract me from the message.

CAPITALS IN PLACE
Thanks, Ahmed, for attaching a copy of the 2001 **P**lant **S**afety Guidelines. I'll review this file by **T**uesday.

If you ignore conventions for capitals, readers may assume that you are careless. Be especially alert to conventions at your workplace for capitalizing titles, company divisions, and the like.

40a Recognizing and proofreading for capitals that begin sentences

Sentences begin with capital letters, whether complete sentences or fragments used appropriately as partial sentences. (See 21c.)

Two national parks, Yellowstone and Grand Teton, are in Wyoming.

1 Capitalize the opening word in a quoted sentence

Capitalization varies with the completeness of a quotation. The following examples include MLA style page citations (see 51a).

STRATEGY Adjust capitalization as you integrate a quotation.

Capitalize when a quotation is a complete sentence or begins your sentence.

QUOTED SENTENCE
As Galloway observes, "**T**he novel opens with an unusual chapter" (18).

SENTENCE OPENER
"**A**n unusual chapter" (Galloway 18) opens the novel.

211

Do not capitalize after you interrupt a quotation with your own words or you integrate a quotation into the structure of your own sentence.

INTERRUPTED QUOTATION   "**T**he novel," claims Galloway, "**o**pens with an unusual chapter" (18).

INTEGRATED QUOTATION   Galloway notes that the book "**o**pens with an unusual chapter" (18).

2 Capitalize a freestanding sentence in parentheses

Capitalize the first word of a sentence if it stands on its own in parentheses but not if it falls *inside* another sentence.

FREESTANDING SENTENCE   The Union forces were split up into nineteen sections. (**N**evertheless, Grant was determined to unite them.)

ENCLOSED SENTENCE   Saskatchewan's economy depends on farming (**o**ver half of Canada's wheat crop comes from the province).

3 Capitalize the first word of a line of poetry

Lines of poetry traditionally begin with a capital letter.

We said goodbye at the barrier,
And she slipped away. . . .

—ROBERT DASELER, "At the Barrier," *Levering Avenue*

If a poem ignores this or other conventions, follow the poet's practice.

new hampshire explodes into radio primary,
newspaper headlines & beer—
well-weathered tag-lines from lips of schoolchildren.

—T. R. MAYERS, "(snap)shots"

4 Use consistent capitalization

When capitalization is flexible, be consistent within a document.

Complete sentence after a colon. When a *sentence* follows a colon (see 35b), you can use lowercase (as for other words after a colon) or capitalize.

OPTION 1   The population of New Brunswick is bilingual: **o**ne-third is French-speaking and the rest English-speaking.

OPTION 2   The population of New Brunswick is bilingual: **O**ne-third is French-speaking and the rest English-speaking.

Questions in a series. Capitalize or lowercase a sequence of questions.

OPTION 1   Should we order posters? **B**illboards? **F**lyers?

OPTION 2   Should we order posters? **b**illboards? **f**lyers?

run-in lists. When items are not listed on separate lines, you may separate them with commas, semicolons (if they are complex), or periods (if they are sentences). Capitalize the first letters of sentences standing alone. Don't capitalize words, partial sentences, or a series of embedded sentences.

> In estimating costs, remember the following: (a) **l**ab facilities must be rented, (b) **u**tilities are charged to the project's account, and (c) **m**easuring equipment has to be leased.

> In estimating costs, remember to include (a) **l**ab facilities, (b) **u**tilities, and (c) **m**easuring equipment.

vertical lists. Choose whether to capitalize words or partial sentences, but capitalize complete sentences except in an outline without periods.

40b
cap

OPTION 1
1. **L**ab facilities
2. **U**tilities
3. **M**easuring equipment

OPTION 2
1. **l**ab facilities
2. **u**tilities
3. **m**easuring equipment

40b Recognizing and proofreading for capitals in proper names and titles

www
40.1

Capitalize the names of specific people, places, and things (**proper nouns**) as well as **proper adjectives** derived from them.

> Brazil, Dickens   Brazilian music, Dickensian plot

In titles, capitalize the first word, the last word, and all words in between *except* articles (*a, an, the*), prepositions under five letters (*in, of, to*), and coordinating conjunctions (*and, but*). These rules apply to titles of long, short, and partial works as well as your own papers. Capitalize the first word after a colon that divides the title.

> *The Mill on the Floss*   "Civil Rights: What Now?"

> Developing a Growth Plan for a Small Business [your own title]

In an APA reference list, however, capitalize only proper nouns and the first letters of titles and subtitles of full works (books, articles) (see 52b).

CAPITALIZATION OF NOUNS AND ADJECTIVES

CAPITALIZED   LOWERCASE

INDIVIDUALS AND RELATIVES
Georgia O'Keeffe   my teacher's father
Uncle Jack, Mother   my cousin, her dad

CAPITALIZED	LOWERCASE
GROUPS OF PEOPLE AND LANGUAGES	
Maori, African American	the language, the people
TIME PERIODS AND SEASONS	
October, Fall Orientation	spring, summer, fall, winter
Easter, Ramadan	holiday
RELIGIONS AND RELATED SUBJECTS	
Buddhism, Catholic	catholic (meaning "universal")
Talmud, Bible, God	talmudic, biblical, a god
ORGANIZATIONS, INSTITUTIONS, AND MEMBERS	
U.S. Senate, Senator Hayes	a senator
Air Line Pilots Association	the union, a union member
PLACES, THEIR RESIDENTS, AND GEOGRAPHIC REGIONS	
Malaysia, Erie County	the country, the county
the Southwest, East Coast	southwestern, eastern
BUILDINGS AND MONUMENTS	
Taj Mahal, Getty Museum	the tower, a museum
HISTORICAL PERIODS, EVENTS, AND MOVEMENTS	
Algerian Revolution, Jazz Age	the revolution, a trend
ACADEMIC INSTITUTIONS AND COURSES	
Auburn University	a university, the college
Sociology 203, Art 101	sociology or art course
VEHICLES	
Pontiac Bonneville SSE	my car, an automobile
COMPANY NAMES AND TRADE NAMES	
Siemens, Kleenex	the company, tissues
SCIENTIFIC, TECHNICAL, AND MEDICAL TERMS	
Big Dipper, Earth (planet)	star, earth (ground)

41 | Italicizing (Underlining)

Type that slants to the right—***italic type***—emphasizes words and ideas. In texts that are handwritten, typed, or prepared in MLA style (see 51c), underlining is its equivalent: The Color Purple = *The Color Purple*.

DERLINING   Walker's novel <u>The Color Purple</u> has been praised since 1982.

READER'S REACTION: I can spot the title right away.

me readers, including many college instructors, prefer underlining because
s easy to see. Observe the conventions your community expects.

1a Recognizing and proofreading for italics (underlining) in titles

Italicize (underline) titles of most long works (books, magazines, films)
nd complete works (paintings, sculptures). Enclose parts of works and short
works (stories, reports, articles) in quotation marks (see 37b).

41b
it/und

41b Recognizing and proofreading for conventions for emphasizing terms

Italicize (underline) the names of specific ships, airplanes, trains, and
spacecraft (*Voyager VI, Orient Express*) but not *types* of vehicles (Boeing 767,
Chris Craft) or *USS* and *SS* (USS *Corpus Christi*). Italicize a foreign word or
phrase that has not moved into common use (*omertà*) but not common words
such as quiche, junta, taco, and kvetch. Italicize scientific names for plants
(*Chrodus crispus*) and animals (*Gazella dorcas*) but not common names (sea-
weed, gazelle).

Focus attention on a word, letter, number as itself, or defined term by
italicizing it.

41.1

In Boston, <u>r</u> is pronounced <u>ah</u> so that the word <u>car</u> becomes <u>cah</u> and
<u>park</u> becomes <u>pahk</u>.

A <u>piezoelectric crystal</u> is a piece of quartz or similar material that responds to pressure by producing electric current.

You may italicize a word or phrase for stylistic emphasis, but readers
become annoyed if you do this too often.

EMPHASIS   The letter's praise is <u>faint</u>, not fulsome.

STRATEGY   Rewrite to eliminate excessive underlining.

Notes, personal letters, and other informal writing may use underlining to add "oral" emphasis. Avoid this in formal writing.

INFORMAL   <u>Hand</u> the receipts to me.

MORE FORMAL   Give the receipts to me personally.

TREATMENT OF TITLES

UNDERLINING OR ITALICS QUOTATION MARKS

BOOKS AND PAMPHLETS

Maggie: A Girl of the Streets (book) "Youth" (chapter in book)
Beetroot (story collection) "The Purloined Letter" (story)
The White Album (essay collection) "Once More to the Lake" (essay)
Guide for Surgery Patients (pamphlet) "Anesthesia" (section of
  pamphlet)

POEMS

Paradise Lost (long poem) "Richard Cory" (short poem)
The One Day (long poem) "Whoso list to hunt" (first line as
  title)

PLAYS AND FILMS

King Lear (play)
Star Wars (film)

RADIO AND TELEVISION PROGRAMS

The West Wing (TV series) "Gone Quiet" (episode)
20/20 (TV news show) "Binge Drinking" (news report)

PAINTINGS AND SCULPTURES

Winged Victory (sculpture)

MUSICAL WORKS

Nutcracker Suite (work for "Waltz of the Flowers" (section of
  orchestra) longer work)
Master of Puppets (CD) "Orion" (song on CD)
Camille Saint-Saëns's BUT Saint-Saëns, Symphony no. 3
  Organ Symphony in C Minor, op. 78

MAGAZINES AND NEWSPAPERS

Discover (magazine) "How Baby Learns" (article)
Review of Contemporary Fiction "Our Students Write with
  (scholarly journal) Accents" (scholarly article)
the *Denver Post* (newspaper) "All the Rage" (article)

NO UNDERLINING, ITALICS, OR QUOTATION MARKS

SACRED BOOKS AND PUBLIC, LEGAL, OR WELL-KNOWN DOCUMENTS
Bible, Koran, Talmud, United States Constitution

TITLE OF YOUR OWN PAPER (UNLESS PUBLISHED)
Attitudes of College Students Toward Intramural Sports
Verbal Abuse in The Color Purple (title of work discussed is underlined)

42 | Hyphenating

Readers expect hyphens to play two different roles—dividing words and ~~join~~ing them together.

~~CO~~NFUSING   The Japanese language proposal is well prepared.
READER'S REACTION: Is the proposal *in* Japanese or *about* the Japanese language?

~~C~~LARIFIED   The Japanese-language proposal is well prepared.

~~T~~ype a hyphen as a *single* line (-) with no space on either side.

~~F~~AULTY HYPHEN   well ▬ trained engineer

~~E~~DITED   well▬trained engineer

42a Recognizing and proofreading for hyphens that join words

A **compound word** is made from two or more words tied together by hyphens (*double-decker*), combined as one word (*timekeeper*), or treated as separate words (*letter carrier*). These conventions may vary or change rapidly; check an academic style guide, observe accepted practice in work or public contexts, or use an up-to-date dictionary.

Numbers. In general writing, hyphenate numbers between twenty-one and ninety-nine, even if the number is part of a larger one. Academic and workplace readers in certain fields, however, expect numbers in figures (not spelled out) (see 43b).

forty▬one   fifty▬eight thousand   sixty▬three million

Use a hyphen for inclusive numbers (pages 163▬78, volumes 9▬14) and generally for fractions spelled out (one▬half).

Prefixes and suffixes. Hyphenate a prefix that comes before a capitalized word or a number.

Cro▬Magnon   non▬Euclidean   post▬Victorian   pre▬1989

Hyphenate with *ex-, self-, all-, -elect*, and *-odd*.

self▬centered   all▬encompassing   president▬elect

217

Letters with words. Hyphenate a letter and a word forming a compound except in music terms.

A-frame   T-shirt   A minor   G sharp

Compound modifiers. Hyphenate two or more words working as a single modifier when you place them *before* a noun. When the modifiers come *after* a noun, generally do not hyphenate them.

BEFORE NOUN   The **second-largest** supplier of crude oil is Nigeria.

AFTER NOUN   Many cancer treatments are **nausea inducing**.

Do not hyphenate *-ly* adverbs or comparative and superlative forms.

Our **highly regarded** research team developed them.

Hyphens help readers know which meaning to assign a compound.

The scene required three **extra wild** monkeys.

The scene required three **extra-wild** monkeys.

STRATEGY Try suspended hyphens with strings of modifiers.

Reduce repetition with hyphens that signal the suspension of an element until the end of a series of parallel compound modifiers. Leave a space after the hyphen and before *and*, but not before a comma.

The process works with **oil- and water-based** compounds.

42b Recognizing and proofreading for hyphens that divide words

Hyphens help distinguish different words with the same spelling.

For **recreation,** they staged a comic **re-creation** of events.

They clarify words with repeated or odd combinations of letters.

anti-imperialism   post-traumatic   co-owner

Traditionally you could use a hyphen to split a word at the end of a line, marking a break *between syllables*. Now word processors include **automatic hyphenation**, dividing words at the ends of lines but sometimes creating hard-to-read lines or splitting words incorrectly. Many writers turn off this feature, preferring a "ragged" (unjustified) right margin.

- Divide words only between syllables (for example, *ad-just-able*).
- Check divisions in a dictionary (*ir-re-vo-ca-ble*, not *ir-rev-oc-able*).

- Leave more than one letter at the end of a line and more than two at the beginning (not *a-greement* or *disconnect-ed*).
- Divide at natural breaks between words in compounds (*Volks-wagen*, not *Volkswa-gen*) or after hyphens (*accident-prone*, not *acci-dent-prone*).
- Don't divide one-syllable words (*touched, drought, kicked, through*).
- Avoid confusing divisions that form distracting words (*sin-gle*).
- Don't split acronyms and abbreviations (*NATO, NCAA*), numerals (*100,000*), and contractions (*didn't*).
- Don't hyphenate an electronic address; divide it after a slash.

43a
num

43 | Using Numbers

You can convey numbers with numerals (*37, 18.6*), words (*eighty-one, two million*), or a combination (*7th, 2nd, 25 billion*).

GENERAL TEXT   These **fifty-nine** scientists represented **fourteen** states.

> READER'S REACTION: In general academic or other texts, I expect most numbers to be spelled out.

TECHNICAL   These **59** scientists represented **14** states.

> READER'S REACTION: When I read a scientific or technical report, I expect more numerals.

This chapter shows you how to present numbers in general writing. For conventions expected in specific technical, business, or scientific contexts, seek advice from your instructor, supervisor, colleagues, or style guide (see Chapters 51–54). Unconventional or inconsistent usage can mislead readers or undermine your authority as a writer.

43a Recognizing when to spell out numbers or use numerals

Spell out a number of one or two words, counting hyphenated compounds as a single word.

twenty-two computers   **seventy thousand** eggs   **306** books

Treat numbers in the same category consistently in a passage, either as numerals (if required for one number, use them for all) or as words.

CONSISTENT   Café Luna's menu soon expanded from **48** to **104** items.

STRATEGY Spell out an opening number, or rewrite.

INAPPROPRIATE **428** houses in Talcott are built on leased land.

DISTRACTING **Four hundred twenty-eight** houses in Talcott are built on leased land.

EASY TO READ **In Talcott, 428** houses are built on leased land.

43.1

43b Proofreading numbers

43b
num

Use numerals and spell numbers as readers expect.

1 Use numerals when appropriate

ADDRESSES, ROUTES
2450 Ridge Road, Alhambra, CA 91801   Interstate 6

DATES
September 7, 1976   1880–1910   from 1955 to 1957
1930s   class of '97,   the '80s (informal)
486 B.C. (or B.C.E.)   A.D. (or C.E.) 980

PARTS OF A WRITTEN WORK
Chapter 12   Genesis 1:1–6 or Gen. 1.1–6 (MLA style)
Macbeth 2.4.25–28 (or act II, scene iv, lines 25–28)

MEASUREMENTS WITH ABBREVIATIONS
55 mph   6'4"   47 psi   21 ml   80 kph

FRACTIONS, DECIMALS, PERCENTAGES
7 5/8   27.3   67 percent (or 67%)

TIME OF DAY
10:52   6:17 a.m.   12 p.m. (noon)   12 a.m. (midnight)

MONEY (SPECIFIC AMOUNTS)
$7,883 (or $7883) $4.29 $7.2 million (or $7,200,000)

SURVEYS, RATIOS, STATISTICS, SCORES
7 out of 10   3 to 1   a mean of 23
a standard deviation of 2.5   won 21 to 17

CLUSTERED NUMBERS
paragraphs 2, 9, and 13 through 15 (or 13–15)
units 23, 145, and 210

RANGES OF NUMBERS
LESS THAN 100   Supply the complete second number.
9–13   27–34   58–79   94–95

OVER 100   Simply supply the last two figures in the second number unless readers need more to avoid confusion. Do not use commas in four-digit page numbers.

134–45   95–102 (not 95–02)   370–420
1534–620 (not 1534–20)   1007–09

YEARS   Supply all digits of both years in a range unless they belong to the same century.

1890–1920   1770–86   476–823   42–38 B.C.

Spell out numbers when appropriate

DATES AND TIMES

October seventh   nineteenth century   the sixties
four o'clock, *not* 4 o'clock   four in the morning
half past eight, a quarter after one (rounded to the quarter hour)

ROUNDED NUMBERS OR ROUNDED AMOUNTS OF MONEY

three hundred thousand citizens   nearly eleven thousand dollars
sixty cents (and other small dollar or cent amounts)

LARGE NUMBERS

For large numbers, combine numerals and words.
75 million years   2.3 million members

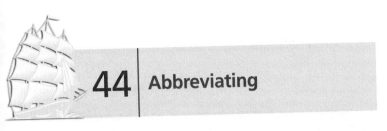

44 | Abbreviating

When they are accepted by both writer and reader, abbreviations act as a shorthand, making a sentence easy to write and read. Inappropriate or badly placed abbreviations, however, can make a sentence *harder* to read.

CONFUSING   **Jg. Rich.** Posner was a **U of C** law **prof.**

    READER'S REACTION: Am I supposed to know all these abbreviations? What is "Jg."? Is "U of C" the University of California?

CLEAR   **Judge Richard** Posner was a **University of Chicago** law **professor**.

Abbreviations should aid readers, not baffle them.

44a Recognizing familiar abbreviations

Use standard abbreviations widely accepted by your readers.

1 Abbreviate titles with proper names

Abbreviate titles just before or after people's names.

> **Ms.** Rutkowski   Cathy Harr, **D.V.M.**   James Guptil, **Sr.**

With a person's full name, you may abbreviate a title. Spell out a title used a
part of your reference to the person or placed away from a proper name.

FAULTY   We invited **Prof.** Leves and **Rep.** Drew.

ACCEPTABLE   We invited **Professor** Leves and **Representative** Drew.

ALTERNATIVE   We invited **Prof. Roland** Leves and **Rep. John** Drew.

EXCEPTIONS   **Rev.** Mills and **Dr.** Smith were not invited.

Use only one form of a person's title at a time.

FAULTY   **Dr.** Vonetta McGee, **D.D.S.**

EDITED   **Dr.** Vonetta McGee or Vonetta McGee, **D.D.S.**

Abbreviated academic degrees such as *M.A.*, *Ph.D.*, *B.S.*, and *M.D.* can be used
as titles or on their own.

ACCEPTABLE   The **Ed.D.** is designed for school administrators.

ESL ADVICE: ABBREVIATED TITLES

In some languages, abbreviated titles such as *Dr.* or *Mrs.* do not require
periods as they do in English. If so in your first language, proofread carefully.

2 Abbreviate references to people and organizations

Readers generally accept abbreviations that are familiar (*3M*, *IBM*),
simple (*AFL-CIO*), or standard in specific contexts (*FAFSA*). Abbreviations in
which the letters are pronounced singly (*USDA*) and **acronyms** in which
they form a pronounceable word (*NATO*) usually use capitals without periods (but note *laser*, *radar*).

ORGANIZATIONS   NAACP, AMA, NBA, FDA, NCAA, UNESCO, IBEW

CORPORATIONS   GTE, USX, PBS, GM, CNN, AT&T, CBS, BBC

COUNTRIES   USA (*or* U.S.A.), UK (*or* U.K.)

PEOPLE   JFK, LBJ, FDR, MLK

THINGS OR EVENTS   FM, AM, TB, MRI, AWOL, DUI, TGIF

TRATEGY | **Introduce an unfamiliar abbreviation.**

Give the full term when you first use it; show the abbreviation in paren-
eses. From then on, use the abbreviation to avoid tedious repetition.

The **American Library Association (ALA)** has taken stands on access to information. For example, the **ALA** opposes book censorship.

Abbreviate terms with dates and numbers

Abbreviations that *specify* a number or amount may be used with dates
nd numbers; don't substitute them for general terms. For example, use *the
horning*, not *the a.m.* (See 43b.)

ABBREVIATION	MEANING
A.D. or AD	*anno Domini*, meaning "in the year of Our Lord"
B.C. or BC	*before Christ*
B.C.E. or BCE	*before common era* (alternative to B.C.)
C.E. or CE	*common era* (alternative to A.D.)
a.m. or A.M.	*ante meridiem* for "morning" (A.M. in print)
p.m. or P.M.	*post meridiem* for "after noon" (P.M. in print)
no., $	number, dollars

44b Proofreading for appropriate abbreviations

In most formal writing, readers expect words in full form except for familiar abbreviations. In research, scientific, or technical writing, you can use
more abbreviations to save space, particularly in documenting sources (see
Chapters 51–54). Abbreviations may also be accepted in specific contexts—
for example, OT (occupational therapy) in medical reports.

44.1

DAYS, MONTHS, AND HOLIDAYS

DRAFT	Thurs., Thur., Th	Oct.	Xmas
EDITED	Thursday	October	Christmas

PLACES

DRAFT	Wasatch Mts.	Lk. Erie	Ont. Ave.
EDITED	Wasatch Mountains	Lake Erie	Ontario Avenue
EXCEPTION	988 Dunkerhook Road, Paramus, **NJ** 07652		

Use accepted postal abbreviations in all addresses with zip codes.

COMPANY NAMES

QUESTIONABLE	LaForce Bros. Electrical Conts.
EDITED	LaForce Brothers Electrical Contractors

Use abbreviations only if they are part of the official name.

PEOPLE'S NAMES

DRAFT	Wm. and Kath. Newholtz will attend.
EDITED	William and Katherine Newholtz will attend.

DISCIPLINES AND PROFESSIONS

DRAFT	econ., bio.	poli. sci.	phys. ed.	PT
EDITED	economics, biology	political science	physical education	physical therapy

SYMBOLS AND UNITS OF MEASUREMENT

In general writing, reserve symbols (@, #, =, −, +) for tables or graphs. Spe[ll] out units of measurement (*mile*). Abbreviate phrases such as *rpm* and *mpl[?]* with or without periods, but be consistent in a text.

AVOID IN TEXT	pt.	qt.	in.	mi.	kg.
USE IN TEXT	pint	quart	inch	mile	kilogram

PARTS OF WRITTEN WORKS

Follow your instructor's advice or the style guide for the field.

IN DOCUMENTATION	ch.	p.	pp.	fig.
IN WRITTEN TEXT	chapter	page	pages	figure

LATIN ABBREVIATIONS

Reserve these for documentation and parenthetical comments.

cf.	compare (*confer*)	i.e.	that is (*id est*)	e.g.	for example (*exempli gratia*)
N.B.	note well (*nota bene*)	et al.	and others (*et alii*)	etc.	and so forth (*et cetera*)

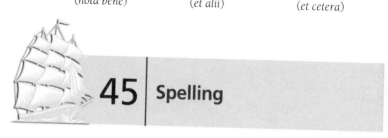

45 | Spelling

Readers in all communities notice how accurately you spell.

INCORRECT	The city will not **except** any late bids for the project.
	READER'S REACTION: I get annoyed when careless or lazy writers won't correct their spelling.
PROOFREAD	The city will not **accept** any late bids for the project.

aders may ignore or laugh at a newspaper misspelling. For academic and
ork documents, however, they may consider a writer who misspells lazy, ig-
rant, or disrespectful.

45a Recognizing spelling errors

Correct the errors you see; then ask readers to spot others.

Start with your spelling checker

When you use a spelling checker, the computer compares the words in
our text with those in its dictionary. If it finds a match, it assumes your word
s correctly spelled. If it does *not* find a match, it questions the word so you
an select an alternative spelling or make a correction. What it can't reveal
re words properly spelled but used incorrectly, such as *lead* for *led*. When in
oubt, check a dictionary.

STRATEGY **Go beyond the spelling checker.**

- List as many possible spellings as you can. Look them up. Once you're
  in the right area in the dictionary, you may find the word.
- Try a special dictionary for poor spellers, listing words under both cor-
  rect spelling (*phantom*) and likely misspellings (*fantom*).
- Try a thesaurus (see 33b); the word may be listed with a synonym.
- Ask classmates or co-workers about the spelling, especially for techni-
  cal terms; verify their information in the dictionary.
- Check the indexes of books that treat the topic the word relates to.
- Look for the word in textbooks, company materials, or newspapers.
- Add tricky words to your own spelling list. Look for ways to recall
  them. For example, you might associate the two *z*'s in *quizzes* with
  boredom (*zzzz*).

2 Watch for common patterns of misspelling

Many groups of letters can trip up even the best spellers.

45.1

Plurals. You form most plurals simply by adding *-s* (*novel, novels*).

- For words ending in a consonant plus *-o*, often add *-es*.

ADD -es	potato, potatoes	hero, heroes
ADD -s	cello, cellos	memo, memos

When a vowel comes before the *-o*, add *-s*.

ADD -s	stereo, stereos	video, videos

45a
spell

- For words ending in a consonant plus -*y*, change *y* to *i*, and add -

  etiology, etiologies   gallery, galleries   notary, notaries

  EXCEPTION   Add -*s* for proper nouns (*Kennedy, Kennedys*).

- For words ending in a vowel plus -*y*, keep the *y*, and add -*s*.

  day, days   journey, journeys   pulley, pulleys

- For words ending in -*f* or -*fe*, often change *f* to *v*, and add -*s* or -*es*.

  knife, knives   life, lives   self, selves

  Some words simply add -*s*.

  belief, beliefs   roof, roofs   turf, turfs

- For words ending with a hiss (-*ch*, -*s*, -*ss*, -*sh*, -*x*, -*z*), usually add -*es*

  bench, benches   bus, buses   bush, bushes
  buzz, buzzes   fox, foxes   kiss, kisses

  One-syllable words may double a final -*s* or -*z*: *quiz, quizzes*.

- Words with foreign roots often follow the original language.

  alumna, alumnae   criterion, criteria   datum, data

- Some familiar plurals are irregular: *foot, feet; mouse, mice; man, men*.
- In a compound, make the last word plural unless the first is more important.

  basketball, basketballs   sister-in-law, sisters-in-law

Word beginnings and endings. Prefixes do not change the spelling of the root word that follows: *precut, post-traumatic, misspell*.

- *In-* and *im-* have the same meaning; use *im-* before *b, m,* and *p*.

  | **USE** *in-* | incorrect | inadequate | incumbent |
  | **USE** *im-* | immobile | impatient | imbalance |

Suffixes may change the root word that comes before, or they may pose spelling problems in themselves.

- Retain a word's final silent -*e* when a suffix begins with a consonant.

  | **KEEP** -*e* | fate, fateful | gentle, gentleness |
  | **EXCEPTIONS** | words like *judgment, argument, truly,* and *ninth* |

- Drop the silent *-e* when a suffix begins with a vowel.

  DROP *-e*   imagine, imaginary   decrease, decreasing

  EXCEPTIONS   words like *noticeable* and *changeable*

- Four familiar words end in *-ery*: *stationery* (paper), *cemetery*, *monastery*, *millinery*. Most others end in *-ary*: *stationary* (fixed in place), *secretary*, *primary*, *military*, *culinary*.
- Most words with a final "seed" sound end in *-cede*, such as *precede*, *recede*, and *intercede*. Only three are spelled *-ceed*: *proceed*, *succeed*, and *exceed*. One is spelled *-sede*: *supersede*.
- Add *-able* if word roots can stand on their own and *-ible* if they can't.

  USE *-able*   charitable, habitable, advisable, mendable
  Drop the *e* for word roots ending in one *e* (*comparable*, *debatable*), but keep it for words ending in double *e* (*agreeable*).

  USE *-ible*   credible, irreducible

Words containing *ie* and *ei*. Most words follow the old rhyme: *I before e / Except after c, / Or when sounding like a / As in n*ei*ghbor and w*ei*gh.*

USE *ie*   believe, thief, grief, friend, chief, field, niece

USE *ei*   receive, deceit, perceive, ceiling, conceited

EXCEPTIONS   weird, seize, foreign, ancient, height, either, neither, their, leisure, forfeit

45b
spell

45b Proofreading for commonly misspelled words

Words that sound like each other but are spelled differently (*accept/except, assent/ascent*) are known as **homophones**.

COMMONLY MISSPELLED OR CONFUSED WORD PAIRS	
WORD	**MEANING**
accept	receive
except	other than
affect	to influence; an emotional response
effect	result
all ready	prepared
already	by this time
allusion	indirect reference
illusion	faulty belief or perception

(Continued)

COMMONLY MISSPELLED OR CONFUSED WORD PAIRS *(Continued)*

WORD	MEANING
assure	state positively
ensure	make certain
insure	indemnify
bare	naked
bear	carry; an animal
board	get on; flat piece of wood
bored	not interested
brake	stop
break	shatter, destroy; a gap; a pause
capital	seat of government; monetary resources
capitol	building that houses government
cite	credit an authority
sight	ability to see; a view
site	a place
complement	to complete or supplement
compliment	to praise
desert	abandon; sandy wasteland
dessert	sweet course at conclusion of meal
discreet	tactful, reserved
discrete	separate or distinct
elicit	draw out, evoke
illicit	illegal
eminent	well known, respected
immanent	inherent
imminent	about to happen
fair	lovely; light-colored; just
fare	fee for transportation
forth	forward
fourth	after *third*
gorilla	an ape
guerrilla	kind of soldier or warfare
hear	perceive sound
here	in this place
heard	past tense of *hear*
herd	group of animals
hole	opening
whole	complete

its	possessive form of *it*
it's	contraction for *it is*
know	understand or be aware of
no	negative
later	following in time
latter	last in a series
lessen	make less
lesson	something learned
loose	not tight
lose	misplace
passed	past tense of *pass*
past	after; events occurring at a prior time
patience	calm endurance
patients	people getting medical treatment
peace	calm or absence of war
piece	part of something
plain	clear, unadorned
plane	woodworking tool; airplane
persecute	harass
prosecute	take legal action against
personal	relating to oneself
personnel	employees
precede	come before
proceed	go ahead, continue
principal	most important; head of a school
principle	basic truth, rule of behavior
raise	lift up or build up
raze	tear down
right	correct
rite	ritual
write	compose; put words into a text
scene	section of a play; setting of an action
seen	visible
stationary	fixed in place or still
stationery	paper for writing
straight	unbending
strait	water passageway
than	compared with
then	at that time; next

45b
spell

(Continued)

COMMONLY MISSPELLED OR CONFUSED WORD PAIRS *(Continued)*

WORD	MEANING
their	possessive form of *they*
there	in that place
they're	contraction for *they are*
to	toward
too	in addition, also
two	number after *one*
waist	middle of body
waste	leftover or discarded material
which	one of a group
witch	person with magical powers
who's	contraction for *who is*
whose	possessive of *who*
your	possessive of *you*
you're	contraction for *you are*

45b
spell

TAKING IT ONLINE

SEVEN STEPS TO EFFECTIVE LIBRARY RESEARCH

http://www.library.cornell.edu/okuref/research/tutorial.html

This hypertext guide to library research offers advice on how to develop research topics, locate background material, and find and evaluate books, periodical articles, recordings, and Internet resources.

INTERNET TUTORIALS

http://library.albany.edu/internet

This helpful site can improve your search skills whether you need to pick a search engine, select search terms, or evaluate what you find.

SINK OR SWIM: INTERNET SEARCH TOOLS AND TECHNIQUES

http://www.ouc.bc.ca/libr/connect96/search.htm

Probably the most accessible search engine tutorial on the Web, this site presents a full workshop on doing electronic research with ease.

INTERNET SEARCH STRATEGIES

http://www.rice.edu/fondren/etext/howto/search.html

Try this page for a quick look at types of search engines, search engine evaluations, search techniques, and source evaluation.

COMMUNITY INFORMATION BY ZIP CODE

http://library.csun.edu/mfinley/zipstats.html

When you're conducting research on your own community, visit this site for sources of local information, accessible by zip code.

TYPES OF SURVEYS

http://trochim.human.cornell.edu/kb/survtype.htm

This Web site clearly explains the various types of surveys you might use if you do field research.

46 | Participating in Research Communities: Academic, Work, and Public

Are you working in the library on your psychology paper on stress? Are you interviewing people about company-financed child care? Are you searching the Web for a local group, seeking ways to deal with school bullies? Each task raises different questions and calls for different research strategies, sources of information, and forms for turning inquiry into writing. (See the chart on p. 232.) Each is shaped by the curiosity and concerns of its own narrow research community but also addresses goals shared by a broader audience—academic, work, or public.

46a Recognizing research communities

46.1

Successful research writing goes beyond simply conveying information. By blending their own insights with information and ideas from print, electronic, or field sources, researchers increase readers' understanding. Together, writers and readers form a **research community**, a web of people and texts preserving and adding to the understanding of a subject.

In one sense, everyone engaged by a subject like "cosmetics" has a common interest, even if individual reasons for inquiry differ. In a more important sense, however, a researcher's setting defines a specific community of readers and writers whose consensus extends far beyond a general subject. These readers and writers share a perspective on the scope and focus of a matter of interest—a **research topic**. They agree on what's worth asking about the topic, **research questions** that set goals for gathering and examining information. They use common terms, **keywords** that form a research thread linking topics, questions, and resources.

46b Identifying research topics and keywords

Whatever problem you investigate, you'll want to shape your topic around questions that intrigue you and your community.

1 Develop your topic for your readers

Research often begins with an assignment or task that helps identify the expectations of your audience, whether a teacher, a supervisor, or an organization. It may establish how much time you have, what kind of docu-

GENERAL COMMUNITY GOALS FOR PRINT, ELECTRONIC, AND FIELD RESEARCH

	ACADEMIC	WORK	PUBLIC
GOALS	Explain or prove, offer well-supported interpretations or conclusions, advance knowledge, analyze or synthesize information for use in other settings	Document problems, propose a project or a policy or course of action, compare information, improve performance	Support arguments for a policy or course of action, inform or advise for the public good
AUDIENCE EXPECTATIONS	Detailed evidence from varied sources (summary, paraphrase, quotation); documented sources that acknowledge scholarship	Clear, direct, and precise information; appropriate detail; less formal documentation	Accessible, fair, and persuasive information with evidence; informal documentation
TYPICAL QUESTIONS	What does it mean? What happened? How does it occur? How might it be modified?	What is the problem? How can we solve it? What course of action will help us achieve our goals?	How can this policy or situation be improved? What do people need or want to know?
TYPICAL FORMS	Interpretive (thesis) paper, informative paper, research report, grant report	Proposal, report, feasibility study, memorandum	Position paper, editorial, proposal, informative article, pamphlet, guidelines, letter
SAMPLE RESEARCH TOPIC (COSMETICS)	Gender roles in cosmetics advertising (refer to *Social Sciences Index*)	International marketing strategies for cosmetics (refer to *BIZZ—Business Index*)	Animal testing of cosmetics (refer to *Readers' Guide to Periodical Literature*)
SAMPLE RESEARCH QUESTION (COSMETICS)	What roles for women and men are reinforced by advertising?	How should trade-marked packaging be modified for regional markets?	Is animal testing necessary for safe products? How good are the alternatives?

ment you are creating, and what kind of research you need to do. It also may trigger your curiosity and help you define a topic to investigate.

STRATEGY Expand suggestions in your assignment.

- Read your assignment or notes carefully, looking for words that specify a topic or question, limiting or opening up your choices (see 4a).
- List any topic ideas along with synonyms or alternative terms. Draw on this list as you identify keywords to describe your topic (see 46b-3).
- If you don't identify a topic, begin with whatever you have. Try listing or clustering (see 3a–b) to generate related terms or potential topics.
- Consider asking the person who made the assignment for an opinion on a potential topic—and for more topic suggestions.

In an intermediate composition course, Jennifer Figliozzi and Summer
rrigo-Nelson underlined important words in their assignment to "investi-
te the <u>psychological or social dimensions</u> of a <u>local or campus problem.</u>"
ney then listed some campus problems.

canceled classes	student fees	date rape	parking
library hours	role of sports	student alcohol use	crime

ney chose "student alcohol use" because the topic sounded interesting with
>urces readily available and the field research manageable.

Try to balance your interests with readers' expectations. For example,
nnifer and Summer knew that their audience wanted an academic report
sing print and electronic sources with field research on a problem.

STRATEGY Map your community as you focus and plan.

- What academic, workplace, or public goals motivate readers? What issues engage, concern, or benefit them? Why?
- What do they want to know: What happened? What it means? Why or
  how it occurred? How to solve or improve it? What to do?
- Are they interested in the past (history), present (current events), or
  future (trends, predictions)?
- Which individuals, organizations, sources, methods, or evidence do
  they consider most authoritative and reliable?
- What type of written or oral presentation—with what organization or
  approach—do they expect? When is it due? How do you need to plan
  your research to meet these expectations?

46b
resrc

2 Write, read, and browse for topic ideas

Try planning strategies (see 3a) to explore intriguing problems, do
some preliminary reading (see 2a), or browse online.

STRATEGY Read and browse to begin your inquiry.

- For academic projects, turn to specialized encyclopedias and scholarly
  journals in the field (see 47b). For work-related topics, try business
  magazines or publications from industry or professional groups. For
  topics of public interest, turn to popular magazines like *Time, Discover,*
  and *The Nation.*
- Use the "Search" button on your Web browser to find useful Internet
  search engines, Web sites where you can look for information or
  browse through collections of **links** or connections to other sites (see
  47d). Search engines can be especially useful when they categorize
  links in **subject trees**, presenting a broad category with more specific
  subcategories that may suggest issues and questions.
- As you read or browse, look for new (perhaps contradictory) research,
  unanswered questions, unsolved problems, intriguing ideas, unresolved

issues, inconsistencies, policies or ideas with which you disagree, or u
convincing interpretations.

After Jennifer and Summer selected "student alcohol use" as a focus, their in
tial reading and browsing led them to wonder about the role of parents in d
termining the drinking habits of students.

3 Use keywords to help define your topic

Note recurring words (*exercise*, *beauty*), names (*John Glenn, Snow White*
and phrases (*student drinking, alcohol use*). Libraries use such terms to catalc
resources. Web and electronic databases use them to categorize and access in
formation. Field researchers use them in interviews or questionnaires. In shor
research communities rely on shared terms—**keywords**—to maintain the
focus on a topic and its associated issues.

STRATEGY Begin a list of keywords used in your community.

Write down all the keywords, names, and phrases that might refer t
your topic. Note synonyms, such as *maturation* for *growth*. Add words use
by print resources or search engines to break down subjects. Initially, you
keywords can help you define your topic and join the dialogue of your re
search community. Later they can help you develop research questions (se
46c), follow a research thread (see 46d), and plan your project (see 46g).

46c
esrch

46c Recognizing research questions

Research questions, or **guiding questions**, focus your attention a
you gather and filter information from print, electronic, or field sources. Consider typical audience concerns as you design questions.

Academic. What have other scholars and researchers concluded about your
topic? Do you agree or disagree? Why? What can you add?

Work. What are the pertinent details of the problem? What action are you
proposing? Why is it workable, efficient, or cost effective?

Public. Who needs your information? Why? What are you proposing? What
might its effects be? How do you account for other views?

STRATEGY State your research questions.

- Aim to arrive at two or three research questions relatively early. A
  longer set may lack focus or may be unrealistic, given your deadline.
- Given your preliminary writing, reading, and browsing, consider which
  questions matter to your research community.

- Relate your questions to your general goals (to inform, to persuade) and your specific ones (to get a policy adopted, to interpret plausibly).
- Pose questions about issues or problems without clear answers.
- Design your questions to enlighten both you and your readers.
- State your questions simply, integrating keywords of your community.

nnifer and Summer developed these research questions for their project on rental behaviors and college student drinking.

- Will students with permission to drink at home have different drinking behaviors at college than those without such permission?
- Do students feel that a correlation exists between drinking behaviors at home and at college?

46d Following a community research thread

Identify a **research thread**, a limited set of keywords, names, and hrases that connects your topic to your research questions. Follow this road ap from source to source, across search engines, or through a series of links. dd any unusual or technical keywords preferred by your sources, such as *hysical development* for *bodybuilding*.

STRATEGY **Refine your list of keywords.**

As you discover sources, revise your list of keywords (see 46b-3). Record those used repeatedly in sources, and drop those used infrequently. Use this list to search (see 47a and e) systematically through library catalogs, ibliographies, databases, and the Internet. If your keywords produce too nany sources, look for more limited terms. If they produce too few, try alternatives more common in your research community.

46e Building a working bibliography

Keep track of possible resources in a **working bibliography**, listing tems likely to address your research questions. (See Chapter 47 on finding sources.)

1 Decide what to include in a working bibliography

As you consult reference works, note possible sources that will help you address your questions. Write your research questions at the head of your working bibliography (or keep a copy close at hand).

INCLUDE
- More sources than you'll need (for some won't be available or useful)
- Items with descriptive titles or lengths suggesting rich, relevant sources

- Recent sources to provide up-to-date information
- Varied sources for broad surveys and specific treatments
- Sources from bibliographies, search engines, or indexes with annota-
  tions or abstracts summarizing content

EXCLUDE

- Sources that may be very difficult to obtain
- Sources with a questionable relationship to your research questions
- Sources with doubtful credibility

2 Choose a format to record bibliography entries

Select a system for recording bibliographic information so you can
quickly identify the source each time you take reading notes and easily document your sources once you finish (see Chapters 51–54).

Note cards. If you write out each entry on a 3" × 5" card, you can arrange
the cards by category or alphabetize them when you prepare your list of
works cited or references. Adding and eliminating items is simple.

Research notebook. For a handy bibliography, use a notebook with pockets for printouts from electronic indexes. Rearranging and alphabetizing is
less convenient, though you can add marginal comments or numbers, highlight, or duplicate and cut up the pages.

46e
esrch

Electronic notes. Electronic card file systems and database programs have
most of the advantages of the 3" × 5" cards they often resemble. These entries can be easily transferred to your reference list. Some databases even rearrange information about sources using the documentation style you select.

3 Make complete and accurate entries

Entries in a working bibliography should contain the following.

BOOKS	ARTICLES	ELECTRONIC INFORMATION
Call number	Author(s)	Name of person
Author(s), editor(s),	Title and subtitle	writing, posting,
translator(s)	Periodical name	or sending
Title and subtitle	Volume and issue	information
City of publication,	number (if used)	Name of source
name of publisher,	Date	Date of online
and date of	Page number(s)	publication or
publication		revision
		Date of access
		Address/URL/access
		route/database
		Any original publication
		information (online
		or print)

6f Taking notes as you read analytically and critically

Reading and research go hand in hand. (See 2b and 48a–b.)

Take analytical and critical notes

Because analytical reading (see 2b and 48a) concentrates on understanding information, **analytical notes** record facts, details, concepts, interpretations, and quotations from your sources, focusing on what's relevant to
our research questions. **Critical notes** often accompany them, adding your
comments, interpretations, or assessments of a source in relation to your research questions. (See 2b and 48b.)

STRATEGY Double-check quotations for accuracy.

When you're using actual books and journals, not photocopies, be *absolutely certain* that you copy quotations word for word and record the exact
page number where each quotation appears. If a quotation runs on to a second page in the source, note both numbers and the place where the page
changes. (After all, you don't know what you might finally quote; see 49b.)

Choose a format for recording notes

Develop an easy, efficient system for keeping notes.

46f
resrch

Note cards. Many writers prefer portable, convenient index cards, generally
4" × 6" or 5" × 7". If you identify the card's topic clearly at the top and re-
strict each card to one kind of note (quotation, summary, paraphrase, synthesis), you can group, add, or rearrange cards as you plan or write.

Research journal. A research journal (usually a notebook) provides space
to record information, reflect on new knowledge, and begin assembling your
project. Add headings or marginal comments to identify the topics of the
notes. Store photocopies or printouts in any pockets or folder.

Electronic notes. You can use software designed for note taking or set up
word-processing files like a research journal or set of note cards (one page =
one card). If you specify a subtopic or research question for each entry, you
can use these labels to sort, reorganize, or retrieve material.

STRATEGY Organize and link your notes as you take them.

- **Link notes to your keywords or research questions.** At the top of
  each card, page, or entry, use your keywords, research questions, or
  subtopics to identify how material relates to your topic.
- **Link notes to sources.** Clearly note the source on each card, page, or
  entry. Use the author's last name or a short version of the title to connect each note to its corresponding full bibliography entry (see 46e-3).

- **Link notes to exact locations.** Include the page numbers of t
source, especially for any material quoted or paraphrased. If an ele
tronic source uses paragraph numbers instead of page numbers, no
these.

---

3 Duplicate only especially useful materials

Before you duplicate or print material, assess whether it responds
your research questions. (See also 48c–d on evaluating sources.)

STRATEGY Be selective as you download electronic resources.

Use the menu of your browser to save or print useful online materia
because Web sites can change rapidly. In your notes or on the printou
record the date you accessed the resource, any information about its creato
or sponsor, and its Web address. Pay attention to copyright issues, too. Som
resources explicitly state that they are not to be redistributed, others are pai
tially restricted, and still others are freely available. In many cases you ca
collect information for academic work, but if you plan to republish what yo
gather or have questions, discuss the issues with your instructor.

46g Turning research into writing

How do you know when to begin *writing* your research paper? Actu
ally, there's no set time. If you've been recording your responses as a critica
reader and assembling material as answers to your research questions, you've
already begun drafting. Think strategically about your task as you move to
ward a more complete text.

1 Review your research questions

Return to your research questions (see 46c) to plan your draft.

STRATEGY Let your research questions guide your draft.

Arrange your research questions in a logical sequence, adding any others that you now think you ought to address. Answer the questions, and use
them to determine the order of material in your draft.

---

2 Focus on your readers and purpose

Review your readers' expectations, values, questions, and likely reactions to your project (see 4c and 46b). Try to respond with clear explanations, arguments, and supporting evidence. Also consider the goals that your
research questions reflect (see 46c).

TRATEGY **Use your purpose to clarify your form.**

Ask yourself what you want your research project to *do*. Then ask what
~m it might take, given this purpose. What do you want your audience to
rn, to do, or to feel? Does your research suggest a position paper, interpre-
ion, history, case study, proposal, or report?

___

y working out a **purpose structure**, a series of statements briefly describ-
g what you intend to do in each section of your paper.

GINNING	Explain the importance of copyrights, patents, and intellec- tual property rights, especially for computer software.
IDDLE	Discuss intellectual property rights in three cases: Sun Micro- system's Java language versus Microsoft's, *Excel* versus similar spreadsheets, and Apple's Macintosh user interface versus Micro- soft's *Windows*.
IDING	Describe recently proposed solutions to the problem of estab- lishing ownership of software designs.

Build from a thesis to a draft

Begin with a thesis statement (see 4b), based on your research ques-
ions. Modify it as you draft, perhaps breaking it into several sentences, or or-
anize around its parts, repeated at key points. Instead of a detailed tradi-
ional outline, try a working outline, blocking out the general sequence and
elating the segments (see 3b). Pull together the materials that belong in each
part using whatever method of grouping suits your resources and notes.

46g
resrc

STRATEGY **Group your materials in sequence.**

- Arrange your cards or notes in relation to one another. As patterns
  emerge, you may see how other material fits.
- Prepare pieces of paper describing available information—major points
  from sources, paraphrases, summaries, or ideas to include. Arrange
  these in relation to each other until you find a workable grouping (see
  49b on integrating sources).
- Photocopy your research journal if you've written on both sides of the
  pages or don't want to cut it up. Then cut out the separate entries,
  arrange them in a sequence, and draft transitions to connect them.
- Use your word processing program to cut and paste relevant electronic
  notes into a new file wherever they seem to fit.

___

Once you have chunks of related materials, move from the largest units to
the smaller sections, interweaving notes, source materials, and additions.
Write transitions between the chunks, explaining how they fit together. Use
your research questions to focus your introduction and conclusion, but direct these key parts to your readers as you draft.

STRATEGY Design an introduction and a conclusion for readers.

For the introduction, ask, "How can I make readers want to read on For the conclusion, ask, "How can I keep readers thinking about my topic Try several versions of each, experimenting with style and content.

4 Revise and edit

Allow time to revise what you've written based on your audience's need the community for which you're writing, your research questions, and you purposes (see 6a–b). Ask others to respond to your draft (see 6c). Careful edit (see 14b–c), proofread (see 14e), and design your document (see 13c–f Make sure that any quotations are accurate and that page numbers and a thors are cited correctly (see 49b). Double-check your documentation for (see Chapters 51–54).

If your project is collaborative, organize these tasks as a group.

STRATEGY Research collaboratively within your community.

- Work together to define your topic or issue, identify keywords, an state your research questions.
- Organize as your teacher, supervisor, or group expects.
- Divide responsibilities for building a working bibliography, capitaliz ing on individual strengths, background, and expertise.
- Meet regularly to stay on track, assessing what you've found and wha you need to find. Come to meetings ready to compare, connect, sup plement, exchange, and critique.
- Try strategies for collaborative drafting (see 5c), revising (see 6c), and editing (see 14c). Organize and rehearse together for any oral presenta tion (see Chapter 11 and 55h).

47 | Using Print and Electronic Resources

With a careful search strategy, you'll probably uncover more sources than you can use—plenty to help you write with authority.

47a Developing search strategies

A **search strategy** begins with your topic and your research questions (see 46b–c), helping you select the most appropriate resources.

Consider *where* research might take place

- **Library research** focuses on print or electronic resources: books, articles, pamphlets, microforms, databases, recordings, films, and art works. It calls on your skill with indexing and reference systems. It also rewards your effort with sources gathered and screened by library professionals.
- **Electronic or online research** focuses on resources available through networks: texts, data, graphics, audio, film, and electronic messages. It calls on your skill with software and search engines.
- **Field research** focuses on artifacts, events, and oral texts gathered through observations, interviews, surveys, and recordings. It calls on your skill at organizing, conducting, and interpreting field contacts.

STRATEGY Decide what kinds of research suit your topic.

- Has your topic been covered in books and articles, on Web sites, or in newspapers? Do library and electronic research to build on what others know and say.
- Is your subject a text (book, poem, Web page, video, film, document), an object (painting, sculpture), or an event (play, musical performance)? Do research in a library, museum, or theater. Obtain the subject in print or electronic form along with responses of others to it. Do field research by witnessing a performance and the audience's reaction.
- Is your subject a historical event that you can study only through documents, films, or pictures? Do library or electronic research.
- Is your subject an event, a situation, a set of attitudes, or a pattern of behavior that has not been widely studied and that you can investigate directly? Do field research (see Chapter 50).
- Has your subject been debated online? Cautiously consult electronic mailing lists, newsgroups, and Web forums (see 48d-3).

47a
sour

2 Distinguish between *primary* and *secondary* sources

Primary sources consist of information and ideas in original (or close-to-original) form: historical documents, literary works, electronic messages, letters, taped interviews, survey data, videotapes, raw statistics, and other basic information with little or no interpretation by the observer or gatherer. Analyze and interpret such sources to clarify how they respond to your research questions. **Secondary sources** consist of works that analyze, summarize, interpret, or explain primary sources, telling you what others have said and what issues are debated in a given community. Interpret, synthesize, and evaluate such sources as you integrate them.

3 Move from preliminary to general to specialized sources

Begin by skimming the most broadly informative sources such as encyclopedias, magazine articles, ready references, general information books, or

47.1

Web pages. These **preliminary sources** can help you focus on a topic, arr
at research questions, and identify keywords for searching.

Next, **general sources** provide background and help identify issue
problems, and ideas you might examine more closely. They include boo
articles in general-interest magazines and academic journals, online ne
sites, Web pages on a specific topic, database introductions, or postings to
electronic mailing list, newsgroup, or Web forum.

Finally, **specialized sources** provide substantial support for the exp
nations, interpretations, and arguments you advance in a paper. They inclu
research or project reports, scientific studies, technical documents, survey
entries in a specialized database, field notes, theoretical books, specialize
newsletters, topic-centered electronic discussions, industry or public-intere
reports, and scholarly articles.

STRATEGY Design your own search strategy.

Plan. Identify possible research directions, types of research, and kinc
of sources.

List. Jot down the steps in your research process (see Chapter 46
including which sources you might consult first and which later.

Focus. Review your research questions and keywords each time yo
go to the library or online so you stick to the same research threac

Direct your work. Look for varied, fair sources. Balance tradition
library resources (probably evaluated prior to publication) with onlin
resources such as Web sites (possibly narrow or less reliable). Wor
from broad, general sources to narrower, specific ones. In an academ
ic setting, use any required kind or number of sources.

Reflect and redirect. Review and revise your research questions, searcl
strategy, and keywords as your research evolves.

47b Finding references and indexes

Your search strategy should lead to varied resources, often already as-
sembled for you. Many will be available online, but some only in print or
through library terminals. Visit your library as well as using its home page to
discover what is readily available.

1 Begin with general and specialized references

In almost all fields of academic, work, or public interest, you can turn
to references for a broad overview of a topic, relevant background, useful
keywords, and bibliographies of sources.

General encyclopedias, ready references, maps, and dictionaries. These
references provide basic information on a range of topics. Look for resources
as varied as *The New Encyclopaedia Britannica*, *Grolier Multimedia Encyclopedia*,

tistical Abstract of the United States, National Geographic Atlas of the World, or bster's New World Dictionary of the American Language.

ecialized encyclopedias. Works such as the Encyclopedia of Pop, Rock, and ul or the McGraw-Hill Encyclopedia of Science and Technology cover a specific pic or area in depth.

bliographies. Save time by using organized lists (sometimes annotated) references on a topic. Look for specialized works as well as major compila- ns such as the International Bibliography of the Social Sciences; Film Research: Critical Bibliography with Annotations and Essays; and the MLA International bliography of Books and Articles on the Modern Languages and Literature.

STRATEGY Talk to information specialists.

The librarians at your school, your company, or your public library can elp you develop your search strategy, conduct effective keyword searches, nd locate materials. As the people in an organization with the most training finding and managing information, they can help you tap available re- ources or turn to a lending service called interlibrary loan.

Consult indexes to periodicals and books as you focus

47b
sour

Periodicals are published at specified periods of time and contain articles y different authors. **General-interest magazines** often appear monthly or veekly, with each issue paginated separately. Many **scholarly journals** appear ss frequently than magazines, perhaps four times a year, and number pages ontinuously through the issues in an annual volume. **Newspapers** generally ppear daily or weekly with numbered or lettered sections. **Online (electronic) eriodicals** may supply past issues or selected articles in electronic archives; ther **Web sites** act like periodicals, offering a selection of articles. These sites nay add material irregularly as it's available or as the site maintainer decides to update.

Through your library, Internet services, and search engines, you can access **periodical indexes**, and some include related resources, links, or **ab- stracts** (brief summaries). Refine your list of keywords (see 46b) as you search. Try indexes from varied fields or perspectives to bring your research the benefits of **triangulation**, using multiple sources to enhance accuracy.

General and newspaper indexes. Each indexing particular publications or topics, these resources help you find articles in newspapers and general- interest magazines. Select from references such as Academic Index, Editorials on File, Facts on File, InfoTrac, PAIS (Public Affairs Information Services), Readers' Guide to Periodical Literature, and New York Times Index.

Specialized indexes and abstracts. Designed for specific fields or academic areas, these indexes are as varied as Anthropological Literature, EconLit, ERIC

TYPES OF PERIODICALS

	MAGAZINES	JOURNALS	NEWSPAPERS
READERS	General public, special interest	Academics, professionals	Local, national, special interest
WRITERS	Staff, freelancers	Experts	Journalists
REVIEWERS	Editors	Peers	Section editors
FREQUENCY	Month, week	Quarter, month	Day, week, month
PAGINATION	Issue	Volume, issue	Section
FOCUS	Useful, short articles	Research, theory, or application	Current events and timely information
FORMAT	Cover, color, sidebars, photos	Little color, table of contents, data displays	Some color, large pages, columns, headlines, photos
ADS	General, topical	Professional, scholarly	General, local, topical

47c
ource

(Educational Resources Information Center), *Current Index to Journals in Edu-cation*, *Government Documents Catalog Service* (*GDCS/GPO Index*), *Social Science Index*, *Biological and Agricultural Index*, *Medline*, *Abstracts of English Studies*, and *Psychological Abstracts* (*PsycINFO*).

Indexes of databases. Databases are files of information available in elec-tronic form. To find those covering your topic, you might consult catalogs such as the *Gale Directory of Databases* or the *Federal Database Finder: A Directory of Free and Fee-Based Data Bases and Files Available from the Federal Government*.

47c Tapping library resources

Turn to your library's home page, catalog, and special collections.

1 Use the catalog to locate sources

The online catalog may be available on campus and off through your library's home page. You can use exact names or keywords to search by *author's name*; *title* of a work, periodical, or series; or *subject area*. (See Figure 47.1 on p. 247.) If your search locates several items (each listed in a *brief display*), click on one to call up its *full display*. You may expand a search to related topics, au-thors, or works, or follow links to indexes, bibliographies, encyclopedias, and other materials (see 47b). Print or record your search results, including each source's call number and location.

Seek out government documents and special collections

Libraries have a variety of resources other than books and articles, such **special collections** of rare books, manuscripts, and documents; **audio-sual collections** of videotapes, films, and audio recordings; and **microform ollections** of many sources on microfilm and microfiche. **Government doc-ments** include reports, pamphlets, and regulations issued by Congress, fed-al agencies, and state or local governments. The *Monthly Catalog of U.S. overnment Publications* can aid your search for these as can the *Govern-ent Information Sharing Project* at <http://govinfo.kerr.orst.edu>, the *Library of ongress* at <http://www.loc.gov>, the *National Archives and Records Adminis-ation* at <http://www.archives.gov>, and the *Thomas Legislative Information on e Internet* site at <http://thomas.loc.gov>.

47d Finding Internet and Web resources

The **Internet** links researchers through email, discussion groups, re-ource sites, and the Web. The Web consists of documents (*pages*) or collec-ions of pages (*sites*) that you can access using a **browser**, navigational soft-vare such as *Netscape Navigator* or *Internet Explorer*. To access a Web page, you :an enter its address, known as a **URL** (uniform resource locator), into a Web :rowser, or you can follow links embedded in an online document (usually narked by an icon or highlighted line). Materials online range from well-researched studies to hasty opinions, from personal Web pages to corporate ind organizational sites promoting an idea or a product. (See 47f and 48d.)

47d
sour

1 Use search engines

Web sites that categorize links and provide keyword search tools for finding resources are called **search engines**. Access these through the search button on your browser or their URLs.

All the Web	http://alltheweb.com
AltaVista	http://www.altavista.com
Ask Jeeves	http://www.ask.com
DogPile	http://www.dogpile.com/
Excite	http://search/excite.com/info.xcite
Google	http://www.google.com
HotBot	http://hotbot.lycos.com/
Lycos	http://www.lycos.com/
MetaCrawler	http://www.go2net.com
Yahoo!	http://www.yahoo.com

Although you'll find more information using a large search engine, you may find more that's worthwhile by searching at smaller scholarly sites with pre-screened and categorized information such as these.

BUBL Information Service	http://bubl.ac.uk

Infomine	http://infomine.ucr.edu
Internet Scout Project	http://www.ilrt.bris.ac.uk/mirrors/scout/index.html
Librarians' Index to the Internet	http://lii.org
The WWW Virtual Library	http://www.vlib.org

STRATEGY Test and assess several search engines.

When you conduct a search, the search engine goes to its own data bases, not the Internet directly. Thus each may find different information, or ganized differently as well. Save time by learning what several search engine offer and how to use them efficiently.

- Try the same search using identical terms with several search engine to find out what each produces. (See 47e.)
- Find out how the search engine is organized, how it searches, and wha it offers (many items, selected items, advanced searches, topic groups special collections, or other features).
- Get advice from others in your community—teachers, peers, librarians co-workers—about search engines they use for both quick searches and extensive research.
- Visit sites such as <http://www.searchenginewatch.com> for current re views and links, including specialized search engines such as *AltaVista'* multimedia options, *FirstGov*, or *SpeechBot*.

2 Join electronic discussions

Email allows you to contact individuals or organizations that can answer specific questions or provide information (see 12b). Use the directory services of search engines to locate email addresses of individuals, and check Web pages for contact information to email the author or sponsor. Newsgroups, Web-based forums, and electronic mailing lists (see 12c) are all conversational sources that may or may not supply reliable information (see 48d-3).

47e Making the most of your keyword searches

Whether you're exploring specialized indexes (see 47b), library hold ings (see 47c), or the Internet (see 47d), an efficient keyword search uses a string of keywords or specific terms called a **query**. Figure 47.1 shows a key word search conducted through the online interface to a university library catalog using the keywords "college" and "alcohol." This search illustrates how to move from keywords to a general list of materials to a specific catalog entry.

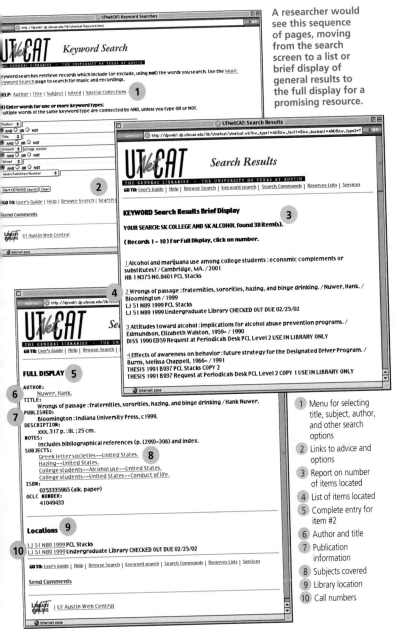

A researcher would see this sequence of pages, moving from the search screen to a list or brief display of general results to the full display for a promising resource.

1 Menu for selecting title, subject, author, and other search options

2 Links to advice and options

3 Report on number of items located

4 List of items located

5 Complete entry for item #2

6 Author and title

7 Publication information

8 Subjects covered

9 Library location

10 Call numbers

47e
sour

FIGURE 47.1 A keyword library catalog search

STRATEGY Select keywords to focus your search.

- Use your list of keywords (see 46b and d) and your research question to select your first set of search terms. Consider various word forms.
- Submit them to the catalog, index, search engine, or other database. Type and spell carefully. If the database contains a keyword that matches your query, it will display the items as the results of the search.
- Repeat your search, looking for the most useful keywords, combinations, synonyms, or related terms. Use effective clusters again to search different databases.

If your results seem uneven—too many or too few items—click on the advanced search advice for the search engine, catalog, or index. Find out how to search most productively, using specific words, math signs (+, −), symbols (* to look for all variations using part of a word), or automatic default combinations (as in Figure 47.1 on p. 247).

STRATEGY Learn advanced search strategies.

Use your query to narrow a search, specifying terms you want to combine, rule out, or treat as alternatives. Use these principles of Boolean logic to help focus on what you actually want to know.

OR (expands): X OR Y	Search for either term (documents referring to either X or Y)
AND (restricts): X AND Y	Search for both terms (documents referring to both X and Y, but not to either alone)
NOT (excludes): X NOT Y	Search for X unless X includes the term Y (documents referring to X except for those documents that also refer to Y)

Figure 47.2 shows the results of a query sent to the *Google* search engine using two keywords, "college" and "alcohol," to find only documents associated with both terms. For this widely discussed topic, the search turned up an overwhelming 757,000 items. Narrowing the search (college + alcohol + parents) only reduced the results to 239,000. Repeating the query at *AllTheWeb* produced 27,740 items, though this search engine narrows by categorizing the first two hundred results. Often your research dilemma may be focusing and selecting, not simply finding sources.

STRATEGY Search for fewer but more useful results.

- **Try hit-or-miss.** Compare the first pages of results from several search engines, sampling resources with useful descriptions.

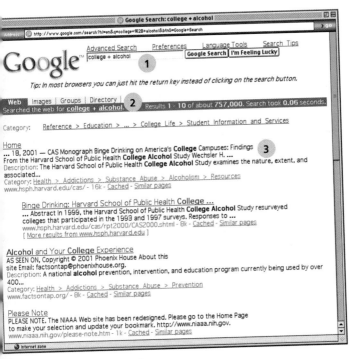

1. Boolean logic used to combine search items
2. Count of items found
3. Search returns with title, brief description, and location

FIGURE 47.2 A keyword Web search

- **Narrow further.** Follow the search engine's advice for other search limits or options and related terms or groups of links.
- **Define a community edge.** Search for terms with an academic, workplace, or civic slant, not just a topic.
- **Go to a specialty database.** Turn to prescreened databases such as the library's catalog (see the search in Figure 47.1, identifying 38 items). Use specialized search engines respected by your research community. (A "college alcohol" search at the scholarly *Infomine* produced only five items—all clearinghouses or agencies likely to supply reliable information and leads to other sources.)
- **Seek help.** Ask librarians or others doing related research to recommend useful resources or sites with relevant links.
- **Screen.** Begin to assess resources as you search. Ask how each possible resource relates to your research questions.

47f Evaluating Web search results

Although you must judge all your sources critically, Internet resources require more careful evaluation than library materials, which have been evaluated prior to publication. Because anyone can place materials online, the Internet provides the largest repository of information—and much questionable information. Further, conversational and multimedia resources complicate critical evaluation (see 48d).

Academic audiences generally expect you to find authoritative sites produced by people aware of the scholarly discussion. Work audiences expect you to use sites that address a problem directly, produced by people or organizations known for their accuracy. Public audiences expect you to rely on sites with careful reasoning and reliable information. For all three communities, you'll need to decide whether your results are authoritative, current, verifiable, and credible.

STRATEGY Screen your search results.

- Categorize what you've found. Is each source a business or organizational site, a personal Web page, an academic article, or something else? Are your results balanced? Are they appropriate for your project and community?
- Begin to connect and relate your sources. Plan to use only information you have found in at least two credible places. Identify what you need to corroborate or reconsider.
- Assess what you still need to locate. Consider quality and quantity. Continue to search for sources to fill gaps in your research.
- Be sure you've printed key pages in case they disappear, recorded URLs and dates of access, and noted sources of nonpublic messages in case you need permission to quote.

47g Pulling your research materials together

Besides finding resources, you also have to manage what you find.

STRATEGY Organize your information.

- Gather your materials—notes, photocopies, printouts, and files.
- Sort your resources; note missing material, and track it down.
- Use major points and subtopics, keywords, color codes, stacks of material, or some other method to categorize your resources.
- If a category seems scant, drop it or do further research.
- If a category seems very full, consider breaking it into subtopics.
- If you have not found enough appropriate material, ask for help from a librarian, your instructor, a colleague, or a specialist in the field.
- Reexamine and regroup your resources until you are ready to plan and draft.

48 | Reading Critically and Evaluating Sources

A research project calls for two types of reading, analytical and critical (see 2b). When you read **analytically**, you aim to understand the ideas and information presented in a source. When you read **critically**, however, you interact with the source. You assess its strengths and limitations, investigate how it relates to other texts, and identify what it doesn't address. This interaction also helps you determine how to use its information within your own writing.

Of course, both analytical and critical reading take place within the context of a research community and are intertwined. And both contribute to the outcome of a research project. Analytical reading leads to the summaries, paraphrases, syntheses, quotations, and details you develop into much of your content. But your analytical selection of quotations, for example, depends on your critical assessment of the text. This critical reading rests, in turn, on your clear understanding of the ideas and information in your source.

48a Reading analytically: Summarizing, paraphrasing, and synthesizing

Analytical reading encourages your understanding of sources as you sum up, restate, and relate what they present.

1 Summarize your source

Because a summary is much shorter than the original, it helps you focus on key content in an article, book chapter, or passage. It presents the essentials in your own words without interpretation or unnecessary detail.

STRATEGY Compress main ideas in a summary.

- **Read.** Read the selection, looking for the key ideas, evidence, and information. Underline, highlight, or note these.
- **Scan.** Scan (reread) the selection to decide which of the ideas you've noted are the *most* important. Look for the writer's main purpose and the major sections of the discussion.
- **Write** (1). Sum up each section (each stage in the argument or explanation) in a *single sentence* that focuses on the key ideas.
- **Write** (2). Sum up the entire selection in a *single sentence* that captures its main point.
- **Combine.** Combine your section summaries and overall summary.

251

- **Revise.** Rewrite for logic and ease of reading. Check against the sour for accuracy.
- **Document.** Indicate clearly the source of your summary using a sta dard style of documentation (see Chapters 51–54).

Jennifer Figliozzi and Summer Arrigo-Nelson use two one-sentence sum maries to help introduce the first research question in their paper (see par graph 2 on p. 316). They use APA style to cite sources (see 52a).

First, research has shown that adolescents who have open and close re lationships with their parents use alcohol less often than do those wit conflictual relationships (Sieving, 1996). For example, a survey of stu dents in seventh through twelfth grades reported that approximatel 35% of adolescent drinkers were under parental supervision whil drinking (Department of Education, 1993).

2 Paraphrase your source

A good paraphrase may help you understand a source by putting its content into your own words. Although a paraphrase doesn't add to or de tract from the original, it can help you incorporate detailed information in your writing without a dense or confusing quotation. To paraphrase pictures, drawings, or graphics, you need to "extract" their information and concepts and "translate" the material into your own words.

STRATEGY   Restate a source's ideas in a paraphrase.

- **Read.** Read the selection carefully, noting wording and content.
- **Write.** Draft your paraphrase, using your own words, phrases, and sentence patterns in place of the original wording. Rely on synonyms and equivalent expressions. You can retain names, proper nouns, and the like.
- **Revise.** Rewrite so your version is easier to read than your source.
- **Double-check.** Avoid accidental plagiarism; be sure your sentence structures and phrasing don't echo the original (see 49c–d).
- **Document.** Indicate clearly the source of your paraphrase using a standard style of documentation (see Chapters 51–54).

Jennifer Figliozzi encountered the following passage in a report on current alcohol abuse programs at various schools.

The university also now notifies parents when their sons or daughters violate the alcohol policy, or any other aspect of the student code of con- duct. "We were hoping that the support of parents would help change

students' behavior, and we believe it has," says Timothy F. Brooks, an as-
sistant vice-president and the dean of students.

because she wanted to avoid long quotations and integrate the information
smoothly, Jennifer paraphrased part of the passage, combining it with a brief
quotation.

> Officials at the University of Delaware thought that letting parents know
> when students violate regulations on alcohol use would alter students'
> drinking habits, and one administrator now says, "we believe it has"
> (Reisberg, 1998, p. A42).

Synthesize your sources

A synthesis pulls together summaries of several sources and points out
their relationships. It enables you to provide background, explore causes and
effects, contrast explanations, or consolidate support for your thesis.

STRATEGY Relate ideas in a synthesis of sources.

- **Read.** Gather and read your sources, preparing a summary of each.
- **Focus.** Decide on the purpose of your synthesis, and sum up your con-
  clusions about how the sources relate.
- **Arrange.** Select a sequence for the sources in your synthesis.
- **Write.** Draft your synthesis, combining your summaries of the sources
  with your conclusions about their relationships.
- **Revise.** Rewrite so that your synthesis is easy to read and readers can
  easily identify the sources of the various ideas.
- **Document.** Indicate clearly the sources for your synthesis using a
  standard style of documentation (see Chapters 51–54).

48a
read

Work and public writing often use synthesis to identify a problem or policy
that needs to be examined. Similarly, many academic papers summarize prior
studies to identify the need for more research and to justify research questions, as in the opening of Jennifer and Summer's paper (see 52c.)

> Studies conducted with high school students have supported the hy-
> pothesis that positive family relationships are more likely to be associ-
> ated with less frequent alcohol use among adolescents than are negative
> relationships. Adolescents model the limited substance use of their par-
> ents where there is a good or moderate parent-adolescent relationship
> (Andrews, Hops, & Duncan, 1997). Other factors the studies found to
> be associated with positive family relationships, along with substance
> use, were academic achievement, family structure, place of residence,
> self-esteem, and emotional tone (Martsh & Miller, 1997; Wechsler,
> Dowdall, Davenport, & Castillo, 1995).

48b Reading critically: Questioning, synthesizing, interpreting, and assessing

Critical reading encourages your interaction with sources—asking questions, unifying varied perspectives, relating sources to your own views, and making judgments.

1 Identify unanswered questions

A research report or essay often begins by identifying an unanswered academic question, an unsolved work problem, or an unsettled public issue—highlighting its importance for readers.

STRATEGY **Prepare a problem paragraph on what's unaddressed.**

On note cards, in your research journal, or in the margins of photocopies, record whatever is unresolved or unexamined—questions, problems, evidence, perspectives, ideas. Then state them concisely in a **problem paragraph**, which may suggest how to develop your paper.

Here's Lily Germaine's note card on bodybuilding.

> Tucker, pp. 389-91   *Weight training & self-concept*
>
> Tucker uses "although" at least four times when summarizing other studies and phrases such as "only a few studies have shown...." He's nice on the surface but sets his readers up to find fault with the other studies. That basic fault is their lack of objective methodology, which he seems to plan on rectifying by using mathematical measurements and rigid definitions of terms. He seems to think he can be completely objective in determining such a slippery thing as "self-concept." I really have to question this assumption.

Her problem paragraph incorporated her insights and wording.

Does bodybuilding affect self-concept? Before we can answer this question, we need to ask if we can accurately measure such a slippery thing as "self-concept." Some researchers, like Tucker, believe that self-concept can be accurately gauged using mathematical measurements and rigid definitions of terms. For several reasons, however, this assumption is questionable. . . .

2 Synthesize perspectives

Use a **critical synthesis** to bring together opinions, interpretations, and evidence from a variety of sources. Like an **analytical synthesis** (see

a-3), a critical synthesis provides a unified discussion of various perspec-
ves. But a critical synthesis goes further—summarizing agreements, differ-
ces, and limitations while presenting conclusions.

STRATEGY **Synthesize to connect perspectives.**

- Consider your purpose, perhaps reviewing prior research, possible so-
  lutions to a problem, or positions on a public issue.
- Focus on material that relates directly to your topic or point.
- Be true to the ideas and information in your sources.
- Use your own ideas to go beyond your sources as you relate conclu-
  sions, opinions, ideas, and facts.
- Write a statement, summarizing the relationships you observe.
- Acknowledge contradictory facts, opinions, and perspectives.

Here is an analytical synthesis Kimlee Cunningham used in the second paragraph of her MLA-style paper on recent Disney animated films. It expands a
simpler statement of her key idea in paragraph 1: "By contrasting *Snow White
and the Seven Dwarfs* with the recent animated features *Beauty and the Beast*
(1991) and *Aladdin* (1992), we can see the leading female characters becoming more independent and assertive." (See 51c.)

> It is probably an exaggeration to say that a character like Belle in
> *Beauty and the Beast* is a lot like a contemporary feminist, as one critic sug-
> gests (Showalter). However, we should not simply ignore an interpreta-
> tion like this. Even if many people view a film like *Beauty and the Beast*
> (or *Aladdin*) as a simple love story (Hoffman), the films nonetheless grow
> out of the complicated values and roles that shape relationships today.
> Disney's contemporary portrayal of women characters shows a willing-
> ness to change with the times but also a reluctance to abandon traditional
> values and stereotypes.

3 Interpret your source

Your research paper or report should present your point of view about
the topic: your conclusion about its meaning or causes (academic), your commitment to a course of action (work), or your stand on an issue (public). At
the same time, you need to interpret the outlooks of your sources. Note how
views, values, background, or advocacy affect trustworthiness. Point out im-
balances, misrepresentations, or distortions of other views. Indicate why readers should accept your view instead.

An **interpretation** builds on synthesis (see 48a-3 and b-2) by explicitly
including your opinions and giving priority to your point of view. Interpreting
involves **generalizing** (reaching broad conclusions about what your research
says) and **extending** (going beyond this to present your own views based on
what you've discovered).

48b
read

> **STRATEGY** Interpret a source's outlook and balance.

- State your source's point of view as accurately as possible. Take into account any strong advocacy (or questionable bias).
- Present your point of view with supporting evidence, perhaps comparing the perspective of one source to that of another and to your own.
- Add your own conclusions, missing or differently presented in sources.

4 Assess your source

Sources aren't equally accurate, complete, or persuasive. And even the most reliable may not be relevant for a project. Decide what material to treat as authoritative and what to reject or refute. (See 47f, 48c, and 48d.)

> **STRATEGY** Assess accuracy, credibility, and value.

- Support your judgments with examples.
- Explain your judgments by comparing one text or body of data to others.
- Base your assessment on your own ideas, but feel free also to draw on assessments from sources.

48c Evaluating sources critically

48c
eval

In contrast to many Web sites (see 48d), books from reputable publishers and articles in scholarly journals or well-known magazines generally are reviewed and produced with editorial checks and balances. Even so, each source has its own bias and motivation.

> **STRATEGY** Evaluate every source, print or online.

- Does the publisher, journal, or sponsor have a reputation for balance and accuracy? Is it an advocate whose views require caution?
- Is the author's reputation clear? What do other sources think of the author's trustworthiness, fairness, and importance?
- How accurate is your source, especially if it presents facts as truth? Can you spot obvious errors? Which points are well documented?
- How does the writer support generalizations? Do they go beyond the facts? Are they consistent with your knowledge?
- Are the ideas generally consistent with those in your other sources? If different, do they seem insightful or misleading and eccentric?
- Does the source meet the expectations of your research community?
- Does the source appropriately document information, quotations, and ideas or clearly attribute them to the author?
- Has the source appeared without an editorial or review process? Does it apply only to a specific setting? Is its information outdated? Does it cite experts who have political or financial interests? Does it try to obscure its own bias? If so, consider it questionable; use it with caution.

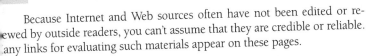

48d Evaluating Internet and Web sources critically

48.1

Because Internet and Web sources often have not been edited or re-
ewed by outside readers, you can't assume that they are credible or reliable.
.any links for evaluating such materials appear on these pages.

> "Bibliography on Evaluating Web Information"
>   http://www.lib.vt.edu/research/libinst/evalbiblio.html
> "Evaluation of Information Sources"
>   http://www.vuw.ac.nz/~agsmith/evaln/evaln.htm

he following pages explain how to examine a Web site critically.

> "The Good, the Bad and the Ugly: or, Why It's a Good Idea to
>   Evaluate Web Sources"
>   http://lib.nmsu.edu/instruction/eval.html
> "Thinking Critically about World Wide Web Resources"
>   http://www.library.ucla.edu/libraries/college/help/critical/index.htm
> "Evaluating Web Resources" (with links to checklists and examples)
>   http://www2.widener.edu/Wolfgram-Memorial-Library/
>   webevaluation/webeval.htm

1 Approach Web materials critically

48c
eval

Because Web research may uncover a variety of materials, adapt the
general guidelines for evaluating sources (see 48c). For instance, ask questions about the authority and relevance of articles in an online journal as you
would about traditional printed essays. Pay attention to affiliations, biases,
authors or sponsors, design, and content. Evaluate credibility, evidence, support, and documentation.

STRATEGY **Examine the types of Web materials you find.**

- Is the material documentary (films, sounds, images, surveys)? If so,
  consider authenticity, biases, and relevance to your research questions.
- Is the resource textual (essays, narratives, studies, articles)? If so, consider its authorship, construction, level of detail, support for reasoning, complexity, fairness, sources, and documentation.
- Is the resource peculiar to the Web (personal, educational, corporate, organizational sites)? If so, consider its genre, affiliation, reputation, possible motivation, construction, design, and value in terms of content.
- Is the resource conversational? If so, analyze it as primary material (see
  48d-3).

2 Ask critical questions about Web materials

To evaluate the strengths, weaknesses, and credibility of Web resources
such as personal pages and organizational sites, ask the following questions

developed by Paula Mathieu and Ken McAllister at the University of Illinois
Chicago as part of the *Critical Resources in Teaching with Technology* (CRIT
project.

- **Who benefits? What difference does that make?** The Web pages
  <http://www.whymilk.com>, for example, seem dedicated entirely
  the reader's health, as Figure 48.1 illustrates. But because this site pro
  motes drinking milk every day, critical readers can easily see that mil
  producers and distributors will also benefit from these milk sales.
- **Who's talking? What difference does that make?** The "speaker" re
  sponsible for all the site's positive facts about milk is identified as "us" i
  the invitation to request more information. The site's privacy statemen
  however, identifies the site owner as the California Fluid Milk Processor

48d
eval

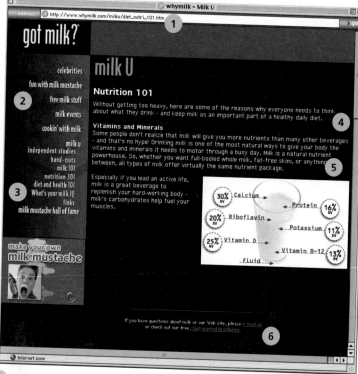

1 Commercial site
2 Includes features designed to appeal to readers
3 Offers quizzes on milk
4 Advocates drinking milk
5 Uses graphics to convey information
6 Offers more information

READER'S REACTION: **Why are you sharing
all this? How do you benefit? How
do I know this is accurate, complete
information?**

FIGURE 48.1   "Milk U" Web page

Advisory Board. What might be the point of view of this group? Will all the "facts" appear on the pages, especially any that might question milk's goodness?

In contrast, the Web page at <http://liberator.enviroweb.org/fall94/milk.html> links milk drinking to disease (Figure 48.2). This article was published in *AnimaLife,* founded by an advocacy group, Cornell Students for the Ethical Treatment of Animals (CSETA). The author doesn't supply his background, leaving readers to judge his evidence and reasoning. He does seem to provide scientific support, but readers may find the reasoning strained and the tone impassioned.

Yet another perspective is offered by "Why Does Milk Bother Me?" at <http://www.niddk.nih.gov/health/digest/pubs/whymilk/index.htm> (see Figure 48.3 on p. 260). Sponsored by the National Digestive Diseases Information Clearinghouse, part of the National Institutes of

48d
eval

1 Organizational site
2 Uses title to introduce position
3 Adds graphics to highlight point of view
4 Includes statistics
5 Cites authority

READER'S REACTION: Given the number of milk drinkers, how serious is this risk? Isn't this view a bit extreme?

FIGURE 48.2 "Milk . . . Help Yourself" Web page

Health, this site presents impartial information about lactose intoleance, an inability to digest milk sugar that affects millions of people. T "speaker," an authoritative government agency, clearly answers questio about dairy products. The page appeals to a wide range of readers wi direct language, visuals, and food lists. Elsewhere on the site, the agen supplies a more technical discussion as well.

- **What's missing? What difference does that make?** The *Why Mil* site is a commercial venture promoting cow's milk. Naturally, it ignor

48d
eval

① Government site
② Identifies topic in title
③ Uses simple questions and answers to explain
④ Supplies link to more detailed information
⑤ Adds informative graphics

READER'S REACTION: This consumer-oriented explanation is very clear. The sponsor is identified later, too.

FIGURE 48.3   "Why Does Milk Bother Me?" Web page

soy, goat, and other milk (and nonmilk) options. In contrast, "Milk . . . Help Yourself," published by an animal rights group, omits data on milk's safety and health benefits. On the other hand, "Why Does Milk Bother Me?" does not promote or attack dairy products; instead, it aims to inform, giving the public reliable advice and ignoring commercial or organizational interests. Each of these—like every resource—has a point of view that guides its selection and presentation of information. Examining who benefits, who speaks, and what is omitted can help you critically evaluate this point of view.

Evaluate conversational resources

Electronic mailing lists, newsgroups, or Web-based forums can provide you with instant access to firsthand information. However, you need extra vigilance to distinguish authoritative comments, backed by genuine expertise, from unsupported opinions (see 10a–b and 56c–e). One strategy is to treat conversational materials as primary resources, data which you need to analyze and interpret for your readers. Ask critical questions: What do you know about the author's expertise, credibility, fairness, logical reasoning, or supporting evidence? Do other resources substantiate the author's claims? How does the author's view relate to your research thread? How would your research community react to the material? (See also 48c and 48d-1.)

49a
integ

49 | Integrating and Crediting Sources

By distinguishing your contributions from those of your sources, you'll gain recognition for your own insights and hard work. You'll also avoid inadvertently taking credit for the work of others—a form of theft called **plagiarism**. Crediting sources boosts your credibility as a writer and researcher; it substantiates your knowledge of other studies and allows readers to draw on or check your research.

49a Documenting and citing sources as readers expect

Each community shares its own expectations about how to use and cite sources. As you read, notice what is drawn from sources, how such material is incorporated, and how sources are acknowledged.

Academic. Readers generally expect you to acknowledge prior work, show-ing how your ideas fit into a research tradition. They look for authoritative evidence, data, and a formal documentation style. Try to integrate sources—emphasizing quotations, summaries, findings, currency, or other matters—readers in a field expect.

Work. Readers expect brief treatment of what they know and extended treat-ment of what they don't (but need to). They may expect quotations, para-phrases, summaries, or visuals—all appropriately documented.

Public. Readers may appreciate source material but be content with informal citations. But when you advocate a policy or controversial view, readers ex-pect fair play and accurate facts, figures, and details.

49b Integrating your reading into your writing

Each time you quote, paraphrase, or summarize, you retain something of the original: the exact wording, the sequence, or the general point. Distinguish your source materials from your own ideas by identifying each source with an in-text citation (see Chapters 51–54).

1 Integrate quotations

Use quotations sparingly; select them for these reasons.

- To support your conclusions with a recognized or insightful authority
- To represent accurately ideas you wish to modify, extend, or dispute
- To present something stylishly, persuasively, or concisely
- To illustrate vividly and dramatically what other people think
- To provide a change of pace or a jumping-off point

Short quotations. Set off the precise words of a source with quotation marks as you blend them into your discussion. For example, introduce an entire sen-tence by interpreting it and relating it to your point.

> Celebrities can also play roles in our fantasy lives: "Many people ad-mire, but do not mimic, the rebellious rock star" (McVey 32).

Or you can use an **embedded quotation**, weaving in key wording.

> Many teenagers were "riveted by the fast-paced lyrical cynicism" (Low 124) of Bob Dylan's early vocal style.

STRATEGY **Present quotations following accepted practice.**

If you are following a specific documentation style (see Chapters 51–54), check its advice on source citations and punctuation with parenthetical citations or note numbers. Here are some general guidelines.

- Put the exact spoken or written words of your source within quotation marks. Introduce the quotation smoothly, and identify its source.

- Follow your introductory line with a colon only if it is a complete sentence. Use commas to set off a tag such as "X says" that introduces or interrupts a quotation; vary *says* with other verbs (*claims, explains, shows*).
- If you work a quotation into your own sentence, use the context to decide whether it should be separated with a comma.
- If you leave out words or add to a quotation, use ellipses (see 39d) or brackets (see 39b) to identify your changes.
- Position these punctuation marks *inside* concluding single or double quotation marks: commas, periods, and question or exclamation marks that apply to the quoted material.
- Position these punctuation marks *outside* concluding single or double quotation marks: semicolons, colons, and question or exclamation marks that apply to the whole sentence.

Block quotations. When you use a **block quotation**, a longer passage from a source, readers expect you to *do* something with the quotation, not just insert it. Explain or interpret by drawing conclusions, highlighting key points, or connecting them to your ideas.

If you quote a passage longer than four lines typed (MLA style) or forty words or more (APA style), set it off from your prose. Begin on the line after your introduction. Indent one inch or ten spaces (MLA style, see 51a) or five spaces (APA style, shown below). Double-space the quotation; do not use quotation marks (unless they appear in the source).

49b
inte

> Perez (1998) anticipates profound shifts in staff training.
>> The greatest challenge for most school districts is to
>> earmark sufficient funds for training personnel, not for
>> purchasing or upgrading hardware and software. The
>> technological revolution in the average classroom will
>> depend to a large degree on innovation in professional
>> development. (p. 64)

Begin the first line without further indentation if you are quoting from one paragraph. Otherwise, indent all paragraphs 1/4" or three spaces (MLA style) or any additional paragraphs 1/2" or five spaces (APA style).

Also present four or more lines of poetry in a double-spaced block quotation. On the line after your introduction, indent ten spaces or an inch from the left margin (MLA style, shown below). Do not use any quotation marks unless the verse contains them.

> Donald Hall also varies line length and rhythm, as "The Black-
> Faced Sheep" illustrates.
>> My grandfather spent all day searching the valley
>> and edges of Ragged Mountain,
>> calling "Ke-<u>day</u>!" as if he brought you salt,
>> "Ke-<u>day</u>! Ke-<u>day</u>!" (lines 9-12)

2 Integrate information in your own words

To make your writing more sophisticated, quote selectively. Paraphrase, summarize, or synthesize instead (see 48a), blending in points or details from sources—properly credited, of course.

STRATEGY **Embed sources to strengthen your reasoning.**

- Select sound evidence that supports your thesis.
- Paraphrase to speak consistently in your own voice.
- Summarize to credit sources but focus on your own points.
- Synthesize to relate several sources to your thesis or to consolidate supporting or varied evidence.
- Alternate striking short quotations with paraphrase and summary.
- Add examples, or shape supporting paragraphs around facts, details, and statistics. Credit these as well as ideas and expressions.
- Build on sources, but let your interpretation, reasoning, and voice as an author dominate. Don't just tack sources together assuming readers will figure out how to interpret or connect them.

3 Integrate visuals

Visuals (drawings, photos, graphs, icons, charts) can present, explore, or emphasize data. Whether you create a visual or take it from a source, be sure it adds to your text, explaining or extending your point rather than substituting for it (see 13b–f). If you copy a visual from print or download it, you will need to cite its source and may need permission to use it.

STRATEGY **Integrate visuals for readers.**

- Position the visual as close to the relevant written text as you can without disrupting the flow of the text or distorting the visual.
- Do not interrupt the writing in ways that make it hard to read.
- Use visuals of good quality and appropriate size for the page.
- Ask peer readers whether your visuals are easy to follow and whether they add to the text.
- Plan spacing and document design (see 13b–f).
- Label each visual (Table 1, Figure 1 in APA style; Fig. 1 in MLA style).

49.1

49c Recognizing plagiarism

Plagiarism—treating someone else's work as your own—is a serious ethical breach. It can lead to paper or course failure, strong college penalties, or legal action in work and public settings. Going to a "paper mill" on the Web or to a social group's file for a paper is an example of wholesale plagiarism. Besides the moral implications and the damage to your learning, remember that your instructor may have had prior experience with your source, access

the same material, or access to plagiarism detection sites. Plagiarism also
includes lapses in attention and inadvertent errors which this chapter can help
you avoid.

STRATEGY **Avoid situations that can lead to accidental plagiarism.**

- Plan ahead, and take careful notes (see 46e–f) to avoid problems caused
  by missing, inaccurate, or sloppy notes and references. If you can't credit
  your source, don't use the material.
- When you cut and paste online material into your own file, identify
  your sources so you don't mistake the file for your own work.
- Start reading and drafting early so you allow time to get help with a
  difficult source. Don't copy complex material into your paper.
- Record sources as you draft. Note authors and pages in parentheses;
  add a reminder (* or FIX) to edit later for correct form.
- If you aren't sure whether—or how—to cite sources in a college paper,
  ask your teacher's advice. For examples from four major documentation systems, see Chapters 51–54.
- At work, consult your supervisor or legal department about how to use
  and cite sources in internal and external documents.
- For public documents, acknowledge sources clearly, even when readers accept an informal documentation style.

**49d
plag**

49d Avoiding plagiarism

When you use quotations, paraphrases, and summaries, you *must* credit
your sources. The following paraphrase is too close to the original to be presented without quotation marks and would be considered plagiarized.

ORIGINAL PASSAGE
Malnutrition was a widespread and increasingly severe problem
throughout the least developed parts of the world in the 1970s, and
would continue to be serious, occasionally reaching famine conditions, as the millennium approached. Among the cells of the human
body most dependent upon a steady source of nutrients are those of
the immune system, most of which live, even under ideal conditions,
for only days at a time. (From Laurie Garrett, *The Coming Plague,* New
York: Penguin, 1994, p. 199.)

PLAGIARIZED VERSION
In her book about emerging global diseases, Garrett points out that malnutrition can give microbes an advantage as they spread through the
population. Malnutrition continues to be a **severe problem throughout the least developed parts of the world**. The human immune system contains cells that are **dependent upon a steady source of nutrients**. These cells may **live, even under ideal conditions, for only
days at a time**.

The writer of the plagiarized version made only minor changes in some phra
and "lifted" others verbatim.

APPROPRIATE PARAPHRASE

In her book about emerging global diseases, Garrett points out th
malnutrition can give microbes an advantage as they spread throu
the population. The human body contains immune cells that help
fight off various diseases. When the body is deprived of nutrients, the
immune cells will weaken (Garrett 199).

The writer also could have simply summarized the passage.

APPROPRIATE SUMMARY

Malnutrition can so weaken people's immune systems that diseases the
would otherwise fight off can gain an advantage (Garrett 199).

STRATEGY Edit to avoid inadvertent plagiarism.

- After a break, check your draft against your source or your notes. Mak
  sure that you weren't so absorbed that you accidentally echoed or r
  peated words. Quote or reword anything questionable.
- When you don't quote but adapt arguments, explanations, evidence,
  a sequence of ideas, cite your source.
- Check your in-text citations for accurate page numbers.
- Request permission if you want to cite an electronic message not poste
  publicly or use other restricted material.
- Take another break, and then proofread your list of sources. Concentrat
  on the details such as punctuation, capitals, and spaces.

49e Deciding what to document, what not to document

In general, you need to document the words, ideas, and informatior
you draw from another person's work. Document sources (1) to add suppor
and credibility to your points by showing they are based on careful research
(2) to acknowledge another person's hard work, and (3) to give other researchers access to your sources. What needs documenting may vary with
your audience. General academic readers might expect you to cite sources
when you discuss subatomic particles; an audience of physicists would probably see such matters as common knowledge.

YOU MUST DOCUMENT

- Word-for-word (direct) quotations taken from someone else's work
- Paraphrases or summaries of someone else's work, whether published
  or presented informally in an interview or electronically
- Ideas, opinions, and interpretations that others have developed and
  presented, even if they are based on common knowledge
- Facts or data that someone else has gathered or identified if the information is not considered common knowledge

- Information that is not widely accepted or that is disputed
- Illustrations, charts, graphs, photographs, recordings, original software, performances, interviews, and the like

DO NOT DOCUMENT
- Ideas, opinions, and interpretations that are your own
- Widely known ideas and information—available in common reference works or usually presented as common knowledge
- Commonly used quotations ("To be, or not to be")

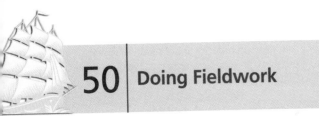

50 | Doing Fieldwork

Field research is firsthand research, gathering material directly from people you interview or survey or from events and places you observe. Your fieldwork addresses your research questions with original material that's the product of your own work, not somebody else's research.

Good field research also involves interpretation. Give the data you collect the same critical "reading" and analysis you give to all other sources (see 8a–b). Secondary sources from your research may suggest how to use and what to conclude from your data. Of course, your fieldwork goals and methods depend on your task and research community.

Academic settings. Field research in sociology, psychology, business, education, or urban planning generally means studying people's behaviors or outlooks to find patterns or causes and effects. In chemistry, engineering, or pharmacy, it inquires into how substances, organisms, objects, or machines work. Ask about any institutional approval needed for research involving other people.

Work settings. Field research in businesses and organizations often looks at how customers (or staff) act and interact.

Public settings. Field research in public settings often gathers (and measures) people's opinions on issues or policies.

STRATEGY **Prepare for your fieldwork.**

Do background research, and plan your fieldwork carefully. To identify worthwhile questions or problems, look over research already conducted. Use the methods of others as models for your own.

50a Conducting an ethnographic study

You can use **ethnographic research** to interpret practices, behavic
language, and attitudes of groups connected by interests or ways of understar
ing and acting. Because an **ethnography**—the written report of this cultu
analysis—aims for in-depth understanding, you may use several methods
gather detailed information about your subject, including **observations** of pe
ple, events, and settings; **interviews** with **informants** (people who provi
information about the group to which they belong); and collection of **artifac**
(characteristic material objects).

Focus your fieldwork on a specific setting, activity, person, or grou
Conduct **structured observations** in which you objectively watch a situatio
behavior, or relationship in order to understand its elements and processes. F
instance, to study how preschoolers use language during play, you might co
duct a series of structured observations at a day-care center.

STRATEGY   Plan a structured observation.

- Choose the site; if necessary, get permission to observe.
- Decide how to situate yourself (in one spot or moving). How will yc
  explain your presence to those observed?
- Decide what information or artifacts you want to gather and why. Ho'
  will you use this material in your report?
- Consider what equipment you will use to record information: tape re
  corder, camera, notepad, or video camera.
- Anticipate problems, and plan strategies for dealing with them.

The following notes were transcribed from an audiotape for an anthro
pology study of a person with an unusual occupation.

Dave Glovsky—Palace Playland: Dave's Guessing Stand
(Sound of game, the Striker: hammer swings in background)
[First interchange between Brian Schwegler and Dave Glovsky is in
audible because of background noise.]
BS: So, Dave, can you tell me a little something about how you guess
Can you tell me how you guess?
DG: Ages? I read the lower lids. I read the lower lid. It deteriorates a:
we get older. The more it gets darker, they get older. Even chil
dren of sixteen can fool me with the deterioration under the eyes
They can have beautiful skin, but I don't check the skin. I check
the lower lid of their eyes.
[The interview continues until a customer arrives.]
DG: Hey, come on in, have fun. What do you want me to guess?
Female cust: My age.
DG: All right, that's a dollar. (Holds up one dollar bill.) A hundred dol-
lar bill. Step into the office here. (Points to a patch of pavement.)

hen you report ethnographic data, be precise. Offer interpretations that go
yond simply presenting details.

First Draft: Dave the Guesser
by Brian Schwegler

"Come on in, have some fun with the famous guesser of Old
chard," says Dave "The Guesser" Glovsky. Relying on his voice and
rsonality to attract customers, he seems out of place in this
chanized wonderland. Hand-painted signs covered with cramped
iting are his advertisement. . . .

As I stand in front of his stand and read his signs, a young
man approaches Dave.

"Hey, come on in, have fun. What do you want me to guess?" Dave
ks.

"My age," says the young woman.

"All right, that's a dollar." Holding up the dollar bill that
e woman gives him, Dave examines it the way a jeweler examines a
recious stone. "A hundred dollar bill." Pointing to a space on the
avement, Dave says, "Step into the office here." Dave checks her out
rom all angles, looking for the clue that will let him know her age
ithin two years, his margin of error. . . .

50c
field

50b Conducting an interview

Talk with experts or people with pertinent experiences to test or sup-
lement your other sources.

STRATEGY   Organize a productive interview.

- List potential interviewees and possible questions. Consider whether
  you will need a lengthy interview or just a few short answers.
- Write out your questions, arranging them logically. Avoid those that
  can be answered by *yes* or *no* and that are unclear or leading.
- Use your questions, but don't be shackled by them. In the interview,
  follow up on new information and ideas that serve your purpose.
- If you wish to tape-record instead of take notes, always ask permission.
  Bring extra tapes and batteries as well as backup paper and pen.
- After an interview, send a thank-you note—both to be polite and in
  case you need a follow-up interview.

50c Using a survey, poll, or questionnaire

Surveys, polls, and questionnaires gather opinions or information about
specific behaviors and possible future actions.

50.1

1 Use surveys and polls

Surveys and **polls** collect short answers, often in *yes/no* form, prov
ing statistics for charts, comparisons, or support.

STRATEGY Prepare for a survey or poll.

- Decide who you want to survey or poll. How many people do y
  need to contact? Of what gender, age, or occupation?
- Always draft, test, and revise your questions in advance.
- Select your location; it may determine who answers your questions.

Shane Hand marked answers to his recycling questions on a tally sheet.

```
Do you . . .
Use coffee mugs instead of polystyrene cups?        Yes   N
Reuse plastic wrap, foil, and plastic bags?         Yes   N
Recycle newspapers and/or magazines?                Yes   N

Are you willing to . . .
Take your own bags to the store?                    Yes   N
```

2 Use questionnaires

Usually mailed, **questionnaires** can gather in-depth information from
many people but need careful preparation for clarity. (See the sample ques
tionnaire at the end of the research paper in 52c.)

STRATEGY Design your questionnaire.

Consider form: Will you ask respondents to write out explanations
check boxes, or circle answers? Will you use multiple-choice items or a rat
ing scale? How will you analyze answers?

- Draft your questions, and test them on several people. Ask your tester
  to identify where they were confused or lacked information.
- Revise the questionnaire, and prepare it for distribution. Try to fit you
  questions on one page (front and back), but leave room for comments

TAKING IT ONLINE

MLA STYLE

http://www.mla.org/style/style_main.htm

For reliable information on MLA documentation style and for sample citations that will complement what you'll find in the upcoming section, visit the official site of the Modern Language Association (MLA), an organization that encourages the study of English, American, and other literatures and languages. Click on "MLA Style," and then visit the FAQ page for advice on specific issues such as documenting Web sources.

For more advice on using MLA style, check the home page for your library or tutoring center, or go to one of the sites below. Be certain that any site you use is updated to reflect the most current MLA style.

MLA CITATION EXAMPLES WRITTEN BY HCC LIBRARY

http://www.hcc.hawaii.edu/education/hcc/library/mlahcc.html

This site, sponsored by the Honolulu Community College Library, provides general formats and typical examples for entries for an MLA list of works cited.

USING MODERN LANGUAGE ASSOCIATION (MLA) FORMAT

http://owl.english.purdue.edu/handouts/research/r_mla.html

One of the many useful documents supplied by the Purdue University Online Writing Lab, this page explains how to lay out your paper, prepare Works Cited entries, and present long and short quotations in MLA style.

SECTION 9
Documenting Sources: MLA Style

Guide to MLA Formats for In-Text (Parenthetical) Citations

Guide to MLA Formats for List of Works Cited

51 | Using MLA Documentation Style

The MLA (Modern Language Association) documentation style offers a convenient system for acknowledging and directing readers to your sources for ideas, information, and quotations. It consists of an in-text citation (generally in parentheses) and a list of works cited (at the end of the text). (For advice on what to document, see 49e.)

51
MLA

STRATEGY Use MLA style in the humanities to emphasize exact sources.

ACADEMIC SETTINGS

When readers expect MLA style or simple parenthetical documentation

WORK AND PUBLIC SETTINGS

When your subject and readers would be well served by a simple documentation style that seldom uses footnotes or endnotes

When you need an easy way to identify exact sources of quotations, paraphrases, or summaries

When other writers or publications in your setting use MLA, modified MLA, or a similar informal style

51.1

271

For more on MLA style, see the *MLA Handbook for Writers of Research Pape* (5th ed., New York: MLA, 1999), the *MLA Style Manual and Guide to Scholar Publishing* (2nd ed., New York: MLA, 1998), or updates posted on the MI Web site at <http://www.mla.org/style/style_main.htm>.

51a Using MLA in-text (parenthetical) citations

The MLA documentation style uses a citation in the text (usually a author's name) to identify a source. Readers can easily locate this source, de scribed in full, in the list of works cited that ends the paper. In-text citation follow standard patterns, and many note the exact page in the source whe readers can find the particular information mentioned.

DRAFT   Even costumes convey the film's theme (Dell, p. 134).

  READER'S REACTION: Why does a comma follow the author's name Why is *p.* used before the page number?

EDITED   Even costumes convey the film's theme (Dell 134).

1. Author's Name in Parentheses

You can provide the author's name in parentheses. For a quotation c specific detail, give the page number in the source.

IN PARENTHESES   When people marry now "there is an important sense in which they don't know what they are doing" (Giddens 46).

2. Author's Name in Discussion

You can include the author's name (or other information) in your dis cussion, clarifying which observations are your source's.

IN DISCUSSION   Giddens claims that when people marry now "there is an important sense in which they don't know what they are doing" (46).

3. General Reference

A **general reference** refers to a source as a whole, to its main ideas, or to information throughout; it needs no page number.

IN PARENTHESES   Many species of animals have complex systems of communication (Bright).

IN DISCUSSION   As Michael Bright observes, many species of animals have complex systems of communication.

Specific Reference

A **specific reference** documents words, ideas, or facts from a particular place in a source, such as the page for a quotation or paraphrase.

QUOTATION   Dolphins can perceive clicking sounds "made up of 700
units of sound per second" (Bright 52).

**PARAPHRASE
FACTS**   Bright reports that dolphins recognize patterns
consisting of seven hundred clicks each second (52).

One Author

Provide the author's last name in parentheses, or integrate either the
full name or last name alone into the discussion.

According to Maureen Honey, government posters during World War
II often portrayed homemakers "as vital defenders of the
nation's homes" (135).

Two or Three Authors

Name all the authors in parentheses or in the discussion.

The item is noted in a partial list of Francis Bacon's debts
from 1603 on (Jardine and Stewart 275).

For three authors, do the same: (Norman, Fraser, and Jenko 209).

More Than Three Authors

Within parentheses, name the first author and add *et al.* ("and others").
Within your discussion, use a phrase like "Chen and his colleagues point out
. . ." or something similar. If you name all the authors in the works cited list
rather than using *et al.*, do the same in the text citation (see Entry 3 on
p. 278).

More funding would encourage creative research on complementary
medicine (Chen et al. 82).

8. Corporate or Group Author

When an organization is the author, name it, but shorten a cumbersome name such as *Committee of Concerned Journalists*.

The consortium gathers journalists at "a critical moment"
(Committee 187).

9. No Author Given

When no author is named, use the title instead. Shorten a long title as
in this version of *Baedeker's Czech/Slovak Republics*.

In 1993, Czechoslovakia split into the Czech Republic and the
Slovak Republic (Baedeker's 67).

10. More Than One Work by the Same Author

When the list of works cited includes more than one work by an author, add a shortened form of the title to your citation.

One writer claims that "quaintness glorifies the unassuming
industriousness" in these social classes (Harris, Cute 46).

11. Authors with the Same Name

When authors have the same last name, identify each by first initial (or entire first name, if necessary for clarity).

Despite improved health information systems (J. Adams 308),
a recent report indicates that medical errors continue to
increase (D. Adams 1).

12. Indirect Source

Use *qtd. in* ("quoted in") to indicate when your source provides you with a quotation (or paraphrase) taken from yet another source. Here, Feuch is the source of the quotation from Vitz.

For Vitz, "art, especially great art, must engage all or almost
all of the major capacities of the nervous system" (qtd. in
Feuch 65).

13. Multivolume Work

To cite a whole volume, add a comma after the author's name and *vol.* before the number (Cao, vol. 4). To specify one of several volumes that you cite, add volume and page numbers (Cao 4: 177).

In 1888, Lewis Carroll let two students call their school
paper Jabberwock, a made-up word from Alice's Adventures in
Wonderland (Cohen 2: 695).

14. Literary Work

After the page number in your edition, add the chapter (*ch.*), part (*pt.*), or section (*sec.*) number to help readers find the passage in any edition.

In Huckleberry Finn, Mark Twain ridicules an actor who "would
squeeze his hand on his forehead and stagger back and kind of
moan" (178; ch. 21).

entify a part as in (386; pt. 3, ch. 2) or, for a play, the act, scene, and line
mbers, as in (Ham. 1.2.76). For poems, give line numbers (lines 55–57)
both part and line numbers (4.220–23).

. Bible

Place a period between the chapter and verse numbers (Mark 2.3–4).
. parenthetical citations, abbreviate names with five or more letters, as in
e case of Deuteronomy (Deut. 16.21–22).

6. Two or More Sources in a Citation

Separate sources within a citation with a semicolon.

```
Differences in the ways men and women use language can often be
traced to who has power (Tanner 83-86; Tavris 297-301).
```

7. Selection in Anthology

For an essay, story, poem, or other work in an anthology, cite the work's
uthor (not the anthology's editor), but give page numbers in the anthology.

```
According to Corry, the battle for Internet censorship has
crossed party lines (112).
```

8. Electronic or Other Nonprint Source

After identifying the author or title, add numbers for the page, paragraph (*par.*, *pars.*), section (*sec.*), or screen (*screen*) if given. Otherwise, no
number is needed.

```
Offspringmag.com summarizes current research on adolescent
behavior (Boynton 2).
The heroine's mother in the film Clueless died as the result of
an accident during liposuction.
```

**51a
MLA**

19. Informative Footnote or Endnote

Use a note when you wish to comment on a source, provide background details, or supply lengthy information of use to only a few readers.
Place a superscript number (raised slightly above the line of text) at a suitable
point in your paper. Label the note itself with a corresponding number, and
provide it as a footnote at the bottom of the page or as an endnote at the end
of the paper, before the list of works cited, on a page titled "Notes."

```
1 Before changing your eating habits or beginning an
exercise program, check with your doctor.
```

> ### PLACEMENT AND PUNCTUATION OF PARENTHETICAL CITATIONS
>
> Put parenthetical citations close to the quotation, information, paraphrase, or summary you are documenting.
>
> - At the end of a sentence before the final punctuation
>
> ```
> Wayland Hand reports on a folk belief that going to sleep on
> a rug made of bearskin can relieve backache (183).
> ```
>
> - After the part of the sentence to which the citation applies, at a natural pause in the sentence so that you do not disrupt it, or after the last of several quotations in a paragraph, all from one page of the same source
>
> ```
> The folk belief that "sleeping on a bear rug will cure
> backache" (Hand 183) illustrates the magic of external
> objects producing results inside the body.
> ```
>
> - At the end of a long quotation set off as a block (see 49b-1), after the end punctuation with a space before the parentheses
>
> ```
> Many baseball players are superstitious, especially pitchers.
>             Some pitchers refuse to walk anywhere on the day of
>             the game in the belief that every little exertion
>             subtracts from their playing strength. One pitcher
>             would never put on his cap until the game started
>             and would not wear it at all on the days he did
>             not pitch. (Gmelch 280)
> ```

51b Creating an MLA list of works cited

Provide readers with full detail about your sources in an alphabetical list following the last page of your text.

- **Page format.** Use the heading "Works Cited" (or "Works Consulted," for all sources used) centered one inch below the top edge of a new page. Continue the page numbering from the body of the paper.
- **Indentation.** Do not indent the first line of each entry. Indent additional lines one-half inch or five spaces.
- **Spacing.** Double-space all lines within and between the entries. Leave a single space after a period within an entry.

- **Alphabetizing.** Alphabetize by last names of authors (or first names for authors with the same last name); then alphabetize by title multiple works by the same author. For sources without an author, use the first word in the title (other than *A*, *An*, or *The*).

DRAFT Fem. and Polit. Theory, by C. Sunstein. UCP, 1990.

READER'S REACTION: Entries that follow the MLA pattern are easy to understand. Are these notes?

EDITED Sunstein, Cass R. <u>Feminism and Political Theory</u>.

Chicago: U of Chicago P, 1990.

STRATEGY Find and match the MLA models.

- Take bibliographic notes as you use a source (see 46e).
- Figure out what type of source you've used—book, article, or other form. Use the Guide on the Section 9 divider to find the sample entry for that type. Prepare your entry following this pattern.
- Identify how many authors or other features your source has. Find the patterns for these, and rework your entry as needed.
- Check your entry for the sequence of information, capitalization, punctuation, abbreviations, and other details.

Books and Works Treated as Books

- **Author.** Give the last name first, followed by a comma, and then the first name and any middle name or initial. End with a period.
- **Title.** Underline the title (and any subtitle), and capitalize the main words (see 40b). End with a period (unless the title concludes with a dash or a question or exclamation mark).
- **Publication information.** Begin with city of publication, a colon, and a space. Give the publisher's name in shortened form (*U of Chicago P* for *University of Chicago Press* or *McGraw* for *McGraw-Hill, Inc.*) followed by a comma, the year of publication, and a period.

51b
MLA

1. One Author

Twitchell, James B. <u>ADCULTusa: The Triumph of Advertising in</u>

<u>American Culture</u>. New York: Columbia UP, 1996.

2. Two or Three Authors

Begin with the first author's last name. Add other names in regular order, separated by commas with *and* before the final name.

Kress, Gunther, and Theo van Leeuwen. <u>Reading Images: The</u>

<u>Grammar of Graphic Design</u>. London: Routledge, 1996.

3. Four or More Authors

After the first name, add *et al.* ("and others"). You may give all the names; if so, list them in the text citations too (see Entry 7 on p. 273).

> Bellah, Robert N., et al. Habits of the Heart: Individualism and Commitment in American Life. Berkeley: U of California P, 1985.

> Bellah, Robert N., Richard Madsen, William M. Sullivan, Ann Swidler, and Steven M. Tipton. Habits of the Heart: Individualism and Commitment in American Life. Berkeley: U of California P, 1985.

4. Corporate or Group Author

Alphabetize by the first main word of the group's name. If this body is also the publisher, repeat its name, abbreviated if appropriate.

> Nemours Children's Clinic. Diabetes and Me. Wilmington, DE: Nemours, 2001.

5. No Author Given

Alphabetize by the first main word of the title.

> Guide for Authors. Oxford: Blackwell, 1985.

6. More Than One Work by the Same Author

List multiple works by an author alphabetically by the first main word of each title. For the first entry, include the name of the author. For additional entries, use three hyphens instead of the name, ending with a period. If the author or authors are not *exactly* the same for each work, include the names in full.

> Tannen, Deborah. The Argument Culture: Moving from Debate to Dialogue. New York: Random, 1998.

> ---. You Just Don't Understand: Women and Men in Conversation. New York: Ballantine, 1991.

7. One or More Editors

Begin with the editor's name followed by *ed.* (or *eds.*).

> Achebe, Chinua, and C. L. Innes, eds. African Short Stories. London: Heinemann, 1985.

Author and Editor

Begin with either the author's or the editor's name depending on whether you are using the text itself or the editor's contributions.

Wardlow, Gayle Dean. Chasin' That Devil Music: Searching for
    the Blues. Ed. Edward Komara. San Francisco: Miller, 1998.

Translator

Begin with the author unless you emphasize the translator's work.

Baudrillard, Jean. Cool Memories II: 1978-1990. Trans. Chris
    Turner. Durham: Duke UP, 1996.

0. Edition Following the First

Note the edition (*Rev. ed.*, *1998 ed.*) after the title.

Coe, Michael D. The Maya. 6th ed. New York: Thames, 1999.

1. Reprint

Supply the original publication date after the title; follow with the publication information from the version you are using.

Ondaatje, Michael. The Collected Works of Billy the Kid. 1970.
    Harmondsworth, Eng.: Penguin, 1984.

12. Multivolume Work

Indicate the total number of volumes after the title (or after the editor's or translator's name).

Tsao, Hsueh-chin. The Story of the Stone. Trans. David Hawkes.
    5 vols. Harmondsworth, Eng.: Penguin, 1983-86.

If you cite only one of several volumes, supply the specific volume number and publication information. End with the total number if you wish.

Tsao, Hsueh-chin. The Story of the Stone. Trans. David Hawkes.
    Vol. 1. Harmondsworth, Eng.: Penguin, 1983. 5 vols.

13. Work in a Series

Add the series (*Ser.*) name and any item number after the title.

Hess, Gary R. Vietnam and the United States: Origins and Legacy
    of War. Intl. Hist. Ser. 7. Boston: Twayne, 1990.

51b
MLA

14. Book Pre-1900

The publisher's name is optional.

Darwin, Charles. <u>Descent of Man and Selection in Relation to Sex</u>. New York, 1896.

15. Book with Publisher's Imprint

Give the imprint name, a hyphen, and the publisher's name.

Sikes, Gini. <u>8 Ball Chicks: A Year in the Violent World of Gir</u> <u>Gangs</u>. New York: Anchor-Doubleday, 1997.

16. Anthology or Collection of Articles

Supply the editor's name, with *ed.*, and then the title of the collectio (To cite a selection, see Entry 34 on pp. 283–84.)

Zipes, Jack, ed. <u>Don't Bet on the Prince: Contemporary Feminist</u> <u>Fairy Tales in North America and England</u>. New York: Methuen, 1986.

17. Conference Proceedings

Begin with the title unless an editor is named. Follow with details abou the conference, including name and date.

<u>Childhood Obesity: Causes and Prevention</u>. Symposium Proc., 27 Oct. 1998. Washington: Center for Nutrition Policy and Promotion, 1999.

18. Title Within a Title

Within a book title, don't underline another book's title, but underline a title normally in quotation marks.

MacPherson, Pat. <u>Reflecting on</u> Jane Eyre. London: Routledge, 1989.

Golden, Catherine, ed. <u>The Captive Imagination: A Casebook on "The Yellow Wallpaper."</u> New York: Feminist, 1992.

19. Pamphlet

Use the same form for a pamphlet as for a book.

Vareika, William. <u>John La Farge: An American Master (1835-1910)</u>. Newport: Gallery of American Art, 1989.

. Dissertation (Published)

When published, a doctoral dissertation is treated as a book. Add *Diss.*, school, and the date of the degree.

Said, Edward W. <u>Joseph Conrad and the Fiction of Autobiography</u>.

Diss. Harvard U, 1964. Cambridge: Harvard UP, 1966.

. Dissertation (Unpublished)

Use quotation marks for the title; add *Diss.*, the school, and the date.

Anku, William Oscar. "Procedures in African Drumming: A Study

of Akan/Ewe Traditions and African Drumming in

Pittsburgh." Diss. U of Pittsburgh, 1988.

2. Government Document

Begin with the name of the government and agency, the independent agency, or the author, if any. Start with *United States* for a report from a federal agency or for congressional documents, adding *Cong.* (*Congress*), the branch (*Senate* or *House*), and the number and session (*101st Cong., 1st sess.*). Include the titles of both the document and any book in which it is printed. Use *GPO* for the federal Government Printing Office.

Sheppard, David I., and Shay Bilchick, comps. <u>Promising

Strategies to Reduce Gun Violence Report</u>. US Dept. of

Justice. Office of Juvenile Justice and Delinquency

Prevention. Washington: GPO, 1999.

United States. Cong. House. <u>Anti-Spamming Act of 2001</u>. 107th

Cong., 1st sess. Washington: GPO, 2001.

Articles and Selections from Periodicals and Books

- **Author.** Give the last name first, followed by a comma. Add the first name and any middle name or initial. End with a period.
- **Article title.** Give the full title in quotation marks, with the main words capitalized. Conclude with a period inside the quotation marks (unless the title ends in a question mark or an exclamation point).
- **Publication information.** Underline the journal or book title. Supply volume number (and sometimes issue number), year of publication, and page numbers. The volume number appears on the publication's title page or cover; use Arabic numerals even if the periodical uses Roman numerals. Introduce page numbers with a colon except for selections from books and in a few other situations shown in entries that follow.

23. Article in Journal Paginated by Volume

When each volume consists of several issues paginated continuous[ly], give the volume number right after the journal's title.

> Rockwood, Bruce L. "Law, Literature, and Science Fiction: New
>   Possibilities." <u>Legal Studies Forum</u> 23 (1999): 267-80.

24. Article in Journal Paginated by Issue

When the issues making up a volume are paginated separately, follo[w] the volume number with a period and the issue number.

> Adams, Jessica. "Local Color: The Southern Plantation in
>   Popular Culture." <u>Cultural Critique</u> 42.1 (1999): 171-87.

25. Article in Weekly Magazine

Note the day, month (abbreviated except for May, June, and July), an[d] year followed by a colon. Give the sequence of page numbers (27–38). If th[e] pages are not consecutive, give the first page with a plus sign (23+).

> Wright, Robert. "The Power of Their Peers." <u>Time</u> 24 Aug. 1998:
>   67.

26. Article in Monthly Magazine

> Jacobson, Doranne. "Doing Lunch." <u>Natural History</u> Mar. 2000:
>   66-69.

27. Article with No Author Given

Alphabetize by title, excluding *A, An,* and *The.*

> "Horseplay." <u>New Yorker</u> 5 Apr. 1993: 36-38.

28. Article in Newspaper

Cite pages as you would for a magazine (see Entry 25), but add any section number or letter. Omit *The, A,* or *An* beginning a newspaper's name. For a local paper, add the city in brackets after the title unless it's named there.

> Willis, Ellen. "Steal This Myth: Why We Still Try to Re-create
>   the Rush of the 60's." <u>New York Times</u> 20 Aug. 2000: AR1+.

29. Editorial

Start with the author or, if none, with the title.

> "A False Choice." Editorial. <u>Charlotte Observer</u> 16 Aug. 1998: 2C.

30. Letter to the Editor

> Varley, Colin. Letter. <u>Archaeology</u> May-June 1993: 10.

. Interview (Published)

Identify the person interviewed, not the interviewer, first. For untitled
terviews, supply *Interview* (without underlining or quotation marks) in place
a title.

```
Stewart, Martha. "I Do Have a Brain." Interview with Kevin

     Kelly. Wired Aug. 1998: 114.
```

2. Review

Begin with the name of the reviewer or the title, for an unsigned re-
ew. For an untitled review, follow the reviewer's name with *Rev. of* ("Review
`"), the work's title, *by*, and the work's author.

```
Muñoz, José Esteban. "Citizens and Superheroes." Rev. of The

     Queen of America Goes to Washington City, by Lauren

     Berlant. American Quarterly 52 (2000): 397-404.

Hadjor, Kofi Buenor. Rev. of The Silent War: Imperialism and

     the Changing Perception of Race, by Frank Furendi. Journal

     of Black Studies 30 (1999): 133-35.
```

33. Article in Encyclopedia or Reference Work

Begin with the author's name or an unsigned article's title. Note only
he edition and date for a common reference work or series. If entries appear
alphabetically, you may leave out the volume or page.

```
Oliver, Paul, and Barry Kernfeld. "Blues." The New Grove

     Dictionary of Jazz. Ed. Barry Kernfeld. New York: St.

     Martin's, 1994.

"The History of Western Theatre." The New Encyclopaedia

     Britannica: Macropedia. 15th ed. 1987. Vol. 28.
```

34. Chapter in Edited Book or Selection in Anthology

List the author of the selection or chapter, then its title (in quotation
marks, but underline titles of novels, plays, and so on; see 37b, 41a). Next,
provide the underlined title of the book containing the selection or chapter.
If the book is edited, follow with *Ed.* and the names of the editors. Add publication information and page numbers for the selection.

```
Atwood, Margaret. "Bluebeard's Egg." "Bluebeard's Egg" and

     Other Stories. New York: Fawcett-Random, 1987. 131-64.
```

Use *Rpt. in* ("Reprinted in") to introduce a subsequent reprint.

```
Atwood, Margaret. "Bluebeard's Egg." "Bluebeard's Egg" and

     Other Stories. New York: Fawcett-Random, 1987. 131-64.
```

Rpt. in <u>Don't Bet on the Prince: Contemporary Feminist
Fairy Tales in North America and England</u>. Ed. Jack Zipes.
New York: Methuen, 1986. 160-82.

35. More Than One Selection from Anthology or Collection

Include an entry for the collection. Use its author's name for cross references from individual selections.

Goldberg, Jonathan. "Speculation: <u>Macbeth</u> and Source." Howard
and O'Connor 242-64.

Howard, Jean E., and Marion F. O'Connor, eds. <u>Shakespeare
Reproduced: The Text in History and Ideology</u>. New York:
Methuen, 1987.

36. Preface, Foreword, Introduction, or Afterword

Identify the section as a preface, foreword, introduction, or afterword. Add the title of the work and its author, following *By*.

Tomlin, Janice. Foreword. <u>The Complete Guide to Foreign
Adoption</u>. By Barbara Brooke Bascom and Carole A. McKelvey.
New York: Pocket, 1997.

37. Letter (Published)

Name the letter writer as the author. Include the letter's date or any collection number.

Garland, Hamlin. "To Fred Lewis Pattee." 30 Dec. 1914. Letter
206 of <u>Selected Letters of Hamlin Garland</u>. Ed. Keith Newlin
and Joseph B. McCullough. Lincoln: U of Nebraska P, 1998.

38. Dissertation Abstract

For an abstract in *Dissertation Abstracts International (DAI)* or *Dissertation Abstracts (DA)*, include *Diss.* ("Dissertation"), the institution's name, and the date of the degree. Add publication information for that volume of abstracts.

Hawkins, Joanne Berning. "Horror Cinema and the Avant-Garde."
Diss. U of California, Berkeley, 1993. <u>DAI</u> 55 (1995): 1712A.

Field and Media Resources

39. Interview (Unpublished)

First identify the person interviewed and the type of interview: *Personal interview* (you conducted it in person), *Telephone interview* (you talked to the

rson over the telephone), or *Interview* (someone else conducted the inter-
w, perhaps on radio or television). If the interview has a title, use it to re-
ace *Interview*. Give the date of the interview or other detail.

> Schutt, Robin. Personal interview. 7 Oct. 2001.
>
> Coppola, Francis Ford. Interview with James Lipton. Inside the
>
> > Actors Studio. Bravo, New York. 10 July 2001.

). Survey or Questionnaire

MLA does not specify a form for these field resources. When citing
ur own research, you may wish to use this format.

> Figliozzi, Jennifer Emily, and Summer J. Arrigo-Nelson.
>
> > Questionnaire on Student Alcohol Use and Parental Values.
> >
> > University of Rhode Island, Kingston. 15-20 Apr. 1998.

1. Observation

Because MLA does not specify a form, you may wish to cite your field
otes in this way.

> Ba, Ed. Ski Run Observation. Vail, CO. 26 Jan. 2002.

2. Letter or Memo (Unpublished)

Give the author's name, a brief description (*Memo to Jane Cote* or, for a
etter to you, *Letter to the author*), and the date. For letters between other peo-
le, identify any library holding the letter in its collection.

> Hall, Donald. Letter to the author. 24 Jan. 1990.

43. Oral Presentation

Identify the speaker, title or type of presentation, and meeting details,
including sponsor, place, and date.

> Shields, Carolyn. "Can Perrogies, Potlatches, and Polkas Combat
>
> > Racism?" Leadership in Culturally Diverse Schools. Amer.
> >
> > Educ. Research Assn. Sheraton Hotel, New Orleans. 27 Apr.
> >
> > 2000.

44. Performance

Following the title of the play, opera, dance, or other performance, note
the composer, director, writer, theater or location, city, and date. (Include ac-
tors when relevant.)

> Cabaret. By Joe Masteroff. Dir. Sam Mendes. Studio 54, New
>
> > York. 2 July 2001.

45. Videotape or Film

Alphabetize by title, and generally name the director. Name others ir portant for identifying the work or for your discussion. Identify the distrib tor, date, and other relevant information.

> Rosencrantz and Guildenstern Are Dead. Dir. Tom Stoppard. Perf
>
>> Gary Oldman, Tim Roth, and Richard Dreyfuss.
>>
>> Videocassette. Buena Vista Home Video, 1990.
>
> Rosencrantz and Guildenstern Are Dead. Dir. Tom Stoppard. Perf
>
>> Gary Oldman, Tim Roth, and Richard Dreyfuss. Cinecom
>>
>> Entertainment, 1990.

46. Television or Radio Program

> "The Tour." I Love Lucy. Dir. William Asher. Nickelodeon. 2
>
>> July 2001.

47. Recording

Identify the form of the recording unless it is a compact disc.

> The Goo-Goo Dolls. Dizzy Up the Girl. Warner, 1998.
>
> Mozart, Wolfgang Amadeus. Symphony no. 40 in G minor. Vienna
>
>> Philharmonic. Cond. Leonard Bernstein. Audiocassette.
>>
>> Deutsche Grammophon, 1984.

48. Artwork or Photograph

> Leonardo da Vinci. Mona Lisa. Louvre, Paris.
>
> Larimer Street, Denver. Personal photograph by author. 5 May
>
>> 1999.

49. Map or Chart

> Arkansas. Map. Comfort, TX: Gousha, 1996.

50. Cartoon

Provide the cartoonist's name, any title, and *Cartoon*.

> Cochran, Tony. "Agnes." Cartoon. Denver Post 10 June 1999: 10E.

51. Advertisement

First, name the product or organization advertised.

> Toyota. Advertisement. GQ July 2001: 8.

ternet, Web, and Electronic Resources

- **Author, title, and publication information.** Supply detail like that for a print source so a reader could identify or find the item.
- **Dates.** Give the date the material was posted, revised, or updated and then, before the URL, the date you accessed the source.
- **Uniform resource locator (URL).** Enclose the complete URL (beginning with *http, gopher, telnet,* or *ftp*) in angle brackets (< >). Include the path, links, or file name needed to reach the page or frame you used. Split the URL only after a slash; do not add a hyphen.
- **Page numbering.** Include any page, paragraph (*par., pars.*), or section numbers provided.

2. Professional Web Site

History of the American West, 1860-1920. 25 July 2000. Denver
      Public Library. 16 Oct. 2001 <http://memory.loc.gov/
      ammem/award97/codhtml>.

3. Individual Web Site

Note the creator, title or description such as *Home page*, and sponsor.

Baron, Dennis. Home page. 16 Aug. 2000. Dept. of English,
      U of Illinois, Urbana-Champaign. 23 Aug. 2000
      <http://www.english.uiuc.edu/baron/index.htm>.

54. Online Book

Add any available information about print publication.

London, Jack. The Iron Heel. New York: Macmillan, 1908. The
      Jack London Collection. 10 Dec. 1999. Berkeley Digital
      Library SunSITE. 15 July 2001 <http://sunsite.berkeley.edu/
      London/Writing/IronHeel/>.

55. Selection from Online Book

Muir, John. "The City of the Saints." Steep Trails. 1918. 17
      July 2001 <http://encyclopediaindex.com/b/sttrl10.htm>.

56. Online Journal Article

Dugdale, Timothy. "The Fan and (Auto)Biography: Writing the
      Self in the Stars." Journal of Mundane Behavior 1.2
      (2000). 19 Sept. 2000 <http://www.mundanebehavior.org/
      issues/v1n2/dugdale.htm>.

57. Online Magazine Article

Rickford, John R. "Suite for Ebony and Phonics." <u>Discover</u> Dec.
 1997. 15 Aug. 2000 <http://www.discover.com/archive/
 index.html>.

58. Online Newspaper or News Service Article

Mulvihill, Kim. "Childhood Obesity." <u>San Francisco Chronicle</u> 1
 July 2001. 15 July 2001 <http://www.sfgate.com/cgi-bin/
 article.cgi?file=/kron/archive/2001/07/12/obesity.DTL>.

59. Online Government Document

United States. Dept. of Commerce. Bureau of the Census. <u>Census</u>
 <u>Brief: Disabilities Affect One-Fifth of All Americans</u>.
 Dec. 1997. 18 July 2001 <http://www.census.gov/prod/
 3/97pubs/cenbr975.pdf>.

60. Online Editorial

Ely, Jane. "For the Young, Get Houston the Games." Editorial.
 <u>Houston Chronicle</u> 17 July 2001. 17 July 2001 <http://
 www.chron.com/cs/CDA/story.hts/editorial/970112>.

61. Online Letter to the Editor

Hadjiargyrou, Michael. "Stem Cells and Delicate Questions."
 Letter. <u>New York Times on the Web</u> 17 July 2001. 18 July
 2001 <http://www.nytimes.com/2001/07/18/opinion/
 L18STEM.html>.

62. Online Interview

Rikker, David. Interview with Victor Payan. <u>San Diego</u>
 <u>Latino Film Festival</u>. 1999. 20 Jan. 2002 <http://
 www.sdlatinofilm.com/video.html#Anchor-David-64709>.

63. Online Review

Chaudhury, Parama. Rev. of <u>Kandahar</u>, dir. Mohsen Makhmalbaf.
 <u>Film Monthly</u> 3.4 (2002). 19 Jan. 2002 <http://
 www.filmmonthly.com/Playing/Articles/Kandahar/
 Kandahar.html>.

. Online Database, Information Service, or Scholarly Project

You can cite a database or a text it contains, beginning with author and
le. Identify any sponsoring group before your access date.

The On-Line Books Page Presents Banned Books On-Line. Ed. John

Mark Ockerbloom. 7 Feb. 1999 <http://www.cs.cmu.edu/

People/spok/banned-books.html>.

5. Online Source from Computer Service

Include, as available, the URL or your access route (introduced by *Key-
ord* or *Path*), the name of any subscribing library, and your access date.

"Native American Food Guide." Health Finder. 16 July 2001.

America Online. 16 July 2001. Keyword: Health.

6. Online Abstract

Prelow, Hazel, and Charles A. Guarnaccia. "Ethnic and Racial

Differences in Life Stress among High School Adolescents."

Journal of Counseling & Development 75.6 (1997). Abstract.

6 Apr. 1998 <http://www.counseling.org/journals/

jcdjul197.htm#Prelow>.

67. Online Videotape or Film

Coppola, Francis Ford, dir. Apocalypse Now. 1979. Film.com. 17

July 2001 <http://ramhurl.film.com/

smildemohurl.ram?file=screen/2001/clips/apoca.smi>.

68. Online Television or Radio Program

Edwards, Bob. "Adoption: Redefining Family." Morning Edition.

Natl. Public Radio. 28-29 June 2001. 17 July 2001

<http://www.npr.org/programs/morning/features/2001/

jun/010628.cfoa.html>.

69. Online Recording

Malcolm X. "The Definition of Black Power." 8 Mar. 1964. Great

Speeches. 2000. 18 July 2001 <http://www.chicago-law.net/

speeches/speech.html#1m>.

70. Online Artwork

> Elamite Goddess. 2100 BC (?). Louvre, Paris. 16 July 2001
> > <http://www.louvre.fr/louvrea.htm>.

71. Online Map or Chart

> "Beirut [Beyrout] 1912." Map. Perry-Castañeda Library Map
> > Collection. 16 July 2000. <http://www.lib.utexas.edu/
> > maps/historical/beirut2_1912.jpg>.

72. Online Cartoon

> Auth, Tony. "Spending Goals." Cartoon. Slate 7 Sept. 2001. 16
> > Oct. 2001 <http://cagle.slate.msn.com/politicalcartoons/
> > pccartoons/archives/auth.asp>.

73. Online Advertisement

> Mazda Miata. Advertisement. 16 July 2001 <http://
> > www.mazdausa.com/miata/>.

74. Other Online Sources

When citing a source not shown here (such as a photo, painting, o
recording), adapt the nonelectronic MLA model.

> NASA/JPL. "Martian Meteorite." Views of the Solar System:
> > Meteoroids and Meteorites. Ed. Calvin J. Hamilton. 1999. 13
> > June 1999 <http://spaceart.com/solar/eng/meteor.htm#views>.

75. FTP, Telnet, or Gopher Site

Treat a source obtained through FTP (file transfer protocol), telnet, or
gopher as you would a similar Web source.

> Lewis, Deanna L., and Ron Chepesuik. "The International Trade
> > in Toxic Waste: A Selected Bibliography." Electronic Green
> > Journal 1.2 (1994). 29 Apr. 1996 <ftp.uiadaho.edupub/docs/
> > pub/publications/EGJ>.

76. Email

Give the writer's name, message title or type, and date. Be sure to hyphenate *e-mail* in MLA style.

> Trimbur, John. E-mail to the author. 17 Sept. 2000.

. **Online Posting**

Aid readers (if you can) by citing an archived version.

Brock, Stephen E. "School Crisis." Online posting. 27 Apr.

　　2001. Special Events Chat Transcripts. Lycos Communities.

　　18 July 2001 <http://clubs.lycos.com/live/Events/

　　transcripts/school_crisis_tscript.asp>.

8. **Synchronous Communication**

When citing material from a MUD, a MOO, or another form of synchronous communication, identify the speaker, the event, its date, its forum uch as *CollegeTownMOO*), and your access date. End with *telnet* and the address. Cite an archived version if possible.

Finch, Jeremy. Online debate "Can Proust Save Your Life?"

　　3 Apr. 1998. CollegeTownMOO. 3 Apr. 1998

　　<telnet://next.cs.bvc.edu.7777>.

9. **CD-ROM, Diskette, or Magnetic Tape**

Note the medium (*CD-ROM, Diskette, Magnetic tape*), the name of the endor, and the publication date.

Shakespeare, William. All's Well That Ends Well. William

　　Shakespeare: The Complete Works on CD-ROM. CD-ROM.

　　Abingdon, Eng.: Andromeda Interactive, 1994.

30. **CD-ROM Abstract**

Add information for any parallel printed source. Identify the database and medium (*CD-ROM, Diskette*), vendor, and publication date.

Blich, Baruch. "Pictorial Representation and Its Cognitive

　　Status." Visual Arts Research 15 (1989): 68-75. Abstract.

　　PsycLIT. CD-ROM. SilverPlatter. 3 Mar. 1996.

51c MLA

51c Sample MLA paper

The *MLA Handbook* recommends beginning a research paper with the first page of the text, using the format shown on page 292. Refer to the features of Kimlee Cunningham's paper, noted in the margins, as you prepare your paper.

↕ ½" from top
Cunningham 1

↕ 1" from top of page

Kimlee Cunningham   **Heading format without a title page**

Professor N. Reynolds   **Double-spaced heading and paper**

English 201

5 May 1999   **Title reflects key ideas and catches readers' attention**

Disney's Magic Mirror Reflects Traditions of Old

1   Since Disney Studio's first animated feature, Snow White and the Seven Dwarfs (1937), the portrayal of female characters has changed in some obvious ways but has also remained the same in some key respects. By contrasting Snow White and the Seven Dwarfs with the recent animated features Beauty and the Beast (1991) and Aladdin (1992), we can see the leading female characters becoming more independent and assertive. At the same time, a comparison of the three movies reveals the studio's continuing appeal to its audiences' sense of feminine physical beauty.

2   It is probably an exaggeration to say that a character like Belle in Beauty and the Beast is a lot like a contemporary feminist, as one critic suggests (Showalter). However, we should not simply ignore an interpretation like this. Even if many people view a film like Beauty and the Beast (or Aladdin) as a simple love story (Hoffman), the films nonetheless grow out of the complicated values and roles that shape relationships today. Disney's contemporary portrayal of women characters shows a willingness to change with the times but also a reluctance to abandon traditional values and stereotypes.

↑ 1" margin at bottom

Left margin annotations:

1" margin on each side

¶ indented 5 spaces

Introduces key ideas to be developed

Gives background

Synthesizes varied points of view

51c MLA

Omits page numbers for 1-page (Showalter) and electronic (Hoffman) sources

Cunningham 2

3   Nearly sixty years separate <u>Snow White and the Seven Dwarfs</u> from <u>Beauty and the Beast</u> and <u>Aladdin</u>. During this time of great social change, the roles of women have expanded. The shift has been from American women as housewives to American women as workers, college students, and corporate executives. By contrasting the main female character in <u>Snow White</u> with those in <u>Beauty</u> and <u>Aladdin</u>, we can see that they reflect both their own times and the social changes separating the different time periods.

4   In <u>Snow White and the Seven Dwarfs</u>, Snow White is portrayed as a homemaker when she and her furry and feathered companions in the forest come upon the Dwarfs' cabin. Her first reaction upon seeing the inside of the cabin is "We'll clean the house and surprise them. Then maybe I can stay." Snow White also becomes a mother to the Dwarfs. Before dinner, she checks their hands and sends them out to wash. Later in the evening, she calls out, "Bedtime! Right upstairs to bed." Visually, Snow White looks like an adolescent girl with wide doe eyes, tiny mouth, and pure ivory skin (Allan 161) instead of looking like a woman.

5   The facial features of both Belle in <u>Beauty and the Beast</u> and Jasmine in <u>Aladdin</u> are more realistic and womanly. Instead of looking like porcelain figurines, both Belle and Jasmine look like vigorous young women. Their skin has a realistic tone, their cheeks are not as artificially rounded as Snow White's,

---

Repeats and develops key ideas while indicating method of analysis

|

Refers to films listed in Works Cited

Supplies supporting evidence

|

Explains values implied in portrait of Snow White

|

Identifies details of appearance

|

Reaches conclusion

51c
MLA

Introduces both *Beauty* and *Aladdin*

|

Contrasts appearances of other characters

Supplies supporting detail

and their eyes are still wide but are not exaggerated. Their roles and personality traits are also very different from Snow White's.

Leads into discussion of contrasting values and characters

6   <u>Beauty and the Beast</u> is an unusual fairy tale in which the woman is the hero (McKenna A13). Belle's intelligence allows her to defeat her enemy, Gaston.

More on ¶3 discussion of Belle's personality, actions, and implied values

Gaston, her would-be suitor, offers a masculine parallel to Belle's beauty but no equivalent to her intelligence. Gaston, the brawny, bluff beefcake figure, is nothing short of brainless. Wisely, Belle cannot be wooed by looks alone, and Gaston's words would disappoint any intelligent woman. Gaston also manages to alienate Belle when he criticizes her zest for reading and books by saying, "It's not right for a woman to read. Soon she starts getting ideas and thinking."

Leads to start of next ¶

7   While Snow White has to wait passively for a man, her prince, to release her from her imprisonment in an unnatural sleep, Belle is an active agent in her fate. Belle's compassion is her father's salvation from death and the Beast's salvation from his curse. To release her father from the Beast's imprisonment, Belle offers her own eternal freedom in return for her father's. This action is also the first step toward the Beast's salvation from himself and the curse.

8   The curse that has been placed upon the Beast has severely altered his appearance, turning a handsome prince into a hairy creature mixing the features of a lion and a buffalo. In order for the spell to be

**51c
MLA**

Cunningham 4

broken, someone must be able to see past this appearance and love the Beast for his inner qualities before the last petal of an enchanted rose falls. It is Belle, through her compassion and understanding, who changes the spirit of the man who has been turned into a beast. He learns to control his temper and becomes kind and forbearing. Belle conquers adversity with her quick wit, compassion, understanding, and love. This is truly a refreshing contrast to the familiar "'battle or conquest'" approach of most heroes (McKenna A13).

9   Jasmine of Aladdin has been acclaimed by some critics as the "most independent-minded Disney heroine yet" (Rosenberg). The rebellious spirit within causes her to do things that would be considered daring and bold for a princess. She escapes from her father's palace walls to assert her freedom by exploring the streets of Agrabah, but most significantly, she refuses to marry for politics or the tradition that the sultan's daughter must marry a prince. Jasmine rejects her princely suitors by saying that they lack character and that she does not love them. Jasmine's desire for true love is nothing new to Disney films; Snow White desires a true love as well, but in Aladdin, the terms of love are dictated by the female character. She is someone to be wooed, but not a prize to be won. It is she who makes the real choice.

10   At the same time, by comparing Snow White with Beauty and Aladdin, we can see how Disney films still

Summarizes preceding discussion

Uses source to support conclusion

Picks up theme that concludes ¶8

Develops idea introduced in quotation

Summarizes events

51c
MLA

Could have added quotations

Supplies transition to discussion of similarities

Might have developed key element of appearance in more detail

try to preserve some traditional attitudes. Although Snow White, Belle, and Jasmine may have different appearances, they all appeal to our culture's traditional sense of physical beauty. They are fragile

Mentions selected details from all three films

and thin with perfect skin, hair, and teeth. Their figures are also proportioned in traditionally attractive ways. Snow White's looks draw a kiss from a prince; Belle's beauty (as the name itself implies) is

Reaches strong conclusion that seems to undermine earlier assertions of independence

part of her power to change the Beast; and Jasmine's looks are an essential part of her power, as illustrated by her ability to distract the evil vizier Jafar while Aladdin attempts to steal back the lamp.

11   None of the heroines is active or involved in any modern sense. Snow White cooks, cleans, and hums; Belle

Could discuss further, though interpretation is consistent with main idea

buries her nose in a book and takes care of her father; Jasmine sits in her father's palace and mopes, rejecting suitor after suitor. Their lives take a positive or active turn only when they are introduced to the men they will come to love. Regarding Beauty and the Beast as "a liberated love story for the '90s" (Showalter) seems to miss the film's balance of contemporary and traditional values.

12   Disney has frequently been criticized for its

Broadens focus to look at films in culture

powerful ability to adapt reality to fit its own purposes (Baudrillard). But perhaps Disney's retention of stereotypes of feminine beauty and passivity reflects our culture's reluctance to let go of traditions. Many men and women are still trying to define their priorities in life, especially in terms of work and relationships.

**51c
MLA**

Cunningham 6

For many, this struggle becomes a battle between family and work. Like many people, Americans may need to focus on traditional values when they believe that their culture and their lives are undergoing painful change and potential disorder. Could it be possible that <u>Beauty</u> and <u>Aladdin</u> reflect the need of many in their audiences to retain certain traditional values and behavior patterns while simultaneously endorsing new roles and perspectives?

13   Despite the fact that <u>Snow White and the Seven Dwarfs</u> was made roughly sixty years earlier than <u>Beauty and the Beast</u> and <u>Aladdin</u>, many things in the movies remain the same. There is a formula that Disney animators seem to follow in creating the appearance of female characters, one of conventional feminine beauty. The writers have also chosen fairy tale patterns for the story lines with such familiar features as the "happily-ever-after ending" and the image of a woman swept away by a man's love. What is different is that <u>Beauty and the Beast</u> and <u>Aladdin</u> weave themes of independence, intelligence, and action into the stories, centering them on the female characters. In contrast, the character and actions of Snow White emphasize themes of innocence, naiveté, and motherliness. While the continuing popularity of <u>Snow White</u> reveals at the very least a nostalgia for these themes, the shift to the more contemporary themes of <u>Beauty</u> and <u>Aladdin</u> is probably a sign of Disney's accurate perception of a society endorsing change yet looking for reassurance.

Returns to ideas introduced in opening ¶s

Raises question tentatively answered at end of paper

Restates opening observations, then summarizes key points

**51c
MLA**

Answers question raised in ¶12

Page numbers continue

↑ 1" from top of page

↕ ½" from top
Cunningham 7

Works Cited   Heading centered

Sources from paper listed alphabetically

All lines double-spaced

First line of each entry not indented

Additional lines indented 5 spaces

<u>Aladdin</u>. 1992. Videocassette. Walt Disney Company, 1993.

Allan, Robin. "Fifty Years of Snow White." <u>Journal of
    Popular Film and Television</u> 24 (1988): 155-63.

Baudrillard, Jean. "Disneyworld Company." Trans.
    Francois Debrix. <u>CTHEORY</u> 27 Mar. 1996.
    20 Mar. 1999 <http://www.ctheory.com/
    e25-disneyworld_ comp.html>.

<u>Beauty and the Beast</u>. 1991. Videocassette. Walt Disney
    Company, 1991.

Hoffman, Loreen. "Feminism in a Disney Film." Online
    posting. 2 Feb. 1998. 26 Aug. 1998
    <wysiwyg://22/http://faculty.ucr.edu/wcb/
    s. . .t/master/2/forums/forum2/messages/7.htm>.

McKenna, M. A. J. "Film Provides 'Beauty'-ful Role
    Models." <u>Boston Herald</u> 1 Dec. 1991: A13+.

Rosenberg, Scott. "The Genie-us of Aladdin." <u>San
    Francisco Examiner</u> 25 Nov. 1992: B2.

Showalter, Elaine. "Beauty and the Beast: Disney Meets
    Feminism in a Liberated Love Story for the '90s."
    <u>Premiere</u> Oct. 1997: 66.

<u>Snow White and the Seven Dwarfs</u>. 1937. Videocassette.
    Walt Disney Company, 1994.

TAKING IT ONLINE

APASTYLE.ORG
http://www.apastyle.org

Visit this official Web site of the American Psychological Association for current, accurate information about APA style. For special issues, click on topics such as electronic references or style tips, including an archive of previous Tips of the Week. Changes and updates in APA style are announced here as well.

For further advice on using APA style, check the home page for your library or tutoring center or other academic sites such as the one below. Be certain that any site you use has been revised and updated to reflect the most current APA style.

USING AMERICAN PSYCHOLOGICAL ASSOCIATION (APA) FORMAT (UPDATED TO 5TH EDITION)
http://owl.english.purdue.edu/handouts/research/r_apa.html

Sponsored by the Purdue University Online Writing Lab, this page explains how to lay out a paper, present quotations, and prepare entries for a reference list following APA style.

CITATION STYLE GUIDES
http://www.libraries.wright.edu/libnet/referen/citation.html

This page offers links to help you with the style guides for several fields, including the *WSU Writing Center Mini-Manual for Using APA Style in Research Papers.*

SECTION 10
Documenting Sources: APA Style

Guide to APA Formats for In-Text (Parenthetical) Citations

Guide to APA Formats for References

46. Online Organization or Agency Document
47. Online Government Document
48. Online Document from Academic Site
49. Online Report
50. Online Report from Academic Site
51. Online Abstract
52. Journal Article from Online Database

53. Newspaper Article from Online Database
54. Presentation from Virtual Conference
55. Email
56. Online Posting
57. Computer Program
58. CD-ROM Database

52 | Using APA Documentation Style

The documentation style developed by the APA (American Psychological Association) identifies a source by providing its author's name and its date of publication within parentheses. For this reason, the APA style is often called a name-and-date style. The information in the parenthetical citation guides readers to more detail about the source in a reference list at the end of the paper or report.

STRATEGY Use APA style in the social sciences to emphasize current sources.

52.1

ACADEMIC SETTINGS

When readers expect APA or a name-and-date style

WORK AND PUBLIC SETTINGS

When business or professional readers prefer a name-and-date system or want to see at once how current your sources are

When you need a simple way to identify sources and dates

When other writers or publications in your setting use APA style, modified APA style, or a similar informal system

For more on this documentation style, consult the *Publication Manual of the American Psychological Association* (5th ed., Washington, DC: APA, 2001). Updates are posted on the APA Web site at <http://www.apastyle.org>.

52 APA

52a **Using APA in-text citations**

The APA system provides in-text parenthetical citations for quotation paraphrases, summaries, and other specific information from a source. (F advice on what to document, see 49e.) APA style makes the year of public tion part of an in-text citation which refers to a reference list.

DRAFT   The current argumentative climate impedes exchanges among

those with differing ideas (Tannen).

READER'S REACTION: Is this source up to date?

EDITED   The current argumentative climate impedes exchanges among

those with differing ideas (Tannen, 1998).

1. Author's Name in Parentheses

When you include both the author's name and the year of publicatic in parentheses, separate them with a comma. To specify the location of quotation, paraphrase, summary, or other information, add a comma, *p.* *pp.*, and the page number(s) on which the material appears in the source.

One recent study points out that "women radio news directors

have exceeded the men in yearly salary" (Cramer, 1993, p. 161)

2. Author's Name in Discussion

When you include an author's name in your discussion, give the dat of the source in parentheses after the name. Provide the page number in th source following any quotation or paraphrase.

As Cramer (1993) points out, "Although women radio news

directors have exceeded the men in yearly salary, that may not

be the case in other radio news positions" (p. 161).

3. Specific Reference

Indicate what you are citing: *p.* ("page"), *chap.* ("chapter"), *figure, para* or *¶* (paragraphs) in electronic sources. Spell potentially confusing words For classical works always indicate the part (chap. 5), not the page.

Teenagers who survive suicide attempts experience distinct

stages of recovery (Mauk & Weber, 1991, Table 1).

4. One Author

You can vary your in-text citations as you present both the name and date in parentheses, both in the text, or the name in the text.

```
Mallory's 1999 study of magnet schools confirmed trends
identified earlier (Jacobson, 1989) and also updated the
classification by Bailey (1996).
```

Two Authors

In a parenthetical citation, separate the names with an ampersand (&); your text, use the word *and*.

```
Given evidence that married men earn more than unmarried men
(Chun & Lee, 2001), Nakosteen and Zimmer (2001) investigate how
earnings affect spousal selection.
```

. Three to Five Authors

Include all the names, separated by commas, in the first citation. In arenthetical citations, use an ampersand (&) rather than *and*.

```
Sadeh, Raviv, and Gruber (2000) related "sleep problems and
neuropsychological functioning in children" (p. 292).
```

ı any following references, give only the first author's name and *et al.* ("and thers"): Sadeh et al. (2000) reported their findings.

. Six or More Authors

In all text citations, follow the first author with *et al.*: (Berg et al., 998). For your reference list, see Entry 2 on page 304.

. Corporate or Group Author

Spell out the name of the organization, corporation, or agency in the irst citation. Follow any cumbersome name with an abbreviation in brack-ts, and use the shorter form in later citations.

IRST CITATION	Besides instilling fear, hate crimes limit where women live and work (National Organization of Women [NOW], 2001).
ATER CITATION	Pending legislation would strengthen the statutes on bias-motivated crimes (NOW, 2001).

9. No Author Given

Give the title or the first few words of a long title.

52a
APA

```
These photographs represent people from all walks of life
(Friendship, 2001).
```

Full title: *Friendship: Celebration of humanity.*

10. Work Cited More Than Once

When you cite the same source more than once in a paragraph, repeat the source as necessary to clarify a page reference or specify one of several sources. If a second reference is clear, don't repeat the date.

```
Much of the increase in personal debt can be linked to
unrestrained use of credit cards (Schor, 1998, p. 73). In fact
according to Schor, roughly a third of consumers "describe
themselves as either heavily or moderately in financial debt"
(p. 72).
```

11. Authors with the Same Name

When your references include works by two authors who share the same last name, provide the author's initials for each in-text citation.

```
Scholars have examined the development of African American
culture during slavery and reconstruction (E. Foner, 1988),
including the role of Frederick Douglass in this process
(P. Foner, 1950).
```

12. Personal Communications, Including Interviews and Email

In your text, cite letters, interviews, memos, email, telephone calls and so on using the name of the person, the expression *personal communication*, and the full date. Readers have no access to such sources, so you can omit them from your reference list.

```
According to J. M. Hostos, the state no longer funds services
duplicated by county agencies (personal communication, October
7, 2001).
```

13. Two or More Sources in a Citation

If you sum up information from several sources, include them all in your citation. Separate the authors and years with commas; separate the sources with semicolons. List the sources alphabetically, then oldest to most recent for several by the same author.

```
Several studies have related work performance and personality
(Furnham, 1992; Gilmer, 1961, 1977).
```

4. Two or More Works by the Same Author in the Same Year

If you use works published in the same year by the same author or author team, alphabetize the works, and add letters after the year to distinguish them.

```
Gould (1987a, p. 73) makes a similar point.
```

5. Content Footnote

You may use a content footnote to expand material in the text. Place a superscript number above the related line of text; number the notes consecutively. On a separate page at the end, below the centered heading "Footnotes," present the notes in numerical order. Begin each with its superscript number. Indent five to seven spaces for the first line only of each note, and double-space all notes.

```
TEXT          I tape-recorded and transcribed all interviews.[1]

NOTE                [1]Although background noise obscured some parts of

              the tapes, these gaps did not substantially affect the

              material studied.
```

52b Creating an APA reference list

On a separate page at the end of your text (before notes or appendixes), provide a list of references to the sources you've cited.

- **Page format.** Allow a one-inch margin, and center the heading "References" without underlining or quotation marks.
- **Alphabetizing.** List the works alphabetically by author or by the first main word of the title if there is no author. Arrange two or more works by the same author from oldest to most recent, by year of publication.
- **Spacing.** Double-space within and between all entries.
- **Indentation.** Do not indent the first line, but indent all additional lines like paragraphs, a half inch or five to seven spaces.

```
DRAFT     Carlson, NR., and Buskist, Wm. (1997), Psychology: The
          Science of Behavior. Boston, Allyn & Bacon.
```
          READER'S REACTION: This writer seems very careless about detail. I wonder if the research is this sloppy, too.

```
EDITED    Carlson, N. R., & Buskist, W. (1997). Psychology: The
          science of behavior (5th ed.). Boston: Allyn &
          Bacon.
```

52b APA

Books and Works Treated as Books

- **Author.** Give the author's last name followed by a comma and the initials *only* of the first and middle names. Use the same inverted order for all the names of co-authors. Separate the names of co-authors with commas, and use an ampersand (&) before the name of the last author.
- **Date.** Put the year of publication in parentheses followed by a period.
- **Title.** Italicize the title, but capitalize only proper names and the first word of the main title and any subtitle.
- **Publication information.** Name the city (and the country or the state's postal abbreviation except for major cities) followed by a colon and a space. Supply the publisher's name without words such as *Inc.* or *Publishers.*

1. One Author

Wilson, W. J. (1996). *When work disappears: The world of the new urban poor.* New York: Knopf.

2. Two or More Authors

List up to six authors; add *et al.* to indicate any others.

Biber, D., Conrad, S., & Reppen, R. (1998). *Corpus linguistics: Investigating language structure and use.* Cambridge, England: Cambridge University Press.

3. Corporate or Group Author

Treat the group as an author. When author and publisher are the same, give the word *Author* after the place instead of repeating the name.

Amnesty International. (2001). *Annual report 2001* [Brochure]. London: Author.

4. No Author Given

Boas anniversary volume: Anthropological papers written in honor of Franz Boas. (1906). New York: Stechert.

5. More Than One Work by the Same Author

List works chronologically with the author's name in each entry.

Aronowitz, S. (1993). *Roll over Beethoven: The return of cultural strife.* Hanover, NH: Wesleyan University Press.

Aronowitz, S. (2000). *From the ashes of the old: American labor and America's future.* New York: Basic Books.

More Than One Work by the Same Author in the Same Year

If works by the same author appear in the same year, list them alphabetically based on the first main word in the title. Add lowercase letters after the dates to distinguish them in text citations: (Gould, 1987b).

Gould, S. J. (1987a). *Time's arrow, time's cycle: Myth and metaphor in the discovery of geological time.* Cambridge, MA: Harvard University Press.

Gould, S. J. (1987b). *An urchin in the storm: Essays about books and ideas.* New York: Norton.

. One or More Editors

Include (*Ed.*) or (*Eds.*) after the names of the editor or editors.

Bowe, J., Bowe, M., & Streeter, S. C. (Eds.). (2001). *Gig: Americans talk about their jobs.* New York: Three Rivers Press.

. Translator

Bourdieu, P. (1990). *In other words: Essays towards a reflexive sociology.* (M. Adamson, Trans.). Stanford, CA: Stanford University Press.

. Edition Following the First

Identify the edition in parentheses after the title (for example, *3rd ed.* or *Rev. ed.* for "revised edition").

Groth-Marnat, G. (1996). *Handbook of psychological assessment* (3rd ed.). New York: Wiley.

10. Reprint

Butler, J. (1999). *Gender trouble.* New York: Routledge. (Original work published 1990)

11. Multivolume Work

> Strachey, J., Freud, A., Strachey, A., & Tyson, A. (Eds.).
> (1966-1974). *The standard edition of the complete
> psychological works of Sigmund Freud* (J. Strachey et al.,
> Trans.) (Vols. 3-5). London: Hogarth Press and the
> Institute of Psycho-Analysis.

12. Anthology or Collection of Articles

> Cobley, P. (Ed.). (1996). *The communication theory reader*.
> London: Routledge.

13. Encyclopedia or Reference Work

> Winn, P. (Ed.). (2001). *Dictionary of biological psychology*.
> London: Routledge.

14. *Diagnostic and Statistical Manual of Mental Disorders*

After an initial full in-text citation, you may use standard abbreviations: *DSM-III* (1980), *DSM-III-R* (1987), *DSM-IV* (1994), or *DSM-IV-T* (2000).

> American Psychiatric Association. (1994). *Diagnostic and
> statistical manual of mental disorders* (4th ed.).
> Washington, DC: Author.

15. Dissertation (Unpublished)

> Gomes, C. S. (2001). *Selection and treatment effects in managed
> care*. Unpublished doctoral dissertation, Boston
> University.

16. Government Document

> Select Committee on Aging, Subcommittee on Human Services,
> House of Representatives. (1991). *Grandparents' rights:
> Preserving generational bonds* (Com. Rep. No. 102-833).
> Washington, DC: U.S. Government Printing Office.

. Report

Begin with the individual, group, or agency that has written the report. he same body publishes the report, use *Author* in the publication informa- n. If the report has a number, put it in parentheses after the title but before e period.

```
Dossey, J. A. (1988). Mathematics: Are we measuring up? (Report
    No. 17-M-02). Princeton, NJ: Educational Testing Service.
    (ERIC Document Reproduction Service No. ED300207)
```

rticles and Selections from Periodicals and Books

- **Author.** Follow the author's last name and initials with a period.
- **Date.** Supply the date in parentheses followed by a period.
- **Title of article.** Capitalize only proper names and the first word of the title and any subtitle. Do not use quotation marks or italics. End with a period.
- **Title of journal, periodical, or book.** Italicize the journal title, with all main words capitalized, and the volume number. Follow with page numbers. Capitalize a book title like an article title, but italicize it.

8. Article in Journal Paginated by Volume

Omit the issue number when the page numbers run continuously hroughout the different issues making up a volume.

```
Macklin, M. C. (1996). Preschoolers' learning of brand names
    from visual cues. Journal of Consumer Research, 23,
    251-261.
```

9. Article in Journal Paginated by Issue

When page 1 begins each issue, include the issue number in parenthe- es, but not italicized, directly after the volume number.

```
Sadeh, A., Raviv, A., & Gruber, R. (2000). Sleep patterns and
    sleep disruptions in school-age children. Developmental
    Psychology, 36(3), 291-301.
```

20. Special Issue of Journal

Begin with the special issue's editor (if other than the regular editor). If no editor is indicated, begin with the title.

```
Balk, D. E. (Ed.). (1991). Death and adolescent bereavement
    [Special issue]. Journal of Adolescent Research, 6(1).
```

21. Article in Weekly Magazine

> Adler, J. (1995, July 31). The rise of the overclass. *Newsweek*
> *126*, 33-34, 39-40, 43, 45-46.

22. Article in Monthly Magazine

> Dold, C. (1998, September). Needles and nerves. *Discover, 19*,
> 59-62.

23. Article with No Author Given

> True tales of false memories. (1993, July/August). *Psychology*
> *Today, 26*, 11-12.

24. Article in Newspaper

Use *p.* or *pp.* to introduce the article's page numbers.

> Murtaugh, P. (1998, August 10). Finding a brand's real essence
> *Advertising Age*, p. 12.

25. Editorial or Letter to the Editor

> Ellis, S. (2001, September 7). Adults are problem with youth
> sports [Letter to the editor]. *USA Today*, p. 14A.

26. Interview (Published)

Although APA does not specify a form for published interviews, you
may wish to employ the following form.

> Dess, N. K. (2001). The new body-mind connection (John T.
> Cacioppo) [Interview]. *Psychology Today, 34*(4), 30-31.

27. Review with Title

Following the title of the review, describe in brackets the kind of work
(*book, film, television program*), and give the work's title.

> McMahon, R. J. (2000). The Pentagon's war, the media's
> war [Review of the book *Reporting Vietnam: Media and*
> *military at war*]. *Reviews in American History, 28*,
> 303-308.

8. Review Without Title

> Van Meter, E. J. (1994). [Review of the book *Preparing
> tomorrow's school leaders: Alternative designs*].
> *Educational Administration Quarterly, 30,* 112-117.

9. Article in Encyclopedia or Reference Work

> Chernoff, H. (1978). Decision theory. In *International
> encyclopedia of statistics* (Vol. 1, pp. 131-135). New
> York: Free Press.

0. Chapter in Edited Book or Selection in Anthology

> Chisholm, J. S. (1999). Steps to an evolutionary ecology of
> mind. In A. L. Hinton (Ed.), *Biocultural approaches to the
> emotions* (pp. 117-150). Cambridge, England: Cambridge
> University Press.

1. Dissertation Abstract

> Yamada, H. (1989). American and Japanese topic management
> strategies in business conversations. *Dissertation
> Abstracts International, 50*(09), 2982B.

If you consult the dissertation on microfilm, end with the University Microfilms
number in parentheses: (University Microfilms No. AAC–9004751).

Field and Media Resources

32. Unpublished Raw Data

When you use data from field research, briefly describe its topic within
brackets, and end with *Unpublished raw data.*

> Hernandez, J. (1998). [Survey of attitudes on unemployment
> benefits]. Unpublished raw data.

33. Interview (Unpublished)

If you have conducted an interview, cite it only in the text: (R. Gelles,
personal communication, November 20, 2001).

34. Personal Communications (Including Email)

Cite letters, email, phone calls, and other communications unavailable to readers only in your text (see Entry 12 on p. 302).

35. Paper Presented at a Meeting

Nelson, J. S. (1993, August). *Political argument in political science: A meditation on the disappointment of political theory.* Paper presented at the annual meeting of the American Political Science Association, Chicago.

36. Videotape or Film

Musen, K. (Producer/Writer), & Zimbardo, P. (Writer). (1990). *Quiet rage: The Stanford prison study* [Motion picture]. (Available from Insight Media, New York)

37. Television or Radio Program

Siceloff, J. L. (Executive Producer). (2002). *Now with Bill Moyers* [Television series]. New York: WNET.

38. Recording

Begin with the name of the writer and the copyright date.

Freeman, R. (1994). Porscha [Recorded by R. Freeman & The Rippingtons]. On *Sahara* [CD]. New York: GRP Records.

Internet, Web, and Electronic Resources

39. Web Site

Brown, D. K. (1998, April 1). *The children's literature Web guide.* Calgary: Author. Retrieved August 23, 1998, from http://www.acs.UCalgary.ca/~dkbrown/

40. Online Book or Document

If you can't pinpoint a date of publication, use *n.d.* ("no date").

Frary, R. B. (n.d.). *A brief guide to questionnaire development.* Retrieved August 8, 1998, from http://ericae.net/ft/tamu/upiques3.htm

41. Selection from Online Book or Document

Lasswell, H. D. (1971). Professional training. In *A pre-view of policy sciences* (chap. 8). Retrieved May 4, 2002, from http://www.policysciences.org/spsresources.htm

42. Online Journal Article

Sheridan, J., & McAuley, J. D. (1998). Rhythm as a cognitive skill: Temporal processing deficits in autism. *Noetica, 3*(8). Retrieved December 31, 1998, from http://www.cs .indiana.edu/Noetica/OpenForumIssue8/McAuley.html

43. Online Article Identical to Print Version

If online and print articles are identical, you may use the print format but identify the online version you used.

Epstein, R. (2001). Physiologist Laura [Electronic version]. *Psychology Today, 34*(4), 5.

If the online article differs in format or content, add your retrieval date with the URL.

44. Online Newsletter Article

Cashel, J. (2001, July 16). Top ten trends for online communities. *Online Community Report*. Retrieved October 18, 2001, from http://www.onlinecommunityreport.com/ features/10/

45. Online Newspaper or News Service Article

Phillips, D. (1999, June 13). 21 days, 18 flights. *Washington Post Online*. Retrieved June 13, 1999, from http://www.washingtonpost.com/wp-srv/business/ daily/june99/odyssey13.htm

46. Online Organization or Agency Document

Arizona Public Health Association. (n.d.). *Indigenous health section*. Retrieved September 6, 2001, from http:// www.geocities.com/native_health_az/AzPHA.htm

47. Online Government Document

U.S. Department of Labor, Women's Bureau. (2001). *Women's jobs 1964-1999: More than 30 years of progress*. Retrieved September 7, 2001, from http://www.dol.gov/dol/ wb/public/jobs6497.htm

48. Online Document from Academic Site

Cultural Studies Program. (n.d.). Retrieved September 9, 2001, from Drake University, Cultural Studies Web site: http://www.multimedia.drake.edu/cs/

49. Online Report

Amnesty International. (1998). *The death penalty in Texas: Lethal injustice*. Retrieved September 7, 2001, from http://www.web.amnesty.org/ai.nsf/index/AMR510101998

50. Online Report from Academic Site

Use "Available from" rather than "Retrieved from" if the URL will take your reader to access information rather than the source itself.

Vandell, D. L., & Wolfe, B. (2000). *Child care quality: Does it matter and does it need to be improved?* (Special Report No. 78). Available from University of Wisconsin, Institute for Research on Poverty Web site: http://www.ssc.wisc.edu/ irp/sr/sr78.pdf

51. Online Abstract

Include the source of the original work.

National Bureau of Economic Research. (1998). Tax incentives for higher education. *Tax Policy and the Economy, 12*, 49-81. Abstract retrieved August 24, 1998, from http://www-mitpress.mit.edu/journal-editor .tcl?ISSN=08928649

2. Journal Article from Online Database

Piko, B. (2001). Gender differences and similarities in adolescents' ways of coping. *The Psychological Record, 51*(2), 223-236. Retrieved August 31, 2001, from InfoTrac Expanded Academic database.

3. Newspaper Article from Online Database

Li, R. J. (1999, May 4). Ohio State U. Greeks "aware" alcohol not necessary for fun. *The Lantern*. Retrieved July 22, 1999, from Electric Library database.

54. Presentation from Virtual Conference

Brown, D. J., Stewart, D. S., & Wilson, J. R. (1995). *Ethical pathways to virtual learning*. Paper presented at the Center on Disabilities 1995 virtual conference. Retrieved September 7, 2001, from http://www.csun.edu/cod/95virt/0010.html

55. Email

Cite email only in your text. (See Entry 12, p. 302.)

56. Online Posting

Treat these as personal communications (see Entry 12, p. 302) unless they are archived and accessible.

Lanbehn, K. (2001, May 9). Effective rural outreach. Message posted to State Independent Living Council Discussion Newsgroup, archived at http://www.acils.com/silc/

57. Computer Program

Begin with the name of an author who owns rights to a program or with its title (without italics).

Family Tree Maker (Version 9.0) [Computer software]. (2001). Fremont, CA: Learning Company.

52
APA

58. CD-ROM Database

Hall, Edward T. (1998). In *Current biography: 1940-1997*.

Retrieved March 14, 1999, from Wilson database.

52c Sample APA paper

The APA manual recommends beginning a paper with a separate title page, as illustrated below. The students also included an abstract before the paper and their questionnaire in the appendix following it.

Number title page and all others using short title   Alcohol Use   1

Abbreviate title (50 characters maximum) for heading
Running head: ALCOHOL USE

Center title and all other lines
Alcohol Use: Correlations Between College Drinking

and Previous Parental Permissiveness

Supply names and institution
Jennifer Emily Figliozzi and Summer J. Arrigo-Nelson

The University of Rhode Island

Supply course information and date if requested by your instructor
Professor Robert Schwegler

Writing 201

Section 1

May 1, 1998

Center heading

Abstract

Do not indent

College students at a medium-sized state university were asked to fill out a questionnaire on their parents' attitudes toward alcohol use and their own drinking behaviors. The study addressed two research questions: (a) Do students given permission to drink while still living at home exhibit different college drinking behaviors than those who were not given permission? and (b) Do students feel there is a correlation between college drinking behaviors and permission to drink while still living at home? The study found evidence both of a correlation between parental permission and drinking behaviors and of student belief that such a correlation exists.

Begin on new page

Summarize paper in one ¶, no more than 120 words

Double-space abstract and paper

[Besides the abstract, typical sections in an APA paper are Introduction, Method, Results, and Discussion.]

52 APA

1" from top of new page

Alcohol Use: Correlations Between College Drinking
and Previous Parental Permissiveness

1" margin on each side

Indent ¶s and reference list consistently, ½" or 5 to 7 spaces

Opening presents problem, background, and hypothesis or research question

1   Research dealing with student alcohol use most often focuses on children's perceptions of their parents' actions and on the relationship between child and parent. Studies conducted with high school students have supported the hypothesis that positive family relationships are more likely to be associated with less frequent alcohol use among adolescents than are negative relationships. Adolescents model the limited substance use of their parents where there is a good or moderate parent-adolescent relationship (Andrews, Hops, & Duncan, 1997). Other factors the studies found to be associated with positive family relationships, along with substance use, were academic achievement, family structure, place of residence, self-esteem, and emotional tone (Martsh & Miller, 1997; Wechsler, Dowdall, Davenport, & Castillo, 1995).

Citation includes more than one source

Center subheading Introduction

2   The focus of our study is twofold. First, research has shown that adolescents who have open and close relationships with their parents use alcohol less often than do those with conflictual relationships (Sieving, 1996). For example, a survey of students in seventh through twelfth grades reported that approximately 35% of adolescent drinkers were under parental supervision while drinking (Department of Education, 1993). On the basis of this research, we

Research question 1

Builds on previous studies but adds question of relationship with parents

1" margin at bottom

52c
APA

Alcohol Use   4

are interested in determining if students who were given permission to drink while living with their parents would have different drinking patterns upon reaching college than those who did not previously have permission to drink.

3   Second, studies have demonstrated that student perception of parental drinking behavior and parental restrictiveness shapes student behavior as much as, if not more than, actual parental behavior (Aas, Jakobsen, & Anderssen, 1996). Considering this, we are also interested in learning if students feel that a correlation exists between having permission to drink at home and their behavior once in college.

Method

Sample

4   We distributed our questionnaire to a group of students from a medium-sized land grant university in a rural New England town. Our sample consisted of 8 male and 6 female students for a total of 14 participants.

Materials

5   Our questionnaire was designed to gather self-reported data from students on their drinking behaviors, the actions of their parents, and their perceptions of their parents' views on alcohol (see Appendix). For each participant, we compared parental behavior and student drinking behavior in relation to each other and to the responses from the other questionnaires. An open-response section was also

Research question 2

Discusses participants, materials, and procedure for research study

Cross-references Appendix

52 AP.

included in order to compare each student's perception of the correlation between parental actions and his or her own drinking behavior to the more objective correlation as calculated by the students' responses to the binary (yes/no) and multiple-choice questions.

Procedure

6   We distributed our questionnaire to members of the sample group and asked them to fill it out as honestly and accurately as possible. Once the questionnaires were completed, they placed them in a pile on a designated desk.

Follows same order as questionnaire

|

Provides detailed summary of responses

Results

7   The first question on our survey asked the participants if they were offered alcohol by their parents as children. The outcome was that 86% were offered alcohol at home while 14% were not. With a yes or no option, we designated a value of (1) to yes and (2) to no. Taken from these values, the mean for question 1 is 1.14, which shows a tendency toward alcohol consumption at home among the study participants.

[The results section goes on to discuss questions 2 through 9.]

8   Questions 10 and 11 return to the students' thoughts rather than their actions. Question 10 revealed that 36% of the participants felt that their parents' views on drinking affected their drinking habits at college, and 64% felt that they acted independently of their parents' views. Question 11

found that 57% saw a direct correlation between
students' drinking behavior and their behavior at home
while 43% felt that there is no such correlation.
For this question, 83% of the female participants,
but only 37% of the male, saw a correlation.

9   Question 14 was an open-ended question asking
participants to explain their answers for question 11.
Responses to this question were mixed: 24% felt that
children tend to emulate their parents' views and
behavior; 5% felt that the real influence on student
behavior is from friends; 9% said that when parents
allow children to drink at home, the students' tendency
is to abstain from drinking excessively at school;
24% felt that student drinking is rebellious toward
the parents who didn't allow it to occur in the home;
38% said that growing up with permission to consume
alcohol in the house turns the thought of drinking
into something that is not a big issue, therefore
making the child a responsible drinker.

10   While we were reviewing the results of the survey,
it became apparent that a majority of the participants
did voice support for the existence of a correlation
between permission to drink at home and drinking habits
away from home. Although 57% agreed with this theory,
opinions varied as to how it affected drinking habits.
Of the 57%, 38% said being raised with permission to
drink gave them a sense of responsibility when at
college; 24% said that they follow their parents'

> Highlights
> interesting
> pattern in
> data

> Includes
> results that
> are not
> easy to
> interpret

52
AP.

influence and do as they do; 24% felt that being forbidden to drink alcohol at home forces the student to drink as a form of rebellion; 9% reported that being permitted to drink at home sets a pattern of nonexcessive drinking at college; and 5% said that peers influenced student behavior more than upbringing.

Discussion

11   Despite differences in student drinking behavior, this survey demonstrates that many similarities are revealed when multiple answers to the same questions are grouped and analyzed. In many cases, the results seem to indicate that trends exist in student behavior and thought. Further administrations of this questionnaire would have clarified these trends, however. Two examples, in particular, demonstrate the need for further clarification.

12   First, although both questions 1 and 4 looked to determine student alcohol use within the home, we observed a discrepancy between the percentage of people who replied that they were offered alcohol at home and those who said that their parents believed that alcohol was only for those over 21 years of age. This discrepancy could have arisen if the students in the sample were not thorough in their evaluation of parental views, in which case correlations drawn from this data should not be relied upon (Aas, Jakobsen, & Anderssen, 1996). Second, a strong correlation between gender and response was seen in questions 7 and 11.

In both cases, it is likely that cultural influences beyond the scope of this study have shaped male and female adolescents in ways that would account for the disparities within the answers.

Suggests need for further research

13   Our first research question asked if those students who had permission to drink at home would have different drinking behaviors at college than those who were not given permission to drink. The results show that there is a strong correlation between the availability of alcohol in the home and a student's decision to drink in college (86% were offered liquor in the home, and 86% now drink). However, a lesser percentage of the students who were allowed to drink in the home, when compared to those who were not allowed, get drunk when they drink.

Considers extent to which data answers research questions

14   Our second research question looked to determine if students feel that a correlation exists between drinking behaviors at home and at college. Although 57% of students felt such a correlation existed when answering question 11 (a yes-no question), 80% gave the same response when answering question 14 (an open-ended question). These findings indicate that over 20% of the students surveyed do not consciously recognize the correlation which they, themselves, indicate exists. Out of those students who reported a correlation, the majority felt that it made students more responsible drinkers while only 20% of the students argued that a negative correlation exists

(where students rebel against their parents' teachings at the first available opportunity).

Returns to broader view in conclusion

15   We conclude that within the context of a medium-sized university setting, there are correlations between student drinking behavior in college and parental permissiveness toward drinking in the home. It is obvious that more research is needed to determine definite patterns and correlations. For example, a recent appeal for greater parental involvement (Wechsler, Dowdall, Davenport, & DeJong, n.d.) signals a recognition that parents can have an important impact not just before but also during their children's college years. This study supports the argument that a student's drinking behavior, upon entering college, is strongly determined by the environment in which the student has grown up. Further research could examine how these behaviors correlate with the level of parental permissiveness (or involvement) during the college years.

References

Aas, H., Jakobsen, R., & Anderssen, N. (1996). Predicting 13-year-olds' drinking using parents' self-reported alcohol use and restrictiveness compared with offspring's perception. *Scandinavian Journal of Psychology, 37,* 113-120.

Andrews, J. A., Hops, H., & Duncan, S. C. (1997). Adolescent modeling of parent substance use: The moderating effect of the relationship with the parent. *Journal of Family Psychology, 11,* 259-270.

Department of Education. (1993). *Youth and alcohol. Selected reports to the Surgeon General* (Report No. OESC-92-38). Washington, DC: Author. (ERIC Document Reproduction Service No. ED361616)

Martsh, C. T., & Miller, W. R. (1997). Extraversion predicts heavy drinking in college students. *Personality and Individual Differences, 23,* 153-155.

Sieving, R. E. (1996, Fall). Parental influence on alcohol use among young adolescents. *GSAN Newsletter.* Retrieved April 25, 1998, from http://www.nursing.umn.edu/MS/Adolescent/ Newsletter/fall1996.html

Wechsler, H., Dowdall, G. W., Davenport, A., & Castillo, S. (1995). Correlates of college student binge drinking. *American Journal of Public Health, 85,* 921-926.

Begin on new page

52
AP

Wechsler, H., Dowdall, G. W., Davenport, A., & DeJong, W. (n.d.). Binge drinking on campus: Results of a national study. *Bulletin Series: Alcohol and Other Drug Prevention.* Newton, MA: The Higher Education Center for Alcohol and Other Drug Prevention. Retrieved April 29, 1998, from http://www.edc.org/hec/pubs/binge.htm

Appendix

Questionnaire

Circle one answer.

1. As a child, did your parents ever offer you

   alcohol?   Yes   No

Check as many as apply.

2. My parents offered me:

   sips of their own drinks

   half servings of alcoholic beverages

   full servings of alcoholic beverages

   more than one full serving on a given occasion

Circle one answer.

3. As a child, were you allowed to drink at family

   functions? (for example, weddings, birthdays,

   holidays)   Yes   No

Circle the statement that most reflects the attitude
of your parents toward alcohol.

4. a. Drinking is only for those who are 21 or older.

   b. Drinking is only for those who are responsible

      enough to drink, regardless of their age.

   c. My parent(s) completely abstained from drinking

      any alcohol.

Circle one answer (per question).

5. Do you agree with the way in which your parents

   handled the issues of alcohol and your consumption

   of alcohol within your household?   Yes   No

6. Have you had an alcoholic drink since coming

   to college?   Yes   No

Check as many as apply.

7. In a typical week I will drink:

    on weekdays

    on weekends

    once a week

    only on special occasions

Circle one answer (per question).

8. On average, I will drink _____ alcoholic drinks in one sitting:

    1   2-3   4-6   7 or more

9. Is the quantity consumed in one sitting enough to give you some or all of the effects of drunkenness?

                                      Yes   No

10. Do you let the views your parents hold on drinking affect your drinking behavior?   Yes   No

11. Do you feel that there is a correlation between students' drinking behavior in college and their drinking behavior in their homes?   Yes   No

12. I am: Male   Female

13. I am in my _____ year of college:

    First   Second   Third   Fourth

    Fifth or More

14. Please take a few moments to explain why you chose the answer you did for question 11. If you answered yes, please explain what type of correlation you feel exists. (Please continue on the back of this page if you need more room.)

TAKING IT ONLINE

THE CHICAGO MANUAL OF STYLE FAQ (AND NOT SO FAQ)
http://www.press.uchicago.edu/Misc/Chicago/cmosfaq.html
This official Web site for *The Chicago Manual of Style* answers detailed questions from students, writers, and editors on topics such as commas, compounds, numbers, quotations, URLs, and usage.

COUNCIL OF SCIENCE EDITORS WEB SITE
http://www.councilscienceeditors.org
Formerly the Council of Biology Editors (CBE) and now the Council of Science Editors (CSE), this group sponsors *Scientific Style and Format,* the guide to CSE style. This official Web site supplies updates on the style and access to the latest electronic formats of the National Library of Medicine, which CSE generally follows.

For more advice on using the CMS and CSE styles, check the home page for your library or tutoring center, or refer to other reliable academic sites. Check the revision date for any site you use; rely on sites that reflect the most current editions of these style guides. Visit the following sites for information on many academic or professional style guides.

RESOURCES FOR DOCUMENTING SOURCES
http://owl.english.purdue.edu/handouts/research/r_docsources.html
This site lists style guides for about twenty fields, noting both the official sites of the organizations sponsoring the style guides and helpful academic and other sites with explanations useful to students.

CITATION STYLE GUIDES
http://www.libraries.wright.edu/libnet/referen/citation.html
Sponsored by the Wright State University Libraries, this page offers links to style guides and aids for citing sources in a variety of fields.

SECTION 11
Documenting Sources: CMS and CSE Styles

Guide to CMS Formats for Endnotes and Footnotes

Books and Works Treated as Books
1. One Author
2. Two Authors
3. Three Authors
4. Four or More Authors
5. No Author Given
6. One Editor
7. Two or More Editors
8. Author and Editor
9. Edition Following the First
10. Reprint
11. Multivolume Work

Articles and Selections from Periodicals and Books
12. Article in Journal Paginated by Volume
13. Article in Journal Paginated by Issue

14. Article in Magazine
15. Article in Newspaper
16. Chapter in Edited Book
17. Selection in Anthology

Field and Media Resources
18. Interview (Unpublished)
19. Audio or Video Recording

Internet, Web, and Electronic Resources
20. Online Book
21. Online Article
22. CD-ROM

Multiple Sources and Sources Cited in Prior Notes
23. Multiple Sources
24. Work Cited More Than Once

Guide to CMS Formats for Bibliography Entries

Books and Works Treated as Books
1. One Author
2. Two Authors
3. Three Authors
4. Four or More Authors
5. No Author Given
6. One Editor
7. Two or More Editors
8. Author and Editor
9. Edition Following the First
10. Reprint
11. Multivolume Work

Articles and Selections from Periodicals and Books
12. Article in Journal Paginated by Volume

13. Article in Journal Paginated by Issue
14. Article in Magazine
15. Article in Newspaper
16. Chapter in Edited Book
17. Selection in Anthology

Field and Media Resources
18. Interview (Unpublished)
19. Audio or Video Recording

Internet, Web, and Electronic Resources
20. Online Book
21. Online Article
22. CD-ROM

Multiple Sources
23. Multiple Sources

53 | Using CMS Documentation Style

The CMS (*Chicago Manual of Style*) outlines a system for references using endnotes or footnotes. These notes are less compact than parenthetical references and may distract a reader, but they allow detailed citations.

STRATEGY Use CMS style in the arts and sciences to place citations in notes.

53.1

ACADEMIC SETTINGS
When readers expect "Turabian," "Chicago," or footnotes or endnotes

WORK AND PUBLIC SETTINGS
When your readers expect footnotes or endnotes
When readers won't need to consult each note as they read and might be distracted by names, page numbers, or dates in parentheses
When other writers or publications addressing your readers use CMS

The CMS style is one of two systems of documentation outlined in *The Chicago Manual of Style* (14th edition, Chicago: University of Chicago Press, 1993), a reliable guide often simply called "Chicago." Its Web site at <http://www.press.uchicago.edu/Misc/Chicago/cmosfaq.html> answers many questions for writers and editors who routinely use CMS. This style is detailed for students in Kate L. Turabian's *A Manual for Writers of Term Papers, Theses, and*

**53a
CMS**

Dissertations (6th ed., rev. John Grossman and Alice Bennett, Chicago: Unive sity of Chicago Press, 1996). This popular student manual accounts for t wide identification of CMS style as "Turabian."

53a Using CMS endnotes and footnotes

To indicate a reference in your text, add a superscript number abov the line; number the references consecutively. Provide the details about th source at the end of the paper (in an endnote) or at the bottom of the pag (in a footnote). (For advice on what to document, see 49e.)

TEXT   Wideman describes his impoverished childhood neighborhood

as being not simply on "the wrong side of the tracks" but

actually "*under* the tracks."[1]

NOTE   1. John Edgar Wideman, *Brothers and Keepers* (New York

Penguin Books, 1984), 39.

Your word processor may position footnotes between the text and the bottor margin. Otherwise, you'll probably prefer endnotes. Most readers mark th endnote page for easy reference, but you should put all necessary informa tion in the text, not the notes, in case a reader skips a note.

Place endnotes following your paper, after any appendix but before th bibliography, which alphabetically orders your sources. Supply the notes on separate page with the centered heading "Notes." Indent the first line of each note like a paragraph; type its number on the line, followed by a period and space. Do not indent any following lines. CMS suggests double-spacing all o your text, but Turabian suggests single-spaced notes. Though both alterna tives appear in this chapter, we advise double-spacing for ease of reading.

Notes can also supply material of interest to only a few readers, but avoid excessive detail that may obscure a source reference.

TEXT   Another potential source of workplace misunderstanding

comes from differences in the ways orders are given by men

(directly) and women (indirectly, often as requests or

questions).[2]

NOTE   2. Deborah Tannen, "How to Give Orders Like a Man,"

New York Times Magazine, 18 August 1994, 46. Tannen

provides a detailed and balanced discussion of the ways

men and women use language in *Talking from 9 to 5*

(New York: William Morrow, 1994).

53b Creating CMS endnotes or footnotes

A typical note provides the author's name in regular order, the title, publication information, and the page reference.

Books and Works Treated as Books

One Author

> 1. Iris Chang, *The Rape of Nanking: The Forgotten Holocaust of World War II* (New York: Basic Books, 1997), 83.

Two Authors

> 2. William H. Gerdts and Will South, *California Impressionism* (New York: Abbeville Press, 1998), 214.

Three Authors

> 3. Michael Wood, Bruce Cole, and Adelheid Gealt, *Art of the Western World* (New York: Summit Books, 1989), 206-10.

Four or More Authors

Follow the name of the first author with *and others*. (Generally supply all the names in the bibliography entry.)

> 4. Anthony Slide and others, *The American Film Industry: A Historical Dictionary* (New York: Greenwood Press, 1986), 124.

No Author Given

> 5. *The Great Utopia* (New York: Guggenheim Museum, 1992), 661.

One Editor

To emphasize the editor, translator, or compiler, begin with that name.

> 6. Robert H. Ferrell, ed., *Dear Bess: The Letters from Harry to Bess Truman 1910-1959* (New York: W. W. Norton, 1983), 71-2.

The word *by* with the author's name may follow the title but isn't needed if the name appears in the title.

Two or More Editors

> 7. Cris Mazza, Jeffrey DeShell, and Elisabeth Sheffield, eds., *Chick-Lit 2: No Chick Vics* (Normal, Ill.: Black Ice Books, 1996), 173-86.

8. Author and Editor

Name any editor (*ed.*), translator (*trans.*), compiler (*comp.*), or som
combination of these after the title.

> 8. Francis Bacon, *The New Organon*, ed. Lisa Jardine,
> trans. Michael Silverthorne (Cambridge: Cambridge University
> Press, 2000), 45.

9. Edition Following the First

After the title, abbreviate the edition: *4th ed.* ("fourth edition") or *re
and enl. ed.* ("revised and enlarged edition").

> 9. John D. La Plante, *Asian Art*, 3d ed. (Dubuque, Iowa:
> Wm. C. Brown, 1992), 7.

10. Reprint

Note original publication of a reprint or paperback edition.

> 10. Henri Frankfort and others, *The Intellectual Adventur*
> *of Ancient Man* (Chicago: University of Chicago Press, 1946;
> reprint, Chicago: University of Chicago Press, 1977), 202-4.

11. Multivolume Work

If you cite the whole work, include the total number of volumes afte
the title. Separate volume and page numbers for a specific volume with
colon. For a separately titled volume, give the volume number and name af
ter the main title and only a page reference at the end.

> 11. Sigmund Freud, *The Standard Edition of the Complete*
> *Psychological Works of Sigmund Freud*, trans. James Strachey
> (London: Hogarth Press, 1953), 11: 180.

Articles and Selections from Periodicals and Books

12. Article in Journal Paginated by Volume

When page numbers run continuously through the issues in a volume
give only the volume number. Supply specific page numbers for part or in
clusive numbers for all of an article, such as 98–114.

> 12. C. Anita Tarr, "'A Man Can Stand Up': Johnny Tremain
> and the Rebel Pose," *The Lion and the Unicorn: A Critical*
> *Journal of Children's Literature* 18 (1994): 181.

13. Article in Journal Paginated by Issue

If each issue of a journal begins with page 1, give the volume number
and *no.* ("number") with the issue number. If the issue is identified by month

season, include this inside the parentheses with the year: (winter 1994) or
February 1996).

13. Jose Pinera, "A Chilean Model for Russia," *Foreign Affairs* 79, no. 5 (2000): 62-73.

4. Article in Magazine

Follow the magazine title with the date: 25 November 2001.

14. Joan W. Gandy, "Portrait of Natchez," *American Legacy*, fall 2000, 51-52.

5. Article in Newspaper

Identify newspapers by date: 4 February 2002. Provide the section (*sec.*) number or letter and page (*p.*) or pages (*pp.*). Add the city, state, or country, as needed: *Westerly (R.I.) Sun, Times* (London).

15. Janny Scott, "A Bull Market for Grant, A Bear Market for Lee," *New York Times*, 30 September 2000, sec. A, pp. 17, 19.

6. Chapter in Edited Book

Follow the title with *ed.* and the editor's name.

16. Julie D'Acci, "Defining Women: The Case of *Cagney and Lacey*," in *Private Screenings: Television and the Female Consumer*, ed. Lynn Spigel and Denise Mann (Minneapolis: University of Minnesota Press, 1992), 169.

7. Selection in Anthology

17. W. E. B. Du Bois, "The Call of Kansas," in *W. E. B. Du Bois: A Reader*, ed. David Levering Lewis (New York: Henry Holt, 1995), 173.

Field and Media Resources

8. Interview (Unpublished)

For unpublished interviews by someone else, supply the name of the person interviewed, *interview by*, the name of the interviewer, the date, any file number, the medium (such as *tape recording* or *transcript*), and the place where the interview is stored (*Erie County Historical Society, Buffalo, New York*). Identify interviews you conduct as *interview by author*; include the medium, place, and date of the interview.

18. Shawon Kelley, interview by author, transcript, Tempe, Ariz., 22 May 2000.

19. Audio or Video Recording

Start with the title unless the recording features a particular individu[al]. Give names and roles (if appropriate) of performers or others. Add any record[ing] number (audio) after the company.

> 19. *James Baldwin*, prod. and dir. Karen Thorsen, 87 min., Resolution Inc./California Newsreel, 1990, videocassette.

Internet, Web, and Electronic Resources

20. Online Book

For a book previously in print, include all standard information, an[d] add the medium in brackets after the title: [book online]. Supply your acce[ss] date, the URL, and the network: INTERNET.

> 20. Charles Darwin, *On the Origin of Species by Means of Natural Selection, or the Preservation of Favoured Races in the Struggle for Life* [book online] (London: Down, Bromley, Kent, 1859 [cited 12 February 1999]); available from ftp://sailor.gutenberg.org/pub/gutenberg/etext98/otoos10.txt; INTERNET.

21. Online Article

Supply standard information, but add the medium [journal online], the URL, your access date, and the network: INTERNET.

> 21. Alfred Willis, "A Survey of Surviving Buildings of the Krotona Colony in Hollywood," *Architronic* 8, no. 1 (1999) [journal online] [cited 29 September 2000]; available from http://architronic.saed.kent.edu/; INTERNET.

22. CD-ROM

Add the medium [*CD-ROM*] in brackets.

> 22. Rose, Mark, ed., "Elements of Theater," *The Norton Shakespeare Workshop CD-ROM*, Vers. 1.1 [CD-ROM] (New York: Norton Publishing, 1997).

Multiple Sources and Sources Cited in Prior Notes

23. Multiple Sources

Separate several references with semicolons. Give the entries in the order in which they are cited in the text.

> 23. See Greil Marcus, *Mystery Train: Images of America in Rock 'n Roll Music* (New York: E. P. Dutton, 1975), 119; Susan Orlean, "All Mixed Up," *New Yorker,* 22 June 1992, 90; and Cornel West, "Learning to Talk of Race," *New York Times Magazine,* 2 August 1992, 24.

. **Work Cited More Than Once**

In your first reference, provide full information. Later, provide only the thor's last name, a short title, and the page.

24. Pinera, "Chilean," 63.

25. Wood, Cole, and Gealt, *Art*, 207.

two notes in a row refer to the same source, you can use the traditional *ibid.* atin for "in the same place") for the second note. Add a new page reference the specific page is different.

26. Tarr, "'A Man,'" 183.

27. Ibid.

28. Ibid., 186.

53c Creating a CMS bibliography

In addition to your notes, provide an alphabetical list of sources, titled Selected Bibliography," "Works Cited," "References," or something similar. lace this list on a separate page at the end of your paper; center the title two iches from the top. Continue the page numbering used for the text. Al-hough we show single-spaced entries below to conserve space, we recom-nend double-spacing throughout for ease of reading. (Check with your in-tructor.) Do not indent the first line, but indent any subsequent lines five paces. Alphabetize by authors' last names or by the first word of the title, ex-luding *A*, *An*, and *The*, if the author is unknown.

Books and Works Treated as Books

1. **One Author**

Chang, Iris. *The Rape of Nanking: The Forgotten Holocaust of World War II*. New York: Basic Books, 1997.

2. **Two Authors**

Gerdts, William H., and Will South. *California Impressionism*. New York: Abbeville Press, 1998.

3. **Three Authors**

Wood, Michael, Bruce Cole, and Adelheid Gealt. *Art of the Western World*. New York: Summit Books, 1989.

4. **Four or More Authors**

Slide, Anthony, Val Almen Darez, Robert Gitt, and Susan Perez Prichard. *The American Film Industry: A Historical Dictionary*. New York: Greenwood Press, 1986.

5. No Author Given

The Great Utopia. New York: Guggenheim Museum, 1992.

6. One Editor

Ferrell, Robert H., ed. *Dear Bess: The Letters from Harry to Bess Truman 1910-1959.* New York: W. W. Norton, 1983.

7. Two or More Editors

Mazza, Cris, Jeffrey DeShell, and Elisabeth Sheffield, eds. *Chick-Lit 2: No Chick Vics.* Normal, Ill.: Black Ice Books 1996.

8. Author and Editor

Bacon, Francis. *The New Organon.* Ed. Lisa Jardine, trans. Michael Silverthorne. Cambridge: Cambridge University Press, 2000.

9. Edition Following the First

La Plante, John D. *Asian Art.* 3d ed. Dubuque, Iowa: Wm. C. Brown, 1992.

10. Reprint

Frankfort, Henri, H. A. Frankfort, John A. Wilson, Thorkild Jacobsen, and William A. Irving. *The Intellectual Adventure of Ancient Man.* Chicago: University of Chicago Press, 1946. Reprint, Chicago: University of Chicago Press, 1977.

11. Multivolume Work

Freud, Sigmund. *The Standard Edition of the Complete Psychological Works of Sigmund Freud.* Translated by James Strachey. Vol. 11. London: Hogarth Press, 1953.

Articles and Selections from Periodicals and Books

12. Article in Journal Paginated by Volume

Tarr, Anita C. "'A Man Can Stand Up': Johnny Tremain and the Rebel Pose." *The Lion and the Unicorn: A Critical Journal of Children's Literature* 18 (1994): 178-89.

3. Article in Journal Paginated by Issue

Pinera, Jose. "A Chilean Model for Russia." *Foreign Affairs* 79, no. 5 (2000): 62-73.

4. Article in Magazine

Gandy, Joan W. "Portrait of Natchez." *American Legacy,* fall 2000, 51-52.

5. Article in Newspaper

Scott, Janny. "A Bull Market for Grant, A Bear Market for Lee." *New York Times,* 30 September 2000, sec. A, pp. 17, 19.

6. Chapter in Edited Book

D'Acci, Julie. "Defining Women: The Case of *Cagney and Lacey*." In *Private Screenings: Television and the Female Consumer,* edited by Lynn Spigel and Denise Mann, 169-201. Minneapolis: University of Minnesota Press, 1992.

7. Selection in Anthology

Du Bois, W. E. B. "The Call of Kansas." In *W. E. B. Du Bois: A Reader,* edited by David Levering Lewis, 101-121. New York: Henry Holt, 1995.

Field and Media Resources

18. Interview (Unpublished)

Kelley, Shawon. Interview by author. Transcript. Tempe, Ariz., 22 May 2000.

19. Audio or Video Recording

James Baldwin. Produced and directed by Karen Thorsen. 87 min. Resolution Inc./California Newsreel, 1990. Videocassette.

Internet, Web, and Electronic Resources

20. Online Book

Darwin, Charles. *On the Origin of Species by Means of Natural Selection, or the Preservation of Favoured Races in the Struggle for Life* [book online]. London: Down, Bromley, Kent, 1859 [cited 12 February 1999]. Available from ftp://sailor.gutenberg.org/pub/gutenberg/etext98/ otoos10.txt; INTERNET.

21. Online Article

Willis, Alfred. "A Survey of Surviving Buildings of the Kroton
    Colony in Hollywood." *Architronic* 8, no. 1 (1999) [journal
    online] [cited 29 September 2000]. Available from
    http://architronic.saed.kent.edu/; INTERNET.

22. CD-ROM

Rose, Mark, ed. "Elements of Theater." *The Norton Shakespeare
    Workshop CD-ROM.* Vers. 1.1. [CD-ROM]. New York: Norton
    Publishing, 1997.

Multiple Sources

23. Multiple Sources

When a note mentions more than one source, list each one separately
in your bibliography.

54 | Using CSE Documentation Style

One widely used form of documentation in the sciences is the CSE
(Council of Science Editors) style, formerly called CBE (Council of Biology
Editors) style. This guide advocates a simplified international scientific style
and presents two options for documentation: a name-and-year and a number
system.

STRATEGY Use CSE style in physical, life, and technical sciences.

54.1

ACADEMIC SETTINGS

When readers expect CSE (CBE) or "scientific documentation"

WORK AND PUBLIC SETTINGS

When a professional group or company division expects you to use
    CSE or some type of scientific documentation

When readers prefer a name-and-year or number system

When other writers or publications addressing audiences like yours
    use CSE, modified CSE, or a similar style

E style tends to vary more than the other styles, mainly because different entific and engineering fields have different requirements. Check expectations with your instructor or your readers. If you are advised to follow the rule of a specific journal, find its guidelines for authors, or compare examples from it with general CSE advice. For more information, see *Scientific Style and Format: The CBE Manual for Authors, Editors, and Publishers* (6th ed., Cambridge, Eng.: Cambridge University Press, 1994) or the CSE Web site at <http://www.councilscienceeditors.org>.

54a Using CSE in-text citations

You can use one of two methods for CSE in-text references.

Use the name-and-year method

With this method, include the name of the author and the publication date in parentheses unless you mention the name in the text.

PARENTHETICAL   Decreases in the use of lead, cadmium, and zinc have resulted in a "very large decrease in the large-scale pollution of the troposphere" (Boutron and others 1991, p 64).

NAMED IN TEXT   Boutron and others (1991) found that decreases in the use of lead, cadmium, and zinc have resulted in a "very large decrease in the large-scale pollution of the troposphere" (p 64).

Distinguish several works by the same author, all dated in a single year, by letters (*a*, *b*, and so forth) after the date.

2 Use the number method

With this method, use numbers instead of names of authors. The numbers can be placed in parentheses in the text or raised above the line; they correspond to numbered works in your reference list.

Decreases in the use of lead, cadmium, and zinc have reduced pollution in the troposphere (1).

Your first option is to number your in-text citations consecutively as they appear and to arrange them accordingly on the references page. Your second is to alphabetize your references first, number them, and then use the corresponding number in your paper. Because only the number appears in your text, you should mention the author's name if it is important.

54b Creating a CSE reference list

You may use "References" to head your list. The samples below follo[w] the number method. If you use the consecutive number method, arran[ge] your references according to which work comes first in your paper, whi[ch] second, and so on. If you use the alphabetized number method, arrange yo[ur] list alphabetically, and then number the entries. If you use the name-and-ye[ar] method instead, alphabetize the references by the last name of the main a[u-] thor, and then order works by the same author by date of publication. Pla[ce] the date after the author's name, followed by a period.

Books and Works Treated as Books

1. One Author

Include the total number of pages at the end of the entry for a boo[k.]

1. Bishop RH. Modern control systems analysis and design using MATLAB and SIMULINK. Menlo Park (CA): Addison Wesley; 1997. 251 p.

2. Two or More Authors

2. Freeman JM, Kelly MT, Freeman JB. The epilepsy diet treatment: an introduction to the ketogenic diet. New York: Demo; 1994. 180 p.

3. Corporate or Group Author

If an organization is also the publisher, include the name in both places. You can replace the name with a well-known acronym.

3. Intergovernmental Panel on Climate Change. Climate change 1995: the science of climate change. Cambridge: Cambridge University Press; 1996. 572 p.

4. Editor

4. Dolphin D, editor. Biomimetic chemistry. Washington: American Chemical Soc; 1980. 437 p.

5. Translator

If the work has an editor as well as a translator, place a semicolon after *translator*, name the editor, and add *editor*.

5. Jacob F. The logic of life: a history of heredity. Spillmann BE, translator. New York: Pantheon Books; 1982. 348 p. Translation of: Logique du vivant.

Conference Proceedings

6. Witt I, editor. Protein C: biochemical and medical
    aspects. Proceedings of the International Workshop; 1984
    Jul 9-11; Titisee, Germany. Berlin: De Gruyter; 1985.
    195 p.

Report

Include the information a reader would need to order a report. Bracket widely accepted acronym following an agency's name.

7. Environmental Protection Agency (US) [EPA]. Guides to
    pollution prevention: the automotive repair industry.
    Washington: US EPA; 1991. 46 p. Available from: EPA Office
    of Research and Development; EPA/625/7-91/013.

Articles and Selections from Periodicals and Books

. Article in Journal Paginated by Volume

8. Yousef YA, Yu LL. Potential contamination of groundwater
    from Cu, Pb, and Zn in wet detention ponds receiving
    highway runoff. J Environ Sci Hlth 1992;27:1033-44.

. Article in Journal Paginated by Issue

Give the issue number in parentheses with no space after the volume number.

9. Boutron CF. Decrease in anthropogenic lead, cadmium and
    zinc in Greenland snows since the late 1960's. Nature
    1991;353(6340):153-5, 160.

10. Article with Corporate or Group Author

10. Derek Sims Associates. Why and how of acoustic testing.
    Environ Eng 1991;4(1):10-12.

11. Entire Issue of Journal

11. Savage A, editor. Proceedings of the workshop on the zoo-
    university connection: collaborative efforts in the
    conservation of endangered primates. Zoo Biol
    1989;1(Suppl).

12. Chapter in Edited Book or Selection in Anthology

The first name and title refer to the selection and the second to the book in which it appears.

12. Moro M. Supply and conservation efforts for nonhuman primates. In: Gengozian N, Deinhardt F, editors. Marmoset in experimental medicine. Basel: S. Karger AG; 1978. p 37-40.

13. Figure from Article

Identify a figure (or graphic) by name, number, and page.

13. Kanaori Y, Kawakami SI, Yairi K. Space-time distribution patterns of destructive earthquakes in the inner belt of central Japan. Engng Geol 1991;31(3-4):209-30 (p 216, table 1).

Internet, Web, and Electronic Resources

CSE recommends following the National Library of Medicine formats fc Internet sources, reflected here and available through the CSE Web site.

14. Patent from Database or Information Service

14. Collins FS, Drumm ML, Dawson DC, Wilkinson DJ, inventors. Method of testing potential cystic fibrosis treating compounds using cells in culture. US patent 5,434,086. 1995 Jul 18. Available from: Lexis/Nexis/Lexpat library/ALL file.

15. Online Article

15. Grolmusz V. On the weak mod m representation of Boolean functions. Chi J Theor Comp Sci [Internet] 1995 [cited 1996 May 3];100-5. Available from: http://www.csuchicago .edu/publication/cjtcs/articles/1995/2/contents.html

16. Online Abstract

16. Smithies O, Maeda N. Gene targeting approaches to complex genetic diseases: atherosclerosis and essential hypertension [abstract]. Proc Natl Acad Sci USA [Internet]. 1995 [cited 1996 Jan 21];92(12):5266-72. 1 screen. Available from: Lexis/Medline/ABST.

17. CD-ROM Abstract

17. MacDonald R, Fleming MF, Barry KL. Risk factors associated with alcohol abuse in college students [abstract]. Am J Drug and Alc Abuse [CD-ROM];17:439-49. Available from: SilverPlatter File: PsycLIT Item: 79-13172.

TAKING IT ONLINE

TEACHING TIPS: A STUDENT GUIDE TO ESSAY EXAMS
http://www.cte.iastate.edu/tips/essay.html
This site, sponsored by Iowa State University, provides practical advice
on preparing for and taking essay exams.

THE BASIC PRINCIPLES OF PERSUASIVE WRITING
http://www.cstudies.ubc.ca/wc/workshop/tools/argument.htm
Review logical, emotional, and ethical appeals along with the characteristics
of sound evidence for persuasive writing.

STEPHEN'S GUIDE TO THE LOGICAL FALLACIES
http://datanation.com/fallacies
This comprehensive site explores various logical fallacies.

11 WAYS TO IMPROVE YOUR WRITING AND YOUR BUSINESS
http://www.editorialservice.com/roberts/11ways.html
These tips, written for participants in a business writing seminar,
can help you write memos, business letters, reports, and news releases.

OCCUPATIONAL OUTLOOK QUARTERLY
http://stats.bls.gov/opub/ooq/ooqindex.htm
Check the index or search for articles (with examples) on job
alternatives, applications, résumés, and interviews.

DEVELOPING A LETTER OF APPLICATION
**http://www.raycomm.com/techwhirl/magazine/gettingstarted/
lettersofapplication.html**
At this site for technical writers, click on "Employment" for articles
on job hunting, letters of application, résumés, and interviews.

CIVNET: A WEBSITE OF CIVITAS INTERNATIONAL
http://www.civnet.org
Follow the links here to many sites on civic involvement and
volunteer organizations.

Writing
in Action

55 | Addressing the Academic Community

Academic settings are places for both learning and teaching—for taking in knowledge and for communicating it.

55a Recognizing the goals of academic writing

Academic writers are often apprentices—students writing to learn in history, plant biology, or nursing. At the other end of a continuum are professionals (and some students) presenting new, specialized knowledge.

Apprentice with teachers and mentors	**ROLE**	Professional with colleagues
Practice and learn	**GOAL**	Contribute to knowledge
General, introductory	**LEVEL**	Highly specialized

General education courses (often called surveys or introductions) usually require writing that helps you learn the subject matter, practice the field's ways of thinking, and show a teacher what you've learned. As you specialize within a major, you move toward professional conversations in your field.

> **STRATEGY** Analyze your academic writing situation.
> - Where would you place yourself on the continuum?
> - Why are you writing? to learn something new? to show what you've learned? to inform others about new knowledge?
> - What expertise or knowledge is expected at your level?

55b Analyzing academic audiences

Like the goals of academic writing, academic readers vary from experts with considerable knowledge in a field to general readers with little or none.

General ⟶ Greater knowledge and expertise ⟶ Expert

Nevertheless, academic writing often addresses multiple audiences.

- Your instructor is an expert, and you've done specialized research, but your assignment is to explain key concepts to novices.

341

- You know your topic well, but you need to address general reade (your classmates) and to offer new ideas to experts (your teacher).
- Your course journal is intended to help you learn, yet it is read by you instructor, who may be influenced by your reactions and insights.

STRATEGY **Consider what your academic readers expect.**

- What does your main reader want—the person whose assessment coun the most? What do your secondary readers expect?
- How will your main reader evaluate your writing: in terms of his or he own expertise or in terms of a specified secondary audience?

55c Understanding academic writing tasks

Academic writing tasks come as handouts, directions on a board, on line postings, textbook assignments, or explanations during class.

STRATEGY **Read and "unpack" the assignment.**

- Examine its main verbs (such as *analyze* or *show*) and main nouns (the *causes* of the *stock market crash*). (See 4a.)
- Figure out its goals: the primary goal, secondary goals, and any as sumed or "hidden" goals that appear as additions or explanations.

Instead of fearing evaluation or resigning yourself to guesswork and hope, use the course standards to guide your writing process.

STRATEGY **Identify and use evaluation criteria.**

- How will your writing be judged? What are the explicit criteria, writ ten or oral, such as a description of strong and weak papers?
- Are there any implicit criteria (such as precision rather than elegance)?
- List the criteria you have identified. Turn the evaluative statements ("Your paper should begin with a clear point or thesis") into questions ("Does my paper begin with a clear point or thesis?").
- Use your questions as a drafting guide and a revision checklist.

55d Recognizing types of academic writing

Most forms of academic writing fall into one of five categories though assignments may have mixed goals or expect several forms of writing. When academic writing *reflects*, it draws on personal experience and insight in re sponse to events, readings, and ideas. In contrast, writing that *draws on sources* goes outside personal experience to integrate information and ideas from arti cles, reports, books, or Web sites. Academic writing may also *interpret* mean-

g or significance—of a historical event, a text, a painting, a cultural pattern,
a social phenomenon—or grow from *observing and experimenting*, examin-
g human behavior or the natural world. The final activity, *testing*, often
monstrates a student's mastery of a subject though experts, too, are rou-
nely evaluated by colleagues as they present conference papers, publish arti-
es, or submit grant proposals.

TYPES OF WRITING IN THE ACADEMIC COMMUNITY

TYPE	CHARACTERISTIC ACTIVITIES	COMMON FORMS
REFLECTING	Responding, reacting, speculating, exploring, inquiring	Reading journals, logs (data observations and insights), personal essays, reaction papers, autobiographies, reflexive writing (self-observing and self-critical)
DRAWING ON SOURCES	Summarizing, paraphrasing, synthesizing, analyzing, comparing, compiling, evaluating	Summaries and abstracts, reviews and syntheses (research, ideas, or information), book reviews and reports, annotated bibliographies, informative research papers, poster presentations, analyses of issues or controversies
INTERPRETING	Analyzing, defining key ideas and meanings, identifying causes and effects, describing patterns, applying a theory, drawing a conclusion, taking a stand on an issue	Interpretations of a text or work of art (documented or not), analyses of phenomena (historical, social, or cultural), "thesis" papers taking a stand on scholarly issues, documented arguments drawing on research
OBSERVING/ EXPERIMENTING	Making observations; designing surveys and experiments; collecting, synthesizing, and anayzing data; recognizing patterns	Scientific reports and articles, logs of observations and experiments, lab reports, field research reports, project evaluations
TESTING	Explaining, supporting, defining, presenting information and ideas, offering conclusions	Essay tests, take-home exams, tests requiring sentence- or paragraph-length answers, written responses to readings

55e Writing a short documented paper

In many courses, you may write a short paper that draws on a few
sources and argues, interprets, or simply presents information.

ELEMENTS OF A SHORT DOCUMENTED PAPER

- It summarizes or synthesizes others' views, results, or positions.
- It presents information fairly in your own words.

- It may provide reasoned conclusions or interpretations based on cit[ed]
  sources but allow readers to apply these to their actions or beliefs.
- It is well organized and easy to read.

Following are excerpts from a short documented paper. Though the pap[er]
cites facts and statistics from four articles, it also has its own thesis.

Desperate Times for Teachers

by David Aharonian

55e
acad

1   There is a major controversy regarding teacher

salaries presently in this country. Many people feel that

Synthesizes
opposing
positions

teachers are overpaid because they have summers off from

work. They feel that teachers do not truly work year-

round and therefore are either getting a fair rate of pay

or getting too much. Many teachers, however, disagree

with this assessment. They feel that they are underpaid

Thesis

for the work that they do. Most teachers find it very

difficult just to make ends meet on a teacher's salary,

and often they resort to moonlighting.

Defines
key term

2–6   Moonlighting means that a person holds another job

in addition to his or her career. . . .

[Four additional paragraphs supply information and data from
two sources on moonlighting teachers.]

Presents
alternatives,
leaving
reader to
decide

7   But there really are no easy solutions to the

problem. One obvious answer would be to increase teacher

salaries (Alley 21). This would lead to less moonlighting

and allow teachers to concentrate more on their primary

occupation. But there are still plenty of people who

Supplies
detail

oppose raising teacher salaries. Many times teachers may

go two or three years without any raise in their pay.

Then when the teachers do get a raise, it may only be 2

or 4 percent. This certainly lowers the morale of the

teachers and can cause teachers to become frustrated
(Henderson 12). As one teacher in Oklahoma put it, "It's   **Concludes
with pertinent
quotation**
hard to look across the hall and see a teacher who's
taught 14 years, making only $4,000 more than you are"
(Wisniewski and Kleine 1).

[The paper ends with a list of works cited.]

55f Writing a lab report

In fields like biology, chemistry, or engineering, you are likely to write
lab reports on experiments. Lab reports need to be clear and concise, describing exactly what you did and what happened as a result.

Lab reports vary in style and format, depending on the field. Check
with each instructor about requirements, such as section numbers and headings. A typical structure begins with an overview or abstract of the focus or
goal (why it was done), introduces the problem or principles (what it shows),
describes the methods (how it was done), explains the results (what happened), discusses the outcomes (what the results mean), and states a conclusion (what it shows).

ELEMENTS OF A LAB REPORT
- It strictly follows the format required by the instructor or field.
- It does not digress into unnecessary commentary on the experiment.
- It uses specific terminology and unambiguous language.
- It presents data and results accurately, without distortion.

Typical sections of a lab report include the Abstract, Introduction, Experiment
(Materials and Procedure), Results, Discussion, and Conclusion. Here is a selection from the closing section of a chemistry lab report.

Butane: Determining Molecular Weight from Vapor

by Melanie Dedecker

[The report follows the brief assigned format, beginning with
Materials, Procedure, and Calculations.]

<u>Conclusion</u>. The purpose of this experiment was to   **Includes
required
section
headings**
determine the molecular weight of butane gas through the
use of the ideal gas law and to learn how to write an
accurate procedure. In order to determine the molecular

Uses specific terms

weight of butane gas, a lighter was weighed and then lighted underneath a graduated cylinder full of water. The gas that was emitted from the lighter displaced the water in the graduated cylinder. From this data and the mass of used butane gas, the density of the gas was

Supplies detailed results

determined. This value was used in an altered form of the ideal gas law to ascertain the molecular weight of butane gas. Although the actual molar mass of butane gas is 58 g/mol, this experiment determined the molar mass of butane to be 61.4 g/mol, resulting in a 5.86% error.

55g acad

[The report ends with possible reasons for this result.]

55.2

55g Writing an essay exam

When you work on an essay exam, even a take-home exam, you have only a short time to write. Read the question carefully, and jot down a working thesis and specific evidence. State your points clearly, especially beginning each paragraph. Watch your time.

ELEMENTS OF AN ESSAY EXAM ANSWER
- It addresses all parts of the exam question directly.
- It follows directions about the approach (such as comparison or explanation) and covers the number of points or examples expected.
- It uses references—quotations, facts, and other information—efficiently, illustrating the point without overloading the essay.
- It connects references and synthesizes material to show significance.
- It interprets, supporting a point, not merely listing details.

Here are selections from an open-book essay exam that asked students to identify a common theme running through a survey of American literature and to discuss this theme in two stories.

Moral Perfection in "Young Goodman Brown"

and "The Birthmark"

by Ted Wolfe

States theme selected

1   Hawthorne's "Young Goodman Brown" explores the conflict between good and evil. Young Goodman Brown has his religious faith tested during a journey into the

woods. In what may or may not be a dream, he is shown by the devil that everyone he believed to be good is evil. . . . When the devil is about to baptize him, Brown calls out for Faith, his wife, telling her to resist the temptation. He is really calling out for faith, as in faith in God. When he does this, the hellish vision passes, and he is alone in the woods. From this, I think we can conclude that Hawthorne believes that people should try to resist temptation and live moral lives.

Refers to events in story

Interprets events and character's name

Draws conclusion about story

55h acad

2   But Goodman Brown is never the same after the experience, be it dream or reality. He becomes "a stern, a sad, a darkly meditative, if not a desperate man." In his heart he doubts the goodness of Faith/faith, Deacon Gookin, Goody Cloyse, and everyone else. . . . Symbolically, the experience in the woods causes him to give up his faith. The overriding message that Hawthorne is trying to convey is that one should try to keep one's faith, to believe in others' inherent goodness, and to live morally. If one doesn't, life becomes as barren and miserable as it became for Goodman Brown.

Uses short supporting quotation

Develops conclusion further

3   Hawthorne's "The Birthmark" also addresses . . .

Follows directions to discuss two stories

[Continues with second short story.]

4   . . . Hawthorne's point is that one should not get so caught up in trying to be morally perfect that it ruins one's life. People must learn to "find the perfect future in the present."

Concludes essay

55h Speaking in the academic community

Planning a presentation with a partner or team takes time but provides valuable experience for work and public communities. (See 58g, 59f.)

> **STRATEGY** **Work together as a speaking team.**
>
> - Split up research responsibilities; collaborate as you create and e change talking points; rehearse as a group (see 11c).
> - Unify around your purpose, theme, and organization.
> - Coordinate all contributions, and divide the time evenly; plan how monitor and cue each other on time limits.
> - Have the first presenter introduce the team; then have each speak create a transition to the next. Create a single presentation that revea differences in the subject, not oppositions in the team.

56a
arg

56 | Making Persuasive Arguments

Argument can persuade a foundation to support an academic researc grant, encourage a production team to alter a process at work, or convince county airport to curtail expansion in the public community. Because valu judgments, policy questions, and proposed actions seldom lend themselves t proof or absolute certainty, readers are aware of other opinions and evidence They'll expect you to argue with good reasons, logic, evidence, and attention to other opinions before they decide to agree with you. You'll need to encour age them to share your perspective or values, convincing them that your line of reasoning—your argument—is fair and justifiable. (See Chapter 10.)

56a Recognizing an issue in a community of readers and writers

Argumentative writing begins with an *issue*—a subject or situation about which opinions clearly differ. Such disagreements are common in public settings, where people with different values, cultures, and perspectives meet to address problems. Serious differences about policies, interpretations, and solutions are frequent in academic and work settings, too. Your argument develops around *your* opinion, that is, the value judgment, action, or interpretation you propose and wish your readers to endorse. Your aim initially is to answer two questions: What issue am I arguing about? What, precisely, is my opinion?

1 Identify an issue

To find (or more sharply focus) an issue that interests you, look for significant problems, judgments, and disagreements.

STRATEGY   Get involved in the flow of opinions.

- List current local or general problems, controversies, or trends that concern you or your academic, work, or public community.
- Turn to news and opinion magazines (such as *The Nation*, *National Review*, or the online *Salon*); editorials in local and national newspapers (in libraries or online); periodical databases that index a wide range of articles; and professional, business, or academic publications.
- Interview people (see 50b) about issues that inspire strong opinions.
- "Talk" to yourself by writing a one- or two-sentence summary of at least two different opinions on a possible issue. Look for a focused issue, even a limited or local one such as parking or garbage problems.

56b
arg

2 Evaluate the issue

A problem is not automatically an issue, nor is every opinion worth arguing about. Drunk driving, for example, is certainly a problem but is not in itself an issue. Anyone advocating drunk driving would seem foolish, but reasonable people do disagree about how to discourage it.

STRATEGY   Test the issue.

- Is the issue clearly debatable? Are there two or more reasonable contrasting opinions? Is there evidence to back opinion?
- Is the issue more than individual preference or personal taste? Reasoning generally can't change likes and dislikes.
- Does the issue avoid deeply held assumptions that cannot be argued? Social and political issues are arguable unless they rest on systems of belief such as religion.

56b Recognizing and developing your stance

A good argument is positive: you try to persuade people to accept your opinion, but you don't attack them for having another point of view. To do this, you need a clear idea of your own opinion and the reasons why you hold it, and you need to anticipate readers' arguments. (See 10c.)

STRATEGY   Develop your stance.

- Write informally about an issue. Do you feel scornful, fearful, or outraged? Why?
- List key elements of your issue, summarizing your responses.
- Add facts, examples, and ideas that support your reactions.
- Think about other perspectives. Read, talk, and listen. Make a preliminary research plan, or test your views on friends or online.

1 Focus on your purpose

Limit your scope by deciding the kind of opinion to support.

Value judgment. Do you want to argue that some activity, policy, belie[f] performance, book, or situation is good or bad?

Policy. Do you want readers to accept or follow a course of action?

Interpretation. Do you want readers to agree that one point of view about [a] subject is better or weaker than alternatives?

2 Create your thesis

To organize your writing and help readers focus on your outlook an[d] your evidence, state a **proposition** or **claim**—a **thesis** (see 4b) specifyin[g] the issue and your opinion. Look for blurred or illogical propositions, espe cially in a complex thesis.

BLURRED AND ILLOGICAL	Police should stop conducting unconstitutional roadblock[s] to identify drunk drivers and substitute more frequent visua[l] checks of erratic driving.
	READER'S REACTION: This proposition seems to assume that road blocks are unconstitutional. Is the writer supporting this value judgment or proposing a policy?

Make sure your thesis either focuses on one proposition or identifies related propositions you will argue in an appropriate order.

SINGLE PROPOSITIONS	Roadblocks to identify drunk drivers are unconstitutional.
	Police should make more frequent visual checks of erratic driving.
RELATED PROPOSITIONS	The current practice of using roadblocks to identify drunk drivers is unconstitutional; therefore, police should use an-other procedure such as visual checks for erratic driving.

56c Developing reasons and evidence to persuade your community

As you consider your issue or research it, develop reasons and varied, sound evidence that readers will find persuasive (see 10b). Your field study of recycling attitudes might well enlighten academic readers, but readers at work might want evidence of recycling's cost-effectiveness. In a public forum, detailing conditions at the local landfill might help urge a policy change.

Details. Look for statistics, technical information, surveys, interviews, and background or historical information in text or visuals. Be prepared to justify e validity and authority of your sources, especially if they come from the ternet. (See 48c–d.)

mparisons. You can compare a particular issue, problem, policy, or situa- n about which you are uncertain to one about which you are more certain, t avoid far-fetched or unreasonable comparisons.

uotations and ideas from authorities. The words of experts can lend pport, but readers will expect them to be fair and authoritative.

xamples. Drawn from your own or others' experience, events, people, ideas, bjects, feelings, stories, images, and texts all can be used as brief or extended xamples to support a thesis. Supply both *explanation* to make your point and *oncrete detail* to give it power.

56d Recognizing community views

Traditional argument resembles debate: you imagine an adversary and ry to undermine that person's points or **counterarguments**. Most contem- orary approaches to argument, however, expect you to acknowledge other eople's perspectives yet still try to convince them of your views. Especially within a workplace or in public where your opponents on one issue may be our allies on another, treat others respectfully. (See 10c–d.)

STRATEGY Anticipate counterarguments.

Divide a sheet of paper into three columns. On the left, list the main oints supporting your opinion. Write opposing points in the middle. On he right, counter the opposing points.

56e Developing and analyzing a logical argument

Strategies of argument are ways to organize and check the logic of your opinions and supporting evidence (see 10b–c).

1 Use data-warrant-claim (Toulmin) reasoning

In *The Uses of Argument* (1964), Stephen Toulmin proposes **data-warrant-claim reasoning**, which draws on several kinds of statements rea- sonable people usually make when they argue: statements of data, claim, and warrant. A statement of **data** corresponds to your evidence and **claim** to your conclusion or proposition. **Warrant**, however, refers to the mental process by which a reader connects the data to the claim, answering "How?"

In constructing a line of reasoning, you present the data or indisputable facts that lead to your claim, but you also present the warrants, the probable facts and assertions that will encourage readers to accept your claim. This approach does not assume that an argument can provide absolute proof of a proposition. It aims instead at showing readers that an opinion or proposed action is plausible, grounded on good evidence and reasons, and worth the endorsement.

Suppose you are examining the relative safety of cars. As data, you have a study on the odds of injury in different models of cars. To argue effectively, you need to show readers *how* the data and your claim are connected, what patterns (probable facts—warrants) link the data to your claim.

DATA	WARRANT	CLAIM
Ratings of each car model by likelihood of injury (scale: 1 to 10)	• The cars in the ratings fall into three easily recognized groups: small, medium, large. (probable fact) • The large cars as a group have a lower average likelihood of injury to passengers than either of the other groups. (probable fact) • Though some other cars have low likelihood of injury, almost all the large cars seem safe. (assertion + probable fact) • Few consumers will go over the crash ratings to see which models get good or poor scores. (assertion)	For the average consumer, buying a large car is a good way to reduce the likelihood of being injured in an accident.

2 Use Rogerian argument

Effective argument requires a relationship between you and your reader, an issue that **Rogerian argument** considers, based on the theories of psychologist Carl Rogers. Rogers argues that people are more easily persuaded when an opponent seems an ally, not an enemy. To practice Rogerian strategies, imagine the views of someone opposed to your opinion. What is that person's frame of reference? What assumptions are behind those views?

Once you understand the other person's ideas, you may wish to work a **concession** into your argument, acknowledging an opposing view. A concession doesn't have to be so strong that it undermines your argument. But placed strategically, it can show your effort to be fair and help persuade a reader to listen. Highlight brief concessions with *although* or *of course*.

3 Use deductive and inductive reasoning

A **deductive argument** states and then supports an explicit premise (assertion or claim) using syllogistic reasoning as its basic logical format. A **syllogism** includes a major premise, a minor premise, and a conclusion.

MAJOR PREMISE	All landowners in Clarksville must pay taxes.
MINOR PREMISE	Gary Hayes owns land in Clarksville.
CONCLUSION	Therefore, Gary Hayes must pay taxes.

MISLEADING AND ILLOGICAL REASONING: LOGICAL FALLACIES

56e
arg

Faulty Cause-Effect Relationship (*post hoc, ergo propter hoc* reasoning—"after this, therefore because of this"): attempts to persuade you that because one event follows another, the first causes the second.

> The increase in violence on television is making the crime rate soar.
> READER'S REACTION: **This *may* be true, but no evidence here links the two situations.**

False Analogy: compares two things that seem, but aren't, comparable.

> Raising the speed limit is like offering free cocktails at a meeting of recovering alcoholics.
> READER'S REACTION: **I don't see the connection. Most drivers aren't recovering from an addiction to high-speed driving.**

Red Herring: distracts readers from the real argument.

> Gun control laws need to be passed as soon as possible to decrease domestic violence and accidents. The people who think guns should not be controlled are probably criminals themselves.
> READER'S REACTION: **The second sentence doesn't follow logically or add support. It's just a distracting attack on people who disagree.**

Ad Hominem: attacks the person, not the issue.

> Of course Walt Smith would support a bill to aid farmers—he owns several farms in the Midwest.
> READER'S REACTION: **I'd like to hear reactions to his ideas, please.**

Begging the Question: presents assumptions as facts.

> Most people try to be physically fit; obviously, they fear getting old.
> READER'S REACTION: **I don't see any evidence that people fear aging—or that they are working on their physical fitness, either.**

Circular Reasoning: supports an assertion with the assertion itself.

> The university should increase funding of intramural sports because it has a responsibility to back its sports programs financially.
> READER'S REACTION: **So the university should fund sports because it should fund sports?**

A flawed syllogism can often pinpoint faulty reasoning.

MAJOR PREMISE   All Ferraris are fast.

MINOR PREMISE   That car is fast.

CONCLUSION   Therefore, that car is a Ferrari.

In a complex argument your reasoning will be more elaborate, but the syllogistic pattern can frame and test your reasoning.

An **inductive argument** does not explicitly state the premise; rather it leads readers through accumulated evidence to a conclusion. It usually begins with a **hypothesis**, more tentative than an assertion, and the ideas the writer wants to consider. The writer has, but withholds, a conclusion until readers are convinced by the supporting points.

56f
arg

4 Look for logical fallacies

The box on page 353 will help you identify illogical reasoning.

56f Writing a position paper

A short **position paper** defines an issue, considers its audience, and uses evidence and reasoning to advance the writer's thesis.

Animal Rights: The Big Picture

by Zachary Carter

Introduces issue

1   The issue of animal rights is a multifaceted one, and, upon examination, it tends to make one follow a circle of logic that leads from one conclusion to the next, without the benefit of a final outcome or decision. But there is a way out of this circle, and that is to shift the focus of the issue away from small controversies such as animal experiments or the survival of a single species of tiny fish to the true

Presents position

injustice, the large-scale destruction of animals' habitat by the overpopulation of humans. Clearly an intense effort must be made to preserve the rights of

animals for the benefit of every species involved,
including the human race.

2–3 In order to examine this issue thoroughly, we must
find definitions of both "animal" and "rights" and stick
to them. . . .

[Paragraphs define these terms and "balance" in nature.]

If the situation is viewed in this light, then it becomes
not only humanity's right and every other species' right,
but our duty as well . . . to live peacefully within the
balance of nature.

4–6 Humans, driven by natural instinct, are slowly
pushing the balance askew and, in the process, trampling
on the rights of other species to exist inside the
balance. Because of the population boom, humans have
spread across every continent, developing, settling,
industrializing, mining, setting up agriculture, and so
forth. . . . The human race has destroyed vast areas of
native habitat and cut down billions of trees which--at
that volume--are virtually irreplaceable. Predatory
species such as the wolf, coyote, and mountain lion,
which are an important part of the ecosystem (because
they dwell at the apex of the food chain), have been
virtually wiped out in many areas.

[These paragraphs continue with specifics.]

7   We face a future in which there is no longer
physical space on the earth for the human race, much less
the billions of other species that inhabit the planet.
Richard Wagner, author of <u>Environment and Man</u>, states
that "adding four billion more [people] staggers the
imagination, for the earth is barely able to support its

**Defines
terms**

**Restates
position**

**56f
arg**

**Focuses
on key
term
*balance***

**Develops
explanation
of problem**

**Provides
supporting
examples
and detail**

**Projects
consequences
of problem**

**Cites
authority**

Refines position
present population" (553). Clearly the population explosion must be stopped, for the benefit of human beings and the whole of the natural world.

Advocates course of action
8   First, a move must be made to prevent future development of similar problems, and the only way to do this is to curb the population explosion.

[Paragraph outlines specific alternatives, moving from abortion to birth control to sterilization.]

56f arg

Makes concession
9   As for the present, efforts should be made to develop new and streamline old technology in order to make more efficient use of resources. Waste disposal,

Acknowledges counter-arguments
energy production, and manufacturing can be improved significantly. . . .

[Paragraph continues by citing authority.]

Returns to own position
10-11 The first and most important imperative is that all individuals make a conscious effort to improve this relationship to the balance of nature for the sake of animal rights, themselves, and their children. Without this effort to preserve the balance, all members of the human race are on a collision course with destruction, taking millions of innocent species along with them.
. . . An effort to curb these injustices is in order

Concludes with compelling quotation
immediately, for the sake of the balance. For "the earth, like the sun, like the air, belongs to everyone--and to no one" (Abbey 88).

[New page]   Works Cited

Abbey, Edward. The Journey Home. New York: Plume, 1991.

Gore, Albert. Earth in the Balance: Ecology and the Human
       Spirit. New York: Houghton, 1992.

Wagner, Richard H. Environment and Man. New York: Norton,
       1978.

57 | Reading and Writing About Literature

Imagine a world without imagination. Literature—works of fiction, poetry, and drama—gives us a doorway into imaginary worlds, where we can suffer with characters or share their triumphs, feel their misery or their elation. Reading literature critically, however, goes beyond unconsidered experience to new understandings. These insights are the basis for most writing about literature, whether that takes the form of a review for your neighborhood book club or an interpretive paper in an English course.

57a Reading literary texts

When you read a novel, short story, or poem or view a drama or film, pay attention to meaning and to artistic technique.

Read through "lenses" and community responses

Your perspective as a reader may determine your strategies for reading and interpreting. From a psychological view, you might note how a character tries to overcome feelings of childhood abandonment. Or, through a feminist lens, you might examine the portrayal of women in a novel. How particular groups or communities see the world may be reflected in the lenses of academic fields such as psychology or feminist theory or those of other groups bound by occupation, race, culture, or social status.

STRATEGY Shift your reading lens.

After reading a literary work, recall the key events, characters, and settings through a series of lenses appropriate to the work. What happens when you use the lens of economics or, more specifically, capitalism or socialism? What happens if you shift to the lens of technology? or religion? or biology? Test as many lenses as you can to see what insights you gain.

---

2 Read for theme

For many critics and students of literature, to read for meaning is to read for theme. You can view **theme** as an idea, perspective, insight, or cluster of feelings that a work conveys or that permeates a work, organizing the relationships among its parts. Or you can view theme as the insights readers are likely to derive from their experience reading.

357

STRATEGY **Read actively for insights about literature.**

As you read, write down your ideas, responses, or clusters of feelin[g]
Note the techniques writers use to convey meaning (see 57a-3). Look esp[e]
cially for repeated words and ideas, contrasting characters or events, and pa[t]
terns of images, which can signal possible themes.

In reading a short poem, Sevon Randall notes repetitions and contra[s]
that reveal a cluster of feelings and ideas (a theme).

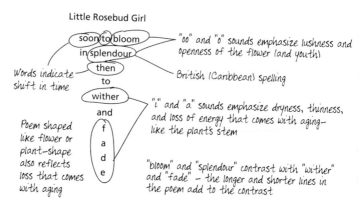

Little Rosebud Girl

soon to bloom
in splendour
then
to
wither
and
f
a
d
e

"oo" and "o" sounds emphasize lushness and openness of the flower (and youth)

British (Caribbean) spelling

Words indicate shift in time

"i" and "a" sounds emphasize dryness, thinness, and loss of energy that comes with aging—like the plant's stem

Poem shaped like flower or plant—shape also reflects loss that comes with aging

"bloom" and "splendour" contrast with "wither" and "fade" – the longer and shorter lines in the poem add to the contrast

—ANSON GONZALEZ, "Little Rosebud Girl" (196[8]

3 Read for technique

When you read for meaning, you inevitably read for technique. A write[r]
can't create events, portray characters, represent scenes, or elicit a reader's re[-]
actions without using techniques of characterization, plot, setting, or imagina[-]
tive language.

STRATEGY **Read actively for key elements of technique.**

57.1

Character. Who are the major and minor characters? What are their
traits? Are the characters complex or one-dimensional? How do they
change—or fail to change—in response to events? How self-aware
are they? Which ones are presented positively, which negatively?

Plot. Are events presented chronologically, or have they been rearranged?
What is the role of conflict in the plot? Do events spring from the characters' personalities or serve mainly to reveal character traits? Is there
a main conflict, a chain of conflicts, or a climax?

Setting. Where and when do events occur? Does the setting help explain
characters' actions or convey a mood that shapes readers' reactions?

Point of view. Who tells the story? Is the narrator a character or a persona, a voice adopted by the writer or poet? Is the story narrated in

the first person (*I*) or in the third person by a narrator who is not identified as *I* but speaks of the characters as *he* or *she*? Is the narrator *omniscient* (all-knowing)? limited in knowledge? reliable?

Language. How does the work use imaginative language—simile, metaphor, understatement, paradox, or irony? Does it use vivid description, unusual wording, rhythms, rhymes, or other sound patterns?

Genre. What's its form: novel, short story, poem, drama, or film? Is it a specific *type* of one of these, such as a novella or allegory? Do its characteristics define a specific genre (such as cinema verité for film)?

57b
lit

57b Writing about literary texts

www
57.2

When you write about a literary text, you interpret and analyze an author's words and techniques. You reach reasonable conclusions—judgments and observations—supported by evidence from the text or secondary sources. Recall the academic conventions for verb tense (see 17b): use present tense to summarize a text ("Falstaff acts . . .") or to discuss what an author does ("Toni Morrison gives her characters . . ."); use past tense for historical context ("During the Vietnam War, Levertov's poetry *took on* a political tone").

Write about meaning

You may explain and support your conclusions about a work's theme or focus on insights you develop by applying a particular perspective to a work (historical, feminist, and so forth).

Develop a thesis. Make sure readers can easily identify your statement of the theme. Try stating your conclusion about it early in a thesis. (See 4b.)

Select evidence. For supporting evidence, you can turn to passages in the text, not just quoting but analyzing them to show readers why they support your interpretation. You can also show how elements such as events, characters, and symbols support your interpretation. If you use outside sources, you can cite the work of critics and scholars.

Organize. Consider two common ways to present an interpretation effectively. You can separate your thesis into parts or subtopics and take up each of these in its own section. Or you can divide your paper to correspond to different segments of the work (beginning, middle, end) or different elements (characters, language, symbols). Then, in each section of your paper, show how the particular segment or element supports your thesis.

2 **Write about technique**

Try to highlight the author's use of language, setting, or characteriztion, drawing conclusions about how the techniques shape the work's meaing and the likely responses of readers.

Develop a thesis. Your thesis should reflect your dual purpose of descriing and analyzing one or more techniques and then relating technique t meaning. In writing about "Young Goodman Brown," for example, you migh say, "Hawthorne uses ambiguity in setting, symbolism, and characterizatic to suggest how excessive concern with the self can alter one's perception everyday events."

Select evidence. Your main evidence about technique is detail from th text itself, presented through quotation, paraphrase, or summary and the connected to the work's meaning. (See 48a.)

Organize. If you examine one technique, try dividing your essay into par corresponding to sections of the work, showing how and why the techniqu is used in each section. If you treat more than one technique, try devoting part of the paper to each different technique.

58 | Addressing the Work Community

Whether you work for a major corporation, run your own small business, join a government agency, or serve in a nonprofit organization, much o your work life will be spent communicating with others. As technology increases the pace and quantity of written exchanges, your ability to write i likely to become even more critical to your success.

58a Recognizing the goals of writing at work

Although workplaces vary greatly, their goals tend to be similar—to meet the needs and expectations of readers by providing and promoting the organization's products or services.

STRATEGY Analyze your writing situation at work.

- What is your purpose? What type of document are you writing?
- What do readers expect you to do: provide information? identify a problem? analyze alternatives? propose a solution?

- What level of information do you have? what level of responsibility?
- How does your company handle writing processes, file exchanges, document templates, or technical specifications?

8b Analyzing audiences at work

Your writing may address very different readers, from your colleague at the next desk to the government official who processes your forms. Because your busy readers value clear, accessible documents, try to meet different needs simultaneously—providing a summary for your overloaded supervisor along with detailed charts in the appendix for the sales team.

58d work

STRATEGY Assess what your readers expect and need.

- How large is your audience? Who does it include? a co-worker? a supervisor? a committee? a customer or client? an outside agency?
- Do readers expect a draft or a finished product? Will they implement your recommendations? Will they rely on your technical data?
- How much time do your readers have? Do they need detailed analysis or focused summary? Will they read carefully or skim the headings?
- What do your readers need to do with your writing? Will they revise it? approve it? implement it? incorporate it in their own writing?

58c Understanding writing tasks at work

You'll want your clarity, tone, and language to represent yourself and your organization well. Many writing tasks will be similarly structured because you'll suppy standard comparable information about comparable situations. For example, using the standard form for a status report or evaluation simplifies your task and aligns your writing with readers' expectations.

When your project is complex or no form is specified, ask others how similar materials have been prepared. Keep samples of well-regarded documents that might be useful models. Notice what characteristics and structures your readers favor in other written materials.

58d Recognizing types of workplace writing

58.1

Reports, memos, and letters are widely adapted to different purposes in the work community. For example, an engineer writes technical reports, while a teacher writes progress reports (or, indeed, report cards). Proposals are adapted to internal and external purposes; memos, however, tend to be used internally and letters externally. Ask advice, and observe existing communication patterns to determine preferred forms. (See also 12b, 13c–g.)

TYPES OF WRITING IN THE WORK COMMUNITY

TYPE	CHARACTERISTIC ACTIVITIES	COMMON FORMS
PROVIDING INFORMATION	Gathering information; exploring issues; comparing competing products or services; tracing background information; summarizing, synthesizing, compiling, and presenting information	Report, study, agenda, minutes, instructions, employee manual, procedural manual, policy guidelines, memo, email message, summary, technical description, organizational chart, brochure, letter (of transmittal, response, adjustment, acknowledgment, good news, bad news, or application), position description, résumé, visuals
REQUESTING INFORMATION OR ACTION	Identifying an issue or a problem, identifying objectives or operational goals, identifying gaps in data or other information, identifying and evaluating potential sources and resources	Memo, email message, directive, letter (of request, inquiry, commitment, or complaint), sales letter, marketing material, advertisements, order form, other forms, letter of application, contract
IDENTIFYING ALTERNATIVES OR RECOMMENDING SOLUTIONS	Analyzing, evaluating, or selecting alternatives; comparing and contrasting; organizing supporting evidence; clarifying implications; advocating	Proposal, report, study, analysis, letter, email message, memo, summary, abstract, projection, evaluation, recommendation

58e   Writing a business letter

The business letter serves many ends but generally follows the practices and format expected by readers. The sample letter included here focuses on the job applicant's accomplishments and abilities. (See p. 364.)

- **Stationery.** The best is 25 or 50 percent white cotton bond, usually twenty-pound weight. Avoid colors and fancy paper.
- **Print quality.** Use a laser printer or a letter-quality impact printer. Your credibility will be damaged by fuzzy print or nonstandard fonts.
- **Format.** In **modified block format**, often used for longer letters, the return address and the closing and signature are centered on the page, but the paragraphs are not indented from the left margin (see p. 364). In **block format**, often used for short letters, all paragraphs (including the greeting and signature) are flush at the left margin.
- **Salutations.** Use the recipient's first name only if you are already on a first-name basis. Use the full name if you don't know the person's gender. Avoid male-specific salutations such as *Dear Sir*. If you don't know which person to address, use salutations such as *Dear Credit Manager*.

- **Notations following the signature.** Place any notations flush left, including initials for writer and typist: *RL: gw, Enc.* or *Enclosure*, *cc: Nancy Harris* (naming a person who is sent a copy).
- **Longer letters.** Use letterhead stationery only for the first page. For subsequent pages, use plain paper of the same weight.
- **Envelope.** Match the letter in color, weight, and type.
- **Electronic transmittal.** If you are expected to email or fax your letter, adapt its features for easy scanning or conversion to a company's word processor. Avoid multiple typefaces and type sizes, underlining, bullets, boxes, columns, or other features that might scramble.

ELEMENTS OF A BUSINESS LETTER

58f work

- It follows conventional form, identifying sender and recipient.
- It is prepared carefully, using appropriate visual features (see 13d–e).
- It has a few well-written paragraphs, each clarifying a specific point.
- It summarizes and synthesizes, respecting the reader's time.
- It specifies what the writer wants, whether information, service, agreement, or employment.

58f Preparing a résumé and application letter

58.2

Your résumé and cover letter sell your most important "product," you and your accomplishments. Develop your résumé around categories: your career objective, education, work or volunteer experience, activities or skills, awards, and references. Arrange information by time order or major skills. Use your cover letter to discuss, highlight, or add to your résumé; to connect the job requirements to your skills; and to express your spirit and interest. (See pp. 364–365.)

Edit, proofread, and design your final documents carefully (see 14b–e, 13c–e). Prepare both for print or electronic submission (plain text without formatting but with searchable keywords). Turn to your campus career center, job-hunting Web sites, or books for advice and samples.

ELEMENTS OF A RÉSUMÉ

- It complements your letter of application by concisely presenting your background, education, experience, skills, and achievements to a prospective employer.
- It uses headings to identify the sections or categories that organize your information.
- It generally arranges the specifics in each section in reverse chronological order, placing the most current information first.
- It is carefully designed and printed for clarity and easy reading.

1" margins on both sides

1⁄2" margin at top above writer's complete address

550 Sundown Ct.
Dayton, OH 45420
June 12, 2001

Recipient's complete address

Jennifer Low, Director of Personnel
Marshall School
232 Willow Way
Huber Heights, OH 45424

Salutation with colon

Dear Ms. Low:

58f work

Identifies job sought

I am seeking employment in elementary education, grades one through eight, and Jan Blake informed me of your junior high opening. During the past year as a student teacher, I have met many people at Marshall School, and I would love the opportunity to work with such a wonderful teaching staff.

Highlights recent training

Single-spaced text with double-spaced ¶s

My recent schooling at Wright State University has equipped me with many strategies that I am excited about implementing into my teaching. One strategy I am ready to try is the use of procedures. If students know what is expected of them, I believe that they can and will live up to those expectations.

Identifies special skills that supplement résumé

My greatest strengths as a teacher are my creativity and time management skills. Both are assets when planning my lessons and keeping students interested while using class time wisely. During one past teaching experience, my task seemed impossible until I designed learning centers to combat time constraints.

Explains benefits of experience

I firmly believe in inquiry teaching, a technique that always worked well during my student teaching. One of the joys of working with children has been seeing their eyes light up when they begin to understand new information.

Supplies contact information

I feel that I would be an asset to Marshall School and hope to start my career in your district next fall. I can be reached at 555-5555 and look forward to an interview with you.

Sincerely,

Tammy Helton

Tammy Helton

Notes enclosure (résumé)

Enclosure

Centers name,
address,
phone, and
email address

Tammy Jo Helton
550 Sundown Ct., Dayton, OH 45420
453-555-5555 TJ@mailnow.com

RTIFICATION

>mentary Education (grades 1-8)
:helor of Arts, August 2001, Wright State University,
▼ton, OH

Begins
with
required
teaching
credential

ICATION

ight State University, 1998-2001, College of Education
nclair Community College, 1997-1998, general education
yne High School, 1997 graduate, college preparatory

Summarizes
education
and awards

**58f
work**

ARDS

i Kappa Phi National Honor Society 2000, 2001
an's list 1999, 2000, 2001

Uses capitals
for main
headings

ACHING EXPERIENCE

udent Teaching
venth grade physical science, L. T. Ball Junior High, Tipp
ty, OH
anned and implemented lessons while maintaining classroom
>ntrol.

Organizes
experience
to show
skills

>servation
▪ilohview, Trotwood, OH
nplemented preplanned lessons.

eaching
▪ixth-grade religious education class, Dayton, OH
urrently responsible for planning and implementing lessons.

ORK EXPERIENCE

>al Line Sports Grill, 1998-present: Server, cash register,
upervisor
risch's Big Boy, 1996-1998: Server, inventory, preparation
hilohview Park, 1995-1997: Park counselor, activity planner

Uses reverse
chronological
order

NTERESTS AND ACTIVITIES

ook dance lessons for ten years; played drums in the school
>and.

Adds optional
information

References available on request.

58g Speaking in the workplace community

Committees and boards have their own conventions for communication, which, if violated, can weaken a member's standing. Observe careful to figure out whether a group interacts formally (using parliamentary procedure), informally (allowing spontaneous comments), or even ineffective (needing guidelines). (See Chapter 11, 55h, and 59f.)

59b public

STRATEGY **Plan your committee participation.**

- Study the agenda ahead; read documents, or gather background.
- Plan, rehearse, and prepare any visuals or materials (see 11c).
- Focus in order to time comments well, advance discussion, offer n ideas, and link your remarks to those of others. Don't dominate.
- Adjust to the group's formality and any shifts to social talk.
- Consider how others may react to assumptions you imply. Cont your emotions to avoid rash or potentially offensive remarks.

59 | Addressing the Public Community

In every public and civic context, people write to convey informatio express their views, organize collective efforts, and challenge injustice. Suc writing not only improves your skills and flexibility but also helps you to b come a better-informed citizen.

59a Recognizing the goals of public writing

When you address the public community, you're likely to think yourself as a volunteer, an activist, or a committee member, not as a write Your first concern will be to organize a beach cleanup or elect a mayor. You write to achieve your civic goals: to motivate others to support your cause, t influence policy decisions, and to promote democratic processes.

59b Analyzing public audiences

When you prepare a meeting reminder for your book club or a news letter for your neighbors, you will know your readers personally. They expec clear information and may appreciate motivation, but they often already agre out issues or activities. But when you begin to draft publicity for the tennis club's pasta dinner—its big fund-raiser—you'll need to address a wider circle, readers you don't know personally and who won't support the dinner unless you can persuade them that your cause is worthwhile.

STRATEGY **Connect your readers with your goals.**

- Why are you writing? What do you hope to accomplish?
- Who are your readers? What do they value? How much do they know or care about your project or issue?
- Do you primarily want to inform or to motivate them? Do you want readers to agree with you or to do something themselves—go to a meeting, contribute time or money, vote "yes" or "no," call an official, or join your group?
- What appeals to your readers' passion, anger, or fear might persuade them to do what you want—your sincerity, testimonials from others, information, or connections to their own interests or community values?
- How might you approach these readers? Will they respond best to impassioned appeals, logical analyses, or combined strategies? Will they expect a neighborly letter, a flyer, or a polished brochure?
- How can you contact prospective readers—through flyers at a meeting, appeals by mail or email, or letters in the newspaper?

59c public

59c Understanding public writing tasks

Community members who are motivated by a cause or by strong civic values are likely to join groups of like-minded people. As a result, public writing is often collaborative, prepared by a committee and revised, as time and bylaws allow, with responses from a wider group. A flyer about an event may be typed by an individual, but its details may report arrangements made by several people. A letter to the editor about a ballot issue may be drafted by one person, but it's likely to reflect the views—if not the campaign strategy—of a larger group. In fact, exactly who signs a letter may be a group decision, taking into account the signer's reputation, credibility, and local stature. Your writing task is likely to require juggling your individual objectives, your group's goals, and your readers' expectations. (See 5c, 6c, 14c, and 46g for collaborative strategies.)

STRATEGY **Work collaboratively to focus your public writing.**

- What is your task? Who will do what as you work on it?
- What's your deadline? How soon will recipients need information? How much time should you allow for printing, mailing, or other steps?
- What type of material should you prepare? What is the usual format? Do you have models or samples of past materials?
- Does your material require approval from anyone?

- Do you need to reserve a meeting room, coordinate with another grou
  or make other arrangements before you can finish your text?
- How will you distribute your material? Do you need to arrange dup
  cation, mailing, or volunteers to deliver or post materials?

59.1

59d Recognizing types of public writing

Many types of public writing—letters, flyers, pamphlets, newsletters
are flexible documents. They can be directed to different readers, such
group members, newspaper readers, officials, or local residents. They can a
dress different—or multiple—goals by providing information, building su
port, motivating to action, or supporting participatory democracy.

59e
public

59e Writing a public flyer

A common form of public writing is the flyer informing people about
meeting, activity, or event. Flyers also supply directions, advice, and inform
tion to residents, citizens, and other groups. (See also Chapter 13.)

TYPES OF WRITING IN THE PUBLIC COMMUNITY		
TYPE	**CHARACTERISTIC ACTIVITIES**	**COMMON FORMS**
PROVIDING INFORMATION	Gathering information, exploring issues, examining other views and alternative solutions, comparing, summarizing, synthesizing, and presenting material	Flyer, newsletter, fact sheet, informative report or article, letter (to group supporters, interested parties, officials, residents, or community in general), pamphlet, poster
BUILDING SUPPORT	Reaching consensus within a group, articulating a stance, defining a problem, proposing a solution, appealing to others with similar or different values, presenting evidence, finding shared values, advocating, persuading	Position paper, letter (to prospective supporters, officials, newspaper, or others concerned or involved), policy guidelines, statement of principles
MOTIVATING TO ACTION	Defining action, orchestrating participation, supplying information about involvement, motivating participants	Action proposal, grant proposal, flyer, letter, call to action in newsletter or other publication
PARTICIPATING IN DEMOCRATIC PROCESSES	Attending public meetings, meeting with officials, understanding legislative processes and timing, advocating civic involvement, distributing information on public or civic actions	Meeting minutes, committee report, legislative update, letter to officials, letter to group members, call to participate in newsletters or other publications, summary or analysis of public actions, petitions

ELEMENTS OF A PUBLIC FLYER

- It may open with its topic ("Hostetler Annual Reunion"), a general appeal ("Light a candle for peace!"), or a greeting ("Dear Choir Members").
- It clearly presents the essentials needed to attend or participate: date, time, place, directions, plans, equipment or supplies, contact and emergency telephone numbers, rain date, and so forth.
- It sticks to essentials and omits long explanations or background.
- It uses visual features, headings, graphics, and white space to highlight the most crucial information. (See 13d–e.)
- It may be informal or formal, depending on the group and the topic.

The following flyer announces a group's special event—a meeting to collect signed petitions for presentation to the school board.

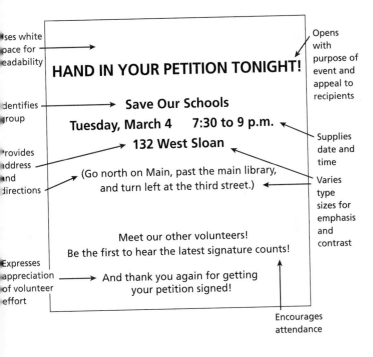

Uses white space for readability

Opens with purpose of event and appeal to recipients

HAND IN YOUR PETITION TONIGHT!

Identifies group

Save Our Schools
Tuesday, March 4   7:30 to 9 p.m.
132 West Sloan

Supplies date and time

Provides address and directions

(Go north on Main, past the main library, and turn left at the third street.)

Varies type sizes for emphasis and contrast

Meet our other volunteers!
Be the first to hear the latest signature counts!

Expresses appreciation of volunteer effort

And thank you again for getting your petition signed!

Encourages attendance

59f   Speaking in the public community

People gather daily to exchange opinions about local concerns. Citizens lobby officials for actions. Campus forums draw students, faculty, and administrators to discuss policies. Interest groups engage members and visitors. (See Chapter 11, 55h, and 58g.)

STRATEGY   **Prepare to speak in a public forum.**

- Attend meetings, listen, and read to get informed about issues.
- Plan and rehearse (see 11c), even to speak for a minute or two.
- Be reasonable; don't alienate those who are undecided or disagree.
- Use facts, details, and other evidence—not emotion—for support.
- Stay calm at a tense meeting so that fear and nervousness don't le
  you to speak angrily, make accusations, or even cry.

Glossary and Index

TAKING IT ONLINE

COMMON ERRORS IN ENGLISH

http://www.wsu.edu/~brians/errors/

Devoted to errors in usage, this site lists hundreds of potentially troublesome words and expressions.

THE SLOT: A SPOT FOR COPY EDITORS

http://www.theslot.com/

Here, you can access usage issues and pesky expressions by searching the site.

THE VOCABULA REVIEW

http://www.vocabula.com/

This electronic publication regularly includes articles on word origins, common errors in grammar and usage, and advice about succinct and stylish writing. Its Language Links will connect you to a wide variety of sites—classics, language resources, periodicals, media sites, and quick references.

THE GLOSSARIST

http://www.glossarist.com

The site collects glossaries of terms for topics and fields— from Arts and Culture to World Regions, Countries, and Travel.

ENGLISH USAGE, STYLE & COMPOSITION

http://www.bartleby.com/usage

At this site, you can search for usage issues or access guides to language and usage.

GUIDE TO GRAMMAR AND STYLE

http://www.andromeda.rutgers.edu/~jlynch/Writing/index.html

Check here for grammar terms, comments on style, and usage notes.

Glossary and Index

GLOSSARY OF USAGE 371-G

Refer to the glossary for advice about how to use confusing words and expressions such as *a lot* or *fewer* and *less*. Terms are arranged alphabetically. Entries include explanations, examples, and cross-references to related sections in the book.

INDEX 383-I

Refer to the index to find topics and terms discussed in this handbook, including advice on writing, grammar, research, and documentation of sources.

GLOSSARY OF USAGE

a, an When the word after *a* or *an* begins with a vowel sound, use *an*: *an outrageous film*. Use *a* before consonants: *a shocking film*. (See 15a.)

accept, except *Accept* means "to take or receive"; *except* means "excluding."

> Everyone **accepted** the invitation **except** Larry.

adverse, averse Someone opposed to something is *averse* to it; if conditions stand in opposition to achieving a goal, they are *adverse*.

advice, advise *Advice* is a noun meaning "counsel" or "recommendations." *Advise* is a verb meaning "to give counsel or recommendations."

> Raul wanted to **advise** his students, but they wanted no **advice**.

affect, effect *Affect* is a verb meaning "to influence." *Effect* is a noun meaning "a result." More rarely, *effect* is a verb meaning "to cause something to happen."

> CFCs may **affect** the deterioration of the ozone layer. The **effect** of that deterioration on global warming is uncertain. Lawmakers need to **effect** changes in public attitudes toward our environment.

aggravate, irritate *Aggravate* means "to worsen"; *irritate* means "to bother or pester."

ain't Although widely used, *ain't* is inappropriate in formal writing. Use *am not*, *is not*, or *are not*; the contracted forms *aren't* and *isn't* are more acceptable than *ain't* but may still be too informal in some contexts. (See 36c.)

all ready, already *All ready* means "prepared for"; *already* means "by that time."

> Sam was **all ready** for the meeting, but it had **already** started.

all right This expression is always spelled as two words, not as *alright*.

all together, altogether Use *all together* to mean "everyone"; use *altogether* to mean "completely."

> We were **all together** on our decision to support the center, but it was **altogether** too hard for us to organize a fund-raiser in a week.

allude, elude *Allude* means "hint at" or "refer to indirectly"; *elude* means "escape."

allusion, illusion An *allusion* is a reference to something; an *illusion* is a vision or a false belief.

a lot This expression is always spelled as two words, not as *alot*. Because *a lot* may be too informal for some writing, consider *many*, *much*, or another modifier instead.

a.m., p.m. These abbreviations may be capital or lowercase letters (see 44a).

among, between Use *between* to describe something involving two people, things, or ideas; use *among* to refer to three or more.

> The fight **between** the umpire and the catcher was followed by a discussion **among** the catcher, the umpire, and the managers.

glo

371-G

amount, number Use *amount* for a quantity of something that can't be divided i[n]
separate units. Use *number* for countable objects.

A large **number** of spices may be used in Thai dishes. This recipe calls fo[r]
small **amount** of coconut milk.

an, a (See **a, an**.)

and etc. (See **etc**.)

and/or Although widely used, *and/or* is usually imprecise and may distract yo[ur]
reader. Choose one of the words, or revise your sentence. (See 39e.)

ante-, anti- Use *ante-* as a prefix to mean "before" or "predating"; use *anti-* to me[an]
"against" or "opposed."

anyone, any one *Anyone* as one word is an indefinite pronoun. Occasionally y[ou]
may want to use *any* to modify *one*, in the sense of "any individual thing or pe[r]-
son." (The same distinction applies to **everyone, every one**; *somebody, so[me]-
body*; and *someone, some one*.)

Anyone can learn to parachute without fear. But the instructors are told not [to]
spend too much time with **any one** person.

anyplace Replace this term in formal writing with *anywhere*, or revise.

anyways, anywheres Avoid these incorrect versions of *anyway* and *anywhere*.

as, like Used as a preposition, *as* indicates a precise comparison. *Like* indicates a r[e]-
semblance or similarity.

Remembered **as** a man of habit, Kant took a walk at the same time each day. H[e]
like many other philosophers, was thoughtful and intense.

as to *As to* is considered informal in many contexts.

INFORMAL   The media speculated **as to** the film's success.

EDITED   The media speculated **about** the film's success.

assure, ensure, insure Use *assure* to imply a promise; use *ensure* to imply a certai[n]
outcome. Use *insure* only when you imply something legal or financial.

The surgeon **assured** the pianist that his fingers would heal in time for the con[-]
cert. To **ensure** that, the pianist did not practice for three weeks and **insure[d]**
his hands with Lloyd's of London.

at In any writing, avoid using *at* in direct and indirect questions.

COLLOQUIAL   Jones wondered where his attorney was **at**.

EDITED   Jones wondered where his attorney **was**.

awful, awfully Use *awful* as an adjective modifying a noun or pronoun; use *awfully*
as an adverb modifying a verb, adjective, or other adverb. (See 20b.)

Sanders played **awfully** at the golf tournament. On the sixth hole, an **awful**
shot landed his ball in the pond.

awhile, a while *Awhile* (as one word) functions as an adverb; it is not preceded by [a]
a preposition. *A while* functions as a noun (preceded by *a*, an article) and is often used in prepositional phrases.

The shelter suggested that the homeless family stay **awhile**. It turned out that
the children had not eaten for **a while**.

OSS

ad, badly Use *bad* as an adjective that modifies nouns or with a linking verb expressing feelings. Use *badly* as an adverb. (See 20b-3.)

because, since In general, avoid using *since* in place of *because*, which is more formal and precise. Use *since* to indicate time, not causality.

being as, being that Avoid both in formal writing when you mean *because*.

beside, besides Use *beside* as a preposition to mean "next to." Use *besides* as an adverb meaning "also" or an adjective meaning "except."

> Betsy placed the documents **beside** Mr. Klein. **Besides** being the best lawyer at the firm, Klein was also the most cautious.

better, had better Avoid using *better* or *had better* in place of *ought to* or *should* in formal writing.

COLLOQUIAL	Fast-food chains **better** realize that Americans are more health-conscious today.
EDITED	Fast-food chains **ought to** realize that Americans are more health-conscious today.

between, among (See **among, between**.)

bring, take *Bring* implies a movement from somewhere else to close at hand; *take* implies a movement in the opposite direction.

> Please **bring** me a coffee refill, and **take** away these leftover muffins.

broke *Broke* is the past tense of *break*; avoid using it as the past participle.

DRAFT	The computer was **broke**.
EDITED	The computer was **broken**.

burst, bursted *Burst* implies an outward explosion. Do not use the form *bursted* for the past tense.

> The gang of boys **burst** the balloon.

bust, busted Avoid the use of *bust* or *busted* to mean "broke."

COLLOQUIAL	The senator's limousine **bust** down on the trip.
EDITED	The senator's limousine **broke** down on the trip.

but however, but yet Choose one word of each pair, not both.

can, may *Can* implies ability; *may* implies permission or uncertainty.

> Bart **can** drive now, but his parents **may** not lend him their new car.

can't hardly, can't scarcely Use these pairs positively, not negatively: *can hardly* and *can scarcely*, or simply *can't*. (See 20b-4.)

capital, capitol *Capital* refers to a government center or to money; *capitol* refers to a government building.

censor, censure *Censor* means the act of shielding something from the public, such as a movie. *Censure* implies punishment or critical labeling.

center around Use *center on* or *focus on*, or reword as *revolve around*.

choose, chose Watch for spelling errors; use *choose* for the present tense form of the verb and *chose* for the past tense.

glo

cite, site *Cite* means to acknowledge someone else's work; *site* means a place or cation.

> Phil decided to **cite** Chomsky's theory of syntax.

> We chose the perfect **site** to pitch our tent.

climactic, climatic *Climactic* refers to the culmination of something; *climatic* ref to weather conditions.

compare to, compare with Use *compare to* when you want to imply similarit between two things—the phrase is close in meaning to *liken to*. Use *compare w* to imply both similarities and differences.

> The doctor **compared** the boy's virus **to** a tiny army in his body. **Compar with** his last illness, this one was mild.

complement, compliment *Complement* means "an accompaniment"; *compliment* mea "words of praise."

> The diplomats **complimented** the ambassador on her menu. The desse **complemented** the main course perfectly.

continual, continuous *Continual* implies that something is recurring; *continuo* implies that something is constant and unceasing.

> Local residents found the **continual** noise of landing jets less annoying tha the traffic that **continuously** circled the airport.

could of, would of These incorrect pairs are common because they are often pro nounced as if they are spelled this way. Use the correct verb forms *could hav* and *would have*.

| DRAFT | I **could of** written a letter to the editor. |
| EDITED | I **could have** written a letter to the editor. |

couple, couple of In formal writing, use *a few* or *two* instead.

| COLLOQUIAL | Watson took a **couple of** days to examine the data. |
| EDITED | Watson took **a few** days to examine the data. |

criteria *Criteria* is the plural form of *criterion*. Make sure your verbs agree in num ber with this noun.

| SINGULAR | One **criterion** for the bonus was selling ten cars. |
| PLURAL | The **criteria** were too strict to follow. |

curriculum *Curriculum* is the singular form of this noun. For the plural, use either *curricula* or *curriculums*, but be consistent.

data Although widely used for both the singular and plural, *data* technically is a plural noun; *datum* refers to a single piece of data. If in doubt, use the formal distinction, and make sure your verbs agree in number.

| SINGULAR | This one **datum** was unexpected. |
| PLURAL | These **data** are not very revealing. |

different from, different than Use *different from* when an object follows, and use *different than* when an entire clause follows.

Jack's proposal is **different from** Marlene's, but his ideas are now **different than** they were when he first joined the sales team.

discreet, discrete *Discreet* means "reserved or cautious"; *discrete* means "distinctive, different, or explicit."

disinterested, uninterested *Uninterested* implies boredom or lack of interest; *disinterested* implies impartiality or objectivity.

done Avoid using *done* as a simple past tense; it is a *past participle* (see 17e).

| DRAFT | The skater **done** the best she could at the Olympics. |
| EDITED | The skater **did** the best she could at the Olympics. |

don't, doesn't Contractions like these may strike some readers as too informal. Err on the side of formality (*do not, does not*) when in doubt. (See 36c.)

due to When meaning "because," use *due to* only after some form of the verb *be*. Avoid *due to the fact that*, which is wordy.

DRAFT	The mayor collapsed **due to** campaign fatigue.
EDITED	The mayor's collapse was **due to** campaign fatigue.
EDITED	The mayor collapsed **because** of campaign fatigue.

effect, affect (See **affect, effect**.)

e.g. Avoid this abbreviation (from Latin, "for example") when possible. (See 44b.)

| AWKWARD | Her positions on major issues, **e.g.**, gun control, abortion, and the death penalty, are very liberal. |
| EDITED | Her positions on major issues **such as** gun control, abortion, and the death penalty are very liberal. |

emigrate from, immigrate to Foreigners *emigrate from* one country and *immigrate to* another. *Migrate* implies moving around (as in *migrant workers*) or settling temporarily.

ensure, assure, insure (See **assure, ensure, insure**.)

enthused Avoid *enthused* to mean *enthusiastic* in formal writing.

especially, specially *Especially* implies "in particular"; *specially* means "for a specific purpose."

It is **especially** important that Jo follow her **specially** designed workouts.

etc. Avoid this abbreviation in formal writing by supplying a complete list of items or by using a phrase like *so forth*. (See 44b.)

| INFORMAL | The Washington march was a disaster: it was cold and rainy, the protesters had no food, **etc.** |
| EDITED | The Washington march was a disaster: the protesters were cold, wet, and hungry. |

eventually, ultimately Use *eventually* to imply that an outcome follows a series of events or a lapse of events. Use *ultimately* to imply that a final or culminating act ends a series of events.

Eventually, the rescue team managed to pull the last of the survivors from wreck, and **ultimately** there were no casualties.

everyday, every day *Everyday* is an adjective that modifies a noun. *Every day* noun (*day*) modified by an adjective (*every*).

Every day in the Peace Corps, Monique faced the **everyday** task of boiling drinking water.

everyone, every one *Everyone* is a pronoun; *every one* is an adjective (*every*) lowed by a noun (*one*). (See also **anyone, any one**.)

Everyone was tantalized by **every one** of the desserts on the menu.

exam In formal writing, some readers may be bothered by this abbreviation of e mination.

except, accept (See **accept, except**.)

explicit, implicit *Explicit* means that something is outwardly or openly stated; *imp* means that it is implied or suggested.

farther, further *Farther* implies a measurable distance; *further* implies someth that cannot be measured.

The **farther** they trekked into the wilderness, the **further** their relationship d teriorated.

female, male Use these terms only when you want to call attention to gender spec ically, as in a research report. Otherwise, use the simpler *man* and *woman* or *b* and *girl* unless such usage is sexist (see 32a).

fewer, less Use *fewer* for things that can be counted, and use *less* for quantities th cannot be divided. (See 15a.)

The new bill had **fewer** supporters and **less** media coverage.

finalize Some readers object to adjectives and nouns that are turned into ver ending in *-ize* (*finalize, prioritize, objectivize*). When in doubt, use *make final* some other construction.

firstly Use *first, second, third*, and so forth when enumerating points in writing.

former, latter *Former* means "the one before" and *latter* means "the one after They can be used only when referring to two things.

freshman, freshmen Many readers consider these terms sexist and archaic. Unles you are citing an established term or group (such as the Freshman Colloquiur at Midwest University), use *first-year student* instead.

get Avoid imprecise or frequent use of *get* in formal writing.

INFORMAL   Martin Luther King had a premonition that he would **get** shot his speeches before his death **got** nostalgic.

EDITED   Martin Luther King had a premonition that he would **be** shot his speeches before his death **waxed** nostalgic.

go, say In very informal contexts, some speakers use **go** and **goes** to mean *say* and *says*. This usage is considered inappropriate in all writing.

INAPPROPRIATE   Hjalmar **goes** to Gregers, "I thought this was my account."

EDITED   Hjalmar **says** to Gregers, "I thought this was my account."

OSS

gone, went Do not use *went* (the past tense of *go*) in place of the past participle form *gone*. (See 17c and d.)

DRAFT   The officers **should have went** to their captain.

EDITED   The officers **should have gone** to their captain.

good, well *Good* is an adjective meaning "favorable" (a *good* trip). *Well* is an adverb meaning "done favorably." (See 20b-3.)

good and This is a colloquial term when used to mean "very" (*good and* tired; *good and* hot). Avoid it in formal writing.

got to Avoid the colloquial use of *got* or *got to* in place of *must* or *have to*.

COLLOQUIAL   I **got to** improve my ratings in the opinion polls.

EDITED   I **must** improve my ratings in the opinion polls.

great In formal writing, avoid using *great* as an adjective meaning "wonderful." Use *great* in the sense of "large" or "monumental."

hanged, hung Although the distinction between these terms is disappearing, some readers may expect you to use **hanged** exclusively to mean execution by hanging and **hung** to refer to anything else.

have, got (See **got to**.)

have, of (See **could of, would of**.)

he, she, he or she, his/her When you use gender-specific pronouns, be careful not to privilege the male versions (see 32a).

hopefully Although the word is widely used to modify entire clauses (as in "Hopefully, her condition will improve"), some readers may object. When in doubt, use *hopefully* only to mean "feeling hopeful."

Bystanders watched **hopefully** as the workers continued to dig.

however, yet, but (See **but however, but yet**.)

hung, hanged (See **hanged, hung**.)

if, whether Use *if* before a specific outcome (either stated or implied); use *whether* when you are considering alternatives.

If holographic technology can be perfected, we may soon be watching three-dimensional television. But **whether** we will be able to afford it is another question.

illusion, allusion (See **allusion, illusion**.)

immigrate to, emigrate from (See **emigrate from, immigrate to**.)

implicit, explicit (See **explicit, implicit**.)

in regard to Although it may sound sophisticated, *in regard to* is wordy. Use *about* instead.

inside of, outside of When you use *inside* or *outside* to mark locations, do not pair them with *of*.

UNNEEDED   **Inside of** the hut was a large stock of rootwater.

EDITED   **Inside** the hut was a large stock of rootwater.

insure, assure, ensure (See **assure, ensure, insure**.)

glo

irregardless Avoid this erroneous form of the word *regardless*, commonly used [be]cause *regardless* and *irrespective* are often used synonymously.

irritate, aggravate (See **aggravate, irritate**.)

its, it's *Its* is a possessive pronoun, and *it's* contracts *it is* (see 18a-3 and 36c). (So[me] readers may also object to *it's* for *it is* in formal writing.)

-ize, -wise Some readers object to nouns or adjectives turned into verbs by add[ing] *-ize* (*finalize, itemize, computerize*). Also avoid adding *-wise* to words, as [in] "Weather-wise, it will be chilly."

kind, sort, type These words are singular nouns; precede them with *this*, not *the[se]*. In general, use more precise words.

kind of, sort of Considered by most readers to be informal, these phrases sho[uld] be avoided in academic and workplace writing.

latter, former (See **former, latter**.)

lay, lie *Lay* is a transitive verb requiring a direct object (but not the self). *Lie*, wh[en] used to mean "place in a resting position," refers to the self but takes the fo[rm] *lay* in the past tense. (See 17f.)

less, fewer (See **fewer, less**.)

lie, lay (See **lay, lie**.)

like, as (See **as, like**.)

literally Avoid using *literally* in a figurative statement (one that is not true to fac[t]). Even when used correctly, *literally* is redundant because the statement will [be] taken as fact anyway.

DRAFT	The visitors **literally** died when they saw their hotel.
REDUNDANT	The visitors **literally gasped** when they saw their hotel.
EDITED	The visitors gasped when they saw their hotel.

loose, lose Commonly misspelled, these words are pronounced differently. *Loos[e]* (rhyming with *moose*) is an adjective meaning "not tight." *Lose* (rhyming wit[h] *snooze*) is a present tense verb meaning "to misplace."

lots, lots of, a lot of (See **a lot**.)

may, can (See **can, may**.)

maybe, may be *Maybe* means *possibly*; *may be* is part of a verb structure.

The President **may be** speaking now, so **maybe** we should turn on the news[.]

media, medium Technically, *media* is a plural noun requiring a verb that agrees i[n] number. Many people now use *media* as a singular noun when referring to the press. *Medium* generally refers to a conduit or method of transmission.

The **media** is not covering the story accurately.

The telephone was not a good **medium** for reviewing the budget.

might of, may of (See **could of, would of**.)

mighty Avoid this adjective in formal writing; omit it or use *very*.

Ms. To avoid the sexist labeling of women as "married" or "unmarried" (a condition not marked in men's titles), use *Ms.* unless you have reason to use *Miss* or *Mrs.* (for example, when giving the name of a character such as *Mrs. Dalloway*). Use profes-sional titles when appropriate (*Doctor, Professor, Senator, Mayor*). (See 32a.)

must of, must have (See **could of, would of**.)

nor, or Use *nor* in negative constructions and *or* in positive ones.

| NEGATIVE | Neither rain **nor** snow will slow the team. |

| POSITIVE | Either rain **or** snow may delay the game. |

nothing like, nowhere near These are considered informal phases when used to compare two things (as in "Gibbon's position is **nowhere near** as justified as Carlyle's"). Avoid them in formal writing.

nowheres Use *nowhere* instead.

number, amount (See **amount, number**.)

of, have (See **could of, would of**.)

off of Use simply *off* instead.

OK When you write formally, use *OK* only in dialogue. If you mean "good" or "acceptable," use these terms.

on account of Avoid this expression in formal writing. Use *because* instead.

outside of, inside of (See **inside of, outside of**.)

per Use *per* only to mean "by the," as in *per hour* or *per day*. Avoid using it to mean "according to," as in "per your instructions."

percent, percentage Use *percent* only with numerical data. Use *percentage* for a statistical part of something, not simply to mean *some* or *part*.

Ten **percent** of the sample returned the questionnaire.

A large **percentage** of the parking revenue was stolen.

plus Avoid using *plus* as a conjunction joining two independent clauses.

| INFORMAL | The school saved money through its "lights off" campaign, **plus** it generated income by recycling aluminum cans. |

| EDITED | The school saved money through its "lights off" campaign and also generated income by recycling aluminum cans. |

Use *plus* only to mean "in addition to."

The wearisome campaign, **plus** the media pressures, exhausted her.

precede, proceed *Precede* means "come before"; *proceed* means "go ahead."

pretty Avoid using *pretty* (as in *pretty good, pretty hungry, pretty sad*) to mean "somewhat" or "rather." Use *pretty* in the sense of "attractive."

principal, principle *Principal* is a noun meaning "an authority" or "head of a school" or an adjective meaning "leading" ("a *principal* objection to the testimony"). *Principle* is a noun meaning "belief or conviction."

proceed, precede (See **precede, proceed**.)

quote, quotation Formally, *quote* is a verb and *quotation* is a noun. *Quote* is sometimes used as a short version of the noun *quotation*, but this may bother some readers. Use *quotation* instead.

raise, rise *Raise* is a transitive verb meaning "to lift up." *Rise* is an intransitive verb (it takes no object) meaning "to get up or move up."

He **raised** his head and watched the fog **rise** from the lake.

glo

rarely ever Use *rarely* alone, not paired with *ever*.

real, really Use *real* as an adjective and *really* as an adverb. (See 20b-3)

reason is because, reason is that Avoid these wordy phrases. (See 26b-1.)

regarding, in regard, with regard to (See **in regard to**.)

regardless, irregardless (See **irregardless**.)

respectfully, respectively *Respectfully* means "with respect"; *respectively* impli
certain order for events or things.

> The senior class **respectfully** submitted the planning document. The admi
> tration considered items 3, 6, and 10, **respectively**.

rise, raise (See **raise, rise**.)

says, goes (See **go, say**.)

set, sit *Set* means "to place"; *sit* means "to place oneself." (See 17f.)

should of (See **could of, would of**.)

since, because (See **because, since**.)

sit, set (See **set, sit**.)

site, cite (See **cite, site**.)

so Some readers object to the use of *so* in place of *very*.

> INFORMAL   The filmmaker is **so** thoughtful about his films' themes.
>
> EDITED   The filmmaker is **very** thoughtful about his films' themes.

somebody, some body (See **anyone, any one**.)

someone, some one (See **anyone, any one**.)

sometime, some time, sometimes *Sometime* refers to an indistinct time in the
ture; *sometimes* means "every once in a while." *Some time* is an adjective (*som
modifying a noun (*time*).

> The probe will reach the nebula **sometime** in the next decade. **Sometimes** su
> probes fail to send back any data. It takes **some time** before images will retu
> from Neptune.

sort, kind, type (See **kind, sort, type**.)

specially, especially (See **especially, specially**.)

stationary, stationery *Stationary* means "standing still"; *stationery* refers to writi
paper.

such Some readers will expect you to avoid using *such* without *that*.

> INFORMAL   Anne Frank had **such** a difficult time.
>
> EDITED   Anne Frank had **such** a difficult time growing up **that** her diar
>   writing became her only solace.

suppose to, supposed to The correct form of this phrase is *supposed to*; the *-d* i
sometimes mistakenly left off because it is not always heard. (See 17c.)

sure, surely In formal writing, use *sure* to mean "certain." *Surely* is an adverb; don'
use *sure* in its place. (See 20b-3.)

> He has **surely** studied hard for the exam; he is **sure** to pass.

sure and, try and With *sure* and *try*, replace *and* with *to*.

take, bring (See **bring, take**.)

than, then *Than* is used to compare; *then* implies a sequence of events or a causal relationship.

West played harder **than** East, but **then** the rain began.

that, which Although the distinction between *that* and *which* is weakening in many contexts, formal writing often requires you to know the difference. Use *that* in a clause that is essential to the meaning of a sentence (restrictive modifier); use *which* with a clause that does not provide essential information (nonrestrictive modifier). (See 34e–f.)

theirself, theirselves, themself All these forms are incorrect; use *themselves* to refer to more than one person, and *himself* or *herself* to refer to one.

them Avoid using *them* as a subject or to modify a subject, as in "*Them* are delicious" or "*Them* apples are very crisp."

then, than (See **than, then**.)

there, their, they're These forms are often confused in spelling because they all sound alike. *There* is a preposition of location; *their* is a possessive pronoun; *they're* is a contraction of *they* and *are*. (See 36c.)

Look **over there**.

Their car ran out of gas.

They're not eager to hike to the nearest gas station.

thusly Avoid this term; use *thus* or *therefore* instead.

till, 'til, until Some readers will find *till* and *'til* too informal; use *until*.

to, too, two Because these words sound the same, they may be confused. *To* is a preposition indicating direction or location. *Too* means "also." *Two* is a number.

The Birdsalls went **to** their lake cabin. They invited the Corbetts **too**. That made **two** trips so far this season.

toward, towards Prefer *toward* in formal writing. (You may see *towards* in England and Canada.)

try and, try to, sure and (See **sure and, try and**.)

ultimately, eventually (See **eventually, ultimately**.)

uninterested, disinterested (See **disinterested, uninterested**.)

unique Use *unique* alone, not *most unique* or *more unique*. (See 20b-4.)

until, till (See **till, 'til, until**.)

use to, used to Like *supposed to*, this phrase may be mistakenly written as *use to* because the *-d* is not always clearly pronounced. Write *used to*. (See 17c.)

wait for, wait on Use *wait on* only to refer to a clerk's or server's job; use *wait for* to mean "to await someone's arrival."

well, good (See **good, well**.)

went, gone (See **gone, went**.)

were, we're *Were* is the past plural form of *was*; *we're* contracts *we are*. (See 36c.)

We're going to the ruins where the fiercest battles **were**.

where . . . at (See **at**.)

whether, if (See **if, whether**.)

which, that (See **that, which**.)

glc

who, whom Although the distinction between these words is slowly disappear[ing] from the language, many readers will expect you to use *whom* as the objec[tive] form. When in doubt, err on the side of formality. (Sometimes editing can el[im]inate the need to choose.) (See 18b-4.)

who's, whose *Who's* contracts *who is*. *Whose* indicates possession. (See 36c.)

The programmer **who's** joining our division hunted for the person **whose** [book?] he took by mistake.

wise, -ize (See **-ize, -wise**.)

would of, could of (See **could of, would of**.)

yet, however, but (See **but however, but yet**.)

your, you're *Your* is a possessive pronoun; *you're* contracts *you are*. (See 18a-3 a[nd] 36c.)

If **you're** going to take physics, you'd better know **your** math.

INDEX

inde.

index

index

index

inde

inde

CREDITS

284: Leo Reisberg, "Colleges Step-Up Efforts to Combat Alcohol Abuse," *The Chronicle of Higher Education*, June 12, 1998, Vol. 44 No. 40. Copyright © 1998 by The Chronicle of Higher Education. Reprinted by permission.

286: Larry A. Tucker, "Effect of Weight Training on Self-Concept: A Profile of Those Influenced Most," *Research Quarterly for Exercise and Sport*, 1983.

290: Paula Mathieu and Ken McAllister, CRITT Web site (Critical Resources in Teaching with Technology), 1997. http://www.engl.uic.edu/~stp.

291: Whymilk.com? Copyright © The National Milk Processor Promotion Board. Used with permission. All rights reserved. http://www.whymilk.com/milku/diet_nutri_101.html.

291: Michael Gregor, "Milk . . . Help Yourself," *AnimaLife*, Fall 1994, Vol. 5, No.1. Reprinted by permission of the publisher.

291: "Why Does Milk Bother Me?" National Digestive Diseases Information Clearinghouse, National Institutes of Health, http://www.niddk.gov/health/digest/pubs/whymilk/index.html. Reprinted with permission.

227: Donald Hall, "A Small Fig Tree," from *Old and New Poems*. Copyright © 1990 by Donald Hall. Reprinted by permission of Ticknor Fields/Houghton Mifflin Co. All rights reserved.

294: Laurie Garrett, *The Coming Plague* (New York: Penguin Books, 1994).

298: Brian Schwegler, "Character Development Sketch: 'Dave the Guesser,'" *Salt Magazine*, August, 1994. Reprinted by permission of the author and SALT Center for Documentary Field Studies.

304: Michael Bright, *Animal Language* (Ithaca, NY: Cornell University Press, 1984).

305: Maureen Honey, *Creating Rosie the Riveter* (University of Massachusetts Press, 1984).

306: Committee of Concerned Journalists, "A Statement of Concern," *The Media & Morality*, edited by Robert M. Baird, William E. Loges, and Stuart E. Rosenbaum (New York: Prometheus Books, 1999).

307: Mark Twain, *Huckleberry Finn* (New York: HarperCollins, 1987).

309: Wayland D. Hand, "Folk Medical Magic and Symbolism in the West," *Magic, Witchcraft, and Religion: An Anthropological Study of the Supernatural*, Third Edition, edited by Arthur C. Lehmann and James E. Myers (Mayfield Publishing, 1993).

309: George Gmelch, "Baseball Magic," *Transaction*, 1971.

329: M. A. J. McKenna, "Film Provides Beauty-ful Role Models," *Boston Herald*, 1991.

329: Scott Rosenberg, "The Genie-us of Aladdin," *San Francisco Examiner*, 1992.

330: Elaine Showalter, "Beauty and the Beast: Disney Meets Feminism in a Liberated Love Story for the 90's," *Premiere Magazine*, Oct. 1997.

336: Judith A. Cramer, "Radio: A Woman's Place Is on the Air," as it appeared in *Women in Mass Communication*, edited by Pamela J. Creedon (Woodland Hills, CA: Sage Publications, 1993).

337: Avi Sadeh, Amiram Raviv, and Reut Gruber, "Sleep Patterns and Sleep Disruptions in School-Age Children," *Developmental Psychology*, Vol. 36, No. 3, May 2000.

338: Juliet B. Schor, *The Overworked American* (New York: HarperCollins, 1998).

367: John Edgar Wideman, *Brothers and Keepers* (New York: Random House, 1984).

377: Claude F. Boutron et al., "Decrease in Anthropogenic Lead, Cadmium, and Zinc in Greenland Snows since the Late 1960's," *Nature*, Vol. 353, 1991.

399: Richard Wisniewski and Paul Kleine, "Teacher Moonlighting: An Unstudied Phenomenon," *ERIC* 1983.

402: Nathaniel Hawthorne, *Young Goodman Brown*.

410: Richard H. Wagner, *Environment and Man* (New York: Norton, 1978).

411: Edward Abbey, *The Journey Home* (New York: Plume, 1991).

413: Anson Gonzalez, "Little Rosebud Girl." Copyright © 1972 by Anson Gonzalez. Reprinted by permission.

Student Acknowledgments: David Aharonian, Summer Arrigo-Nelson, Jeanne Brown, Amy Burns, Zachary Carter, Kimlee Cunningham, Christine Reed-Davis, Robin Edwards, Jenifer Figliozzi, Shane Hand, Tammy Jo Helton, Norrie Herrin, Andrea Herrmann, Kris Lundell, Michael Perry, Brian Schwegler, Meghan Tubridy, Kimberly Tullos, and Ted Wolfe.

GUIDE TO ESL ADVICE

Look for the ESL Advice if your first language is not English. This vice is integrated throughout the handbook, and each ESL Advice section labeled and highlighted so it's easy to spot.

ON ADJECTIVES AND ADVERBS

Adjective Forms (**15d**)
> *See also* Chapter 20: Using Adjectives and Adverbs

Adjective Clauses (**16c-1**)
> *See also* Chapter 28. Using Coordination and Subordination

Adjectives in a Series (**20a**)
Adverb Clauses (**16c-2**)
> Some Words to Introduce Adverb Clauses (**box, p. 94**)

ON AGREEMENT

Subject-Verb Agreement (**19a**)
Paired Conjunctions (**19b-3**)
Separated Subjects and Verbs (**19b-4**)
Present Tense Verb Agreement (**19b-5**)
Quantifiers (**19b-6**)
Other, Others, and *Another* as Pronouns or Adjectives (**19b-6**)
Demonstrative Adjectives or Pronouns (**19c-3**)

ON ARTICLES AND NOUNS

The Articles *A, An,* and *The* (**15a**)
> Nouns and the Use of Articles (**box, p. 78**)
> *See also* Types of Nouns (**box, p. 78**)

Noun Clauses (**16c-3**)

ON CLAUSES

Adjective Clauses (**16c-1**)
Adverb Clauses (**16c-2**)
> Some Words to Introduce Adverb Clauses (**box, p. 94**)

Noun Clauses (**16c-3**)

ON PREPOSITIONS

Prepositions (**15f**)
> Prepositions of Time: *At, On,* and *In* (**p. 84**)
> Prepositions of Place: *At, On,* and *In* (**p. 84**)
> Prepositions of Place: *In, At, On,* and No Preposition (**box, p. 84**)
> *To* or No Preposition to Express Going to a Place (**p. 84**)
> *For* and *Since* in Time Expressions (**p. 84**)
> Prepositions with Nouns, Verbs, and Adjectives (**p. 85**)
> Noun + Preposition Combinations (**box, p. 85**)
> Verb + Preposition Combinations (**box, p. 85**)
> Adjective + Preposition Combinations (**box, p. 85**)

See also Look for Prepositional Phrases (**16b-1**)

Read, Recognize, and Revise
Ten Serious Errors

WHY ARE THESE ERRORS SERIOUS?

These ten errors are identified in our research as among those most likely to confuse or irritate readers in the academic community. Whether errors distort meaning or suggest carelessness, they distract readers from what you want to say. Too many errors can erode your relationship with your readers and diminish the success of your writing.

READ

Pay attention to potential problems as you revise and edit.

Consider the possible reactions of your community of readers.

1. The heavy rain turned the parking area to mud. *And stranded thousands of cars.*
   → READER'S REACTION: **The second part seems disconnected. Now I've got to stop and figure out how it fits.**

2. The promoters called *the insurance company they discovered* their coverage for accidents was limited.
   → READER'S REACTION: **I'm confused. Is this about some new insurance company that the promoters discovered?**

3. After talking with the groundskeeper, the security chief said *he* would not be responsible for the safety of the crowd.
   → READER'S REACTION: **Who's he—the groundskeeper or the security chief?**

4. The local authorities *hadn't scarcely* enough resources to cope with the flooding.
   → READER'S REACTION: *Hadn't scarcely*— **this isn't the way a college graduate or a professional writes.**

5. *After announcing the cancellation from the stage, the crowd* began complaining to the promoters.
   → READER'S REACTION: **I know the crowd didn't announce the cancellation, but that's what this says!**

6. Even the *promoters promise* to reschedule and honor tickets did little to stop the *crowds complaints*.
   → READER'S REACTION: **I can't read this without feeling irritated that apostrophes are missing.**

7. "The grounds are *slippery, the* mayor announced, "so please leave in an orderly manner."
   → READER'S REACTION: **Here are more missing marks! Didn't this writer bother to proofread?**

8. Away from the microphone, the mayor said, "I hope the security chief or the promoters *has* a plan to help everyone leave safely."
   → READER'S REACTION: **Promoters *has*? This careless writer didn't even make the effort to fit subjects and verbs together.**

9. If *people* left the amphitheater quickly, *you* could get to *your* car without standing long in the rain.
   → READER'S REACTION: **Why is this sentence mixing *people* with *you*? Is *you* supposed to mean *me*?**

10. *Although*, the muddy parking area caused problems, all the cars and *people, left* the grounds without incident.
    → READER'S REACTION: **It looks as if the writer just tossed in some commas here—and they make the sentence hard to read.**

◖USING THE "READ, RECOGNIZE, AND REVISE" APPROACH

: **read-recognize-revise pattern** to identify and edit errors. First, *read* the
'e provided (column 1). Consider the Reader's Reaction, showing how
er might respond (column 2). Next use the handbook's advice, the
jies suggested, or your own strategy to help you *recognize* the error
n 3). Finally, select a Strategy to *revise* or repair the error (column 4).

RECOGNIZE	REVISE
ategies for recognizing ms—or invent your own.	Use strategies to edit, repair, or replace errors or problems.
ent: Ask questions. Who (or what) /ho (or what) is? (**21a**) →	The heavy rain turned the parking area to mud and stranded thousands of cars. (**21b**)
Sentence: Look for a long sentence : internal punctuation; count the e statements it contains. (**22b**) →	The promoters called the insurance company, and they discovered their coverage for accidents was limited. (**22c**)
r Pronoun Reference: See whether ntence contains two or more words h a pronoun might refer. (**23a**) →	After talking with the groundskeeper, the security chief said, "I will not be responsible for the safety of the crowd." (**23b**)
e Negative: Check for combinations itive words like *no, not, scarcely,* t. (**20b-4**) →	The local authorities had scarcely enough resources to cope with the flooding. (**20b-4**)
ng Modifier: When a modifier a sentence, consider whether the or thing modified is the subject of in clause. (**24a-2**) →	After the promoters announced the cancellation from the stage, the crowd began complaining about the decision. (**24b**)
g Possessive Apostrophe: Test for sion by trying to turn a noun ending to an *of* phrase. (**36a**) →	Even the promoters' promise to reschedule and honor tickets did little to stop the crowd's complaints. (**36b**)
g Marks: Look for marks often used : such as quotation marks (**37a**) and is. (**34c, 34e, 34j**) →	"The grounds are slippery," the mayor announced, "so please leave in an orderly manner." (**37a**)
f Subject-Verb Agreement: Find iject (especially if separated, plural, ipound); match the verb. (**19a–b**) →	Away from the microphone, the mayor said, "I hope the security chief or the promoters have a plan to help everyone leave safely." (**19b**)
Hunt for illogical or inconsistent shifts j *I, we, you, he, she, it,* or *they.* (**25a**) →	If people left the amphitheater quickly, they could get to their cars without standing long in the rain. (**25b**)
:essary Commas: Check for un- d commas after words like *although* veen subject and verb. (**34l**) →	Although the muddy parking area caused problems, all the cars and people left the grounds without incident. (**34l**)

Contents